D0839387

Marxists in the Face of Fascism

Marxists in the Face of Fascism

Writings by Marxists on Fascism from the Inter-War Period

David Beetham

Haymarket Books
Chicago, Illinois

© 1984 David Beetham
Preface to the New Edition, © 2019 David Beetham

Originally published by Barnes and Noble Books, 1984.

This edition published in 2019 by
Haymarket Books
P.O. Box 180165
Chicago, IL 60618
773-583-7884
www.haymarketbooks.org
info@haymarketbooks.org

ISBN: 978 1 60846-976-5

Trade distribution:
In the US, Consortium Book Sales and Distribution, www.cbsd.com
In Canada, Publishers Group Canada, www.pgcbooks.ca
In the UK, Turnaround Publisher Services, www.turnaround-uk.com
All other countries, Ingram Publisher Services International,
IPS_Intlsales@ingramcontent.com

This book was published with the generous support of Lannan Foundation
and Wallace Action Fund.

Cover design by Eric Kerl.

Printed in Canada by union labor.

Library of Congress Cataloging-in-Publication data is available.

10 9 8 7 6 5 4 3 2 1

Contents

Preface and acknowledgements

The large majority of texts included in this volume have not appeared in English before, though some of them are well known to Continental readers. Where translations already exist, I have used them, though I have re-translated some pieces where it seemed appropriate. In order to make the collection as representative as possible within the space available, I have found it necessary to exclude passages from many of the selected texts. On each occasion I have tried to be as faithful as possible to the main thrust of the writer's argument. These omissions are indicated in the text by an appropriate sign (. . .).

Permission to translate the following items has been kindly given by the copyright holders: articles 32, 51, by Europa Verlag, Zurich; 48, 52, by Professor Richard Löwenthal. Grateful acknowledgement is made for permission to use the following translations: articles 1, 7, 8, English translations © Quintin Hoare 1978, reprinted by permission of Quintin Hoare and Lawrence & Wishart; articles 25–9, English translations © Pathfinder Press Inc., 1971, reprinted by permission.

I am grateful to Christine Phillips for her translations from Spanish, and to Margaret Atack, Raffaella Ferrari and Ken Knight for advice on points of translation from French, Italian and German respectively. D. E. Devreese and V. Kahan of the International Institute of Social History, Amsterdam, provided invaluable biographical information on some of the authors. I am indebted to Colin Barker, Norman Geras, David Howell, Tim Mason, John Schwarzmantel and the late Peter Sedgwick for their comments on an early draft of the Introduction and on the shape of the collection as a whole. Responsibility for the finished work is of course my own. Finally, I should like to express my gratitude to Jeanne Bellovics for typing the manuscript and to my family for their forbearance.

Abbreviations

CNT	National Confederation of Labour (Spain)
CPSU	Communist Party of the Soviet Union
ECCI (EKKI)	Executive Committee of the Communist International (Comintern)
KPD	German Communist Party
KPO	Communist Party Opposition (Germany)
NSDAP	National Socialist Party
PCE	Spanish Communist Party
PCF	French Communist Party
PCI	Italian Communist Party
POUM	United Marxist Workers' Party (Spain)
PSI	Italian Socialist Party
PSU	United Socialist Party (Italy)
SAP	Socialist Workers' Party (Germany)
SDAP	Social Democratic Workers' Party (Austria)
SPD	German Social Democratic Party
USPD	Independent German Social Democratic Party

Preface to the 2019 Edition

This new preface to the unaltered text of the first edition seeks to answer a simple, two-part question: what possible interest can these writings from the 1920s and 1930s hold to justify their republication today; and are they of interest only to historians of Marxism and fascism respectively, or do they have a more general significance for the politics of our own time? Even if we were only to answer "yes" to the first part of this question, these writings would continue to be important documents in the study of fascism's history. Moreover, there is an argument that the resurgence of extreme, right-wing populist movements and regimes in our own time makes the analyses of these former writers helpful in understanding these contemporary formations.

At the outset, it is important to stress that the phenomena we see today are not strictly "fascist," although that term may be loosely applied to them by some commentators, and small neo-Nazi groups, such as PEGIDA in Germany and the rapidly growing National Socialist Movement in the USA, have made their presence felt in several countries. If we were to ignore what these earlier writers and activists saw as most typical of fascist movements and regimes, we would undermine the painful lessons they discovered in their attempts to define and understand fascism. Furthermore, it will be instructive to consider what these contemporary formations have in common with fascism, where they crucially differ from it, and why.

The far-right movements – or rather movement-parties – which we are considering are mainly European: the UK Independence Party in Britain, the Party for Freedom in the Netherlands, the Alternative for Deutschland in Germany, the National Front in France, the Freedom Party in Austria, the Golden Dawn Party in Greece, and many others. What they share with each other, and with earlier fascist parties, is a common political project which gives them their popularity: to cleanse and protect the nation from minority elements defined as alien; to recover a political sovereignty which

they see as infringed or damaged; and to establish elements of autarchy in the face of global economic forces. These parties have been
led by demagogic leaders able to forcefully articulate the concerns
which participants in this project seek to address and resolve, albeit
in highly simplified fashion. These concerns include persistent economic deprivation that mainstream parties have failed to address; resentment at minorities who provide a convenient scapegoat for these
deprivations and are seen as threats to the integrity of the nation; and
finally, the subordination of the country and its policies to external
powers and institutions, such as the European Union and the nexus
of international treaties.

At the same time, the project outlined above is one that is shared
by some more mainstream party leaders who have come to power
through electoral success, such as Viktor Orbán in Hungary, Beatra
Szydło in Poland, and Donald Trump in the USA. The first two have
also sought to reshape the state in a way that is reminiscent of fascism
in power by curbing the independence of institutions that might
serve to check them, from the courts and media to fiscal authorities and non-governmental organisations. They have further glorified
these moves as constituting a new type of regime – illiberal or authoritarian democracy – following the pattern of Turkey and Russia, which they claim is superior to liberal democracy in providing
decisive government and economic development. No doubt Donald Trump would like to emulate them in their refashioning of the
state, but the checks and balances of the US constitution have, so far,
proved too robust, and he is not, as Orbán and Szydło are in their respective parliamentary systems, in full control of the governing party.

If in these respects present-day right-wing parties and governments
exhibit elements of fascism, they also have significant differences. The
writers assembled here were agreed that fascism was characterised by a
distinctive political method—the combination of extra-legal violence
with more conventional forms of political mobilisation, whether as
parties or regimes. In the case of the present-day far-right movements,
the distinctive fascist element of systematic extra-legal violence is
largely absent. This is partly because it would be counterproductive
in the much more secure democracies of the present day; partly also
because electoral methods have proved effective, if not in bringing

them to power, then at least in influencing more mainstream parties to adopt their agendas, as has happened in the UK, Hungary, Austria, and elsewhere.

Perhaps most significant of all, the first victims of fascist violence, directed by both movements and subsequent states, were the institutions of the working class—independent trade unions, Social Democratic and Communist parties, and their leading cadres. Precisely because of their strength, these could only be broken by violent means. This is why fascism came to be tolerated if not actively supported by large-scale capital, however much its methods were looked on with distaste and involved the political subordination of capitalism's representatives. In the present-day context, these and other Left-oriented institutions had already suffered defeat, first at the hands of the Reagan and Thatcher governments, and then by Social Democratic parties accepting the tenets of neoliberalism and its post 2008 programme of austerity. What the writers here saw as the historic role of fascism – to destroy the power of the Left and its institutions – has now been achieved by more conventional means, though we must not forget that in Latin America it required the dictatorships of the 1970s and 1980s to achieve this result.

Here it is worth repeating Ignazio Silone's insistence in his *What is Fascism?* that fascism had to be distinguished from the two other typical forms of capitalist reaction: in developed countries by conservative parties working through parliamentary means, and in less developed countries by military dictatorship. Fascism differed from the latter, he argued, by the mobilisation of a mass movement, and from the former by its hostility to parliamentarism and constitutionality.

These and other conclusions on fascism reached by the writers assembled here will remain relevant reading in a period of resurgence of the far-right and its threat to the pluralisms we have come to take for granted in liberal democracy.

Manchester, UK
2018

Introduction

The purpose of this collection is to make available a wider range of Marxist writing on fascism from the inter-war years than has previously been accessible to readers of English. Over three-quarters of the material here is translated for the first time. One consequence of bringing it together under one cover should be to lay finally to rest the idea that Marxism in this period can be simply equated with Stalinist orthodoxy. That the latter came to exercise an exclusive dominance over the Communist parties after 1928 is not in doubt; nor that its definitions of fascism as the final stage of monopoly capitalism, and of Social Democracy as fascism's left wing, contributed to the defeat of the German working class in 1933. Yet the extent of that dominance and the spectacular character of that defeat have served to obscure the range and subtlety of analyses of fascism within the Communist movement before 1928, and among Communists in opposition thereafter. Of the latter, only Trotsky's work is fully available in English, and even that is often treated as an isolated exception. On the other side of the fence, the rejection by post-1945 Social-Democracy of its Marxist past has allowed a rich vein of theoretical analysis, particularly on the left of the German and Austrian parties, to remain buried. Again there are individual exceptions, such as Otto Bauer, though much of his work still remains to be translated. The first purpose of this collection, then, is to recover the variety and complexity of Marxist work available from this period.[1]

What counts as 'Marxist' is naturally not uncontentious. My criterion has been inclusive rather than exclusive: those writers are included who self-consciously saw themselves as working within a Marxist tradition. That is to say, I do not use the term 'Marxist' prescriptively, to exclude all work which fails to meet some predetermined test of validity, whether of correct socialist strategy or of properly 'scientific' analysis. To adopt such a criterion not only forecloses debate on what such a strategy should be; it also distorts the historical record, and reinforces the illusion that the Marxist method contains some infallible innoculation against error. Perhaps this point needs no emphasis now that the idea of a single Marxist orthodoxy has long since been abandoned. Yet such an idea still has its hold on the history of Marxism, especially in the period of the Third International. As the writings here demonstrate, Marxism has always been pluralistic.

What conclusions emerge from such a collection? First, there is the necessity of a certain re-evaluation at the level of the history of ideas. To recognise the existence of a more subtle analysis of fascism before 1928 in certain sections of the Comintern, particularly in the PCI under Gramsci and Togliatti, sets both the Stalinist orthodoxy after 1928 and the criticisms of its opponents in a somewhat different light. On the one hand, the Comintern's 'third period' line can be seen to involve a conscious rejection of a level of understanding of fascism already available. On the other hand, the theories of its critics did not emerge out of thin air, but represented a continuation and development of an earlier analysis. This continuity was most clearly embodied in those critics who were expelled from the PCI after 1928 (e.g. Tasca, Silone), but is also evident in the writings of Thalheimer and Trotsky. Some of the typical features of this analysis were then taken up by Social Democrats who moved in a revolutionary direction after 1933, and revised their views of fascism as a result of their defeat. This connection is missed by the conventional historiography which treats the history of the Comintern and of Social Democracy in separate compartments, or at least only as a history of antagonism at the institutional level. On this level one can see a Comintern orthodoxy, which viewed fascism as the final stage of capitalism on the road to collapse, challenged by a social-democratic orthodoxy, which viewed fascism as an aberration in the peaceful development of capitalism on the road to socialism. But this misses an alternative and more complex tradition which can be located within the PCI between 1924 and 1928, which was sustained after 1928 by Communists expelled from their national parties, and which was then taken up by left Social Democrats after 1934. This collection is as much concerned with this 'alternative' tradition as with the simple orthodoxies.

Secondly is the content of that analysis. It is a common view that, in comparison with more recent Marxism, accounts of fascism from the inter-war period were crucially flawed by an 'economistic' fallacy, which deduced political structure and ideology directly from the economic system. This failing demonstrated the absence of any adequate theory of the state or of culture, such as it has been precisely the task of more recent Marxism to provide. This judgement is far too sweeping. For example, the idea that fascism, both as movement and as regime, had a certain autonomy from the direct control of capitalist interests, was clearly understood by a number of writers represented here. So too was the idea of the specificity of fascism as a form of reaction, and the explanation of its distinctive characteristics, such as its aggressive nationalism, in terms of the imbalance between different national economic and political structures within the imperialist system, rather than in terms of capitalism *per se*. Such insights were not always articulated at a high theoretical level, yet they existed none the less.[2] They suggest that, in its more complex versions, Marxism has more to offer towards an understanding of fascism than accounts which see it as the product of a uniquely Italian or German history, define it as the cultural malaise of the European spirit, or explain it with reference to theories of mass psychology or totalitarianism. There is not the space to argue this comparison here.[3] The texts must speak for themselves. What they show is that Marxism as a mode of analysis is capable of high degrees both of obfuscation *and* illumination. The tradition is not only a plural, but an ambiguous one.

Thirdly is the practical question of how fascism could be prevented or successfully opposed. None of the writers represented here were concerned with the analysis of fascism simply as an exercise in abstract theory; they were concerned with the urgent practical question of how the working class could be defended against fascism, and how the latter could be defeated. Their strategies all failed, and that failure is instructive. However, a common assumption that the failures were due to an inadequate theory of fascism is over-simple, for two reasons. First, it is possible to have the most profound theoretical understanding, and still fail, because the circumstances themselves are simply too unfavourable. How far 'objective', and how far 'subjective' conditions are responsible is a matter of careful historical investigation in each case. In particular, whether the crucially debilitating split between the Comintern and the parties of the Second International should be assigned to the 'objective' or 'subjective' conditions of working-class defeat in the inter-war period is itself a matter of controversy. Secondly, practice may determine theory as well as vice versa. In this context it is significant that those who had the clearest view of fascism and the strategy for combating it, had either themselves failed in their attempts to prevent it, or been excluded from positions from which they could influence policy, or both. The 'alternative tradition' mentioned above, in other words, was associated with either failure or impotence. To say that its insights were the *product* of the latter would be going too far. Yet it is clear that the relation between theory and practice is a complex one. What we can say is that adequate theory is a *necessary* rather than a *sufficient* condition of successful practice. And to that extent mistakes of theoretical analysis are instructive.

This brings us to the question of the criterion for selection of the material included. I have tried to make the collection reasonably representative of Marxist writings from different perspectives and periods within the years 1921–39. It makes no claim, however, to being comprehensive. It is not a historical record of Marxist struggle against fascism, though due attention is paid to historical sequence and content in the organisation of the selections. I have chosen writings which seem to me intrinsically interesting and instructive, either for the questions they pose, or for the quality of their analysis, or for the exemplary character of their mistakes. The extracts are divided into five parts. The first contains analyses of Italian fascism up to 1928; the second includes more familiar material on Nazism from the Comintern and the KPD; the third is devoted to writings of Communists in opposition after 1928; the fourth includes a wide range of positions within Social Democracy; the fifth addresses what has become a crucial problem in the Marxist analysis of fascism – the relation between the fascist state and the economy. For convenience the introduction follows the same division of material. Its purpose is interpretative rather than historical, in so far as the two can be distinguished. That is to say, it is not intended to provide a detailed historical background to the texts, though readers are invited to consult the chronological table which follows (pp. 64–81). For the rest, a certain historical knowledge is assumed.

Fascism in Italy, 1921–28

Fascism presented itself initially as a complex and puzzling phenomenon, to Marxists no less than to others. The variety of different assessments of it to be found in the writings of Gramsci alone during 1921 bears witness to this.[4] In the articles he published in *L'Ordine Nuovo* in the course of that year, fascism appears successively as the symptom of a specifically Italian political decay and as a form of international reaction; as a criminal conspiracy and a broad social movement; as the instrument of the petty-bourgeois masses and the agent of the most reactionary elements among the major owners of land and capital; as an essentially urban phenomenon, and as a movement to subordinate the towns to the countryside. Such apparently contradictory assessments reflected the actual complexity of fascism itself, and the different phases of its development. It was only gradually that it was possible to integrate these disparate and conflicting elements into a coherent synthesis.

If one problem that had to be overcome in reaching an adequate understanding of fascism was its complexity, another was the opposite: the temptation to cut through the complexity by over-simplification. This failing was evident in the official position of the PCI under Bordiga before Mussolini's march on Rome, when fascism was understood simply as the 'terrorist instrument' or 'military wing' of capitalism. This definition saw no conflict between the fascist movement and the Italian ruling class, and no reason therefore to expect a *coup d'état*. In any case, since according to Bordiga parliament was merely a fig leaf for capitalist dictatorship, a *coup* would make no difference. It was the Socialists, who sustained the democratic illusions of the working class by their support of the parliamentary 'farce', against whom the Communist attack should be most energetically directed.[5] The PCI thus had no strategy for resistance to fascism, and was caught completely unprepared for Mussolini's march on Rome. Even afterwards Bordiga saw no reason to modify his view that all forms of working-class suppression, whether under bourgeois democracy or dictatorship, were essentially the same, a view that was incorporated in official Comintern theses on fascism, most notably in the resolutions of the fifth Comintern Congress in 1924.[6]

Such a simplification undoubtedly represented one strand of Communist thinking in these early years. It did not, however, go unchallenged. Starting with a speech by Radek to the Comintern in November 1922, and developed during 1923 by Klara Zetkin and Gyula Sas,[7] a more subtle analysis emerged which took as its starting point a critique of the earlier position. Through over-simplification, they argued, the PCI had misunderstood the distinctive character of fascism and the seriousness of its threat to the working class; such misconceptions had made their own contribution to the fascist success. The more complex analysis that emerged on the basis of this critique was developed most fully in the writings of Gramsci and Togliatti after 1924, and became the official doctrine of the PCI under their leadership.

Although not identical, these more complex accounts were in broad agreement about the problems of analysis that fascism presented. They accepted the view, put most cogently by Sas, that fascism represented the offensive of capital in a situation of economic crisis, in which the levels of exploitation necessary for capitalist reconstruction could only with great difficulty be imposed on a strongly organised working class within a democratic system. Fascism was thus part of a general capitalist reaction. However, such a characterisation was not seen as sufficient or unproblematic, but as the starting point for a series of further questions, namely: how did fascism differ from other forms of capitalist offensive; how did a movement which served the interests of the largest property owners draw mass support from strata which were ambivalent if not actually hostile to such interests; why was it in Italy, and only there, that fascism proved successful in achieving power in the immediate post-war period? Such questions were not of merely theoretical interest, but crucial to answering urgent problems of political practice: how could fascism be prevented or overcome, and what was the relation between the fight against fascism and the struggle against capitalism itself?

First, then, if fascism was to be located in the wider context of European reaction, it was not synonymous with any and every form of reaction, as Zetkin and Togliatti especially insisted. Terrorism was its distinctive method, but it was not to be equated with terrorism as such. In particular it was to be distinguished from the terrorism of Horthy-type regimes in Hungary and elsewhere, in two decisive respects.[8] Fascist violence was not just counter-revolutionary – i.e. directed against the revolutionary movement – but was levelled at the working class in all its organised forms, including reformist unions and the institutions of Social Democracy. This gave the lie to the reformist theory that fascism was simply a reaction to communism, a revenge by the bourgeoisie for the revolution in Russia. Secondly, unlike the terrorism of the Horthy regime, fascist violence was not perpetrated from above, by a small caste of feudal officers, but from below, with the support of a mass movement. Hence Klara Zetkin's insistence that fascism's characteristic methods combined terrorism with demagogy, and that its victory constituted a *political* and *ideological* defeat for the workers' movement, not merely a military one.

The social location of this defeat was the petty bourgeoisie. Around a hard core of demobilised soldiers in the fascist movement were associated a variety of social groups: white-collar workers, small shopkeepers and small manufacturers in the towns, small landholders and more prosperous peasants and share-croppers in the countryside. Two circumstances combined to make these characteristically 'ambivalent' or 'vacillating' intermediate strata susceptible to fascism. One was the economic crisis, which threatened the long established petty bourgeoisie with proletarianisation, and made the position of newly independent producers precarious. The other was their disillusionment with socialism's failure to realise its promise of a reconstituted society, presenting itself instead as simply a threat to their existence. Whatever the precise definition of this failure – whether the collapse of the factory occupations in northern Italy in the autumn of 1920, or the 'syndicalist' policies of the PSI in the rural areas which alienated the share-croppers and small proprietors – it was agreed that the social strata which subsequently turned to fascism could have been won over, or at least neutralised, by a more intelligent and determined revolutionary movement. Fascism was thus a consequence, not a cause, of socialism's political failure. The failure marked the point at which the middle strata (and sections of the proletariat) turned instead to a movement offering apparently simple solutions to their grievances: the idea that economic problems could be solved 'by machine guns and pistol shots'; that class conflict could be abolished by appeals to national unity and submission to authority; that the power of finance capital could give way before a romanticised conception of the small entrepreneur. As Gramsci put it, fascism had for the first time in history discovered the secret of a mass organisation for the petty bourgeoisie: an ideology of national unity and an organisation modelled on the army in the field.[9]

The identification of fascism as a mass movement of the middle strata raised at once a central problem of analysis. How could it also be the 'organic expression' of large scale property? What was the relationship between the mobilisation of the petty bourgeoisie and the large financial, industrial and landed interests that this mobilisation reputedly served? It was undeniable that the ruthless attacks on the rural workers' organisations were from the first supported by the large agrarian landholders; that the fascist groups were welcomed by the industralists when they moved to the large urban centres; and that they operated everywhere with the connivance of the public authorities. In this sense the idea of 'agent' or 'instrument' had a certain aptness. Yet it is in the nature of agents to be dismissed when they have done their appointed work, of instruments to be discarded when they have served their function. And it was notorious that fascism refused to retire so promptly from the scene. It aspired to go beyond its terrorist activity at the local level, to launch an attack on the bourgeois state itself, and to replace the established ruling groups in power.

It was this fact that led the writers represented here to conclude that the fascist movement could not be simply the tool of the capitalists and landowners, but had a certain autonomy of its own.[10] In so far as the bourgeoisie actually acquiesced in its seizure of power, this could only be, as Zetkin suggested, because the fascists had grown too powerful to be suppressed without the danger of proletarian resurgence. Once in power, however, the fascist regime was dependent for its continuance on satisfying the major industrial and financial interests, even at the expense of the mass of its own supporters. 'The inexorable consequences of capitalist stabilisation impose themselves'. Togliatti wrote, 'and fascism finds itself compelled to carry out the brutal policy of financial capital'.[11] A contrast had therefore to be drawn between the social origins of the fascist *movement* and the policies of the fascist *regime*; between its social base and the objective interests it came to serve.

What began as a problem requiring explanation thus became the central contradiction of fascism itself in power. While it had been engaged in the destructive and essentially localised activity of smashing the workers' movement, a community of interest could emerge between the small and large proprietors. Once it was in power, it soon became evident that capitalist advance could only take place at the expense of the middle strata as well as the workers; policies for the concentration of capital, higher consumer prices, new taxation, etc., all brought fascism into conflict with its mass base. The ideology of national unity was now exposed as a fiction, and 'class conflict was abolished for everyone except the bourgeoisie'. This conflict found its expression within the fascist movement itself, as a conflict between the representatives of finance capital and those of the petty-bourgeois masses, and between the institutions of the state and those of the party to which its members still looked for their protection and advance. Fascism in power, then, was not a 'block of granite' as Zetkin put it, but rent with contradictions.[12] That this conflict was not all on one side was suggested by Gramsci, who highlighted the way in which the terrorist methods intrinsic to fascism continued to operate as a destabilising element after the seizure of power, most conspicuously during the Matteotti crisis:

> Fascism is a movement which the bourgeoisie thought should be a simple 'instrument' of reaction in its hands, but once called up and unleashed is worse than the devil, no longer allowing itself to be controlled . . . but proceeding according to its own internal logic and ending by taking no account of the interests of conserving the existing order.[13]

In an article on fascist 'contradictions' written in 1926, Togliatti identified a number of strategies employed by Mussolini in an attempt to stabilise his regime.[14] Foremost among these was the suppression of the independence of the fascist party, and its fusion with the existing structures of bourgeois class power. Its original cadres (the 'fascists of the first hour') were replaced by members of the bourgeoisie or their representatives; staff were absorbed from other bourgeois political parties; internal party democracy was suppressed and replaced by appointment from above, though not without a struggle. These moves were accompanied by an intensification of the repression of fascism's opponents internally, and a redirection of fascist aggression outwards on to 'the path of nationalism and militarism in struggle against the whole world'. Common to both Gramsci and Togliatti was an insistence that fascist policy had important political as well as economic determinants; and that capitalism's recourse to fascism as a 'solution' to its problems only recreated contradictions on a new plane.

This is an appropriate point to consider the question of why it was only Italy that experienced a fascist regime (though not a fascist movement) in the immediate post-war period. To none of the writers represented here was fascism a uniquely Italian phenomenon, whether as parenthesis in, or necessary consequence of, a uniquely Italian history. Fascism could take root anywhere, given the right combination of circumstances; in this sense it was a 'universal' phenomenon. Yet only in Italy did fascism in fact come to power in this period. The contrast drawn between Italy and other European countries suggested different levels at which an explanation was to be found: first, an especial severity of economic crisis working on a distinctive class structure; secondly, a historic weakness in the bourgeois state.

As to the first, the post-war crisis, so it was argued, had affected Italy more profoundly than any other European country. With a poorly developed industrial base and lack of raw materials, Italy formed one of the 'weakest links' in the capitalist chain after Russia. Objectively it was among the most ripe for revolution; subjectively, however, its proletarian movement was unprepared in both consciousness and organisation to take advantage of the opportunity. Yet it was strong enough in a 'defensive' or 'passive' way to constitute an obstacle to capitalist reconstruction. To these factors was added a further crucial element: the presence of a numerically large petty bourgeoisie, which, so Gramsci argued, because of the scanty development of industry and the regional concentration of what industry there was, constituted the only class that was territorially national. Given such a combination of circumstances, what other European countries might be considered vulnerable to fascism? Significantly Klara Zetkin singled out Germany, on the grounds that its economy had been the most completely shattered at the end of the war, and the SPD responsible for the most complete betrayal and demoralisation of the masses.[15] Gramsci and Togliatti, writing after the apparently conclusive defeat of Hitler's movement in 1923, developed the concept of the capitalist *periphery* to characterise a group of countries with structurally weak economies and large petty-bourgeois strata, including Spain, Portugal, the Balkans, Poland and Lithuania, of which Italy served as the prototype. Such countries, they argued, were most vulnerable to the development of a strong fascist movement[16]

Typical of such 'peripheral' countries was also a weakness of the bourgeois state structure, which meant that economic crisis was immediately reproduced as a crisis in the political sphere. Writing of Italy, Gramsci drew attention to the historical weakness of liberalism, due to the deep division between north and south, and the failure of the bourgeoisie to achieve an ascendancy over the rural landowners. Lacking mass support, and without any cohesion among its ruling classes, the Italian state fell into disarray in face of the economic crisis. Fascism was at once manifestation, contributory cause and beneficiary of this 'decomposition'. Once in power, it offered the prospect of replacing the discredited Giolittian tactic of perpetual compromise with an organic unity of all the bourgeois forces in a single political organism under the control of a single centre.[17] In similar vein Togliatti, contrasting the Italian experience with that of Britain and France, concluded that, where the bourgeoisie was economically and politically strong enough to control the working class by purely economic means, or to inflict defeat on it through the existing political framework, fascism 'moved into the background'. Precisely because the bourgeoisie did not control fascism, it constituted a last resort to which it would only be driven when the existing state proved incapable of sustaining a united political front for the defence of bourgeois class interests. In such a context fascism would have the task not only of destroying working-class autonomy but also of reconstructing the bourgeois political order itself.[18]

Before considering the implications drawn from this analysis for political practice, it would be useful to summarise its main conclusions. In contrast to the view which treated all forms of bourgeois reaction as identical, and every violent suppression of the working class as 'fascist', the position developed by most of the writers in this section, and most fully by Gramsci and Togliatti, involved defining fascism as a distinctive form of capitalist offensive, characterised as follows:

(1) It was a mass movement, drawing support mainly from the petty bourgeoisie, and directing violence at all autonomous institutions of the working class.

(2) Its widespread support was a consequence, not a cause, of revolutionary defeat and of socialist failure to resolve the economic crisis.

(3) It was used, though not always controlled, by the large property owners, who turned to fascism because they were unable to subdue the working class by means of the existing legal and political order.

(4) Once in power, fascism proved unable to promote the interests of its petty-bourgeois followers, in face of the logic of capitalist reconstruction.

(5) This gave rise to internal conflicts, which could only with difficulty be overcome by a reconstitution of the fascist party, and a transference of its militarism on to an external plane.

(6) Fascism was most likely to flourish in those capitalist countries with a weak economic and political structure.

What practical conclusions could be drawn from this analysis for the anti-fascist struggle? A number of different, though interconnected, questions need to be distinguished here. How could a fascist movement be prevented from developing in the first place? How could the working class be protected from it once it had won support? How could it be overthrown once it had seized power? In the context of the writings considered here, the first of these questions was essentially retrospective. All the Communist writers were agreed that it was the failure to carry out the revolution that had provided the fertile soil for fascism, and for this the 'betrayal' by the Socialists in Italy and the Social Democrats elsewhere had been largely responsible.[19] The World War had heralded an 'era of world revolution' and created objectively revolutionary situations in a number of countries in its aftermath, particularly in Italy. What had been lacking was the subjective dimension of an organised and determined revolutionary party capable of taking advantage of this situation. It was this analysis that dictated the logic of the split between the Third and Second Internationals, and the creation of the revolutionary parties on the Bolshevik model.

The logic of this split, however, made it difficult to sustain an effective alliance with Socialists or Social Democrats once fascism had reached the level of a serious danger. According to the analysis of fascism outlined above, it was evident that fascism threatened all autonomous institutions of the working class, reformist as well as revolutionary; indeed the former constituted a particular obstacle to the levels of exploitation necessary for capitalist reconstruction. As Zetkin observed, 'fascism does not enquire whether the factory worker owes his allegiance to the white and blue of Bavaria, to the black, red and gold of the bourgeois Republic, or to the red flag with the hammer and sickle . . . it strikes him down regardless'.[20] Yet it did not prove easy for Communists to make a defensive alliance with parties whose 'betrayal' they saw as responsible for the development of fascism in the first place, and from whom they had only recently split. The tactics required for developing the revolutionary party – ruthless exposure of Social-Democracy's leaders in an attempt to win over the proletarian masses from their influence (the so-called united front 'from below') – were diametrically opposed to those required for a defensive alliance, which demanded genuine co-operation with that selfsame leadership (united front 'from above').[21] To switch from one to the other was not easy, and it depended on an accurate perception of the nature and urgency of the fascist threat. That this was not impossible is exemplified by the writings of Zetkin in 1923, and Thalheimer, Trotsky and others included in later sections of this collection. Yet it proved beyond the capacity of the PCI, which in any case only split off from the Socialists immediately prior to fascism's rise, and became more preoccupied with attacking the PSI than with the threat from fascism itself.

Even after the march on Rome, and subsequently under the leadership of Gramsci and Togliatti, the PCI's approach to the anti-fascist struggle was conditioned by an attitude of unremitting hostility to the Socialist parties. This was predicated on the assumption that a revolutionary conjuncture had only been deferred, not removed by the fascists' seizure of power. On the one hand was the belief, common throughout the parties of the Comintern, that the period of capitalist stabilisation after 1923 was a temporary one only. On the other was the evidence that Mussolini's attempts to remedy the specific structural weaknesses of the Italian economy were intensifying the conflict between the fascist state and the mass of its original supporters. Here one can detect a close parallelism between the PCI's theory of revolution and its analysis of fascism discussed above. It was precisely the countries of the capitalist periphery that were both most vulnerable to fascism and most ripe for revolution; the numerous intermediate strata whose attitudes had determined the success of fascism would also be decisive for the prospects of its revolutionary overthrow. Having 'oscillated' to the right, they were now moving left under the impact of Mussolini's policies. In the first instance the Gramscian strategy of proletarian alliance involved the poor peasants of the south and the Islands, though he saw it in time extending to the middle peasantry and those of other regions.[22] Despite the admitted problems of this strategy – such as the hold exercised over the peasants by the Church, and the problem of reconciling the requirements of agricultural modernisation with the peasants' attachment to private property – it did take seriously the importance of the 'intermediate' strata, both to fascism's success, and to the possibility of its overthrow.

It was this belief in the continuing prospects for revolution that determined the attitude of the PCI to the democratic opposition to Mussolini. The issue crystallised around the question of what sort of regime might follow his fall – a return to bourgeois democracy, or a proletarian dictatorship. In part, as Togliatti observed, this was a question which events and the balance of class forces would determine. Yet in so far as it was a matter of strategy, the policy of the PCI was to oppose those working for a restoration of bourgeois democracy. Gramsci argued the reasons most forcefully: to ally with the bourgeois opposition was to ally with those who had 'acquiesced' in Mussolini's seizure of power; democracy was only acceptable to them now, because fascism had succeeded in rendering the working class impotent ('fascism has restored to democracy the possibility of existing'); for the reformists to accept the restoration of democracy as their goal was to acquiesce in a vicious circle which would one day require the intervention of fascism once more.[23] For these reasons the PCI continued to distance itself from the Socialist parties, and to define them as 'counter-revolutionary' (though, as Togliatti insisted, not themselves actually 'fascist').[24]

At this point the Socialist position was the mirror-image of the Communist one, as the extract from Zibordi makes clear. In fact, Zibordi's analysis of fascism itself was not all that different from the ones already discussed. It was remarkable perhaps for having grasped earlier and set out more systematically the relation between the three component elements of the fascist movement: the hard core of ex-combatants; the mass following from the petty bourgeoisie; the material and personal support of the big bourgeoisie and landowners. Like the others, it recognised the failings of the left as decisive in driving the middle classes into the fascist camp. The crucial difference, however, lay in how these failings were characterised. For Zibordi it was not so much the failure to carry through the revolutionary project, as the fact that it was attempted at all, that was responsible; not so much a 'subjective' inadequacy, as an 'objective' immaturity of economic conditions. Zibordi represented that school of Marxism which held that a political defeat of bourgeois class power was only possible when the economic conditions for socialism had fully matured. Italy's economic backwardness, and the predominance of petty-bourgeois and peasant strata, essentially 'individualist' in outlook, indicated that the country had only reached the stage of political democracy. The Bolshevik revolutionary programme, he argued, as also the Socialists' 'maximalist' programme in those rural areas of north Italy where they held power in 1920, were attempts to 'force the pace of history' beyond what the objective development of the country would allow. Fascism represented the brutal historical reprisal for such an attempt.[25]

This was the mirror image of the Communists' critique of the Socialists. Yet Zibordi could offer no more plausible strategy than they for how to combat fascism once it had become a powerful movement. Indeed, the ideas he did put forward contradicted essential features of his own account of fascism. If, as he argued, the armed defence units of the working class, the *arditi del populo*, were inadequate to take on the fascist gangs, it made no better sense to appeal to the state for protection, when it was admitted that the local apparatus of the state was itself hand in glove with fascism. Then again, for Socialists to adopt a non-provocative economic policy in the rural areas seemed to make no difference; Zibordi acknowledged that fascism was as ruthless in 'moderate' Reggio Emilia as in 'maximalist' Bologna. Finally, the search for 'responsible' elements among the bourgeoisie to construct an anti-fascist alliance was self-defeating, if indeed the advantage they saw in fascism was that it would force the proletariat to 'shoulder the burden' of economic reconstruction. Like many Social Democrats later in Germany, Zibordi was left simply with the *hope* that fascism's characteristic combination of violence with legality would prove self-defeating and internally divisive, and that, like some violent storm, it would eventually blow over.[26]

The example of Zibordi shows that it was possible to have a clear understanding of the nature of fascism and yet embrace an inadequate strategy for resisting it. The Social Democratic commitment to parliamentary legality was too deep-seated easily to be overridden, even when it was clear that the basis of that legality had itself been substantially eroded. This characteristic will be discussed more fully below, in the section on Social Democracy in Germany and Austria. On the Communist side, the obstacles to a defensive alliance with the Socialists were compounded by a massive underestimation of the threat that fascism presented, and a conflation of all forms of capitalist reaction into one and the same mould. As we have seen, the PCI under Gramsci and Togliatti substantially revised its analysis of fascism on the basis of an explicit critique of the Party's earlier mistakes. This more sophisticated understanding was disseminated within the Comintern through Togliatti's writings between 1926 and 1928. It did not, however, prevent the Communist Party in Germany after 1928 from repeating most of the errors of analysis and strategy that the PCI had committed in 1921-2 – indeed, in even more exaggerated form. The reasons for this will be explored in the next section.

The Comintern: From 'Social Fascism' to Popular Front
The theory of fascism developed within the Comintern in its so-called 'third period' after 1928 has become notorious for its contribution to the impotence of the German Communists in face of Hitler's rise to power.[27] What is less well understood is that it represented the surrender of a level of understanding of fascism that had already been attained within the PCI. As will be evident, the type of analysis considered in the first section was not the only one current in the Comintern in the early 1920s. Yet it still requires explanation why the mistakes of the PCI in 1921–2 and its own subsequent self-criticism, made so little impact on the struggle against fascism in Germany.

To start with it is worth pointing out that fascism did not occur a second time in precisely the same way as the first. Among the various differences between Italy and Germany were the following: that Germany possessed an advanced industrial economy and the most strongly organised working class in Europe; that a period of capitalist stabilisation interposed itself between the post-war defeat of revolution and the rise of National Socialism as a mass movement; that Hitler's road to power was prepared by a series of exceptional regimes whose character was not always easy to define; that the disabling of working-class organisations was undertaken after and not before the Nazi seizure of power. To estimate the danger from the Nazis correctly required not only an adequate understanding of fascism in its Italian form, but the flexibility to identify and anticipate its course of development in different surroundings. No such flexibility existed in the official Communist parties in the crucial years after 1928, as Marxist theory became increasingly confined to the straightjacket of Stalinist orthodoxy, and lost the capacity to correct its own mistakes.

Nowhere was this incorrigibility more evident than in the KPD under Thälmann's leadership. Its theory of fascism reasserted the old equation: fascism equals reaction. All capitalist regimes, whether parliamentary or dictatorial, were defined as fascist; at most, they exemplified different degrees of 'fascisation'. The idea that fascism was distinguished by a militant mass movement of the petty bourgeoisie was abandoned. Different factors may have contributed to this conclusion. One was that, as Mussolini's regime moved further in time from its origins and came to resemble more conventional dictatorships, it became easier to overlook the mass movement that was initially its most distinctive characteristic. Probably more influential on the KPD, however, was the Polish experience. In 1926 the Polish Communist Party had supported Pilsudski's *coup* against what was believed to be a 'fascist' government headed by the right wing peasant leader Witos. The subsequent development of Pilsudski's regime showed this support to have been erroneous, and confirmed the view that it was the use of dictatorial powers by governments in the interests of large capital that constituted the essence of fascism.[28]

Most decisive, however, in collapsing the distinction between different bourgeois regimes was the renewed experience of recession after 1928. The Comintern had always taken the view that the post-war stabilisation of capitalism was a temporary one only, and that capitalism's terminal crisis had been merely postponed. This view now appeared vindicated as government policies everywhere became more reactionary under pressure of the recession. Fascism was now defined as the political form of this final stage, the 'political superstructure of capitalism in decay'. Following this definition, the KPD called the Brüning government from 1930 onwards a 'regime for the implementation of fascist dictatorship' and the Papen regime of 1932 a 'more complete form' of that dictatorship.[29] If fascism had already arrived, what worse was there to fear from Hitler? As late as 1932 Thälmann was warning the KPD against any 'opportunistic overestimation of "Hitler-fascism" ', as it was called to distinguish it from 'Brüning-fascism' etc. Moreover if fascism had already arrived, and the KPD had managed to survive it intact, this gave grounds for confidence that it could avoid a repetition of the Italian defeat. Germany, after all, was not Italy.[30] Hence the simultaneous assertion by Thälmann of two otherwise mutually contradictory propositions: that fascism had already arrived, and that 'it can't happen here'.[31]

One reason why it 'couldn't happen here' was provided by the belief that the process of fascisation in Germany did not constitute a threat to the KPD so much as an opportunity. The other side to the reactionary impetus of the recession was that a new era of revolution could be assumed to have opened up. The KPD thus defined itself as being in an offensive rather than a defensive situation. Paradoxically for a revolutionary party, its increased electoral support from 1930 to 1932 was taken as confirmation of this analysis, though its support was drawn largely from the unemployed, rather than from the ranks of organised labour. It was their continued hold over the latter in a new revolutionary period that made the Social Democrats once more appear the main obstacle to revolution, and hence the main target for Communist attack. Now, however, they were seen not merely as counter-revolutionary, but actually fascist.

The notorious concept of 'social-fascism', which became current in the KPD and the Comintern generally from 1929 onwards, embodied two distinct, though overlapping, ideas.[32] One was the idea of Social Democracy as the 'moderate' wing of fascism, because it provided the bourgeoisie with a means for securing consent to reactionary policies which did not involve the use of violence. This idea had already made its appearance at the fifth Comintern Congress in July 1924, which concluded that fascism and Social Democracy were 'two sides of a single instrument of capitalist dictatorship.' Later in the same year Stalin described them as 'twins', as complementary instruments for securing working-class acquiescence in policies for capitalist stabilisation, the one by deception, the other by violence.[33]

It was a different aspect, however, that gave the concept its currency within the KPD itself. This was the resort to violence on the part of Social Democratic ministries in Germany to repress communist activity. The use of the *Freicorps* by Noske in 1919 to crush the Spartacists, including the murder of Luxemburg and Liebknecht, was an early example. Then there was the granting of emergency powers to General Seeckt in 1923 to dismiss the provincial government of Communists and left Social Democrats in Saxony, which first earned the Social Democrats the label 'fascist'. Finally, the massacre of Communists taking part in the prohibited May Day parade in Berlin in 1929 seemed conclusive evidence that Social-Democracy was not merely the 'moderate wing' of bourgeois reaction, nor merely an 'accomplice' in fascism, but actively facist itself. And if fascist, then it was more dangerous even than Hitler, because of its continuing hold over the working masses.[34]

What such a characterisation overlooked, most obviously, was an element in fascism that had been recognised by most of the writers considered in the previous section, namely, that Social Democrats were among fascism's first *victims*, and that fascism threatened all institutions of the working class without distinction. To define Social Democracy as itself fascist was to treat it simply as an agent of capitalist reaction, and not as a potential obstacle to, and hence victim of, that reaction. The concept of 'social-fascism' thus helped confirm the series of disastrous tactical errors committed by the KPD: the alliance with the Nazis in an attempt to bring down the Social Democratic government in Prussia in the so-called 'red referendum' of August 1931; the refusal to consider seriously any joint defensive action with the Social Democrats at an organisational level after the upsurge of Nazi support in 1932; the continued campaigns against them throughout the year after Hitler's accession to power, in the belief that the road to proletarian dictatorship lay open, if only the hold of 'social-fascism' over the masses could be broken.[35]

Why did the theory of social-fascism gain such widespread acceptance within the KPD? At one level it has been held up as an extreme example of the theoretical error of 'economism' − that distortion to which Marxism is prone whereby all political differences become reduced to their common economic base or function. Thus because fascism and Social Democracy both 'served' the interests of capitalist stabilisation, the differences between them came to be seen as unimportant. This is no doubt an accurate characterisation of the theory, but it does not suffice to *explain* why such errors gain ground at one moment and not another; they do not arise out of thin air, without any relation to a practical need or context. At this point a more historical explanation, which ascribes the errors to the requirements of Stalin's domestic and foreign policy, seems more satisfactory. The left turn of the so-called 'third period' of the Comintern which began in 1928 can be closely correlated with Stalin's left turn within the Soviet Union in the same year, in response to the difficulties over the grain supply and the developing struggle with Bukharin. Among other weapons Stalin employed in this struggle was the elimination of any independent bases of support that Bukharin might enjoy in the parties of the Comintern, and the establishment of an inflexible orthodoxy under leaders loyal to Moscow, such as Thälmann. From this point onwards official Marxist theory finally ceased to serve as a critical tool for understanding and changing the world, and became an ideology to be intoned by the faithful and manipulated according to Moscow's interests.[36]

The fact of Stalin's increasing control over the Comintern is incontestable. Yet the above explanation makes insufficient allowance for factors internal to the German situation which contributed to the 'social-fascism' doctrine. Above all was the record of the SPD itself, which since 1918 had largely confirmed the KPD's stereotype of a party concerned to stabilise the capitalist order and suppress working-class militancy, an image that was further underlined by its entry into the grand coalition in 1928, and its 'toleration' of the Brüning regime after 1930. As the economic situation in Germany rapidly deteriorated from 1929 onwards, the KPD confidently expected that the 'traitorous' SPD leadership would be unable to hold its working-class following, and that the united front tactic 'from below' designed to expose such leadership would prove successful. What happened instead was that the KPD drew support from the growing ranks of the unemployed, and this only added a further dimension to its antagonism towards the SPD, which largely represented the organised working class still in employment. The concept of 'social-fascism' both expressed and consolidated this division. The effect of Stalin's influence was thus less to create or disseminate the concept than to make it incorrigible, through the removal of all potential dissenters, particularly from the Party's right wing, who could have given voice in time to the alternative conception of a defensive alliance with the SPD.

In the end it was events themselves that exposed the bankruptcy of the KPD and Comintern policy. By the time Hitler had been in power for twelve months, it was evident to even the most myopic that the KPD had suffered a massive defeat. Pressure from the grass roots for a united front intensified in countries where the workers felt themselves threatened by fascism, most notably in France. However, since the national parties were now completely subordinated to Moscow's direction, any change in policy could only come from outside. When the new united front policy was officially announced, in the summer of 1934, it came with a suddenness 'like scene-shifting in the theatre', Leon Blum remarked, 'before which people sit in open-mouthed surprise'.[37] Stalin by now recognised the danger which an aggressively expansionist Germany presented to the Soviet Union, and the need for a defensive alliance with other bourgeois powers. This interest dictated that Communists should now join not only a *united* front with the previously reviled Social Democrats in defence of working class freedoms, but also in a *popular* front with bourgeois parties and governments in so far as they held peaceful intentions towards the Soviet Union.

The popular front policy was debated at the seventh Comintern Congress in 1935 (the first to be held since 1928), and defined in speeches by Dimitrov and Togliatti. The latter's address was devoted to the international implications of Nazism: to establishing the expansionist dangers of Germany, in particular for the Soviet Union, and to drawing a distinction between the different bourgeois powers according to the militarism or peacefulness of their foreign policy. Dimitrov concentrated on the internal factors that had brought Hitler to power, and the structure of capitalist interests he represented. His definition of fascism as the 'open terrorist dictatorship of the most reactionary, most chauvinist and most imperialist elements of finance capital', provided the necessary analytical basis for the popular front policy. By identifying fascism with a narrow stratum of finance capital, the new definition made the potential class coalition available for inclusion in the popular front as broad as possible, extending to the remainder of the bourgeoisie. Where the ranks of fascism had previously embraced everyone from the left wing of Social Democracy rightwards, they now shrank to a small fraction of capital. Dimitrov spared no criticism of the Social Democrats for their part in Hitler's accession to power, but admitted that Communists had also been in error: in not distinguishing sufficiently between bourgeois democracy and dictatorship; in underestimating the Nazi danger and the extent of national resentment on which they had been able to play; in persisting in left wing sectarianism, which was 'no longer an infantile disorder, but an inveterate tendency'.[38]

In the new phase of Comintern policy there was no more severe critic of past mistakes than Togliatti. During 1935 he conducted a course of 'lessons' on fascism at the Party school in Moscow, the first of which contained a comprehensive critique of Communist errors in the analysis of fascism.[39] This critique was largely a repetition of the one already contained in his writings of 1926–8. And what it was notably silent about was Togliatti's own position during the 'third period'. As I have indicated, the errors of the KPD repeated in exaggerated form the PCI's mistakes in the period of fascist ascendancy in Italy. No one had been better placed than Togliatti to warn the German Party of these mistakes. Yet not only did he keep his 'lessons' to himself after 1928: he also adopted the 'social-fascism' line, and played his own part in the removal of dissenters (most notably Tasca) from the party at Stalin's behest.[40] The silence of Togliatti and other Italian Communists – 'functionaries turned flunkeys' as Trotsky described them – must be added to the other causes of the German disaster as not the least:

> Italian Communists were duty-bound to raise their voices in alarm. But Stalin, with Manuilski, compelled them to disavow the most important lessons of their own annihilation. We have already observed with what diligent alacrity Ercoli (Togliatti) switched over to the position of social fascism, i.e. to the position of passively waiting for the fascist victory in Germany.[41]

Thus although members of the Comintern were prepared to admit past mistakes, the reason for their existence had to be kept quiet. German comrades were made to take the blame, while the structures which had perpetuated their errors went unexamined. Furthermore, the subordination of the individual Communist parties to the interests of Stalinist policy in the USSR, which had characterised the 'third period', now placed its stamp on the popular front policy as well. In practice the revolutionary movement became subordinated to the immediate interests of a defensive alliance at the diplomatic level between the Soviet Union and the governments of France, Czechoslovakia and wherever else might prove necessary. Evidence of this direction was apparent in the readiness of the French Communists to surrender any independent policy upon joining the popular front, to abandon the extra-parliamentary struggle, the workers' militia etc. As Trotsky expressed it, with some exaggeration, the PCF was turned from a revolutionary tiger into a 'trained donkey, with a cargo of patriotism'.[42]

The place where the popular front strategy showed its true character most clearly was in Spain. In his desire not to offend the governments of Britain and France, Stalin was determined that support for the Republican cause in the civil war should not go beyond the limits of the parliamentary republic. Yet in the aftermath of Franco's uprising in July 1936, the revolution had already gone far beyond this point, with the seizure of factories and estates by workers and peasants. In a situation of 'dual power' Stalin ensured that the growing weight of the PCE and the support of Soviet arms was placed firmly behind the restoration of the central government's authority, and the suppression of the revolutionary gains at the place of work. The revolution had to be defined as a popular, democratic, anti-fascist movement, not a socialist one. 'First win the war, then the revolution will look after itself', was the slogan. Anyone opposing this line from the left was seen to be undermining the war effort, and thus objectively 'fascist'.[43]

A critique of the consequences of the popular front strategy in Spain by Andrés Nin is included in the next section, but it would be appropriate to consider it at this point. Nin was one of the leaders of the POUM during the civil war. He had been an orthodox Communist in the 1920s, broke with Stalin in 1928 to join the Trotskyite opposition, then diverged from Trotsky in turn as a result of disagreements over the appropriate revolutionary policy for Spanish conditions. During the period of Primo de Rivera's dictatorship, up to 1930, he had criticised the Comintern for its ultra-leftism – for its definition of the dictatorship as 'fascist', and for arguing that it could only be brought down by a worker–peasant revolution. The only viable strategy, he argued at that time, given the weakness of the revolutionary movement, was to work for the establishment of a bourgeois republic, under which the working classes could gain political experience, and the scattered forces of the left be brought together into a united revolutionary party. Nin believed that the bourgeoisie would prove incapable of solving its problems within the framework of the democratic republic, and that, as in Italy, the choice would eventually be posed between fascism and socialism, between the fascist and the proletarian dictatorship. But the time for this was not yet. The sterile formulae of the Comintern were unable to comprehend the specific conditions of Spain, or the need to see the Spanish revolution as a *lengthy* historical process.

The situation in 1936–7 was very different. Now it was a question of a revolution already in being. Previously the Comintern had urged a revolution in inappropriate circumstances; now it was doing its best to stifle it. The war and the revolution were inextricably linked, he argued; the one was an extension of the other. Only revolutionary policies at the rear, offering the prospect of a different society, could inspire the fighters at the front. The slogan 'First win the war, then the revolution will look after itself' was a formula for the defeat of both. Only two possibilities were now historically available for Spain: socialism or fascism. In working for a third, the 'popular democratic republic', the Communist Party had become effectively counter-revolutionary; paradoxically it constituted a new brand of 'reformism'. This critique formed part of a review of political strategy that Nin prepared for discussion at the POUM national congress in June 1937. By the time it should have taken place, the Party had been suppressed, and Nin himself murdered at the instigation of Stalin's secret police.[11]

In conclusion, the period after 1928 demonstrated the bankruptcy of Marxism, both as a tool of analysis and as a guide to practice, within the official ranks of the Comintern, and its reduction to a series of sterile formulae. Any sense of the specificity of different countries' circumstances was abandoned. What was good for one was good for all. In particular, the flexibility needed to develop the analysis of Italian fascism in the different context of German Nazism was stifled. From now on this development could only take place outside the party. The following section will consider some of these attempts.

Communists in Opposition, 1928–37

It was one of the unfortunate ironies of the Communist movement after 1928 that those who had the clearest understanding of the character of the Nazi threat no longer held positions from which their warnings could be effective. The present section will begin with a comparison between the writings of two of these, Thalheimer and Trotsky. The similarity between their analyses of fascism, and of the strategy needed to combat it, has rarely been acknowledged. One reason for this is that their analyses seem at first sight diametrically opposed: Thalheimer said that fascism resembled Bonapartism, Trotsky said that it did not. As I shall show, this difference was more apparent than real. A more substantial difference lay in their general political orientation. Thalheimer was a member of the right opposition which was expelled from the KPD in 1928 to form a splinter party (KPO). His critique of the 'social-fascism' idea stemmed from a consistent opposition to ultra-leftism within the German Party, and to what he interpreted as the importation of an alien Russian model and strategy to the German struggle. He accepted the wisdom of Stalin's policy for the Soviet Union, but not for elsewhere. Trotsky, who judged everyone by their attitudes towards Stalin and to the principle of internationalism, called Thalheimer 'as hopeless as a corpse'. To him the 'third period' was not a manifestation of ultra-leftism so much as of 'zig-zag centrism' – that erratic course whereby policy veered, now to the right, now to the left, according to the interests of the Stalinist bureaucracy in the Soviet Union. On many issues, therefore, Thalheimer and Trotsky were in disagreement. But where, as on the question of fascism after 1928, German 'ultra-leftism' and Stalinist 'zig-zag centrism' coincided, so too did their opposition to it. This was no *mere* coincidence, however, since their analyses of fascism were based on certain shared theoretical assumptions.

Discussions of Thalheimer's theory of fascism suffer from taking one work in isolation from the whole body of his writings on the subject.[45] The essay in which he developed his well-known comparison between fascism and Bonapartism is undoubtedly important: it represents one of the earliest attempts to treat fascism explicitly as a problem of Marxist *theory*, and to explore Marx's own writings for help in resolving the problem. However, to be evaluated properly, the essay needs to be set in its context. It was written in

1928, on the basis of the Italian experience alone, and before the onset of economic crisis and of National Socialism in Germany.[46] When it came to making sense of the German situation, Thalheimer found himself compelled to modify the Bonapartist model in order to grasp what was happening. To put it paradoxically, the usefulness of the model lay as much in identifying where experience diverged from it, as in where it coincided. It is not enough, therefore, to treat the Bonapartist analogy in Thalheimer as an abstract and isolated contribution to the Marxist theory of fascism; it is necessary also to see what use he made of it in practice.[47]

First, the model itself. In his discussion of Bonapartism Marx had sought to resolve an apparent paradox: how was it possible for a regime which abolished bourgeois parliamentarism and dismissed the bourgeoisie's representatives from power, also to serve the interests of bourgeois class rule? His answer involved showing how, in a situation of acute class conflict and revolutionary threat from the proletariat, the bourgeoisie as a class would tend to lose confidence in the capacity of a parliamentary regime to guarantee order and the security of its property, and would submit to the authoritarian rule of a personal dictator, even against the wishes of its own parliamentary representatives. The distinctive characteristic of the Bonapartist regime was that the power of the executive, of the army and the bureaucracy, became supreme, and this gave it the appearance of standing above all classes. In practice, in establishing order and the security of property, it enabled the bourgeoisie to reassert its domination over society, and thus served its class interests. The key to the paradox thus lay in the distinction Marx drew between social power and political rule, and the conflict of interests that could emerge in a situation of crisis between the bourgeoisie in the country and its representatives in parliament. In order to preserve its social power, it had to allow its political power to be broken, wrote Marx; 'in order to save the purse it had to forfeit the crown'.

In his essay of 1928 Thalheimer used Marx's account to identify a number of parallels between Mussolini's dictatorship and Bonapartism. Like Bonapartism, it embodied 'the autonomisation of the executive power'; its instrument in achieving power, the Fascist Party, paralleled the December bands of Bonaparte in its methods; its militantly nationalist ideology played a similar role, as did its leader, the 'hero' of the *coup d'état*. The dictatorship was the product of a comparable situation of class conflict, an 'onslaught by the proletariat which has ended in its defeat and demoralisation, and a corresponding exhaustion on the part of the bourgeoisie, who cast about for a saviour to secure their social power'. Like Marx before him, Thalheimer distinguished between what he called the political form and the class content of Mussolini's rule, between the visible supremacy of the executive within the political sphere and the social consequences of that supremacy – the re-establishment of the economic and social pre-eminence of the big bourgeoisie and large landowners. This crucial distinction was ignored by Thalheimer's political opponents, who deliberately confused his theory with Otto Bauer's very different use of the Bonapartist analogy to represent fascism as a regime of real independence in a situation of class balance between capitalists and workers.[48] Thalheimer's definition of fascism as 'the open but indirect dictatorship of capital' showed the difference: openly dictatorial in political form, it abolished the direct rule of the bourgeoisie through their political representatives, the more effectively to secure their social dominance by means of the ruthless suppression of all institutions of working-class power.[49]

Critics of Thalheimer from the first argued that the Bonapartist analogy ignored important changes in the development of capitalism since the mid-nineteenth century, much as Marx had originally criticised the application of the term 'Caesarism' to Louis Bonaparte by his contemporaries. In fact Thalheimer was well aware of these differences. Among others, he pointed explicitly to the much greater development of working-class organisation, which required a much more extensive counter-revolutionary instrument for its suppression: 'The fascist party . . . in contrast to the Napoleonic organisation', he wrote, 'has a broad mass following'. Fascism was *not* Bonapartism, but a parallel form of capitalist dictatorship in a period when the advance of working-class organisation gave the class struggle a much greater breadth and intensity.

One effective test of a theory is its usefulness in practice. How far did the Bonapartist analogy help Thalheimer to identify and even anticipate the development of fascism in Germany between 1929 and

1933? The conception of Bonapartism as a particular form of the state – 'the autonomisation of the executive power' – enabled Thalheimer to demarcate fascism clearly from bourgeois democracy and from intermediate forms of authoritarian rule of the Brüning type. The use of bayonets against the workers by a bourgeois parliament certainly helped prepare the ground for fascism, he argued; 'but fascism only begins at the point when the bayonet becomes independent and turns its point against parliamentarism as well'. A disadvantage of this definition, concentrating as it did on the political structure of dictatorship, was that it led Thalheimer in his 1928 essay to include various countries in the category of fascist (e.g. South American dictatorships) which should not have been there. Yet the corrective to this was already present in his recognition that a distinctive feature of fascism (*unlike* Bonapartism) was the terrorist mass movement, acting as counterweight to the organisations of the working class.

From 1930 onwards we can see this latter aspect taking an increasing importance in his writings, as Nazism itself won increasing popular support. The attack on working-class organisations at the grass roots by a combination of infiltration and terrorism, and the winning of a broad if confused mass support by means of a token revolutionary ideology were, he argued, necessary preconditions for a fascist dictatorship. Indeed, the difficulties of establishing a dictatorship in Germany *without* mass support, in view of the strength of its proletarian organisations, led Thalheimer correctly to identify the Papen and Schleicher regimes as unstable and transitory. In sum, Thalheimer's concept of fascism from 1930 onwards combined two different elements, movement and regime: the terrorist mass-organisation directed against the working class from below, the autonomisation of the executive power directed against them from above. Each was complementary to the other. The regimes from Brüning to Schleicher, in their increasing abandonment of parliamentarism, constituted successive moves *towards* the autonomisation of executive power. But it was Hitler's mass movement that provided the necessary basis for the final abrogation of political rights, which was the hallmark of fascist dictatorship, and to which the other regimes were merely a preparation.

Thus far Thalheimer's analysis can be read as a development of positions already established in his essay of 1928. A more significant shift of emphasis lay in his analysis of the crisis out of which National Socialism emerged. As we have seen, Thalheimer had explained fascism as the product of a particular conjuncture in the class struggle – as the direct consequence of proletarian defeat in a revolutionary uprising, whereby the bourgeoisie, itself exhausted and in disarray, turned to counter-revolution to prevent any possibility of proletarian resurgence. The Bonapartist analogy, in other words, inclined Thalheimer to see fascism as essentially counter-revolutionary. What this overlooked was the crisis of profitability within the capitalist economy, which impelled capitalists to attack the living standards, welfare provisions and defensive institutions of the working class. It was this latter dimension of the crisis that was most immediately relevant to Germany in 1929, as Thalheimer increasingly recognised. Of course the crisis increased the possibility of a revolutionary outcome, and also the danger of counter-revolution in turn. Yet Thalheimer argued that the economic logic of the capitalists' own position was driving them towards dictatorship anyway, and that therefore a simple renunciation of revolutionary endeavour offered no protection against the fascist threat.

What was this 'logic'? The depression of world prices from 1929 onwards hit German competitiveness in export markets particularly severely, and intensified capitalist demands for a big reduction in wage levels, the dismantling of welfare provisions and the lowering of company taxation. While certain steps in this direction were compatible with parliamentarism, Thalheimer argued, the point had been reached by 1930 when this was no longer so. The required programme could only be carried through by an onslaught on the ability of workers' economic and political organisations to resist such measures. But democratic rights could not be abolished for one class alone; they had to be abolished generally. Hence the bourgeoisie was objectively impelled towards dictatorship whatever its wishes, and whatever the hesitations on the part of some of its sectors to abandon parliamentarism. The same 'logic of the situation', Thalheimer argued, would impel them to support the Nazis as the most ruthless and determined opponents of working-class autonomy, and so set them on the road to power despite their own misgivings. The Italian bourgeoisie had not originally intended to put the fascists in power; yet such had been the inexorable consequence of supporting their attacks on the working class. 'So the logic of development leads necessarily from the Brüning regime to the open and complete fascist dictatorship.'[50]

One of the chief difficulties confronting anyone analysing the German situation between 1930 and 1933 was how to characterise the Brüning, Papen and Schleicher regimes, and their relationship to National Socialism. Most of those on the left made one of two opposing errors. The first was to insist on the difference between Nazism and the various exceptional regimes, but ignore the connection between them. This was broadly the position of the Social Democrats, who supported (or acquiesced in) Brüning and Hindenburg as less evil alternatives to Hitler, and looked to them for protection against the Nazi menace. The second was to recognise the connection between them, but ignore the differences. This was the position of the KPD, which saw a common logic of capitalist policy at work through the various regimes and a common tendency towards dictatorship, but described them all as fascist. Thalheimer's analysis succeeded in avoiding these errors, by recognising both difference and continuity. His definition of fascism clearly identified the political differences between National Socialism and the other types of regime. His account of the logic of capitalist crisis demonstrated the continuity between them, and the impetus carrying the bourgeoisie towards a fascist dictatorship, to which these other regimes constituted successive transitional steps.

What were the practical implications of this analysis? Although the logic of crisis resolution in Germany led directly towards fascist dictatorship, Thalheimer insisted that this outcome was not inevitable. The logic could be broken, but only the working class could break it, and only by the most determined action. Here Thalheimer's position diverged from both that of the official Communists and of the Social Democrats. It followed from his emphasis on political distinctions that fascist dictatorship and parliamentary democracy could not be treated as equivalents, not least in their implications for workers' rights. In a showdown between the fascists and the bourgeois Republic, he argued, the Communists must defend the democratic institutions of the Republic. But these could not be defended by Parliamentary means, as the leaders of Social Democracy mostly imagined, nor by an alliance with bourgeois parliamentarians, whose position was increasingly being undermined by the growth of fascism, and by the desertion of the bourgeoisie in the country at large. They could only be defended by the most energetic extra-parliamentary action by the class organisations of the workers, if necessary armed. The precedents for a revolutionary defence of bourgeois institutions existed in the defence of the Kerensky government against the Kornilov uprising and the defence of the Weimar Republic against the Kapp *putsch*. These precedents suggested that, once such action was undertaken, it was unlikely to be confined within bourgeois-democratic limits, but would pass over into a struggle for the proletarian dictatorship. It was thus not a question of *choice* between a defensive and an offensive struggle. It was a question of winning positions of strength in the defence of bourgeois parliamentary democracy against fascism, *for* the struggle towards the proletarian dictatorship.[51]

As we have seen, the KPD defined its situation as an entirely offensive one. Perhaps it would be more accurate to say that it treated the offensive and defensive struggles as identical. The only defence against fascism was the revolutionary offensive, preparation for which required an attack on bourgeois democracy and Social Democratic organisations alike. By this strategy, failure to win support for revolution could only end in victory for fascism. Thalheimer, in contrast, distinguished between the defensive and offensive struggles, but pointed to their connection. A successful defence against fascism would put the working class in a strong position to struggle for the proletarian dictatorship. Such a strategy at least left room for an alternative between the success of the revolution and the victory of fascism. This was the possibility that as a result of the defensive struggle 'fascism would be thrown back for a lengthy period', though Thalheimer also insisted that 'only a revolutionary outcome to the economic and political crisis could bring about fascism's permanent liquidation, its final destruction'.

Of central importance to this strategy was the attitude towards

Social Democracy. Thalheimer yielded nothing in his criticism of the Social Democratic leadership for its 'betrayal' of the working class and for helping prepare the soil for fascism; yet this did not make them fascists themselves. The theory of 'social-fascism', he argued, was both wrong and practically disastrous, since it hindered the mobilisation of social-democratic workers in united action against fascism, and isolated the Communist Party from the masses. The most damaging element in the ultra-left strategy had been the formation of separate Communist trade unions, thereby surrendering the terrain on which the struggle against the policies of the Social Democratic leadership had to be fought. The continuation of such a strategy, he concluded, could only end in defeat:

> Whether this development (i.e. towards fascist dictatorship) continues, or is repulsed, now depends entirely on the working class, and in particular on whether the policy of the Communist opposition – of uniting the working class around extra-parliamentary mass activity against fascism and capitalist attacks, and of creating a united front on the basis of a programme combining the most urgent immediate demands with concrete revolutionary propaganda – whether this policy wins the day against the blinkered incompetence of the official party apparat in pursuit of its ultra-left course, on one side, and the Social Democratic party and union apparat pursuing its policies of class betrayal and timid surrender of the workers' democratic rights on the other.[52]

We have moved some way from the Bonapartist model. It is almost as if Thalheimer reached the conclusions he did about fascism in Germany in spite of the analogy as much as because of it. Yet he never actually abandoned it, and it is this that makes his analysis appear superficially different from Trotsky's. Thalheimer held to the analogy between fascism and Bonapartism despite the differences between the two; Trotsky argued that fascism could not be compared with Bonapartism precisely because of these same differences. For example, each recognised the distinctiveness of fascism as a mass terrorist movement. Where for Thalheimer this mass character simply modified the analogy with Bonapartism, to Trotsky it made it wholly inappropriate; Bonapartism properly understood was a dictatorship resting on the executive power alone, in the sense that it lacked any mass support. Thus for Trotsky it was the Brüning–Papen–Schleicher regimes that were the Bonapartist ones, because they stood above, and held the balance between, the mass movements of both left and right; it was crucial to distinguish these regimes from fascism, to which they were but the preliminary. A paradoxical conclusion thus emerges. Both Thalheimer and Trotsky insisted that the Brüning and Papen governments were transitional and not to be identified with fascism; the one did so because they were *not* properly Bonapartist, the other because they *were*.[53]

How did Trotsky justify his use of the concept? As Thalheimer had done, he developed it beyond the limits of the historical parallel, though in a different direction. He distinguished between two types of Bonapartism or 'government of the sabre as judge arbiter of the nation'. The first of these he termed 'pre-fascist' or 'preventive' Bonapartism. This was a dictatorship raised above the rival mass movements of revolution and counter-revolution in a period when the class struggle had reached such an intensity that it could not be contained within parliamentary forms. Bonapartism of this type preceded the decisive confrontation of the contending forces, which it sought to prevent. Hindenburg, Papen, Schleicher (and later Dollfuss in Austria and Doumergue in France), these were the Bonapartes, not Hitler. That they were mostly people of limited ability was irrelevant, since it was the context of class struggle that determined their role, not any personal qualities of their own.

Trotsky's idea of preventive Bonapartism was a considerable departure from any historical parallel, but it did serve an important purpose. This was to emphasise the extent to which fascism constituted a problem, as well as an opportunity, for the bourgeoisie. Thalheimer had recognised their reluctance to allow fascism its head, but had not fully explained it. According to Trotsky their reluctance had two sources. One was the social composition of the fascist movement:

> The petty bourgeoisie regards the bourgeoisie with envy and often with hatred. The bourgeoisie, on the other hand, while utilising the support of the petty bourgeoisie, distrusts it, for it very correctly fears its tendency to break down the barriers set up for it from above.[54]

At the same time the typical fascist methods involved 'shocks and disturbances', and the threat of open civil war with the proletariat, whose outcome was problematic. The 'preventive' Bonapartist regime marked the attempt by the big bourgeoisie to contain the fascist threat in so far as it was a danger to themselves, while at the same time using it to keep the workers submissive. Like Thalheimer, Trotsky regarded these pre-fascist regimes as inherently unstable, because they lacked a mass base of their own, and depended on a precarious balance between the competing class forces like 'two forks stuck symetrically into a cork, standing on the head of a pin'. At most Bonapartism could postpone a decisive confrontation between these forces, not prevent it for good.

The second type of Bonapartism Trotsky called 'Bonapartism of fascist origin'. This followed a decisive struggle in which fascism had proved victorious and won power. Once the task of suppressing the working class organisations had been accomplished, the militancy of the mass movement constituted a threat to social stabilisation, and its petty-bourgeois goals proved increasingly incompatible with the interests of finance capital:

> Having arrived in power, the fascist chiefs are forced to muzzle the masses who follow them by means of the state apparatus . . . But while losing its social mass base, by resting on the bureaucratic apparatus and oscillating between the classes, fascism is regenerated into Bonapartism.[55]

Fascism now itself turned into a dictatorship resting on the executive power alone, but with an important difference: the development followed rather than preceded the exhaustion and defeat of the mass movements. It was therefore a more stable form of regime than the preventive type of Bonapartism. This stability, however, was only relative. Trotsky repeatedly insisted that it was impossible to keep the proletariat in chains indefinitely by use of police power alone – an assumption which would seem to be less plausible when the working class had suffered a massive defeat and had its organisations disbanded. The assumption was, however, connected to another: that in the era of capitalist decline it was impossible for capitalism to survive without mass support of some kind, and that with the suppression of the workers' movement and the erosion of its own petty-bourgeois base, the fascist regime (and with it the structure of monopoly capital) was increasingly vulnerable as it came to reside on the power of the executive alone.[56]

Trotsky's characterisation of the developed fascist regime as Bonapartist (in his sense) raises two difficulties. One was its supposed independence from any mass base. Trotsky followed Gramsci and Togliatti in recognising that the accession of fascism to power would create a crisis in the movement, which could only be resolved by the suppression of the radical petty-bourgeois demands that were incompatible with the interests of finance capital, and by neutralising or eliminating their most vocal representatives. June 1934 in Germany corresponded to a longer drawn-out process within Italian fascism. Nevertheless, the suppression of the radical wing of the movement did not mean the alienation of all support, as Trotsky supposed. Although he admitted the success of the Nazis in focusing the confused resentments of the petty-bourgeois masses on to the substitute target of the Jews, this isolated insight was not supported by any considered theory of the social psychology of Nazism.[57] And he underestimated the strength of its nationalist appeal to a population humiliated by the Versailles settlement. Whether such omissions are intrinsic to a Marxist analysis will be considered in the final section of the Introduction.

The second difficulty is the obverse of the first. In Trotsky's account of Bonapartism, the independence of the executive power was an independence from the mass support necessary to stable rule, not an independence from the direct control of the dominant economic class. While the concept of 'preventive' Bonapartism enabled Trotsky to define the relations between the developing fascist movement and the bourgeoisie as problematic, the application of the term to the developed fascist regime carried the implication that the new regime was merely the instrument of monopoly capital. Hitler was thus seen to make an effortless transition from arch-representative of petty-bourgeois illusions to arch-manipulator of those illusions in the interests of finance capital. This, like the Comintern definition of fascism in power, was more simplistic than the more qualified accounts of Gramsci and Togliatti earlier, according to which the nature and methods of fascism continued to pose a problem for capitalist stabilisation. Such was the sense of Thalheimer's 1928 essay also:

Fascism and Bonapartism both promise bourgeois society 'peace and security'. But in order to prove their indispensability as permanent 'saviours of society', they have to make out that society is constantly under threat; hence proceeds perpetual restlessness and uncertainty.[58]

It is not surprising that recent Marxist theorising, concerned as it is to answer criticism of Marxist analysis of fascism, and to relate that analysis to a more rigorous theory of the state, should find Thalheimer's use of the Bonapartist analogy more acceptable than Trotsky's, because it offers a starting point for a more subtle account of the relationship between fascism in power and capitalist interests. This dimension will be explored more fully in the final section. Yet if we consider the two writers in the urgent practical context of the years 1929–33, with Nazism on the road to power, the balance of advantage is less obvious. In this context the differences in their terminology, and in the precise use they made of the historical parallel with Bonapartism, are less important than the common standpoint they shared. Like Thalheimer, Trotsky saw the ground being prepared for fascism by the anti-parliamentary regimes from Brüning onwards, without confusing these with fascism. He warned the working class as urgently that fascism would prove more violent and barbarous in Germany than in Italy, and would threaten war against the Soviet Union. Both writers exposed the fallacies involved in the theory of social-fascism, and in the tactic of the united front 'from below', aimed at undermining the Social Democratic leadership. As Trotsky argued, the Nazi threat was increasingly a matter of survival for both Communists and Social Democrats; the united front must therefore take the form of a defensive alliance at an organisational as well as at grass-roots level, despite the disagreements about what should follow that defence. Like Thalheimer, Trotsky argued that the defence could only be effectively mounted from outside parliament, and that this would work in a revolutionary direction. The

Communist united front policy', he wrote, 'must proceed from the concern of Social Democracy for its own hide. That will be the most realistic policy, and at the same time the most revolutionary in its consequences'.[59]

This is a convenient point to consider Ignazio Silone's work on fascism, which addresses a central issue confronted by Thalheimer and Trotsky and confused by the Comintern – how to distinguish fascism from other forms of reaction. Unlike the other two, Silone's response to his expulsion from the PCI was to withdraw into literary and historical enquiry. From this perspective he sought to explain the mistakes of Communist analysis, neither by 'ultra-leftism' nor by 'bureaucratic centrism', but by a generic tendency within political movements to subordinate critical enquiry to the immediate requirements of propaganda. His history of Italian fascism, published in German in 1934, was an attempt to free Marxism from these 'distortions'. His last chapter seeks to distinguish fascism from two other forms of reaction: from military dictatorship, which, Silone argued, is the characteristic form of reaction in underdeveloped countries, where the bourgeoisie is weak and the army forms the strongest political organisation; and from reaction carried through by traditional conservative parties within a parliamentary system. Fascism is to be distinguished from the first by its mass political movement, and from the second by its hostility to parliament and the bourgeois parties, which it seeks to replace by its own dictatorship.[60]

Silone's distinctions are clear and straightforward. Like Thalheimer and Trotsky, he recognised the common reactionary impetus underlying the different political forms at the particular conjuncture of the capitalist world economy. The explanation for the *differences*, he argued, was to be found in the Marxist 'law of uneven development', which produced different configurations of social forces in different countries, and ensured that political phenomena did not occur simultaneously across the globe. It was this that the theorists of the Comintern had ignored. It was also overlooked on the other side by the 'fanatical exponents of national particularity', who explained every new phenomenon as uniquely determined by the circumstances of a single country. Following Gramsci and Togliatti, Silone located the origin of fascism in a *class* of countries 'with relatively weak economies, where a unified national state was still a recent creation and lacked any rooted tradition among the masses'.

The distinctions Silone draws between the different political forms of reaction also raise a number of questions. First is the distinction between fascism and other forms of dictatorship. This cannot be said to be quite as clear-cut in practice as Silone makes out. Or rather the categories are to be seen as 'ideal types', which allow for various admixtures in the actual world. Was Franco's uprising fascist? It was perhaps more a conservative counter-revolution that took on fascist trappings and style, and governed with the support of a mass organisation created more from above than from below. From the standpoint of the working classes in Spain after July 1936, however, the distinction between this and 'purer' forms of fascism was unimportant, given the manifest threat its military force posed to them. While necessary for purposes of analysis and strategy, it would be mistaken to insist on the distinction in a way that suggested that fascism constitutes a uniquely damaging threat in comparison with other forms of outright dictatorship.

The distinction between fascism and reaction within a parliamentary system raises a different set of issues. The confusions of the Comintern's 'third period' show the danger of blurring the distinction. Yet there is an opposite danger, that of ignoring the interconnection between the two, as Thalheimer and Trotsky insisted. This connection can take two forms, of succession and simultaneous interaction. A restriction of democratic rights carried out under a parliamentary regime can prepare the ground for their subsequent suspension under a dictatorship. Reaction tends to be fuelled, rather than exhausted, by concessions. A different, and more contemporaneous, process of interaction takes place where the presence of a fascist movement enables a parliamentary regime to win support for reactionary measures that would not otherwise be tolerated. The movement does not have to be large to have this damaging effect. Both forms of connection – successive and reciprocal – were exemplified in Germany between 1929 and 1933. The problems they posed for the Social Democrats' analysis and strategy will be explored in the next section.

Social Democracy and Fascism

So far the discussion has concentrated on Communists' accounts of fascism. The present section will consider analyses by Social Democrats in Germany and Austria. Just as the parties of the Comintern failed, so the parties of Social Democracy in both countries also failed in their strategies to prevent the rise of fascism to power, the one without offering serious resistance, the other after an uprising under unfavourable circumstances. Their failure was less the result of an underestimation of the danger of fascism (though this certainly existed) than the product of a theory and practice of socialism that had been consolidated during the 1920s.[61] A useful point to begin is with the theoretical basis of reformism in its conception of political economy.

A central theme of Social Democratic analysis in the post-war period was the idea of 'organised capitalism', a concept given definitive formulation by Rudolf Hilferding at the SPD Congress in 1927. In his speech to the Congress he offered a quite different account of monopoly capitalism from the one given in his classic work *Finance Capital* published in 1910. The latter had emphasised two features arising from the centralisation and concentration of capital: on the one hand, overseas expansion and imperialist rivalry; on the other, the politicisation of class relations through the direct economic intervention of the state acting in the interests of finance capital.[62] With various modifications by Lenin (in particular the idea that monopoly stifled technical progress, and hence represented the decadence of capitalism), this became the post-war Comintern theory of monopoly capitalism as constituting capitalism's final stage.[63] Communist revolutionary practice, even in the period of capitalist stabilisation in the mid 1920s, was premised on the assumption that the increasing rationalisation of production within capitalist monopolies could only be achieved at the expense of increased anarchy at the level of the international market.

Social Democracy's conception of 'organised capitalism' offered a very different interpretation of capitalism's monopoly stage and its post-war development in Germany. It emphasised, first, the rational planning of production within the monopolistic firm and its capacity for technical innovation even without the immediate pressure of market competition. It was the application of this superior 'socialist' principle of planning that had enabled capitalism to regenerate and stabilise itself in the post-war period. The route to socialism was via the conscious, political extension of this principle to the economy as a whole, not through an autonomously generated crisis within the economic sphere. Secondly, since the establishment of the Weimar Republic the intervention of the state — in social welfare, wage arbitration, industrial reorganisation, etc. — was no longer seen as the instrument of capital but of society as a whole. Or rather, *which* it proved to be depended on the political determination of the ballot box. The state was conceived as 'neutral', and the preservation of the existing political order defined as the supreme aim of Social Democracy, both as a means for extending its own influence, and as an instrument for the future socialist planning of the economy.[64]

The idea of 'organised capitalism' thus developed Hilferding's pre-war themes of monopoly and the politicisation of the economy in a reformist rather than a revolutionary direction, and one that left the Social Democrats unprepared for the economic crisis that hit Germany after 1929. What implications did it have for a theory of fascism? Where the Comintern's theory of monopoly capitalism led it, in the 'third period', to see fascism as the normal political form of capitalism in decay, the Social Democratic theory of 'organised capitalism' led it to view fascism as an aberration, an abnormal interruption in the onward march of technical progress and political democracy. Such a view is particularly evident in Kautsky's work. For Kautsky the use of political violence constituted a historical deviation in an industrialised world where social power was determined by indispensability of economic function, and bourgeois democracy was the appropriate political form for a technically advanced society. Just as violence on the part of the Bolsheviks and putchism by the KPD were a futile attempt to *force* the pace of history, so the violence of fascism was a historical *throwback*, an attempt to hold back economic development and solve its problems by force. (The parallelism between the revolutionary and reactionary forms of dictatorship was significant). Fascism as a movement drew its support from 'reckless and short-sighted capitalist elements' and confused middle strata displaced by economic change. Fascism as a regime was 'economically illiterate' and could only intensify the problems of economic dislocation, not resolve them. Two practical conclusions followed from this analysis for the strategy of the SPD (and later the Austrian SDAP), when the fascist threat unexpectedly moved from backward Italy to Germany. First, the Social Democrats should seek a coalition with the more 'far-sighted' capitalist elements in defence of parliamentary democracy. But, secondly, if this alliance proved inadequate because of the increasing popular support for fascism, the only strategy was to wait, either for the storm to 'blow over', or for the fascists to prove their economic incompetence in power. Not the strategy of 'overthrow' but the 'war of attrition' was the order of the day.[65]

Kautsky's analysis embodied misconceptions frequently to be found in Social Democratic thinking about fascism: that fascist violence was the counterpart of Bolshevik or Communist violence, and was thus essentially counter-revolutionary; that its support was drawn from the petty bourgeoisie and limited 'reactionary' elements of big business; that it did not represent a general thrust by capital as a whole against the working class. Such assumptions were used to justify a policy of quiescence and the search for allies among the bourgeoisie rather than the Communists. However, the same conclusion could be reached by a different route. Hilferding himself was well aware that support for the Nazis was not merely a matter of 'reckless and short-sighted' capitalists, but part of a much broader attack on the social legislation of the Weimar Republic, and on the parliamentary system that was responsible for it. Yet he opposed any determined struggle against the dismantling of social welfare, especially after the Nazi gains in the elections of September 1930, on the grounds that nothing should be done that would alarm the bourgeois parliamentary centre, and encourage it to take the Nazis into the government. Such a move would rapidly lead to outright dictatorship through the Nazi insistence on controlling internal security. It was this calculation as much as inveterate hostility that ruled out any joint programme of extra-parliamentary action with the Communists. It also dictated the SPD's policy of 'tolerating' the Brüning regime as the 'lesser evil', despite its rule by exceptional decree and its progressive dismantling of the welfare system. Better preserve the remnants of parliamentarism until an upturn in the economy took the pressure off, and undermined Nazi support in the country. As late as January 1933 Hilferding was arguing that this tactic had proved successful, and that the decline in the Nazi vote between July and December 1932 marked a decisive turning point in its fortunes. The moment of acute crisis had passed, and the German labour movement remained intact, unlike its counterpart in Italy at the point of fascims's greatest popular support.[66]

This assessment proved tragically mistaken, as the critics of the 'toleration' policy on the left of the SPD had predicted from the outset. Among the crucial weaknesses of the policy, they argued, were that it enabled the parliamentary representatives of capitalist reaction to use the Nazi threat to pressurise the working class into accepting the dismemberment of its social and political rights without the inconvenience of actually allowing the Nazis into government. Yet it gave no guarantee that a Nazi government would not eventually come into being, and at a point when the fighting spirit of the working class would be seriously weakened by the collusion of Social Democracy in the reactionary policies of the Brüning administration. As Max Seydewitz among others acknowledged, any alternative policy would probably bring the Nazis to power. Yet the fact that Social Democracy was confronted with such a woefully limited range of options was a fact of its own making, in having compromised with the reactionary forces in state and society from the onset of the Weimar Republic – a consistent policy of 'toleration' that its theory of the neutral state served to conceal. In their exasperation Seydewitz and others on the left of the SPD broke away from the Party at the end of 1931 to form the SAP, a grouping similar to Thalheimer's right Communist fraction in its perception of the strategy necessary to defend the working class, but equally lacking the support to put it into effect.[67]

The Social Democrats' tactic of legalism at any price came to an end with the discredited attempts to find an accommodation with the Nazis after April 1933, and the final outlawing of the Party in June of the same year. In the circumstances of illegal opposition it was self-evident that the old methods were no longer applicable, and a number of revolutionary groups developed in opposition to the Party's

Executive Committee in exile in Prague. Under pressure from these the latter published its own revolutionary programme in January 1934 (the so-called Prague Manifesto). Drawn up by Hilferding, it rejected Kautsky's view that the goal of the opposition to Hitler should first be the restoration of the democratic republic, so that the struggle for socialism could then resume its peaceful course as in Weimar. Breaking decisively with this traditional Social Democratic perspective, the manifesto sought to unite the struggles against dictatorship and against capitalism in a programme for a transitional revolutionary regime which would expropriate the major social supports of reaction – the large estates, heavy industry, the leading banks – as well as destroying its political structures. Only when all the power bases of reaction had been decisively eliminated would a constitutional assembly be called, and a return to democratic life be possible. Although this model for what was in effect the 'dictatorship of the proletariat' explicitly acknowledged Social Democracy's failure to have carried through the revolution to its conclusion in 1918–19, it was regarded with suspicion by many on the left because it did not admit the reformist practice under the Weimar Republic to have been mistaken, nor was it accompanied by a purge of the Party's discredited leadership. Examples of the debates from this period are included in the collection. For Hilferding himself, one necessary condition for any successful revolutionary movement against Hitler – the intensification of the internal class struggle through pressure on Germany by other Western powers – was never realised.[68]

If the SPD offered the example of a right wing variant of Social Democracy, the SDAP had the reputation of being well to its left, a reputation earned by its more determined opposition to the war, and subsequently by the achievements of municipal socialism in 'red Vienna'. At the ideological level the Party was much less hostile to the Bolshevik model of revolution, which it regarded as appropriate to the circumstances of the USSR, if not to the advanced industrial democracies of Western Europe. Furthermore, its Linz Programme of 1926 had specifically envisaged the possibility of an armed uprising by the bourgeoisie in the event of the Party achieving an electoral majority on a socialist platform.[69] Yet the combined advantages of such preparation, of having a united working-class movement (the Communists were an insignificant factor), and the lessons of the German defeat before its eyes, did not prevent its succumbing to a similar debacle at the hands of the Dollfuss dictatorship in February 1934.

The Austrian political situation was complicated by the presence of two competing fascisms, a weak home-grown movement of clerico-fascism (the *Heimwehr*) and an imported Nazi movement which grew rapidly in strength during 1932. In the context of a parliamentary stalemate the following year, and fearing the further growth of the Nazis in the wake of their electoral success in Germany in March 1933, the right-wing Christian-Social premier, Dollfuss, decided on an anti-parliamentary coup which would enable him to govern by means of emergency powers. The ostensible aim of his dictatorship was to suppress the Nazis, which he did; at the same time he started a drive against the Social Democrats, using the forces of the *Heimwehr* as an auxiliary to the police. The SDAP did not immediately resist the coup, but engaged in a series of attempted negotiations with Dollfuss through 'sympathetic intermediaries'. Otto Bauer, the Party leader, calculated that a general strike would degenerate into civil war, and bring about an alliance between the two strands of fascism, the black and brown, and the armed forces of the state. So 'we offered greater and greater concessions with a view to making a peaceful solution possible . . . all in vain – Dollfuss refused to enter into any negotiations'. Instead he proved adept at dismantling the workers' rights piecemeal, without ever providing the occasion for a decisive confrontation. When an armed rising did eventually break out, in a spontaneous and unco-ordinated manner in Linz in February 1934, the Party had become too weakened to give it effective support.[70]

Immediately after the defeat Bauer concluded that, whatever strategy the working-class movement adopted in the face of fascism – a left tactic as in Italy, a right one as in Germany, or a 'centrist' one as in Austria – seemed to make no difference to the outcome. The explanation for the defeat in each place had therefore to be sought at a deeper level than the subjective question of tactics – in the objective circumstances of the economic crisis. On the one hand was the capitalist necessity to smash Social Democracy because its social legislation had become an intolerable burden in a context of reduced profits. On the other hand the resistance of the working class had been weakened by mass unemployment and the fear of the employed for their jobs. In between was the impoverished and embittered mass of peasants and petty-bourgeoisie, who turned against democracy because it was unable to offer them any protection against the crisis. The causes of the defeat of the working class, he concluded, 'clearly lie deeper than in the tactics of its parties or than in this or that tactical mistake'.[71]

How far was this assertion of impotence after the event justified? Bauer was not alone among Marxists in arguing that the dynamic of economic crisis itself was tending towards dictatorship and the dismantling of parliamentarism. This was in one sense the 'natural' outcome. The extract from Richard Löwenthal's work offers a persuasive analysis of the political aspects of this dynamic.[72] The nature of capitalist crisis, he argued, is to undermine the support for the class parties, whose mutual compromises within the parliamentary arena are a characteristic feature of bourgeois democracy, and essential to its coherence. These now suffer a process of internal fracturing along the lines of antagonism between those economically dependent on the state and those who are not, *within* each class: within the bourgeoisie, between the healthy firms and the 'lame ducks' enjoying public subsidies; within the middle classes, according to whether they depend on state employment; within the working class, between the employed and the unemployed. The consequence of this fragmentation is to make the process of parliamentary compromise unworkable, just at the point when a coherent economic policy is most urgent, and when more people than ever are dependent upon the state. As a result the demand for strong government, for dictatorship, grows, and the balance shifts from parliament to the bureaucracy and the executive, which is now the only source of unified decision within the state. The political system thus breaks apart along its own internal lines of fracture.

The labour movement becomes the particular 'object' or 'victim' of this crisis. Either way it turns it loses out. If it co-operates in capitalist solutions, it undermines its own support, and weakens its capacity for resistance. If it resists, then it only exacerbates the crisis:

The dilemma of its position is expressed above all by the fact that any effective resistance to the attacks of the bourgeoisie only makes a capitalist resolution of the crisis more difficult; it intensifies the crisis and contributes to the further undermining of democracy. On the other hand to make concessions, directly benefits its opponents by weakening its own basis of support.[73]

Once again the slide to dictatorship is the 'natural' outcome. Natural but not inevitable. It can only be prevented, argues Löwenthal, by the conscious organisation of all oppositional elements behind the proletarian class struggle for a socialist resolution of the crisis. And, he adds, 'no labour movement in any country has yet produced a leadership equal to such tasks'.

Löwenthal is not specific about the necessary steps in such a struggle. To take the Austrian situation at the point of Dollfuss' *coup* in March 1933, it is clear that the armed self-defence of the workers around a general strike and the immobilisation of key means of communication could have led to civil war. To hesitate before such an outcome was not despicable. Yet the necessity for precisely such a step in defence of the parliamentary constitution had been envisaged in the Linz Programme. Admittedly that had been seen in the context of a socialist victory, where this was in the first instance defensive. Yet the argument that the fighting capacity of the working class was at a low ebb because of years of economic crisis was contradicted by Bauer's own assertion that the Austrian workers were ashamed by the collapse of the German left without a fight, and were determined that things should happen differently in Austria: a state of mind that was borne out by the massive surge of self-confidence that followed the February uprising, despite its defeat. Such self-confidence harnessed to a more favourable strategic conjuncture might have produced a different outcome. Yet Bauer chose instead the course of negotiations and compromise with an enemy who was prepared to entertain neither.

The outcome, in other words, was not just a question of the dynamic of objective circumstances, tending towards dictatorship. It was also a matter of conscious political choice. And the fact that Social Democrats, whether of left, right or centre, all made the same choices when confronted with the slide to fascist dictatorship cannot be attributed just to the logic of events, but to some basic characteristic of Social Democracy itself. It was the conditioning effect of everyday routines and practices in the parliamentary arena that led them to prefer the familiar processes of negotiation and compromise at the highest level, even with those who were undermining parliament, rather than to rely on the less controllable extra-parliamentary mass struggle, even in defence of parliament. Assumptions made and continually reinforced in a familiar context proved more real than the abstract assertions of a party manifesto, such as the Linz Programme.

Once torn from this context, it is not surprising that Social Democratic leaders should move sharply to the left. Under the pressure of enforced exile Bauer, like Hilferding and the SPD leadership before him, was compelled to reassess his political position. As with the SPD's Prague Manifesto, he argued that the struggle against the fascist dictatorship could only be a struggle for the dictatorship of the proletariat that would overthrow the capitalist classes responsible for fascism 'and make their resurrection impossible for ever'. He drew out the full implications of this position, however, by arguing that the same strategy applied to the struggle against fascism waged within a bourgeois democracy. This defensive struggle would have to move outside the parliamentary arena, he now argued, and must be linked directly with the struggle for socialism. The following passage, written in 1936, and directed to the working class of the democratic countries, implies a clear criticism of the failed strategy of his own Party:

> Today the working class of the democratic countries is compelled to defend bourgeois democracy against fascist attack. In this struggle it must aim to rally the broadest possible masses of the petty bourgeoisie, the peasants and the intellectuals around the proletariat. But when the struggle between democracy and fascism intensifies and reaches its climax, breaking out into open civil war, a revolutionary situation can be generated in which the only defence against fascist counter-revolution is the revolutionary energy of the proletariat. In this way a defensive struggle on behalf of democracy can develop into a dictatorship of the proletariat.[74]

Bauer now believed that a vigorous defence of parliamentary

democracy by extra-parliamentary means could open the way to a proletarian dictatorship. In this his position had moved very close to that of Trotsky and Thalheimer discussed earlier.[75]

It did not follow, however, that Bauer rejected all the reformist past of his own Party. Reformism, he argued, was the product of a particular stage of proletarian development and capitalist stabilisation, for which it was an appropriate strategy. During such a stage it was the task of a socialist party to secure the maximum gains possible both at the workplace and through parliamentary legislation. To deride reformism as 'bourgeois ideology', as the Comintern did, was to misunderstand the limitations necessarily imposed by such a stage, and the roots of reformist practice within the working class itself. Once the capitalist economy moved into slump, however, the capitalist class would launch an offensive against the achievements of the reformist phase, and seek to erode the democratic rights won by the working class. At this point the arena of action would move outside parliament, and the struggle to defend democracy would produce a revolutionary situation. Here the practice of reformism would cease to be appropriate, and could only serve as a brake on the revolutionary process.[76]

By means of this analysis Bauer sought to overcome the split between communism and Social Democracy by integrating them into a comprehensive political strategy that included both. The practice of each was seen to be appropriate to a different stage of capitalist development and of the business cycle; the mistake of each was to assert its own practice as universal, and to persist in it past the point at which it was appropriate. This more comprehensive conception Bauer called *integraler Sozialismus*. Persuasive in outline, it nevertheless left some crucial questions unanswered: how to combine both types of struggle within a single party, and what kind of party it should be; precisely how to move from one type of struggle to the other; how in particular to ensure that the practices and institutional forms of the reformist period did not stifle the revolutionary struggle, as had happened in Austria. These can be recognised as some of the long-standing issues of revolutionary politics.

In considering the development of the Social Democrats' analysis of fascism and their associated strategy, we are confronted by a paradox. At precisely the moment when official Communist opinion was moving towards a reformist position with its popular front strategy, Social Democracy was passing it in the opposite direction with the adoption of a revolutionary programme. The Comintern had arrived at a definition of fascism as the 'terrorist dictatorship of the most reactionary elements of capital' just at the moment when Social Democracy was abandoning this essentially Kautskyite formula as mistaken. The Comintern discovered the existence of a democratic stratum among the bourgeoisie to serve as allies against fascism just when Social Democracy, from its bitter experience, had concluded that the commitment of this stratum to democracy was totally unreliable. As a result there is a quite marked convergence between analyses of fascism by Social Democrats in the mid-to-late 1930s, and many of the earlier Communist accounts we have already considered. Indeed, the line of analysis established by Gramsci and Togliatti in the mid 1920s, and developed by Communists in opposition after 1928, is maintained most clearly by Social Democrats such as Bauer after 1935. Of course the experience of the Nazis in power gave it a broader perspective. The implications of this will be explored in the final section which follows.

The Fascist State, the Economy, and War

Recent Marxist theorising on fascism has been concerned less with the practical issues considered in the preceding section than with the problem that the analysis of fascism in power presents to the Marxist theory of the state.[77] This is because the scope and power of the fascist state, and the nature of its political dynamic, defy attempts to deduce its pattern of development from simple constellations of economic interest. In particular, the standard Comintern theory of the 1930s which defined the fascist regimes as the agent of a particular fraction of capital, dictating policy from behind the scenes, seems implausibly simplistic in the light of what is known about the character of Hitler's and Mussolini's regimes. It should be evident by now, however, that the Comintern orthodoxy did not constitute the totality of Marxism in this period, and there were many theorists who gave a more decisive role to the political domain, and a more complex account of the relationship between state and economic interests than was admitted within the simplified version. It is true that there were few attempts to locate such accounts within a self-conscious theory of the state, in the sense that this is understood in recent Marxist literature. Yet even this deficiency should not be exaggerated. At least the elements of such a theory, I shall argue, existed in the writings considered here, even if it was not always organised or made fully explicit.

As we have already seen, many writers were ready to admit a considerable autonomy to fascism as a movement. It is worth rehearsing the argument briefly. The fascist movement, creature of capitalism's crisis rather than of the capitalists themselves, was recognised as having an independent mass base in the petty bourgeoisie and a rhetoric that was hostile to big business as well as to organised labour. Although it could never have achieved state power without the support of major capitalist interests, it did not do so merely as their agent. Two ideas were typical invoked at this point. One (more appropriate to the Italian experience) was that of 'unintended consequences': once fascism had been encouraged in its attacks on workers' organisations, it emerged too strong to be disbanded without the threat of proletarian resurgence. The other was the idea of 'last resort': the capitalists only acquiesced in fascist participation in government when all other attempts to resolve the crisis had been exhausted.

It was generally agreed, however, that the distinctively petty-bourgeois elements in the fascist economic programme did not long survive its arrival in power, but became subordinated to the interests of large capital and finance, though not without a process of upheaval within the movement itself. This subordination was explained in terms of the incapacity of the petty bourgeoisie as a class to sustain a positive economic policy of its own independently of the major classes of capital and labour, between which it 'oscillated'. Having used its power negatively to demobilise the organisations of the working class, it had inevitably increased the relative social weight of large capital as a result. As an *intermediate* class, comprising a variety of disparate occupations and forms of ownership, it was unable to maintain a distinctive class policy of its own in government, though the individual interests of its members could be satisfied by the expansion of posts in the fascist state. As a *declining* class (at least its small producer element), it was unable to resist the increasing concentration of production in the monopoly stage of capitalism, and any policy devoted to its interests would only serve to depress the economy still further. It was in this sense that Togliatti wrote that 'the laws which determine economic development under the regime of imperialism are inescapable'. And Bauer likewise: 'if you won't create a socialist society, then you must do nothing to disturb the mechanism of the capitalist order, under pain of economic catastrophe'.[78]

To demonstrate that the fascist regimes broadly served the interests of large capital, if necessary at the expense of the petty bourgeoisie, is not necessarily to say that they acted as its agent. The 'laws of capitalist development' generally set limits to the range of possible policy, rather than determine only one outcome. At any one moment there are conflicts of interest between different sectors of capital, between sectional interests and those of the class as a whole, between short-run and long-term interests, and so on. It is precisely such conflicts that allow for a certain autonomy to state policy, within the broad parameters set by the logic of capitalist development as a whole. This is particularly true where, as with fascism, the state takes on a distinctive form, assumes new powers and takes on new functions in relation to the economy.

In the Marxist accounts collected here there are broadly two different types of explanation for the distinctive character and power of the fascist state, though they are not necessarily mutually exclusive. The first locates it within the context of class struggle, and the socio-political crisis that preceded its formation. One origin of the fascist state is to be found in the disintegration of the bourgeois political order. This distinctively political dimension was recognised by both Gramsci and Togliatti, but was formulated most explicitly in Thalheimer's model of Bonapartism. Fearful of the proletariat and unable to organise support for the economic order by means of its own political parties, the bourgeoisie was forced to surrender political power to a fascist dictatorship as the price of preserving its social and economic position. This surrender to the repressive state, while necessary to ensure the security of property and profits, was not without its costs – not only the cost of a massive extension of state posts for members of the fascist party, but the continuation of fascist political methods into government, and the extension of conflicts internal to the fascist movement into the formulation of state policy. Yet the price was tolerated because to abandon fascism once in power would raise the spectre of a renewed resurgence of the working class. Continued submission to the fascist dictatorship was thus the necessary condition for the economic supremacy of capital over labour.

One strand of argument thus identified the fascist state as a special form of capitalist dictatorship arising from a context of class struggle and a breakdown of bourgeois political order. The second derived the necessity of the strong state more directly from the requirements of the capitalist economy itself. A directly interventionist role for the state was already widely acknowledged in the theory of monopoly capitalism. This role was now seen to be massively expanded as a result of the measures necessary to restore profitability in the context of world depression: the artificial stimulation of demand by the state, the reorganisation of finance, the direction of production itself, and so on. This aspect of the strong state derived, not so much from a breakdown of bourgeois political order as from a breakdown of the capitalist market, and its incapability of restoring profitability through the automatic mechanism of the price system. The state was compelled to assume a whole range of functions which the market could no longer perform. This development towards 'state capitalism' was a general phenomenon, but taken furthest in the fascist states. Indeed it was precisely the dictatorial powers needed to resolve the political crisis that also enabled the most far reaching interventions to be made in the economy, compared with what was possible under more democratic regimes.

The distinction between the socio-political dimension of the fascist state, and its economic-interventionist aspect was developed most explicitly by Löwenthal in his article series of 1935. He also offered a distinctive analysis of each. His account of the breakdown of bourgeois democracy, as we saw earlier, particularly emphasised the way the recession undermined the processes of class compromise, and the authority of parliament as the major institution for that compromise. This left the bureaucracy and the executive as the only locus for unity and decisive policy within the state. At the same time the economic crisis required the state to take over functions that could no longer be performed by the market. And it also produced new constellations of interest cutting across classes, which depended on the state for their subsistence. It was precisely the combination of a weakened parliament on the one hand and the economic requirement of a strong state on the other, that made the demand for dictatorship irresistible, a demand that had wide support from the masses, not just from a narrow stratum of the capitalist class.[79]

The concentration of power in the hands of the fascist state was thus determined at two levels, the socio-political and the directly economic. The result, according to Löwenthal, was neither complete autonomy for the fascist state, nor its direct subordination to particular class interests, but a combination of the two which gave it an essentially contradictory character. This took a number of different forms. First, while the concentration of power gave the fascist state much greater control over the economy, it also meant that exercising political influence became much more vital to the survival of economic enterprises: the state was thus subject to the conflicting pressures of intense sectional interests, and its policy pushed this way and that according to their relative influence with the bureaucracy. In particular was the conflict between the subsidy-dependent 'lame ducks', which according to Löwenthal had given particular support to the fascist movement, and the healthy industries on whose profits the possibility of subsidy depended. Here lay a contradiction between the tendencies to stagnation and the forces making for technical development and economic advance, the tendencies to 'autarchy' and those making for an open economy. Finally was the contradiction between the fascist control of economy and society, and the persistence of autonomous forces which eluded that control – class antagonism internally and the anarchy of the international market externally. In sum there was a fundamental contradiction between the potential capacity of the fascist state for the rational co-ordination of economy and society in the general interest, and the actual irrationality of its exercise, subject to the assertion of particular interests, the forces of economic stagnation and the autonomy of class-and national antagonisms. Fascist policy thus had a typically zigzag quality, and its appearance of supreme power was illusory:

> The removal of political opposition makes the bureaucracy appear all
> powerful ... In fact, however, persisting class antagonisms and
> realignments of social forces ensure a continuing autonomy in the depths
> of society, which repeatedly frustrates the attempted co-ordination of the
> nation's energies. The illusion of total power of the state apparatus ...
> creates a distinctive bureaucratic subjectivism that stamps its influence on
> the whole of public life.[80]

The 'contradictions' identified by Löwenthal marked the site of a
number of debates between Marxists in the inter-war period, in
particular over the question whether fascist *étatisme* was capable of
promoting economic development, and whether its control over the
economy was sufficient to overcome the 'laws of motion' of the
capitalist system. In general it was believed in the early years of both
Mussolini and Hitler that the fascist state was incapable of
overcoming the forces of economic crisis and stagnation. As this
judgement proved increasingly questionable, the argument shifted to
the view that whatever economic development occurred could only
take place at the expense of intensified exploitation and by shifting the
location of the crisis on to a different plane (state finances, external
conflict). A purely quantitative conception of capitalist decay thus
gave way to a qualitative one. At first the concept of capitalist decay
implied the idea of some absolute limit beyond which the forces of
production could be developed no further within the capitalist system.
But as the fascist regimes gradually showed themselves capable of
economic expansion and easing the problem of unemployment, so the
idea of an absolute limit to capitalist development gave way to a more
qualitative conception. This was the idea of *distorted* development, the
idea that any further increase of society's productive powers under
capitalism could only take place at the expense of the material and
cultural needs of its members: at the cost of brutal dictatorship, the
depression of mass consumption and the organisation of production
for war. Rosa Luxemburg's alternative of 'socialism or barbarism'
was thus once more explicitly posed.

Otto Bauer's final article on fascism is a characteristic example of
this perspective. The Nazi state, he argued, had taken over essential

functions from the market, determining not only the priorities for investment, but the level of activity in the economy as a whole. The resulting rapid abolition of unemployment in Germany and the sheer speed of its economic recovery convincingly demonstrated the superiority of the planned organisation of production over capitalist anarchy. Yet the massive expansion of production was devoted, not to the satisfaction of consumer needs, but to the preparation of a military machine for war, with intensified exploitation of the working class as its consequence. Furthermore, the central contradiction of monopoly capitalism – the disproportion between the expansion of the productive forces and the limited purchasing power of the masses – was not abolished, merely postponed and transported to a new plane. This was because military preparation generated a once-for-all expansion of employment. Once it was completed, the Nazi regime would confront a choice: either to consign the masses to unemployment, and plunge the economy into severe crisis once more; or 'to set in motion the product of all this immense labour, and direct its military machine on to the path of war'.[81]

Bauer's analysis brings us to a central aspect of the fascist state that all Marxist writers were agreed on – its militarist and expansionist dynamic, which if unchecked would lead to a new world war even bloodier than the last. Here again there were simple and more complex explanations available within the Marxist frame of reference. The simple version saw fascist imperialism as the product of a particular sector of capital which controlled the fascist state. On one side stood the capital goods industries, with interests in armaments production and inclined towards authoritarianism at home and imperialist adventures abroad. On the other side were the consumer industries, opposed to policies which restricted the consumption of the masses, and inclined towards democracy and class collaboration. The onset of economic crisis in both Italy and Germany, so it was argued, drove the former group into the arms of fascism, and ensured it the determination of policy once fascism achieved power.[82]

The special influence of particular sectors of industry on the fascist state cannot be denied. Yet this is not to say that they determined the policies which gave them that influence. Here explanations which derived the aggressive dynamic of fascism from the structure of the

Italian and German economies as a whole, and from the character of the fascist regimes themselves, have greater plausibility. First was the position of the fascist countries within the world economy. Gramsci and Togliatti had used the term 'peripheral' to distinguish a group of European countries with backward economies which were especially susceptible to fascism. In the context of explaining Italian imperialism, a different concept was used, that of 'latecomer': Italy's capitalist development had come too late, when the distribution of colonial markets had already taken place. The absence of guaranteed overseas markets compounded the internal structural weakness of the Italian economy, with its combination of uncompetitive industries, sustained by protectionism, and a restricted home market. According to Tasca, this represented a long-standing problem of Italy's capitalist development, only exacerbated by the rapid expansion of its productive base in the early years of Mussolini's regime. Fascism was forced to resort to preparation for war and external conquest as a consequence of its failure to solve the basic structural weakness of the economy as a whole. This was not the imperialism of the strong, but the aggressive imperialism of the weak, 'imperialism in rags' as Togliatti called it.[83]

The contrast between the peaceful imperialism of the 'satiated' and the aggressive imperialism of the 'dissatisfied' had become a commonplace by the time of the Nazi seizure of power. While the concept of the capitalist 'periphery' did not apply so obviously to the German case, that of 'latecomer' certainly did, especially when the deprivations of the Versailles settlement were added to the account. The contrast between the ability of the established imperialist powers of Britain and France to withstand the recession, and those which lacked their colonial advantages, was especially remarked. 'Fascism exemplifies the imperialism of those who have arrived late at the partition of the world', wrote Löwenthal. 'Behind this imperialism lies a huge need for expansionary opportunities, but none of the traditional means for realising them . . . Fascist imperialism, the imperialism of the bankrupt, is the most aggressive force for war among all the forms of imperialism.' Bauer echoed the same theme. He also pointed to a vicious cycle of inter-action set up by fascist rearmament. The hostile responses of foreign powers impelled the fascist regimes to search for substitute raw materials whose supply they could guarantee in the event of war. This in turn reinforced the tendencies towards the closed economy and protectionism. 'The international division of labour . . . is set back. World trade collapses. The crises of the international economy are exacerbated. The arms race leads everywhere to significant increases in the burden of taxation . . . so fascism plunges the world into an impasse from which it can find no outlet except through war.'[84]

One set of determinations of fascist militarism thus lay at the economic level, in the disadvantaged position of the Italian and German economies as 'latecomers' in the distribution of European imperialism. Another lay in the character of the fascist movement itself. Born out of violent class struggle, so Togliatti argued, the disparate elements of the fascist movement were united around an 'instinctive ideology of conquest', directed first against the enemies at home, and then in struggle against the whole world. If fascism was unable to sustain a distinctive class policy in the economic interests of the petty bourgeoisie, yet it carried a distinctive style of politics with it into government. This political character was reinforced by the conflicts generated within the movement upon its accession to power, which could only be kept in check by redirecting political energies on to external targets. Hence war assumed a 'decisive importance' in all the activities of fascism.[85] In sum, fascist militarism was thus seen as the product of a multiple set of determinations, all of them having their origin in one dimension or another of the capitalist crisis. Even in its slide into war, indeed precisely there, the fascist state showed itself unable to transcend the contradictions of the capitalist mode of production.

This is an appropriate point to refer to the work of the Frankfurt school, whose distinctive emphases demand attention in any overall account of Marxist theorising on fascism. Two features characterised the Frankfurt school's analysis, though they were only fully developed during the 1940s, and hence properly lie outside the scope of the present collection.[86] The first was its explanation of the cultural aspects of fascism and the social-psychological processes involved in its mass appeal. The absence of this dimension is one of the most obvious inadequacies of the Marxist analyses considered here. It is not that their authors were unaware of the character of fascist ideology; they were capable of describing it perfectly accurately. It is rather that the gap between ideology and reality was assumed to be so wide, and the fascist claims so manifestly fraudulent, that they were unable to conceive the possibility of their deep implantation in the popular consciousness, or understand the processes whereby this was effected. Thus the fascist dictatorships were assumed to be based largely on force rather than consent, and hence basically unstable. It was as much the belief that the fascist regimes had alienated their original mass support by their policies, as the assumption of inevitable capitalist collapse, that created the exaggerated optimism about fascism's revolutionary overthrow. The Frankfurt school's investigations into the mass psychology and cultural appeal of fascism thus filled a considerable gap in Marxist analysis. The same could be said about the Gramscian theory of hegemony, though that also was only fully developed much later.

The other characteristic feature of the Frankfurt school's analysis of fascism was its assertion of the 'primacy' of the political. Horkheimer's article on *The Jews and Europe* provides an early statement of this theme. The totalitarian state, he argued, had finally freed itself from the capitalist 'law of value'; the economy no longer had its own independent dynamic, and was therefore no more to be understood with the categories of political economy. Certainly the fascist system was the logical *outcome* of free market capitalism; in this sense 'if you won't talk of capitalism you must remain silent about fascism also'. But the liberal order had given birth to a quite new system, in which social relations were no longer mediated (and obscured) by the market, but took a directly political form; exploitation and social antagonism depended upon the conscious exercise of power. The dominant class was no longer constituted by the ownership of capital, but by the effective disposition and control of the material means of production within both monopolies and the 'leadership' state; the latter was now able to regulate the economy to ensure economic prospects over a long period. The result was not, however, the satisfaction of the general interest, but a competitive struggle whose outcome was determined by the assertion of power and the exercise of arbitrary political decision, not by the impersonality of the market. The Jews, Horkheimer argued, were the first victims of this system. Having lost their function in the market, they were now economically dispensable. 'Previously it was not merely the market's verdict itself that was anonymous; it distinguished the elect and the outcast in the production process without reference to their individual characteristics . . . In the leadership state, however, it is quite deliberately decreed who is to live and who to die.'[87]

Despite obvious similarities, Horkheimer's analysis also differs from the other accounts considered in this section in two decisive respects. First is his assertion of the end of political economy. All the others insisted that, however much the fascist state was able to control the direction of the economy, it could not transcend the contradictions of the capitalist mode of production. The difference becomes even more marked in Horkheimer's subsequent writings, with the idea of a convergence between the USSR and the fascist regimes (the 'authoritarian state') and the further development of the concept of the managerial–administrative ruling class. As with James Burnham and others, these two ideas marked the point where Horkheimer moved outside a Marxist frame of reference.[88] Secondly was his idea that the fascist system represented, not merely the logical end-product of liberal capitalism, but a *universal* principle or tendency, which was not only appropriate to the 'poor or have-not countries'. In this Horkheimer was paradoxically closer to the theory of the Comintern than the other writers considered here, who insisted that fascism was the product of conditions that were specific to certain countries only.

Throughout this collection, in fact, what distinguishes the more from the less simplistic accounts is whether they see fascism as a general phenomenon of a given stage of capitalist development, or as specific to certain countries only. What this in turn depends on is whether capitalism itself is seen as a uniform phenomenon, or subject to a process of uneven development. What distinguished the analyses of Gramsci and Togliatti in the 1920s, and Löwenthal and Bauer in the 1930s, was precisely that they recognised the implications of this uneven development. Does this mean, then, that fascism was not the product of capitalism? Not at all. If it was not accidental that it developed unevenly, then it follows that the possibility of fascism in some countries was as much the product of capitalism as the possibility of democracy in others. Indeed the two were mutually interconnected. The conditions conducive to democracy ('sated and peaceful imperialism') were precisely the conditions that also gave rise to the 'aggressive imperialism' and 'nationalism of the bankrupt' on the part of those who 'arrived too late on the scene'. The full implications of such ideas were perhaps not explicitly worked through in the writings collected here. It has been left to more recent Marxist theorising to bring out their full force.[89]

Postscript

Was fascism a phenomenon confined to the inter-war period in Europe, with no contemporary significance? There are two reasons for thinking it improbable that a fascist movement could come to power in present-day circumstances, both stemming from the analysis considered above. First, the development of capitalism has further reduced the numbers of small independent producers, while the expanding middle strata of white-collar workers are becoming increasingly unionised. This means that there are not the petty-bourgeois masses available for mobilisation behind a fascist movement to the same degree as previously. Secondly, at least as far as western Europe is concerned, parliamentary democracies have a more secure popular implantation than in the earlier period. However, it should be evident from what has been said earlier that a fascist movement does not have to be large to give an immensely damaging impetus to reaction. And it is perfectly possible for deep encroachments to be made into political and social rights within a parliamentary system. Indeed this is now the more likely form of reaction. The effects of a new period of depression and reconstruction of capital working on countries with a weak economic structure and resentful of their relative economic and political decline can be similar to those associated with the rise of fascism: the demand for a diminution of social welfare as an unaffordable luxury; the widespread erosion of civil liberties; the identification of union rights as the chief obstacle to economic recovery; the rekindling of national myths and a resurgence of 'imperialism in rags'.

The lessons that can be drawn from this collection for a successful defence against such a reaction are largely negative. A labour or socialist movement operating at such a capitalist conjuncture faces considerable disadvantages: its strength at the point of work is eroded; it is divided between the employed and the unemployed; it confronts the dilemma that failure to resist produces demoralisation and further encroachments, while successful resistance at individual points of struggle can exacerbate the crisis, without providing the means for its resolution. The extent to which a positive outcome is possible depends on whether the defence of workers' interests at both a parliamentary and extra-parliamentary level can be shown to be a defence, not of narrow sectional interests merely, but of needs which are universal. The arena, in other words, is the one in which fascism in a previous epoch won its earliest victory: that of the broadest ideological and political terrain.

Chronological Table

Date		Italy	Germany
1918	November		Republic proclaimed
	December		KPD founded
1919	January		Spartacist rising in Berlin crushed
	March	PSI affiliates to Comintern	
	April	First *'fasci di combattimento'* burn *Avanti* offices in Milan	Declaration of Munich Soviet
	June		Treaty of Versailles signed
	August		
	September	D'Annunzio seizes Fiume to press Italian Claims to E. Adriatic	
	November	PSI wins 156 of 508 seats in elections	
1920	February		New programme of NSDAP announced by Hitler
	March		'Kapp *putsch*' in Berlin defeated by general strike
	April		
	June	Giolitti prime minister	Reichstag elections: SPD 102, USPD 84, KPD 4, Others 260
	July		SPD leaves government coalition

Austria	Spain	The Comintern
Republic proclaimed Social Democrat–Christian Social coalition		
		Founding Convention: Zinoviov elected President
Failure of Communist rising in Vienna		Soviet Republic declared in Budapest
2nd Communist rising suppressed		
		Downfall of Soviet regime in Hungary: 'white' dictatorship under Horthy
		Lenin's 'Left Wing Communism: an Infantile Disorder'
		Red Army repulses Polish army and invades Poland 2nd World Congress: 21 conditions for affiliation

Date		Italy	Germany
	August		
	September	Employers' lockout in Milan leads to factory occupations	
	October	Normal work resumes after promise of 'workers' control'	
		Fascist attacks begin in rural areas of North	
	November	Clash between socialists and fascists in Bologna	KPD and USPD merge
		Treaty of Rapallo	
	December	D'Annunzio forced to abandon Fiume	
1921	*January*	Livorno Congress of PSI: minority secedes to form PCI under Bordiga	
	March	Fascist terror intensifies	'March action' by KPD ends in fiasco
	May	Elections: PSI 123, PCI 15, Fascists 35, others 335	
	June	Bonomi prime minister	
	August	Conciliation pact between PSI and Fascist deputies	
	December		
1922	*February*	Facta becomes Prime Minister	
	March	PCI Rome Congress	
	April		Rapallo treaty with USSR
	July	New Facta administration	
	September	PSI expels reformists, who form PSU	
	October	Mussolini's 'March on Rome'	
	November		

Austria	Spain	The Comintern
		Red Army retreats from Poland
Elections: SDAP wins 66 of 174 seats and goes into opposition		
	Civil Governor appointed in Barcelona to back employers against CNT	
	'Free syndicates' organised to suppress unions	
		Suppression of Kronstadt rising in USSR New Economic Policy
		3rd World Congress: 'retreat of European revolution; to the masses'
	Spanish defeat in Morocco	
		ECCI announces 'united workers' front' tactic
		4th World Congress: the 'offensive of capital'

Date		Italy	Germany
1923	January		Germany 'in default' on reparations French occupation of the Ruhr
	February	Nationalists unite with Fascists Arrest of PSI and PCI leaderships	Growth of secret armies on the right
	June	New leadership of PCI	Inflation out of control
	August		Stresemann Chancellor at head of grand coalition
	September		State of emergency
	October		KPD joins SDP governments in Saxony & Thuringia to prepare uprising: governments deposed by army
	November	Electoral law guaranteeing 2/3 seats to majority party	Hitler putsch in Munich unsuccessful
1924	February		End of state of emergency
	April	Elections: Fascists win 374 seats after widespread intimidation	
	May	Matteotti condemns intimidation	Reichstag elections: SPD 100, KPD 62, others 301
	June	Matteotti murdered by fascists Opposition parties withdraw from Parliament to Aventine	
	August	3rd Internationalists in PSI fuse with PCI	Dawes plan for reparations payments
	November	Communist deputies leave Aventine opposition	
	December		Reichstag elections: SPD 131, KPD 45, others 287
1925	April		Hindenberg elected President
	November	Attempt on Mussolini's life	

Austria	Spain	The Comintern
	Military coup by General Primo de Rivera	
Elections: SDAP wins 68 seats, others 106		
		5th World Congress: 'democratic–pacifist phase' of capitalist decline, 'Bolshevisation' of CPs
		Stalin announces 'Socialism in one country'

Date		Italy	Germany
	December	Powers of Head of Government extended	
1926	*January*	PCI Lyons Congress	
	April	Right to strike abolished	German–Soviet non-aggression pact
	October	Gramsci arrested New attempt on Mussolini's life Law for defence of state Special tribunal for political crimes	
	November		
1927	*April*	Fascist 'Labour Charter'	
	July		
	November		
1928	*January*	Gramsci condemned to 20 years imprisonment by special tribunal	
	May		Reichstag elections: SPD 154, KPD 54, NSDAP 12, others 218 Grand coalition government under SPD Chancellor Muller
	July		
1929	*January*		
	February	Lateran accords	
	May		May Day demonstration in Berlin suppressed by SPD police chief: 29 workers killed

Austria	Spain	The Comintern
		Victory of Stalin over Zinoviev at 14th Congress of CPSU
Linz Programme of SDAP		
Elections: SDAP 71 seats Armed clashes in Vienna between police and socialist demonstrators: 89 killed		
		Expulsion of Trotsky from CPSU
Growth of fascist *Heimwehr* movement		
		6th World Congress: 'Class vs. class'; 'Right deviation' the greatest danger Stalin's campaign vs. Bukharin intensifies
		Trotsky expelled from USSR
		First Five Year Plan approved in USSR

Date	Italy	Germany
June	Mussolini meets Hitler in Venice	
July		
October		Collapse of stock market in USA
1930 *January*		
March		Brüning appointed Chancellor without Reichstag majority
July		Austerity budget imposed by emergency decree 3 million unemployed
September		Reichstag elections: SPD 143, KPD 77, NSDAP 107, others 229
November	Mussolini subsidises *Heimwehr* elections in Austria	
1931 *April*		
June		
August		'Red referendum' of KPD, supported by Nazis, against SPD government in Prussia
September		

Austria	Spain	The Comintern
		10th ECCI plenum: 'radicalisation of the masses': 'social fascism'; 'liquidation of fractional groups' in CPs Bukharin removed from office
	Primo de Rivera replaced by General Berenguer	
Starhemberg elected leader of *Heimwehr*, and joins cabinet Elections: SDAP 72 seats, Christian Social 66, *Heimwehr* 8		
	Foundation of 2nd Republic Elections to Cortes: Republican majority	11th ECCI plenum: 'development of revolutionary crisis'
Attempted *Heimwehr* putsch Nazi vote increased in provincial elections	Azana ministry with Socialist support	

Date	Italy	Germany
1932 *April*		Hindenberg defeats Hitler for presidency Nazi SA suppressed
May		Papen appointed Chancellor, without Reichstag majority
June		Ban on SA lifted
July		Papen deposes SPD government in Prussia, and takes over its administration 4.7 million unemployed Reichstag elections: SPD 133, KPD 89, NSDAP 230, others 147
October		
November		Reichstag elections: SPD 121, KPD 100, NSDAP 196, others 153 Schleicher appointed Chancellor
1933 *January*		Hitler appointed Chancellor
February		Reichstag fire Decree for protection of people and state 6 million unemployed
March		Reichstag elections: SPD 120, KPD 81, NSDAP 288, others 146 Enabling law giving Hitler power to govern by decree
May		Trade unions abolished
June		SPD outlawed
July		One party state declared
September		
October		Germany leaves League of Nations
November		

Austria	Spain	The Comintern

Dollfuss Chancellor in
Christian–Social
coalition with *Heimwehr*

Heimwehr deputy Fey
appointed security
minister

Parliament suspended by
Dollfuss
Government by decree

Nazis banned

Proclamation of
Christian–Social
authoritarian state

Foundation of *Falange
Española*
Elections to Cortes: victory
for right
Start of 'two black years'

Date	Italy	Germany
December		
1934 *January*		'Prague Manifesto' of SPD in exile
February		
March	Rome protocols on co-peration between Italy, Hungary and Austria	
June		Bloody purge of SA and Nazi opposition
July		
October		
November	Council of Corporations inaugurated in Rome	
1935 *March*		Compulsory military service introduced
May		
July		
September		Nuremburg laws discriminate against Jews
October	Invasion of Abyssinia	
1936 *February*		
March		Reoccupation of Rhineland

Austria	Spain	The Comintern
		13th ECCI plenum: 'fascism and social-fascism still twins'
Indefinite martial law proclaimed Attack on Socialists by *Heimwehr* & government forces Anti-government rising crushed SDAP & unions banned		
Dollfuss killed in attempted Nazi *putsch* and succeeded by Schuschnigg		'United front' agreement between Communists and Socialists in France
	General strike and rising in Asturias: suppressed with 4000 dead	United front in France extended to include Radicals ('popular front')
		Franco–Soviet pact signed 5th World Congress: popular front policy confirmed
	Republican and Socialist popular front wins elections Republican government Falange outlawed	

Date	Italy	Germany
June		
July		
August		
September		New 4 year economic plan for war
October	Rome–Berlin Axis	
December		
1937 *April* *May*		
June *October*		
1938 *March*		*Anschluss* between Germany and Austria
April		
September		Munich agreement over partition of Czechoslovakia
November		
1939 *January*	Chamber of Corporations replaces parliament	
February		

Austria	Spain	The Comintern
		Popular front government elected in France
Agreement between Austria & Germany	Military uprising under Franco begins civil war	
	Spread of collectivisation as government authority disintegrates	
	England and France sign 'non-intervention' pact	First big show trials in USSR
		Zinoviev & Kamenev executed
	CPE joins Caballero government . . . CNT & POUM join regional government in Catalonia	
	Agrarian collectivisation halted	
	POUM expelled from Catalan government	
	Bombing of Guernica	
	Uprising in Barcelona against central government crushed	
	POUM outlawed	
	Central government moves to Barcelona	
Schuschnigg succeeded by Seyss-Inquart		
	Franco reaches coast and cuts republican Spain in two	
	International brigades withdraw from Spain	
	Britain and France recognise Franco	

Date	Italy	Germany
March		
April	Italy seizes Albania	
August		Nazi–Soviet pact signed
September		Germany invades Poland

Austria	Spain	The Comintern
	End of civil war	
		Nazi–Soviet pact signed

I Fascism in Italy 1921–8

1 On Fascism, *Antonio Gramsci*

The following examples from Gramsci's journalistic writing during 1921 illustrate the complexity of fascism in its early stages, and the difficulty of arriving at a definitive assessment of it.

Italy and Spain

What is fascism, observed on an international scale? It is the attempt to resolve the problems of production and exchange with machine-guns and pistol-shots. The productive forces were ruined and dissipated in the imperialist war: twenty million men in the flower of their youth and energies were killed; another twenty million were left invalids. The thousands upon thousands of bonds that united the various world markets were violently broken. The relations between city and countryside, between metropole and colonies, were overturned. The streams of emigration, which periodically re-established the balance between the excess population and the potential of the means of production in individual countries, were profoundly disturbed and no longer function normally. A unity and simultaneity of national crises was created which precisely makes the general crisis acute and incurable. But there exists a stratum of the population in all countries – the petty and middle bourgeoisie – which thinks it can solve these gigantic problems with machine-guns and pistol-shots; and this stratum feeds fascism, provides fascism with its troops.

   In Spain, the organisation of the petty and middle bourgeoisie into armed groups occurred before it did in Italy; it had already begun in 1918 and 1919. The world war cast Spain into a terrible crisis before other countries: the Spanish capitalists had in fact already looted the country and sold all that was saleable in the first years of the conflagration. The Entente paid better than the poor Spanish consumers were able to do, so the owners sold all the wealth and goods which should have provided for the national population to the Entente. By 1916, Spain was already one of the richest European countries financially, but one of the poorest in goods and productive energies. The revolutionary movement surged forward; the unions organised almost the entirety of the industrial masses; strikes, lockouts, states of emergency, the dissolution of Chambers of Labour and peasant associations, massacres, street shootings, became the everyday stuff of political life. Anti-Bolshevik fasces (*somaten*) were formed. Initially, as in Italy, they were made up of military personnel, taken from the officers' clubs (*juntas*), but they swiftly enlarged their base until in Barcelona, for example, they had recruited 40,000 armed men. They followed the same tactics as the fascists in Italy: attacks on trade-union leaders, violent opposition to strikes, terrorism against the masses; opposition to all forms of organisation, help for the regular police in repressive activity and arrests, help for blacklegs in agitation involving strikes or lockouts. For the past three years Spain has floundered in this crisis: public freedom is suspended every fortnight, personal freedom has become a myth, the workers' unions to a great extent function clandestinely, the mass of workers is hungry and angry, the great mass of the people has been reduced to indescribable conditions of savagery and barbarism. Moreover, the crisis is intensifying, and the stage of individual assassination attempts has now been reached.

Spain is an exemplary country. It represents a phase through which all the countries of Western Europe will pass, if economic conditions continue as they are today, with the same tendencies as at present. In Italy, we are passing through the phase which Spain passed through in 1919: the phase of the arming of the middle classes and the introduction into the class struggle of military methods of assault and surprise-attack. In Italy too, the middle class thinks it can resolve economic problems by military violence. It thinks it can cure unemployment by pistol-shots; it thinks it can assuage hunger and dry the tears of the women of the people with bursts of machine-gun fire. Historical experience counts for nothing with petty bourgeois who do not know history. Similar phenomena are repeated and will continue to be repeated in other countries, apart from Italy. Has not the same process affected the Socialist Party in Italy, as had already occurred several years earlier in Austria, Hungary and Germany? Illusion is the most tenacious weed in the collective consciousness; history teaches, but it has no pupils.

Elemental Forces

... It has now become obvious that fascism can only be partially interpreted as a class phenomenon, as a movement of political forces conscious of a real aim. It has spread, it has broken every possible organisational framework, it is above the wishes and proposals of any central or regional Committee, it has become an unchaining of elemental forces which cannot be restrained under the bourgeois system of economic and political government. Fascism is the name of the far-reaching decomposition of the State, and which today can only be explained by reference to the low level of civilisation which the Italian nation had been able to attain in these last sixty years of unitary administration.

Fascism has presented itself as the anti-party; has opened its gates to all applicants; has with its promise of impunity enabled a formless multitude to cover over the savage outpouring of passions, hatreds and desires with a varnish of vague and nebulous political ideals. Fascism has thus become a question of social mores: it has become identified with the barbaric and anti-social psychology of certain strata of the Italian people which have not yet been modified by a new tradition, by education, by living together in a well-ordered and well administered State. To understand the full force of these assertions, it is enough to recall: that Italy holds first place for murders and bloodshed; that Italy is the country where mothers educate their infant children by hitting them on the head with clogs – it is the country where the younger generations are least respected and protected; that in certain Italian regions it seemed natural until a few years ago to put muzzles on grape-pickers, so that they could not eat the grapes; and that in certain regions the landowners locked their labourers up in sheds when the workday was over, to prevent meetings or attendance at evening classes.

The class struggle has always assumed an extremely harsh character in Italy, as a result of this 'human' immaturity of certain strata of the population. Cruelty and the lack of *simpatia* are two traits peculiar to the Italian people, which passes from childish sentimentality to the most brutal and bloody ferocity, from passionate anger to cold-blooded contemplation of other people's ills. The State, though still frail and uncertain in its most vital functions, was with difficulty gradually succeeding in breaking up this semi-barbaric terrain. Today, after the decomposition of the State, every kind of miasma pullulates upon it. There is much truth in the assertion of the fascist papers that not all those who call themselves fascists and operate in the name of the *fasci* belong to the organisation. But what is to be said of an organisation whose symbol can be used to cover actions of the nature of those which disgrace Italy daily? The assertion, moreover, endows these events with a very much more serious and decisive character than those who write in the bourgeois papers would like to accord them. Who will be able to check them, if the State is incapable and the private organisations are impotent?

Thus we can see that the communist thesis is justified. Fascism, as a general phenomenon, as a scourge which transcends the will and the disciplinary means of its exponents – with its violence, with its monstrous and arbitrary actions, with its destruction at once systematic and irrational – can be extirpated only by a new State power, by a 'restored' State in the sense which the communists understand this term, in other words by a State whose power is in the hands of the proletariat, the only class capable of reorganising production and therefore all the social relations which depend on the relations of production.

The Two Fascisms

The crisis of fascism, on whose origins and causes so much is being written these days, can easily be explained by a serious examination of the actual development of the fascist movement.

The *Fasci di combattimento* emerged, in the aftermath of the War, with the petty-bourgeois character of the various war-veterans' associations which appeared in that period. Because of their character of determined opposition to the socialist movement – partly a heritage of the conflicts between the Socialist Party and the interventionist associations during the War period – the *Fasci* won the support of the capitalists and the authorities. The fact that their emergence coincided with the landowners' need to form a white guard against the growing power of the workers' organisations allowed the system of bands created and armed by the big landowners to adopt the same label of *Fasci*. With their subsequent development, these bands conferred upon that label their own characteristic feature as a white guard of capitalism against the class organs of the proletariat.

Fascism has always kept this initial flaw. Until today, the fervour of the armed offensive prevented any exacerbation of the rift between the urban petty-bourgeois nuclei, predominantly parliamentary and collaborationist, and the rural ones formed by big and medium landowners and by the farmers themselves: interested in a struggle against the poor peasants and their organisations; resolutely anti-trade-union and reactionary; putting more trust in direct armed action than in the authority of the State or the efficacy of parliamentarism.

In the agricultural regions (Emilia, Tuscany, Veneto, Umbria), fascism had its greatest development and, with the financial support of the capitalists and the protection of the civil and military authorities of the State, achieved unconditional power. If, on the one hand, the ruthless offensive against the class organisms of the proletariat benefited the capitalists, who in the course of a year saw the entire machinery of struggle of the socialist trade unions break up and lose all efficacy, it is nevertheless undeniable that the worsening violence ended up by creating a widespread attitude of hostility to fascism in the middle and popular strata.

The episodes of Sarzana, Treviso, Viterbo and Roccastrada[1] deeply shook the urban fascist nuclei personified by Mussolini, and these began to see a danger in the exclusively negative tactics of the *Fasci* in the agricultural regions. On the other hand, these tactics had already borne excellent fruit, since they had dragged the Socialist Party on to the terrain of flexibility and readiness to collaborate in the country and in Parliament.

From this moment, the latent rift begins to reveal itself in its full depth. The urban, collaborationist nuclei now see the objective which they set themselves accomplished: the abandonment of class intransigence by the Socialist Party. They are hastening to express their victory in words with the pacification pact. But the agrarian capitalists cannot renounce the only tactic which ensures them 'free' exploitation of the peasant classes, without the nuisance of strikes and organisations. The whole polemic raging in the fascist camp between those in favour of and those opposed to pacification can be reduced to this rift, those origins are to be sought only in the actual origins of the fascist movement.

The claims of the Italian socialists to have themselves brought about the split in the fascist movement, through their skilful policy of compromise, are nothing but a further proof of their demagogy. In reality, the fascist crisis is not new, it has always existed. Once the contingent reasons which held the anti-proletarian ranks firm ceased to operate, it was inevitable that the disagreements would reveal themselves more openly. The crisis is thus nothing other than the clarification of a pre-existing *de facto* situation.

Fascism will get out of the crisis by splitting. The parliamentary part headed by Mussolini, basing itself on the middle layers (white-collar workers, small shop-keepers and small manufacturers), will attempt to organise these politically and will necessarily orient itself towards collaboration with the socialists and the *popolari*.[2] The intransigent part, which expresses the necessity for direct, armed defence of agrarian capitalist interests, will continue with its characteristic anti-proletarian activity. For this latter part – the most important for the working class – the 'truce agreement' which the socialists are boasting of as a victory will have no validity. The 'crisis' will only signal the exit from the *Fasci* movement of a faction of petty bourgeois who have vainly attempted to justify fascism with a general political 'party' programme.

But fascism, the true variety, which the peasants and workers of Emilia, Veneto and Tuscany know through the painful experience of the past two years of white terror, will continue – though it may even change its name.

The internal disputes of the fascist bands have brought about a period of relative calm. The task of the revolutionary workers and peasants is to take advantage of this to infuse the oppressed and defenceless masses with a clear consciousness of the real situation in the class struggle, and of the means needed to defeat arrogant capitalist reaction.

2. Towards a Definition of Fascism, *Giovanni Zibordi*

Zibordi belonged to the reformist wing of the PSI. His book, *Critica socialista del fascismo*, published in 1922, contained one of the earliest systematic analyses of fascism.[3] It was drawn on even by those who opposed the reformist conclusions which, he claimed, followed from a properly Marxist analysis of Italy's stage of development.

The more one seeks to penetrate the fascist phenomenon, and the more its multifarious facets and components are revealed, the more one recognises the dangerous over-simplification of those who define it as the 'white guard' at the service of the bourgeoisie. The bourgeoisie proper undoubtedly makes use of it, but fascism would not have achieved its vitality and strength if it had not been nourished by many other contributory sources of support.

Fascism seems to me to be at one and the same time:

– a counter-revolution of the bourgeoisie proper in response to a *red* revolution which only threatened but never took place (as an insurrectionary act);

– a revolution, or rather an upheaval, of the middle classes, of the disoriented, the deprived and the discontented;

– a military revolution.

Let us examine these three components in turn, beginning with the last.

The Military Revolution

What I call the military revolution – without which fascism would not have even a quarter of its technical efficiency and material power – has manifested itself in a scattered, and one might even say peripheral, form, rather than in the classical form in which we are used to experience or conceive of it; this explains why many are not on their guard against it. Instead of the typical *coup d'état* or the traditional 'palace revolution', carried out by one or more generals at the centre, or effected in military fashion to replace the reigning sovereign by some royal relation – possibilities which were all talked about and still are, though they have not yet occurred – we have experienced in one place after another the moral and material solidarity with fascism of the officers and NCOs of the *carabinieri* and royal guard. This means solidarity with an armed organisation operating outside the law, a state arisen within the state and sometimes against the state, a veritable military sedition.

The adherence of the armed forces to fascism derives from many sources. Apart from the pecuniary factor, which is certainly valid in some cases, the officers sympathise with fascism because it represents a prolongation of the state of war internally, and a possibility of war externally, which always pleases the professional military; also because it signifies a glorification of victory and of the army's achievements, in contrast to the socialist proletariat, which has never been able to acknowledge the sacrifice of those involved in the war. The *carabinieri* and royal guard support fascism partly for the same reasons, but more because the socialist proletariat and the Party press have shown no sympathy at all for these proletarians in uniform, who have often been ready to fire on the crowd, which in turn has too often been ready to attack them with stones etc.

The soldiers who have been demobilised support fascism for all these reasons, and also from pressing economic motives. Among them are many victims of 'war displacement': youths who left for the front before they were 20 years old and returned when they were 23 or 24, and who are no longer able or willing to resume their studies or employment in a regular and profitable way; petty bourgeoisie, of humble circumstances and subordinate position, who became NCOs and even commissioned officers in the war, enjoying the delights of command and the pleasure of being waited on, and who found themselves elevated to a social status that is always held in particular regard, but especially after a victorious war – now they cannot face the return to their previous humble positions; people of varied origin and occupation, who discovered and developed aggressive qualities in the course of the war, becoming attached to the military profession and the exchange of fire, from a spirit of bravado and adventure as well as more dangerous impulses, and who believed that those who had been at the front and suffered in the trenches to save Italy could do with the country whatever they pleased, treat it as if it were their own and arrange it according to their convenience, and could consider themselves free to do anything above or against the law and (in the phrase which exercises such a fascination on the young) 'not give a damn' for anything or anybody.

We Socialists did nothing to attract these military personnel and ex-servicemen towards us, or at least to avert their hostility. Let us recall that to begin with the wounded and the combatants returned home in a touchy and excitable state of mind, inasmuch as their own sacrifice made them want to extol the war, to which the proletariat was opposed; and they appeared to make extravagant claims, and to demand all kinds of privilege for themselves. Yet let us also remember that we did nothing on our part to 'demobilise' this mood, to make them feel that, though we maintained all our reservations about the political fact of the war and the responsibility of those who had decided on it and conducted it, this did not diminish our gratitude and affection for those who had fought and suffered in it.

With that simplistic inclination for symbols that is wholly characteristic of primitive minds, the proletariat identified the war with everything that was its visible reminder; it vented its hatred on the uniform, on the flag, on the soldiers themselves. It failed to understand or appreciate, it did not have the ability or judgement to assess the state of mind of those who had fought with conviction and who returned home with understandable pride. It committed major psychological errors, and multiplied the misunderstandings, the antipathies, the enemies on every side; and now it is paying a heavy price.

The Middle and Petty-Bourgeois Strata

What elements – apart from the criminal ones which always, in all parties and all movements, follow the flag of violence – throng to fill in the outlines, to occupy the spaces in this framework that the ex-combatants have constructed? . . . Before examining these elements, it will be helpful to offer an initial observation about terminology. In its economic sense, the term 'bourgeois' indicates a class or an individual which gains its wealth in whole or in part from the work or consumption of others, by reason of its monopoly of the means of production or distribution. In current parlance, however, the term is used to indicate a number of people who perform useful and necessary intellectual work – professionals, teachers, office workers – who have no reason to fear or oppose socialism, whether as a developing movement or as a definitive future order. In fact we call these the middle bourgeoisie, and the petty bourgeoisie those small traders and shopkeepers who are so numerous. Poor devils they may be, but they exercise a parasitic intermediary function all the more useless and damaging the smaller they are; and their poverty confirms the superfluousness of their function. In other words we confuse, by an inexact terminology (and such imprecision has psychological effects that cannot be ignored) the social composition and *function* of certain classes and individuals, whose present social utility will continue in the future, under another system, with their cultural *circumstances* and conditions of life. We give the term 'bourgeois' to strata that are merely middle-class in intelligence, education, style of life and dress, but which are proletarians and workers with their brain.

Now, fascism is also a movement of social geology, a volcanic fusion of certain classes which found themselves after the war compressed between the weight of the large bourgeoisie and the *nouveau riches* pressing down from above, and the thrust of the working class pushing up from below. Provoked and irritated by the double spectacle of the wealth and extravagance of the profiteers, and the earnings and expenditure of the workers (Is it necessary to say that I am referring to the period when the present raging crisis of unemployment and proletarian reverse was not even in sight?), these classes became agitated and stirred into action, along with the throng of exceptional characters thrown up by the war, who nevertheless demonstrated the fundamental petty-bourgeois characteristics of rebelliousness and revenge. They held the conviction that the biggest part of that substantial social inheritance from which we all live, for better or worse, had been appropriated, though certainly not by the owners, the profiteers, the landed proprietors, the large-scale traders, but by the metal workers, the bricklayers, the labourers; and that the 'massive wages' of these latter were the main cause of the increase in the cost of living and the privations of those classes which, having no means of recuperating their loss, felt its burdensome effects most heavily.

Besides this economic conviction there was a traditional psychological motive. The petty bourgeois who treads his dismal course through life without allowing himself or his children any modest diversion, views the *nouveau riche* driving past in his automobile with less envy and indignation than the worker who sits at the bar or goes to the cinema. There is a powerful custom and tradition which recognises the right of the idle to even the most offensive display of wealth more readily than it admits the right of those who work to even the most basic comfort . . .

Our political and economic movement has generally shown itself indifferent to these classes, if not actually hostile to them. The manual working class in its crudeness and one-sided over-simplification, seemed eager to consider its own work alone as useful and meritorious, and regarded the 'well-dressed' with distrust and suspicion, even if they were employed in necessary professions. It seemed to conceive of socialism as an emancipation of those exploited for their manual labour, who constitute the present day proletariat, and not at all as a universal transformation and a new social order in which all who work today will receive their just deserts. This exclusivity, or this indifference, combined with the congenital superiority of the white-collar workers, has contributed to make them hostile or to keep them apart from us. Many of them passed openly on to the offensive against us when they suffered the displacement of the war, and became discontented and restless when in this crisis and general confusion caused by the cataclysm of war, in this utter reversal of values, these classes fell behind in the socio-economic hierarchy, and saw the manual workers get in front of them. They began to tell stories about the 'huge wages' of the workers, generalising from special cases or the most fortunate families; they eyed the workers with envy and hatred, not from a higher vantage point – as the bourgeoisie proper views the workers, whose demands curtail its profits and whose actions and programmes threaten its privileges – but from below, as if the workers were the 'masters', the new red profiteers, and they, the deprived intellectual classes, were the real oppressed.

If one takes no account of these inversions and psychical aberrations, of these easily mobilised currents, one cannot explain the scale of the fascist phenomenon. The bourgeoisie proper, which has every reason to fear and oppose socialism, would only be a small matter on its own, if it were not shrewd enough to set in motion and draw around itself a wide protective circle of people responsive to sentimental appeals and the inducements of a misguided self-interest. Here in short was the real power of fascism: it brought into combination against the socialist proletariat both the cold, calculating hostility of the authentic bourgeoisie, and the fanatical hatred of these middle classes who were overwhelmed in the post-war crisis, and who directed all the ferment and rancour of their distress on to the proletariat rather than on to the class, or rather regime, that was socially dominant.

I have insisted on this fact, on the predominantly 'non-bourgeois' components of fascism, as a counterweight to the dogmatic over-simplification of those socialists on the extreme left, who define the phenomenon as the fated, natural, inevitable reactionary insurrection of the dominant privileged class against socialism and the proletariat; an insurrection that could no more be effectively resisted than it could be prevented in advance or at least made less formidable. 'Today or tomorrow', say these socialists, 'when the bourgeoisie sees itself reduced to extremities, it puts up a supreme resistance, violent, illegal, unscrupulous, using any means available'.

And so it may. But what kind of power would it have, and what prospect of success, if it were indeed only the 'bourgeoisie', that is the class that dominates in the present order of things, enjoying advantages and privileges that it rightly fears it will see destroyed by a socialist regime? What if, in its anti-socialist offensive, it did not make use, both directly and indirectly, of the collaboration, the approval, the tolerance of surrounding classes and strata, which have nothing to do with the 'bourgeoisie' in the socio-economic sense of the word, but which oppose socialism from an accumulation of suspicions, prejudices, misunderstandings, and outraged sentiments, and because we never did anything to placate them?

It may be objected that these people – the intellectual proletariat, the artisan class, the rural petty bourgeoisie – though not 'bourgeois' in economic circumstance, and not having any reason to fear socialism, is not socialist either. It is individualistic in outlook, from habit and upbringing, or from profession and the kind of work it is engaged in. Each one of its members, like the archetypical 'bourgeois', aspires to rise in the social scale, and believes he can, trusting in his own efforts and his own endowments, not in organisation or solidarity.

True enough. And if such people abound in Italy, it is evidence that Italy is a country whose proletarian development is as yet limited, and hence is politically more 'democratic' than socialist. And if, for various reasons, the democratic parties, which should be the natural political expression for these people, are weak, fragmented and in confusion, it should be the task of socialism, if not actually to assume their direct representation, at least to prevent them shifting to the right and allying with the large, the rich, the genuine bourgeoisie. For this reason it is necessary to remember that socialism in Italy can only be attained gradually, since it is the economic structure of the country that is not socialist; and that we must therefore reconcile ourselves to intermediate stages, corresponding to the actuality of the situation. All this may not satisfy the catastrophic expectations and the impatience of the masses, who have put their trust in story-book miracles; but it is rigorously Marxist, and will secure for socialism's onward march a route which appears less rapid but is actually more secure . . .

So then: the facts show that in Italy it is advisable to proceed in stages, to fight the bourgeoisie proper by attracting around us the so-called 'petty bourgeoisie' and by satisfying their needs, their interests, their rights. The facts show that in a country such as Italy, socialism, the proletariat cannot prosper or endure if it does not try to secure a benevolent atmosphere, a defensive zone of classes who have no reason to fear it. Although unable to give socialism their full support, they would not be hostile and would not align themselves with the bourgeoisie once our Party and the working class, instead of isolating itself and assuming exclusivist attitudes which frighten and repel, instead showed them its true character as a friend of all those who work by hand or brain, and as the protagonist of a social reorganisation in which all honest and useful work will find an appropriate security of life.

Fascism and the Big Bourgeoisie

Many people say that fascism, in its main features and its real, deepest origins, is a movement of the big industrial and profiteering bourgeoisie, seeking to protect its wartime profits against both the claims of the workers and the democratic policies of the government. Certainly if one considers the fantastic expense that the fascist organisation must have cost – because of which there are even those who believe in the instigation of external finance, from a 'friendly' nation interested in undermining revolutionary aspirations and happy to see Italy in the grip of a debilitating unrest – and if one considers also the meanness and relative modesty of resources of the agrarian class in comparison with the industrial, one must conclude without hesitation that it was the latter that played the prevalent part in fascism. It is less evident, though, that they have received proportionate rewards from it, whereas the advantages recouped by the landed and mercantile bourgeoisie in the agricultural provinces are much more obvious and spectacular.

All the same, whether in its initial thrust or its later advance, whether from clear and premeditated purpose or from the prompt exploitation of a movement begun and set in motion with different characteristics, the big, the authentic industrial and agrarian bourgeoisie, and the most typically speculative elements of the mercantile class, large and small, made use of fascism for their own ends, to smash the proletariat wherever it appeared so electorally dominant that there was no hope of a come-back for the bourgeois party, and wherever it was most solidly organised economically.

The threatened revolution contained in the maximalist programme,[4] which had really frightened the bourgeoisie, and the weak, concessive attitude of the government towards the masses, sufficed to make the bourgeoisie look to fascism for its own defence and for a substitute to the state power that was insufficient for its ends. But what drove it in that direction above all, with all the force of instinct and subconscious intuition rather than from any clearly and consciously premeditated plan, was undoubtedly its sense of the gravity of the economic crisis that followed the first gay and thoughtless times immediately after the war. The bourgeoisie felt that the crisis, which Claudio Treves in a memorable parliamentary speech called the 'expiation', was on the way, but it did not want to shoulder the burden of it. It realised that a fully active proletariat would have known how to shift the greater part on to its own shoulders; so it ran for cover and launched an attack before being attacked itself on the same terrain, thinking that once the proletariat was scattered and defeated it would resign itself to carrying the cross like a second Cyrenean of old.

In this sense, then, and because of these features, fascism is a socio-political movement of the big bourgeoisie, or at least a movement that it has successfully used and exploited.

3 Rome Theses, *Amadeo Bordiga* and *Umberto Terracini*

In the theses approved by the Rome Congress of the PCI in March 1922 fascism was accorded only a brief mention at the very end. The following extract shows that the Party was as concerned with attacking and exposing the Socialists as it was with preparing a defence against fascism.

. . .It is possible to recognise in Italy today a characteristic inversion in the manner of the state's operation. The formative period of the bourgeois state, which marked a progressive centralisation of all the functions of government under the authority of a central organisation, finds its check and its negation during the present period. Now the compact unity of all powers, which was once removed from the arbitrary control of private individuals, is being dispersed and fragmented. The state functions revert to being exercised on the basis of individual initiative, and there can be no further necessity for the state to place its institutions, as indeed it does, from the army to the judiciary, and from parliament to the executive, explicitly at the service of bourgeois conservation, since every one of them uses its particular powers to the same end in an autonomous and uncontrollable manner through the person of its own employees.

To prevent any unexpected check on this crisis of dissolution from allowing the state to resume some control over the activity of its individual parts, the bourgeois class hurries to create supplementary organisations. These operate in complete harmony with the constitutional organs, so long as the latter act in accordance with the explicit requirements of bourgeois conservation, but oppose them and take their place when they show anything other than the most servile acquiescence (civil committees, committees of defence, etc.).

The Social Democrats call for a reassertion of state authority and of respect for the law, while at the same time admitting that the democratic-parliamentary state is a class state. This shows their inability to understand that it is precisely because it is a class state that it now performs its essential task, violating the written laws which were necessary for its progressive consolidation, but which would now impair its own conservation.

The present situation in Italy contains in outline all the essential elements of a *coup d'état*, excepting only the decisive external factor of military action. The successive occurrence of acts of violence, nullifying one after another the normal conditions of social life for a whole class of citizens; the imposition of the capricious desires of groups and individuals above the regulations of established law; the immunity they are assured and the persecution guaranteed to their opponents – all this achieves the same results as would have been achieved by a more dramatic and more violent single action that set in train simultaneously much more numerous forces.

The bourgeois class is fully aware of this situation, but its interest requires that the external appearance of formal democracy should not be subjected to the more profound disturbance of a violent upheaval, which in point of fact would provide no greater protection for its privileges than it currently enjoys. It is therefore probable that, being divided on the necessity of a military putsch and still strong enough to render it ineffectual, it would actually oppose any such attempt, initiated as it would be almost entirely by personal ambitions. No new form of government could have a greater contempt than the present one for the lives, liberties and established rights of the workers. Only in a further perfecting of the democratic state, in which the reality of bourgeois dictatorship can be concealed even more successfully, can the bourgeoisie achieve its goal. This will be attained with the formation of a Social Democratic government.

The present situation in Italy is hastening the preparation of precisely this further stage of proletarian martyrdom. Work is proceeding towards this conclusion from two sides: a strong current within the Socialist Party and the parties of the left bourgeoisie are both testing the ground to find the favourable point for coming together in an alliance. Both sides in fact justify their action solely by the necessity of finding protection from the destructive violence of fascism, and on this basis they are asking for the support of all the subversive parties and demanding an end to polemics and mutual attacks.

If a Social Democratic government were to have the power to take on fascism and defeat it – something that both our theoretical convictions and the example of recent history lead us strongly to doubt – and if it were therefore necessary to prepare favourable ground for its formation, this would be achieved all the more rapidly and easily the more the Communists continue their present tireless and persistent polemic against the Socialist Party. The Communist attack gives the Socialist Party credit in the eyes of the bourgeoisie as a target of revolutionary violence, and as an impediment to the unleashing of class conflict, and so makes an agreement and alliance between them more probable. In fact we should not forget that the possibility of Socialist collaboration in Italy was first realistically mooted by the left bourgeois groupings after the Livorno split had removed all communist tendencies from the Socialist party. Any lessening of the struggle between Communists and Socialists would place the latter once more in the false position of appearing to approve the theory and practice of the Third International, and would impede the establishment of the trust necessary to the creation of a Social Democratic bloc. For this reason the most complete intransigence towards the subversive parties is to be practised on the terrain of the political struggle, even allowing for the possibility – in our view mistaken – that a change of personnel in a state structure that otherwise remains unchanged would prove favourable to the proletariat.

As regards fascism, the PCI considers it an inevitable consequence of the development of the present regime. However it does not thereby conclude that a posture of inert passivity should be adopted in face of it. To combat fascism does not imply a belief in the possibility of annulling a function of bourgeois society without destroying the latter's existence; nor does it mean deluding oneself that fascism can be overcome on its own, as if it were a distinct and isolated episode in the complex offensive of capitalism. Its purpose rather is to reduce the damage which the enemy's violence inflicts on this combative and assertive spirit.

The PCI does not exclude the possibility, indeed it keeps it in mind, that the unstable situation may provide the occasion for a violent action by a section of the bourgeoisie. It therefore prepares the minimum means necessary to meet and overcome it, and takes up an attitude of preparedness to the problem of direct action . . .

---

4 Capital's Offensive, *Karl Radek*

Radek's speech was given in November 1922 to the fourth Comintern Congress, shortly after Mussolini's march on Rome. It emphasises the extent of working-class defeat, and seeks to draw lessons from it.

. . . The victory of the fascists in Italy is an element in this policy (sc. of capital's offensive), which is partly conscious, partly a spontaneous product of the circumstances. In my view it is important for the Communist International to understand the character of this victory. I must confess that nothing is more depressing for a Communist than the treatment of this question in the Communist literature, and especially that of our fraternal Italian party. I see in the victory of fascism not merely a mechanical victory for fascist arms, but the heaviest defeat that socialism and communism have suffered since the start of the period of world revolution. When people say that fascism represents the bourgeois counter-revolution, this requires no further demonstration. Whoever smashes the organisations of the workers and establishes the power of the bourgeoisie is counter-revolutionary.

To content ourselves, therefore, with the banal truth that we have here a bourgeois victory, is to abandon the task of understanding anything at all about what may well prove of the greatest importance for the German and Czech movement in the coming months.

How was the victory of fascism possible, what was it based upon and what particularly does it represent in the European counter-revolution? It is perhaps sufficient to ask: 'Is Mussolini to be equated socially and politically with Stinnes and Bonar Law,' or is he something different?' In my view he is something different although his programme is no different from that of Bonar Law and Stinnes – a point of considerable significance. Let us recall what the fascists were originally, and how they emerged. The lower strata of the intelligentsia – schoolteachers, chemists, vets, etc, – returned from the war as disillusioned nationalists, since for all her victory Italy did not gain what the complete national programme had demanded: the Adriatic was not to be *mare nostro*. They returned to an economically ruined country, and the state was in no position to provide for them. They witnessed the growth of a revolutionary workers' movement. They opposed it, not because it was a workers' movement, but because they were enemies of the party that had led the campaign against the war. And the Socialist Party did all it could to alienate these strata – and even the war invalids as well – from itself . . .

The fact that the Socialist Party was unable to give a lead to the workers' struggle was responsible for the emergence of fascist power. When the workers occupied the factories, the Italian bourgeoisie was so impotent that Giolitti said: 'I cannot send the soldiers into the factories, or I will be struck down on the street'. Yet when the Italian reformists helped persuade the workers to leave the factories, the Italian bourgeoisie forgot its fright and went over to the offensive. Now comes the question: why does it not use the state apparatus, the *carabinieri*, the bourgeois courts and bourgeois parties that are on its side? The bourgeois parties have disintegrated; they conducted the war and were responsible for the budgetary deficit; they have nothing more to say to the soldiers. But Mussolini's followers, the nationalist, petty-bourgeois intellectuals, bring a new zest for power. The fascists have the new-born faith of the petty bourgeoisie. They say: 'Socialism was unable to create anything new, but we shall mediate between the workers and capitalists. We shall compel the capitalists to meet the needs of the workers; but you workers have to work, you have to build up the nation'. Since socialism in Italy proved illusory, the fascists could offer them their petty-bourgeois illusions instead. They fell upon the workers' organisations, and these failed to defend themselves. In the towns and industrial centres the masses still kept together, but in the townships and villages, where the workers were scattered, they fell victim to fascism. It first seized their organisations by violence, and then took over their leadership. And there can be no doubt that, although fascism has very few supporters in the industrial centres, in the countryside it has not only overcome the workers by force of arms, but has won them for its nationalist policy as well.

Comrades, if fascism has now conquered, without the slightest resistance from the workers, we can only say that we have reached the lowest point in Italy's development. I have so far refrained from charging individual comrades with this development. But one thing must be said: if our comrades in Italy, and if the Socialist Party fail to understand the reason for fascism's victory and for our own defeat, we shall be in for a long period of fascist rule. This is because the struggle against fascism requires not only the creation of an illegal organisation, not only the courage that Bordiga demonstrated here in his speech: it requires fascism to be defeated *politically*. Only when, in spite of all we have experienced, we can impart a new faith to the working masses, shall we be able to lead the Italian proletariat out of its dangers.

The fascists represent the petty bourgeoisie, which has come to power with the support of capitalism and which will be compelled to carry out capitalism's programme, not that of the petty bourgeoisie. For this reason this crude counter-revolution is the weakest of the counter-revolutionary organisations. Mussolini arrives bringing a host of petty-bourgeois intellectuals in tow, and the first thing he stumbles on is a state deficit of seven billion. Yet behind him stand hundreds of thousands of claimants for government posts. He brings with him a private army on the move, and on the day when the king receives him to confirm him in power he says: 'Demobilise! now there is only one army!' But these people do not travel the length and breadth of Italy for the sake of Mussolini's beautiful eyes! This one did it because he was given food, and that one clothing. And they will be presenting their bill. We can see in fascism an agrarian and an industrial wing. The struggle that the north Italian bourgeoisie has to wage will generate political conflicts which will destroy Mussolini's own policy. In view of his past, Mussolini represents an élitist policy, the antithesis of democracy. Yet in so far as he has succeeded in attracting broad democratic masses, he already has a democratic wing which says typically: We will remain in a democratic party. It is precisely fascism's strength that forms the basis for its downfall. Being a petty-bourgeois party, it has a broad attacking front, but being a large petty-bourgeois party, it cannot carry out the policy of Italian capital without producing revolts in its own camp. Some years ago our friend, comrade Serrati, protested against our agrarian programme; well, the revival of the Italian Party now depends on our ability to mobilise the peasants against Mussolini. If our Italian comrades, the Communists, want to be a small pure party, I can tell them that a small, pure party will easily find room in gaol. It can cultivate the purity of its soul there. But if the PCI wants to be powerful, it will have to oppose Mussolini's victory. Theoretical resolutions about the united front will not help it, nor theoretical discussions about what is possible and impossible under which circumstances. The party has to become the cry of the masses for freedom. It has to be able to unite the widest strata of the population behind the assault on fascist power.

---

5 The Struggle against Fascism, *Klara Zetkin*

In her speech of June 1923 to the Enlarged Executive of the Comintern, the veteran German communist, Klara Zetkin, sought to correct previous simplistic analyses of fascism within the Communist movement, and to link her own analysis to a coherent strategy of united proletarian defence, particularly in Germany. Because of illness she had to be carried into the room and deliver her address seated.

In fascism the proletariat confronts an exceptionally dangerous and terrible foe. Fascism is the classic expression, the most powerful and concentrated form, of the general offensive of the international bourgeoisie at the present time. To overcome it is a basic necessity, not only from the standpoint of the historical existence of the proletariat as a class, whose task is to liberate mankind through the overthrow of capitalism; it is also a matter of life and death for every individual proletarian, a question of food, of working conditions, of living arrangements, for millions and millions of the exploited. For this reason the struggle against fascism must be the concern of the whole proletariat. It is obvious that we shall overcome this insidious enemy all the sooner, the more clearly and precisely we recognise its nature and its typical effects. Up to now there has been considerable confusion about fascism, not only among the proletarian masses but among their revolutionary vanguard, the Communists, as well. The view has been held, and was indeed for a time predominant, that fascism is merely brutal bourgeois terror, and in terms of its character and its effects it was placed on the same historical level as the white terror in Horthy's Hungary. Yet although the bloody terroristic methods of fascism and the Horthy regime are the same, and are directed equally against the proletariat, the historical character of the two is exceedingly different. The terror in Hungary took place after a successful, albeit short-lived, revolutionary struggle of the proletariat; the bourgeoisie had shaken with fright for a while at proletarian power. The Horthy terror came as revenge for the revolution, and the executor of this revenge is the small caste of feudal officers.

It is quite different with fascism. Fascism is in no sense the revenge of the bourgeoisie for the revolutionary advance of the proletariat. Considered historically and objectively, fascism presents itself much more as a punishment on the proletariat for not having continued and extended the revolution that began in Russia. And the 'bearers' of fascism are not a small caste, but broad social strata, popular masses, reaching even into the proletariat. We must be clear about these essential differences if we are to deal with fascism. We will not subdue it by military means alone; we must overcome it on the political and ideological levels as well.

Although the idea that fascism is simply bourgeois terror is entertained even by radical elements of our movement, it partly coincides with the conception held by the reformist Social Democrats. For them fascism is nothing but terror and violence, indeed bourgeois reaction to the violence initiated or threatened by the proletariat against bourgeois society. According to our fine reformists the Russian revolution plays the same role as the apple bitten in Paradise does for believers: it is the starting point for all the terrorist manifestations of the present. As if there had been no imperialist war of plunder, and no class dictatorship of the bourgeoisie existed! So fascism according to the reformists is also the result of the revolutionary original sin of the Russian proletariat . . .

I hold an opposite view, and presumably all Communists do also. Namely, that however tough an image fascism presents, it is in fact the result of the decay and disintegration of the capitalist economy, and a symptom of the dissolution of the bourgeois state. Only when we understand that fascism exercises a stirring and overpowering influence on broad masses of the population, who have lost their earlier security of livelihood and often along with it their confidence in the existing order, will we be able to combat it. One root of fascism, then, is the decomposition of the capitalist economy and the bourgeois state. There were already signs of bourgeois strata being proletarianised by capitalism in the pre-war period. The war has radically disrupted the capitalist economy, as shown not only by the massive immiseration of the proletariat, but equally by the proletarianisation of broad masses of the petty and middle bourgeoisie, by the distress of the peasantry and the unremitting misery of the 'intelligentsia'. The plight of the latter is that much worse since pre-war capitalism did its best to produce a surplus of them. The capitalists wanted to create a mass supply of labour in the white-collar sector as well, so as to unleash a competitive undercutting and depress the level of wages, or should I say salaries. It is precisely from these circles that imperialism and the imperialist world war recruited many of its ideological champions. At present all these strata are experiencing the bankruptcy of the hopes they placed in the war. Their situation has deteriorated enormously. What irks them worst of all is the absence of a secure livelihood which they still enjoyed in the pre-war period . . .

Fascism has a further source. That is the flagging momentum, the standstill in the world revolution, resulting from the betrayal by the reformist leadership of the workers' movement. A large part of the petty and middle bourgeoisie, of the officials and bourgeois intellectuals, were already either proletarianised or threatened by it, and had exchanged their war psychosis for a certain sympathy towards reformist socialism. They expected from it a historical turning point, thanks to 'democracy', but their expectations have been bitterly disappointed. The reformist socialists carry out a bland coalition policy, whose cost falls not only on the proletariat and white-collar workers, but also on the civil servants, the intellectuals, the petty and middle bourgeoisie of all kinds as well. These strata are generally lacking in any theoretical, historical or political education. Their sympathy for reformist socialism was never deeply rooted. The result was that they lost their faith not only in the reformist leaders but in socialism itself. To these bourgeois elements disillusioned with socialism must be added proletarian elements. All of them, whatever their origin, lack a certain valuable inner resource, which enables a person to look in hope from the present gloom towards a brighter future. That is the confidence in the proletariat as the revolutionary class. The betrayal by the reformist leaders has less serious consequences for the attitude of these disillusioned elements than the acquiescence of the proletariat in their betrayal, and their willingness to tolerate the capitalist yoke further without any struggle or resistance, indeed to reconcile themselves to even harsher suffering than previously.

I should add, however, for the sake of accuracy, that the Communist parties outside Russia are not without responsibility for the fact that there are disillusioned elements among the proletariat who throw themselves into the fascist embrace. Their actions have often not been vigorous enough, the scale of their activity insufficient to have any deep or lasting effect on the masses, not to mention specific tactical failures which resulted in defeat. There is no doubt that many of the most active, energetic and revolutionary among the proletariat have not found their way to us, or have got lost on the way because in their view we have not acted vigorously or aggressively enough, and because we have not understood how to explain to them sufficiently clearly the circumstances which compelled us to adopt a justifiable caution at times.

The masses flocked to fascism in their thousands. It offered a refuge for the politically homeless, for the socially uprooted, the destitute and the disillusioned. And the hopes which none of them expected to be met by the revolutionary class of the proletariat and by socialism, they now look to a combination of the cleverest, toughest, most determined and audacious elements from all classes to fulfil. Even they have to be combined into a community, however, and that for the fascists is the nation. They suppose that the determination to create a new and better social order is sufficiently powerful to overcome all class antagonisms. The means for realising their fascist ideal is the state, a strong authoritarian state, which is to be at once their characteristic creation and their willing instrument. It will rule high above all differences of party and conflicts of class, and will fashion the social order according to their ideology and programme.

It is obvious from the social composition of its troops that fascism contains some elements which can prove extremely uncomfortable, even dangerous, for bourgeois society. I would go further and assert that they must become so, if they understand their own interests. Indeed, for them to do so would mean making their own contribution to the early demise of bourgeois society and the realisation of Communism. However, events to date have shown that the revolutionary elements in fascism have been outmanoeuvred and impeded by the reactionary ones. This is analogous to the experience of other revolutions in the past. The petty-bourgeois and middle strata of society at first oscillated hesitantly from one side to the other between the mighty historical forces of the poletariat and the bourgeoisie. The distress of their situation, and partly also their finest aspirations and highest ideals, lead them to sympathise with the proletariat, so long as the latter not only takes a revolutionary line but appear to have prospects of victory. Even the fascist leaders, under pressure from the needs of the masses, have at least to flirt with the revolutionary proletariat, even though they may not inwardly sympathise with them. Yet as soon as it becomes clear that the proletariat has given up any further struggle for revolution, and retreated meekly from the field to make its peace with capitalism under the influence of the reformist leaders, at that point the fascist

masses throw in their lot on the side where most of their leaders have
stood from the start – whether consciously or unconsciously – on the
side of the bourgeoisie.

The bourgeoisie naturally welcomes its new allies with enthusiasm,
seeing in them a strong addition to its power, and are ready to go to
any lengths in the use of mass violence in its service. Unfortunately
the bourgeoisie is accustomed to exercising power, and is much
cleverer and more experienced in addressing a situation and defending
its interests than the proletariat, which is used only to subordination.
From the outset the bourgeoisie grasped the situation very clearly,
and saw the advantage it could gain from fascism. What is it after?
The reconstruction of the capitalist economy and the preservation of
its own class rule. Under present circumstances, however, the
realisation of this goal presupposes a considerable intensification of
exploitation and repression of the proletariat. The bourgeoisie knows
full well that it does not have the means on its own to impose such a
fate on the exploited. Once afflicted by the sudden blows of
destitution, even the most thick-skinned of proletarians finally begins
to rebel against capitalism. The bourgeoisie is forced to admit that
under these circumstances even the bland sermons of the reformist
socialists about class peace are bound to lose their soporific effect. It
calculates that it can only maintain the subordination and exploitation
of the proletariat with the help of force; yet the power available to the
bourgeois state is beginning partially to fail. It is increasingly losing
the financial means and the moral authority to secure blind loyalty
and submission from its slaves. The bourgeoisie can no longer look to
the ordinary powers of the state alone to secure its class domination.
It requires an unofficial, extra-legal structure of power such as fascism
provides with its motley throng of violent followers. For this reason
the bourgeoisie accepts the service of fascism with open arms, and
affords it the most extensive freedom of movement in violation of all
its own written and unwritten laws. It goes even further, nourishing
and sustaining it, and prompting its development with all the means at
its disposal . . .

The question now confronts us – and it is important for the
proletariat everywhere – what has fascism in Italy done to fulfil its
programme since the seizure of state power? What kind of state is it

that it expected to be its instrument? Has it proved to be the promised party-free and class-less state, which guarantees the rights of every stratum of society; or has it also proved to be an instrument of the propertied minority, in particular of the industrial bourgeoisie?

If you compare the programme of Italian fascism with its performance, one thing is already apparent today: the complete ideological bankruptcy of the movement. There is the most blatant contradiction between what fascism has promised and what it actually delivers to the masses. The fresh air of reality has dispersed like a bubble all the chatter about the national interest being supreme in the fascist state. The 'nation' has revealed itself as the bourgeoisie, the fascist ideal state as a vulgar, unscrupulous bourgeois class state. Sooner or later this ideological bankruptcy must be followed by political bankruptcy as well. It is already in process. Fascism is incapable of holding together even the disparate bourgeois forces, with the benefit of whose tacit patronage it came to power. Fascism intended to secure power for the creation of the new society, by seizing control of the state and making the state apparatus conformable to its purposes. It has not yet succeeded in making even the civil service fully submissive. A bitter struggle has broken out between the old established bureaucracy and the new fascist officialdom. The same antagonism exists between the regular army with its career officers and the new leadership of the fascist militia. The conflict between fascism and the bourgeois political parties is intensifying . . .

Behind the conflicts already mentioned and still others, stands the conflict of classes, which cannot be abolished by exhortations and organisation for unity. Class conflicts are more powerful than all the ideologies which deny them, and keep breaking out in spite of fascism, indeed because of fascism and in opposition to it. The attitude of the Popular Party expresses the self-consciousness of the urban petty bourgeoisie and the small peasantry about their class position and their opposition to large scale capital. This is exceedingly important for fascism's maintenance of power in Italy, or rather for the dissolution that confronts it. These strata – particularly the women among them – are deeply religious and deeply Catholic in outlook. For this reason Mussolini has done all he can to win over the

Vatican. But even the Vatican has not dared to oppose the rebellion of the peasant masses against fascism that is emerging within the Popular Party.

When the small peasants see that fascism brings tax relief, tax evasion and lucrative orders for the bourgeoisie, they will surely recognise that heavier burdens will be imposed on themselves by means of indirect taxes and particularly through a new valuation of rural incomes. The same holds for the petty-bourgeois masses in the towns. The source of their strongest opposition is that at the moment of its triumph fascism abolished what limited rent control there was; the landlord once again has unrestricted opportunity for exploitation through high rents. The growing rebellion of peasants and agricultural workers also finds decisive expression in precisely those places where fascism supposed it had broken all resistance by means of its 'squads'. In Boscoreale near Naples, for example, more than one thousand peasants stormed the municipal offices in protest against oppressive taxes. In three places in the province of Novara agricultural workers have been successful in defending their existing wage levels and working conditions against the large landowners, only because they occupied several estates, and that with the support of the fascist squads. This shows that the idea of class struggle is even beginning to take root in the ranks of fascism itself.

Particularly important is the awakening of sections of the proletariat which have been confused and poisoned by fascism. Fascism is incapable of defending the interests of the workers against the bourgeoisie, and incapable of fulfilling the promises it made to the fascist unions. The more victorious it is, the less capable it proves itself as defender of the proletariat. It can never compel the employers to keep their promises about the advantages of a common organisation. Where only a few workers are organised in the fascist unions, it may be possible for the capitalist to improve their wages. But where the masses are enrolled in the fascist organisation, the employers will have no regard for their 'brother fascist', since that would be too costly, and in matters of money and profit 'business is business' for our fine capitalists . . .

There are various conclusions to be drawn from this. First, we should not regard fascism as a homogeneous entity, as a 'granite block' from which all our exertions will simply rebound. Fascism is a disparate formation, comprising various contradictory elements, and hence liable to internal dissolution and disintegration. Our task is to initiate the most energetic campaign for the allegiance not only of those proletarians who have fallen under the influence of fascism, but of the petty and middle bourgeoisie, the peasantry, intellectuals, in short of all those strata whose economic and social situation brings them into increasing opposition to large scale capitalism, and hence into bitter struggle against it.

It would, however, be extremely dangerous to assume that a military collapse must rapidly follow the ideological and political degeneration of Italian fascism. Certainly its military disintegration and collapse must eventually come, but the process can be drawn out for a long time yet by the sheer weight of forces at its disposal. And while the Italian proletariat detaches itself from the influence of fascism, and with increasing self-confidence and clear-sightedness resumes the struggle for its interests, the revolutionary class struggle, it must reckon along with our Italian comrades that fascism in ideological and political decay will throw all its military–terroristic force against them, and will not shrink from the most relentless and unscrupulous violence. They should be prepared! A monster can often dispense devastating blows even in its death struggle. The revolutionary proletarians, the Communists and the Socialists, who take the path of the class struggle with them, must therefore be equipped and prepared for further severe struggles.

It would be a mistake if we allowed ourselves to be induced into inaction or delay, or into a suspension of our mobilisation for the struggle, because of our historical analysis of fascism. Certainly fascism is condemned to an internal process of self-decay and disintegration. It can only serve as a temporary instrument for the bourgeoisie in its class struggle, only temporarily as an illegal or even legal reinforcement for the bourgeois state against the proletariat. Yet it would be fatal for us to play the aesthete's role of knowledgeable spectator and wait around for the disintegration to take place. On the contrary, it is our damned duty to advance and accelerate this process with all the means at our disposal.

This is not only the particular responsibility of the proletariat in

Italy, where this process will probably take place first, but especially also of the German proletariat. Fascism is an international phenomenon; we are all agreed on that. After Italy it has to date achieved probably its firmest hold in Germany. Here the conclusion of the war and the failure of the revolution have favoured its development. This is easy to explain when we bear in mind the ultimate causes of fascism.

In Germany the economy has experienced exceptional disruption as a result of the wartime defeat, the burden of reparations and the Versailles Treaty. The state has been shaken to its foundations. The government is weak and lacking in authority, a plaything in the hands of Stinnes and his associates. In no other country, in my opinion at least, is there such a massive contrast between the objective maturity of the revolutionary situation and the subjective immaturity of the proletariat, in consequence of the treacherous attitudes and behaviour of the reformist leaders. In no country since the outbreak of the war have the Social Democrats collapsed so ignominiously as in Germany. Here we had a highly developed capitalist industry, here the proletariat could pride itself on its sound organisation and its long tradition of Marxist education. The English, the French, the Austrian Social Democrats, indeed all the proletarian organisations assembled in the Second International, had their merits — we acknowledge that. But the foremost party, the one which provided a model for the others, was the German. Its failure is therefore a more shameful, more unforgivable crime than the failure of any other party. All the others have more excuse, more reason to blame the outbreak of war for their bankruptcy than the German Social Democrats. The reaction on the proletarian masses was inevitably exceptionally severe and ill-fated. Combined with the collapse of German imperialism at the hands of the imperialist Entente, it produced here the most favourable conditions for fascism to run riot . . .

The struggle against fascism thus imposes on us an exceptional abundance of new tasks, which it is the duty of every individual section of the Communist International to take in hand and accomplish according to the actual conditions prevalent in each country. We must, however, remain alive to the fact that an ideological and political victory over fascism is insufficient on its own to protect the proletariat in its struggle from the insidious violence of the enemy. Right now the proletariat confronts the urgent necessity of self-defence against the fascist terror, a requirement that must not be postponed even for a moment. It is a matter of life and limb, of the very existence of its organisations. Self-defence of the proletariat is the demand of the hour. Fascism is not to be fought in the manner of the Italian reformists, who entreated with the enemy: 'Don't touch me and I won't touch you!' No. Force against force! Not force in the form of individual terror – that is useless – but force as the power of the organised revolutionary class struggle of the proletariat.

We in Germany have made a start in preparing the self-defence of the proletariat against fascism with the organisation of workshop brigades. When these have been expanded and replicated in other countries, the international defeat of fascism will be assured. But proletarian struggle and self-defence against fascism must mean a proletarian united front. Fascism does not enquire whether the factory worker owes his allegiance to the white and blue of Bavaria, to the black, red and gold of the bourgeois Republic, or to the red flag with the hammer and sickle. It does not ask whether he supports the return of the Wittelsbachs, is enthusiastic about Ebert, or would rather see our comrade Brandler as president of the German soviet republic.[6] It is enough that fascism sees a class-conscious proletarian in front of it; it strikes him down regardless. The workers must therefore make common cause in the struggle, without distinction of party or trade union organisation. The self-defence of the proletariat against fascism is one of the strongest factors making for the organisation and consolidation of the proletarian united front. Without the united front it is impossible for the proletariat to accomplish its own defence successfully. For this reason it is essential for us to extend and deepen our agitation in the factories still further. Only when we set alight a spark of revolutionary class consciousness in every individual worker, and fan it into a flame of class will, shall we succeed in preparing and accomplishing the necessary victory against fascism on the military front as well. Thus however momentarily brutal, because of fascism's support, however virulent the offensive of world capital against the world proletariat may be, the proletariat will finally beat it back. Despite fascism, the days of the capitalist economy, the bourgeois state and the class power of the bourgeoisie are numbered. Fascism itself announces loud and clear the disruption and disintegration of bourgeois society, and the future victory of the proletariat, if only it has the wit and the will to fight in a united front. It must do so! Above the chaos of present conditions the proletariat will rise like a colossus, and cry out: 'I have the will! I have the strength! Mine is the struggle and the victory! The future belongs to me!'

6 The Nature and Historical Significance of Fascism, *Gyula Sas*

Sas, a Hungarian Communist, was living in Italy at the time of the march on Rome, and studied fascism at first hand. This extract is taken from the first chapter of his book, *Der Faschismus in Italien*, published in Hamburg in 1923. It emphasises the international significance of the Italian experience.

The complex political situation and even more its internal contradictions have always made it difficult for the working class to recognise the true nature of Italian fascism. It was not only abroad that people were confused about it – and often still are today – but even in Italy itself people held contradictory views about it. Indeed the tendency was more prevalent in Italy than elsewhere. This was because, while the working class of other countries could make a judgement on the basis of news that trickled out about the destruction of trades councils and the bloody persecution of workers belonging to the Communist and Socialist organisations, and could recognise in that the counter-revolutionary character of fascism, the Italian workers were in too close a contact with the local situation to have a clear perspective. There were some who maintained that fascism was a terrorist guard of the landowners; others said that it was merely a desperate adventurist revolt of *déclassé* elements, lumpen-bourgeois and lumpen-proletarian; others again that fascism was the organisation of the petty bourgeoisie, etc. There was even the view that fascism was actually a revolutionary movement!

How was this possible? Only because of the fact that most people looked at individual phenomena, and confused their particular aspects – and sometimes even individual moments of crisis – for example the mass incursion of landowners into the Fascist Party – with the movement in its totality. Some saw only that the most bloody of the so-called 'punitive expeditions' were those that took place in the typically agrarian provinces of central and northern Italy; others paid attention only to the composition of the fascist gangs, the *squadre*, which in a subsequent phase of fascism's evolution were actually composed mainly of *déclassé* elements; others again drew attention to the fact that the petty bourgeoisie were streaming in increasing numbers into the fascist organisations; and there were some who were deceived by the circumstance that almost all the most visible personalities of fascism had originated from the labour movement. Other factors which helped to obscure a clear view of things for many were the 'programmatic' demands, extremely radical in tone, of the first propagandist period; the 'revolutionary' phraseology of fascism; actions such as, for example, the reductions in the cost of living imposed by terror (albeit in a quite improvised fashion, and always directed only against small shopkeepers and retailers); and also the struggle waged by fascism against the power-holders in the state, against the 'old order', and the demands for the head of Giolitti after the replacement of the ruling monarchy by a republic.

Today lengthy demonstrations are no longer needed to prove that fascism, historically understood, represents an advance of industrial capital. The proof of this is provided in irrefutable manner by the first six months of Mussolini's government. A glance at the economic policy of the fascist government is enough to convince oneself of this. Even so, to establish that fascism is historically an advance of the industrial bourgeoisie is not sufficient to understand its full significance. One might imagine that it is perhaps simply a method of struggle of the bourgeoisie in Italy, without any relevance to the proletariat of other countries. Yet however much the particular economic and political situation of Italy has put its stamp on Italian fascism, fascism itself is not peculiar to Italy, but is realised most fully on the international level. Its roots are embedded in the general economic and political situation of the present time.

The five-year imperialist war has so disrupted the economic foundation of capitalist society throughout the world that an economic reconstruction on the basis of capitalist production, with a 'normal' level of exploitation of the proletariat, is impossible. This remains a fact, despite the 'economic recovery' in the most powerful of the victorious states, despite the economic conjuncture in North America and despite the economic situation in England, which has shown a certain improvement in recent times.

Contemporaneously with the disruption in the economic foundations, and – leaving other factors aside for the moment – also as a result of it, immediately after the war the political power of the bourgeoisie was also disrupted, particularly in central, southern and eastern Europe, although not even the victorious or the neutral states were spared the phenomenon. This weakening of the political power of the bourgeoisie automatically brought with it a corresponding strengthening of the position of the working class. Yet it was only where there existed a politically conscious Communist party, capable of leading the proletariat – i.e. in present Soviet Russia and the Soviet federated Republics – that the proletariat was able to profit from the bourgeois weakness, and extended its own positions of strength to the point of subordinating the bourgeoisie and installing its own dictatorship, in the form of a transition towards the socialist order. In the countries of central and southern Europe, where the objective situation was no less ripe for the proletarian conquest of power, but where the preliminary subjective condition for the proletarian revolution was lacking, that is a well organised Communist party, politically conscious and full of prestige in the eyes of the working masses, the further development of the revolution was frustrated because of the treachery of the reformist Social Democratic leaders. This betrayal took different forms in different countries. In Germany, for example, or in Austria, where the Social Democratic leadership still held by far the greater part of the working masses firmly under its control, it offered the bourgeoisie a coalition with the aim, so it was said, of attaining socialism gradually via the institution of a 'democratic' republic. As if it were the 'democratic' republic and not the dictatorship of the working class that was the ladder to socialism!

In other countries, as in Italy, where the Social Democratic leaders did not yet have the masses behind them, they remained in the party of the revolutionary working class, so as to frustrate and sabotage the further development of the proletarian revolution from inside. Once this task was achieved, they believed that they could follow the glorious example of their German and Austrian colleagues.

However, the 'democratic' republic of the Social Democrats in coalition with the bourgeoisie is a historical absurdity in the existing political and economic situation. This is because the 'normal' level of exploitation of the proletariat in the pre-war period is now insufficient for the reconstruction of the economy on capitalist foundations (and the Social Democrats wanted and still want its reconstruction only on capitalist foundations!). This being so, it is obvious that such a reconstruction is less than ever possible in a 'democratic' republic, given that here (and also in the democratic monarchies such as England and Italy prior to fascism) the working masses have a position of greater strength than they enjoyed before the war. They will certainly not use this position to intensify spontaneously their own exploitation above its 'normal' level, in the interests of capital. They will seek rather to use their increased strength to try and diminish the level of this 'normal' exploitation. They *have* to make this attempt, since their poverty compels them to do so. And the Social Democratic leaders, in their capacity as ministers, can only frustrate these efforts by means of a fresh and repeated betrayal of working class interests.

Now it is clear, and always has been to any thinking person, that a situation of this kind cannot continue in the long run, if it requires both sides to have given in without a fight. The Social Democratic leaders were ready, and still would be now, to abandon the working class to this sort of defeat without a struggle; but they took no account of a second factor, the bourgeoisie. The bourgeoisie is not disposed to perish without a fight! It may be that this comes as a surprise to the Social Democratic leaders, indeed an unpleasant surprise, but for us Communists it is no novelty. We have always expected and predicted that, if the Social Democratic leaders succeeded in frustrating the development of the revolution, the bourgeoisie, which was prostrate and impotent in the first years after the war, would rouse itself from its impotence, and would do everything to re-establish its economic order and its unquestioned class supremacy.

On one side, then, the ruinous economic situation, whose reconstruction required intensified exploitation of the proletariat, on the other the strength of the working class, increased by the circumstances I have described, yet absolutely *passive*, ensured that the bourgeoisie could no longer resolve the problems of economic reconstruction and restoration of its class hegemony by democratic means. The instruments of 'democratic' power, and the legal apparatus of the democratic state no longer suffice, even with the active support of Social Democracy, to subdue a relatively strengthened proletariat in a situation of intensified exploitation. For this reason the bourgeoisie rejects the instruments of 'democratic' power and rejects the legal democratic state (which by now only the Social Democratic leaders believe in with difficulty, if in fact they still do). Indeed the bourgeoisie not only rejects but destroys them, and turns to other instruments which it hopes can enable it to achieve its ends.

This is the historical significance of fascism! In Italy, as in all the other countries of Europe and America, the bourgeoisie cares nothing for the 'superior principle of democracy', and nothing for the 'legal' and 'democratic' state. In its place it puts extra-legal and terroristic methods, which it employs in the political and military struggle to bring the proletariat to its knees, and bind it hand and foot, no longer using 'democratic' instruments of power, but those of a 'fascist order'. In this way it makes the proletariat pay the price of its own capitalist economic reconstruction, and its own bourgeois class domination! . . .

The fact that the working masses of Italy did not perceive the problem clearly, that often they saw in fascism merely a reaction of the landowners, enabled the Social Democratic leaders to convince a considerable number of the Italian working class that *collaboration* with the bourgeoisie could provide them with protection against fascism – against fascism, which was actually the fascism of the bourgeoisie itself! The consequences of this error are far-reaching, since it allowed the Italian reformists to make the first breach in the proletarian ranks, and so to facilitate the victory of fascism.

Other sections of the working class also failed to understand the problem, and saw in fascism the angry outburst of a small adventurist group of *déclassé* bourgeoisie and lumpen proletarians, which was only by chance directed against the workers. This misconception enabled the Socialist Party (the 'maximalists') to recommend to the workers a strategy of unconditional *passivity* in face of fascism 'until the storm blew over'. It enabled it also, at a time when fascism was rent by an acute internal crisis over its constitution and the increase in influence of a section of the landowners, to conclude a 'peace pact' with Mussolini.

There is no reason either to try and cover up the error of the PCI (though one should not forget that it was founded only after the start of the fascist offensive). Its error consisted in not having attributed any particular importance to fascism at an early stage, and in having subsequently seen it merely as an extra-legal *military* force of the bourgeoisie, which the young Communist Party could not yet confront with its own military force. As a consequence of this latter mistake, it failed to confront it *politically*, although the fascist victory even in Italy was not merely a victory of arms, but a political victory as well.

With this observation we now reach the fundamental criterion for assessing the nature of fascism. Even today the opinion is widespread, especially abroad, that the victory of fascism in Italy was simply a victory for armed reaction, like the white terror in Finland or in Horthy's Hungary. Nothing would be more dangerous for the working class than such a totally false conclusion about fascism, since it would remove at the outset the possibility of fighting it with the appropriate weapons, and the only ones that could guarantee success. In so far as the course of fascism in Italy was strewn with the corpses of thousands of proletarians and with the ashes from the ruins of trades councils and workers' associations, its victory was not merely a victory for arms, but also – indeed above all – a *political* victory over the bankrupt policy of Social Democracy, a political victory that alone made possible the military one. The political victory of fascism was the necessary condition for the victory of fascist arms.

This political victory consisted in the fact that fascism succeeded in attracting large sections of the petty bourgeoisie and peasantry, and even a section of the working class as well, especially in the lowlands, and in using them for the political and military struggle against the class-conscious working class. The reason is that while fascism, historically understood, represents an assault by capital on the working class, so as to muzzle it and establish the absolute supremacy of a narrow upper class of the bourgeoisie, yet to outward appearance it does not look – or more precisely did not look before its conquest of power – at all like a movement in reactionary revolt against the interests of the workers, on behalf of a small group of capitalist plutocrats, but more like a progressive movement, even a revolutionary one. Employing a 'revolutionary' phraseology intermingled with abundant nationalistic slogans – 'greatness of our nation', 'national liberty' and so on – it promised to defend the 'security of the nation' and the interests of 'all' the people, in particular those of the middle and working classes, 'upright in outlook and national spirit', *against* the interests of the 'filthy bourgeoisie' and the Bolsheviks, 'enemies' and 'traitors' to the fatherland.

After the fascist conquest of power it naturally soon emerged that the 'fascist revolution' was a cheap trick, and that 'national salvation' meant salvation for the money-bags of the bourgeoisie. The 'superior interests of the nation' signified, not the interests of the people, but exclusively those of the large capitalists. The expression 'filthy bourgeoisie' was merely an astute phrase to trick the middle classes and the workers. By the Bolshevik 'enemies and traitors to the fatherland' was understood not only the communist *and* social democratic workers, but the workers pure and simple, all the workers, not even excluding the fascist ones, who are 'traitors to the fatherland' in so far as they want to see *their* interests defended. And not only the workers, either, but the middle classes, the petty bourgeoisie and the peasants as well are from now on included in the category of 'Bolshevik enemies of the fatherland', and they are slaughtered with the instruments of violence of the 'fascist order', if they do not show themselves disposed to serve the interests of the big bourgeoisie without opposition.

All this is now recognised in Italy by all sections of the proletariat, of the petty bourgeoisie and the peasantry. Indeed, they not only recognise it, they experience it personally every day. But it is already too late, and cannot alter the fact that these are the same petty bourgeoisie and peasants, and in part also confused workers, who delivered to fascism the weight of numbers and the armed strength to defeat the class-conscious proletariat. To have won over these strata of the population for the anti-proletarian struggle constituted the real political victory of fascism . . .

Let us then sum up briefly the lessons that every European and American worker should draw from the example of Italian fascism:
(A) Fascism is neither a terrorist gang of the landed class (or of monarchists, as might appear from some European countries – though this naturally does not exclude the possibility of monarchist currents appearing in the fascist camp) nor is it a revolt of *déclassé* elements, nor a 'revolutionary' movement of the petty bourgeoisie. It is, historically understood, an assault by the bourgeoisie, and for that very reason can only be overcome by means of a conscious struggle against the bourgeoisie itself, and not by attempting a coalition with them.
(B) It is not a special Italian phenomenon, that has no interest for other countries, but an advance of international capital, which will try to make use of fascism in every country of Europe and America to bring the proletariat to its knees, so that it can then extort from it and from the peasantry, and indeed from the petty bourgeoisie, who are all abandoned defenceless to the mercies of the bourgeoisie once the proletariat is defeated, the price of capitalism's reconstruction and of the bourgeoisie's class domination.
(C) It is not merely a victory for arms, but also a political victory over the bankrupt policy of Social Democracy. It can therefore only be decisively overcome by its own methods – military and political – through the immediate establishment of effective organs of proletarian defence, and in the longer term by the development of world revolution, that is by the proletarian conquest of power.

During its evolution in the different countries, fascism will assume a variety of external forms in accordance with their particular economic and political situation. Yet, in so far as the basic features of these economic and political relations are common to all countries, these differences will not detract from the general validity for all more or less capitalist countries of the historical significance of fascism. That is why a more profound understanding of the Italian example is of inestimable importance for the workers of all other countries.

The present short work will allow our class comrades abroad, but also the petty-bourgeois and peasant classes abroad, to understand this example from the precise evidence of the facts, and to draw lessons from it.

---

7 Democracy and Fascism, *Antonio Gramsci*

Gramsci's article of 1924 discusses the political goal of the anti-fascist movement. He justifies the refusal of the PCI to join an opposition bloc for the restoration of bourgeois democracy by pointing to a reciprocal relationship, though not an identity, between bourgeois democracy and fascism.

What service has fascism performed for the bourgeois class and for democracy? It set out to destroy even that minimum to which the democratic system was reduced in Italy – i.e. the concrete possibility to create an organizational link at the base between workers, and to extend this link gradually until it embraced the great masses in movement. It set out too to annihilate the results already achieved in this field. Fascism has accomplished both these aims, by means of an activity perfectly designed for the purpose. Fascism has never manoeuvred, as the reactionary state might have done in 1919 and 1920, when faced with a massive movement in the streets. Rather, it waited to move until working-class organisation had entered a period of passivity and then fell upon it, striking it as such, not for what it 'did' but for what it 'was' – in other words, as the source of links capable of giving the masses a form and physiognomy. The strength and capacity for struggle of the workers for the most part derive from the existence of these links, even if they are not in themselves apparent. What is involved is the possibility of meeting; of discussing; of giving these meetings and discussions some regularity; of choosing leaders through them; of laying the basis for an elementary organic formation, a league, a cooperative or a party section. What is involved is the possibility of giving these organic formations a continuous functionality; of making them into the basic framework for an organized movement. Fascism has systematically worked to destroy these possibilities.

Its most effective activity has, therefore, been that carried on in the localities; at the base of the organizational edifice of the working class; in the provinces, rural centres, workshops and factories. The sacking of subversive workers; the exiling or assassination of workers' and peasants' 'leaders'; the ban on meetings; the prohibition on staying outdoors after working hours; the obstacle thus placed in the way of any 'social' activity on the part of the workers; and then the destruction of the Chambers of Labour and all other centres of organic unity of the working class and peasantry, and the terror disseminated among the masses – all this had more value than a political struggle through which the working class was stripped of the 'rights' which the Constitution guarantees on paper. After three years of this kind of action, the working class has lost all form and all organacity; it has been reduced to a disconnected, fragmented, scattered mass. With no substantial transformation of the Constitution, the political conditions of the country have been changed most profoundly, because the strength of the workers and peasants has been rendered quite ineffective.

When the working class is reduced to such conditions, the political situation is 'democratic'. In such conditions, in fact, so-called liberal bourgeois groups can, without fear of fatal repercussions on the internal cohesion of State and society; (1) separate their responsibilities from those of the fascism which they armed, encouraged and incited to struggle against the workers; (2) restore 'the rule of law', i.e. a state of affairs in which the possibility for a workers' organization to exist is not denied. They can do the first of these two things because the workers, dispersed and disorganized, are not in any position to insert their strength into the bourgeois contradiction deeply enough to transform it into a general crisis of society, prelude to revolution. The second thing is possible for them because fascism has created the conditions for it, by destroying the results of thirty years' organizational work. The freedom to organize is only conceded to the workers by the bourgeois when they are certain that the workers have been reduced to a point where they can no longer make use of it, except to resume elementary organizing work – work which they hope will not have political consequences other than in the very long term.

In short, 'democracy' organized fascism when it felt it could no longer resist the pressure of the working class in conditions even of only formal freedom. Fascism, by shattering the working class, has restored to 'democracy' the possibility of existing. In the intentions of the bourgeoisie, the division of labour should operate perfectly: the alternation of fascism and democracy should serve to exclude for ever any possibility of working-class resurgence. But not only the bourgeois see things in this way. The same point of view is shared by the reformists, by the maximalists, by all those who say that present conditions for the workers of Italy are analogous to those of thirty years ago, those of 1890 and before, when the working-class movement was taking its first steps among us. By all those who believe that the resurgence should take place with the same slogans and in the same forms as at that time. By all those, therefore, who view the conflict between 'democratic' bourgeoisie and fascism in the same way that they then viewed the conflicts between radical and conservative bourgeois. By all those who speak of 'constitutional freedoms' or of 'freedom of work' in the same way that one could speak of these at the outset of the workers' movement.

To adopt this point of view means to weld the working class inexorably within the vicious circle in which the bourgeoisie wishes to confine it. To hear the reformists, the workers and peasants of Italy today have nothing more to hope for than that the bourgeoisie should itself give them back the freedom to reconstruct their organization and make it live; the freedom to re-establish trade unions, peasant leagues, party sections, Chambers of Labour, and then federations, co-operatives, labour exchanges, worker-control offices, committees designed to limit the boss's freedom inside the factory, and so on and so forth – until the pressure of the masses reawoken by the organizations, and that of the organizations themselves, to transcend the boundaries of bourgeois society becomes so strong that 'democracy' can neither resist it nor tolerate it, and will once again arm an army of blackshirts to destroy the menace.

How is the vicious circle to be broken? Solving this problem means

solving, in practice, the problem of revolution. There is only one way:
to succeed in reorganizing the great mass of workers during the very
development of the bourgeois political crisis, and not by concession of
the bourgeois, but through the initiative of a revolutionary minority
and around the latter. The Communist Party, from the day in which
the fascist regime went into crisis, has not set itself any other task than
this . . .

8 The International Situation and the Struggle against Fascism, *Antonio Gramsci*

The notes Gramsci prepared for the Executive Committee meeting of the
PCI in August 1926 constitute one of the last things he wrote on fascism
before his imprisonment. This section of his report situates fascism in its
international context, and identifies three different phases in its
development.

So far as the international situation is concerned, it seems to me to be
dominated especially by the question of the English general strike,
and the conclusions to be drawn from it. The English strike has posed
two fundamental problems for our movement.

The first of these is the problem of general perspectives; i.e. the
problem of a precise assessment of the phase through which the
capitalist order is currently passing. Is the period of so-called
stabilisation over? What point have we reached, with respect to the
capacity of the bourgeois order for resistance? It is clear that not only
from a theoretical and scientific point of view, but also from a
practical and immediate point of view, it is interesting and necessary
to verify precisely the exact point which the capitalist crisis has
reached. But it is also clear that any new political orientation based on
a different assessment of the precise level of the capitalist crisis would
be stupid, if this different assessment is not immediately reflected in
genuinely different political and organizational directives.

The problem to be posed, it seems to me, is the following. In the international field – and this, in practice, means two things: 1. in the field of the group of capitalist states which form the keystone of the bourgeois system; 2. in the field of those states which represent, as it were, the periphery of the capitalist world – are we about to pass from the phase of political organization of the proletarian forces, to the phase of technical organization of the revolution? Or, on the other hand, are we about to pass from the former of the phases mentioned to an intermediate phase, in which a particular form of technical organization can accelerate the political organization of the masses, and hence accelerate the passage to the concluding phase of the conquest of power? These problems in my view should be discussed. But it is obvious that it is not possible to solve them at a purely theoretical level. They can only be solved on the basis of concrete data, with respect to the real effectiveness both of the revolutionary and of the bourgeois forces.

A certain number of observations and criteria must form the basis for this study. The first of these concerns the fact that in the advanced capitalist countries, the ruling class possesses political and organizational reserves which it did not possess, for instance, in Russia. This means that even the most serious economic crises do not have immediate repercussions in the political sphere. Politics always lags behind economics, far behind. The state apparatus is far more resistant than is often possible to believe; and it succeeds, at moments of crisis, in organizing greater forces loyal to the regime than the depth of the crisis might lead one to suppose. This is especially true of the more important capitalist states.

In the typical peripheral states, like Italy, Poland, Spain or Portugal, the state forces are less efficient. But in these countries, one finds a phenomenon of which the greatest account must be taken. This phenomenon, in my view, consists in the following. In these countries, a broad stratum of intermediate classes stretches between the proletariat and capitalism: classes which seek to carry on, and to a certain sense succeed in carrying on, policies of their own, with ideologies which often influence broad strata of the proletariat, but which particularly affect the peasant masses. France too, although it occupies a prominent position in the first group of capitalist States, belongs by virtue of certain of its characteristics to the situation of the peripheral states.

What seems to me to be characteristic of the present phase of the capitalist crisis is the fact that, unlike in 1920–2, today the political and military formations of the middle classes have a left radical character, or at least they present themselves to the masses as left radicals. The development of the Italian situation, given its particular features, seems to me to be able, in a certain sense, to serve as a model for various phases traversed by other countries. In 1919 and 1920, the military and political formations of the middle classes were represented in our country by primitive fascism and by D'Annunzio. It is well known that in those years, the fascist movement and D'Annunzio's movement alike were willing to ally themselves even with the revolutionary proletarian forces in order to overthrow the Nitti government, which appeared as American capital's go-between for the enslavement of Italy (Nitti was the precursor of Dawes in Europe).[7]

The second phase of fascism – 1921 and 1922 – was clearly reactionary. From 1923 on, a molecular process began through which the most active elements of the middle classes moved over from the reactionary fascist camp to the camp of the Aventine opposition. This process crystallized in a manner which might have proved fatal to fascism in the period of the Matteotti crisis. Because of the weakness of our movement, a weakness which moreover was itself significant, the phenomenon was interrupted by fascism and the middle classes were thrown back into a new state of political pulverisation. Today, the molecular phenomenon has begun again, on a scale far greater than that which was started in 1923, and is accompanied by a parallel phenomenon of regroupment of the revolutionary forces around our party, which ensures that a new crisis of the Matteotti type could hardly culminate in a new 3 January.[8]

These phases traversed by Italy, in a form which I would call classical and exemplary, we find in all those countries which we have called peripheral capitalist countries. The present phase in Italy, i.e. a regroupment of the middle classes on the left, we can find in Spain, Portugal, Poland and in the Balkans. Only in two countries, Czechoslovakia and France, do we find a continuity in the permanency of the left bloc – a fact which in my view should be particularly closely studied.

The conclusion to be drawn from these observations, which of course will have to be improved and set out in a systematic manner, it seems to me might be the following. In reality, we are entering a new phase in the development of the capitalist crisis. This phase takes different forms, on the one hand in the countries of the capitalist periphery, and on the other in the advanced capitalist countries. Between these two series of states, Czechoslovakia and France represent the two connecting links. In the peripheral countries, the problem arises of the phase which I have called intermediate between the political and the technical preparation of the revolution. In the other countries, including France and Czechoslovakia, it seems to me that the problem is still one of political preparation. For all the capitalist countries, a fundamental problem is posed – the problem of the transition from the united front tactic, understood in a general sense, to a specific tactic which confronts the concrete problems of national life and operates on the basis of the popular forces as they are historically determined.

9 The Contradictions of Fascism in Power, *Palmiro Togliatti*

This is part of Togliatti's report to the Comintern's commission on fascism in November 1926. He identifies a number of persistent contradictions within the fascist regime, and assesses the likelihood of a repetition of fascist success in other countries.

. . . Let us now turn to the political sphere. I have already mentioned how fascism's campaign against democracy, against the parliamentary system etc., in fact concealed the necessity confronting the large bourgeoisie of overcoming the obstacles that the old state apparatus put in the way of attempts at stabilisation. But the classes which constituted fascism's social base understood this campaign as the advent to power of a new ruling class. During the period of armed struggle against the proletariat it was possible for agreement to exist between the new movement and the old ruling classes of the state. These ruling classes even contributed, in a quite decisive way, to fascism's organisation and victory: but once fascism has achieved power, its very conquest created a new source of contradictions and internal conflicts. Fascism found itself squeezed between the resistance of the old ruling classes, which wanted to hold onto power, and the pressure of the small and middle bourgeoisie. It naturally had to yield to this pressure so as not to lose its base, but the concessions it made to the petty bourgeoisie, while on the one hand they could not completely satisfy it, on the other made the task of stabilising the regime more difficult.

Let us take as an example the fascist campaign against parliament. It is a fact that parliament is the only form in which up to now the petty bourgeoisie has succeeded in organising its participation in political life. How can it participate in political life after the suppression of parliament? It is compelled to seek another solution. But what? One of the directions in which a solution was sought was that of giving the fascist petty bourgeoisie in the different provinces the direction of political life at a local level. But that caused a decomposition of the state apparatus with the creation of a large number of small 'tyrannies' in the different provincial administrative centres.

Another solution that naturally presents itself is for the small and middle bourgeoisie to make the Fascist Party itself the centre of its political life. Moreover this solution is the only one that remains open once all parliamentary discussion has been abolished and all organs of opposition and all the parties except the fascist one have been suppressed. Yet it is clearly a very dangerous solution. It is easy to see why, after the suppression of every party and organ of opposition and the prohibition of every expression of dissent, it was necessary to go as far as suppressing every element of 'freedom' even in the centre of the Fascist Party itself. Following the recent measures all possibility of discussion, all internal democracy has been suppressed in the Fascist Party as well. The Party is a semi-military organisation. All its leaders are nominated from above. The meetings of its local organisations have been suppressed in the sense that they are convened only twice a year, and not to decide or discuss the Party line, but merely to listen to a report made by an official. This is called in fascist language, 'establishing a hierarchy'. In actual fact it signifies a systematic policy of preventing the very people who formed the mass base of fascism from being able to take any part in the political life of the country or deciding its fate. It is the 'struggle against the masses' taken to its logical conclusion.

In connection with these fundamental contradictions in the attempts at a fascist stabilisation of the political domain are a further series of contradictions, at the heart of which the same problem is to be found. For instance:

(A) The contradiction between the apparatus of the Fascist Party and that of the state. According to fascist plans a relationship should be established between them similar to that which exists between the Party and the state in the USSR, country of the dictatorship of the proletariat. But the fascist dictatorship lacks precisely the element that constitutes the strength of the dictatorship of the proletariat, namely the stable foundation provided by the proletariat, by the working class under the leadership of its class party. The relations between the Fascist Party and the state consequently assume the character of continual conflict, of attempts by the one to get the better of the other, that is turmoil and destabilisation, instead of unity and mutual support.

(B) The contradiction between the fascist militia and the army. The army officers, particularly at the top, are largely an expression of a section of the old ruling class, of the monarchists, the clerical reactionaries, all the elements which, once they had made use of fascism to defeat the workers' movement and to give capital its freedom, would now have preferred to dispense with it so as to have a more 'lasting' stabilisation. In the militia by contrast are all the elements which have been made use of to reach the present state of affairs, and which will not allow themselves to be discarded so easily.

(C) The contradiction between the fascist unions, the industrial organisations and the state. The workers' unions have been suppressed, so why create new organisations? This is what the industrialists basically think. But they come up against the plans of fascist syndicalism, which is also, when it is examined thoroughly, the expression of the efforts of a section of the petty bourgeoisie to develop a leading role in the economic and political life of the country by putting itself at the head of a supposedly mass organisation. It is clear that these new organisations have never been mass organisations, have never conceived of or concerned themselves with fighting for the defence of mass interests; on the other hand, however, there are occasions when they have been compelled by their own demagogy to allow the workers some retribution against their bosses. It is to avoid this danger that the fascist law on unions has reduced the fascist union organisation to organs that are to all intents and purposes controlled and administered by the state.

The final result of all these contradictions is the eruption of a crisis in the Fascist Party itself, which is divided into two main currents, one which represents large finance capital more directly, being based on the old 'nationalists' and connected with the reactionary sections of the army, the court, etc., and the other which represents the middle strata from which fascism emerged as a mass movement. Besides this fundamental conflict, there is also a whole series of local crises, which nevertheless reproduce all the conflicts between the two currents that I have mentioned.

How is it, then, that in such a situation fascism avoids the danger of profound internal division, of schisms and disintegration? This danger is avoided on the one side by a continuous intensification of the terror directed against fascism's opponents, on the other by means of an expansionist, imperialist campaign. These twin methods are consciously employed to keep the fascist masses in a state of tension and extreme mobilisation, with the result that they are prevented from succumbing to the influence of those factors that tend to set them against the regime of 'stabilisation' and to cause their disintegration . . .

What conclusions can be drawn from the Italian experience for an assessment of fascism in an international perspective? I think that our foreign comrades should bring forward their own experiences, and then we can attempt to draw general conclusions from them. In the meantime, however, I want to mention some facts which suggest a direction for the study of the general phenomenon.

In the most recent period a disintegration of fascism has taken place in the major capitalist countries, such as France, Germany and England, whereas in a series of smaller countries fascism continues to develop and achieve a certain success, providing the basis for attempts at stabilisation. I believe this tendency shows that, where the bourgeoisie has some possibility of stabilising its regime economically, through the rationalisation of the economy, etc., it quickly abandons the use of fascism as being a source of too deep and too damaging contradictions.

Fascism also takes second place in countries in which there is a reactionary ruling class that conducts its own relentless campaign against the working class. England is a demonstration of this. During the general strike the government itself assumed the defence of the interests of capital, of the large bourgeoisie, and took on the working class in battle. It undertook the function of breaking the strike itself. As a consequence fascism as an autonomous movement took second place.

The third fact of significance is demonstrated in France. During the past year, at the point of the last ministerial crisis, the bourgeoisie failed to unite its own forces to confront the economic crisis that threatened the country. At that point the petty bourgeoisie, organised by fascism, threatened to intervene to break through the obstructions, as it had done in Italy. But once the French ruling classes, in the course of a series of ministerial crises, had themselves realised the danger and attempted to unite their forces to stabilise the economy and the regime on the basis of a bourgeois united front against the working class, at that point fascism started to move into second place in France as well.

These are some of the facts on which I believe we should concentrate our attention. It will be necessary for our commission, on the basis of reports made by comrades from the different countries, to check whether these facts are confirmed by the situation in each country, and to see how far the prospects of fascism have altered in the present period.

10 The Hegemony of the Working Class in the Anti-Fascist Struggle! *Palmiro Togliatti*

Togliatti's report to the Central Committee of the PCI in 1928 addressed two different questions: What was the correct *policy* for the party, and what possible *course* might events take. The fact that Italy's crisis could only be finally resolved by a proletarian dictatorship did not make this outcome the only possibility.

. . . The most serious case of deviation from the Party's political line that one can find oneself confronting in the present period, indeed at this very moment, is that which starts from an examination of the present situation of the working class, and concludes by denying the thesis of proletarian hegemony in the anti-fascist struggle. It retreats instead to the Social Democratic position, according to which the proletarian class struggle can only develop *after* fascism has been overthrown by a bourgeois-democratic or petty-bourgeois movement. It is of particular concern to us to point out this error, because it can only be committed by someone who, in making his assessment of the Italian situation, fails to look beyond the present moment, when the forces of the working class are scattered, disorganised and crushed. It may seem paradoxical to assert that the task of leading the struggle for the overthrow of fascism belongs to the workers, who no longer have a coherent class organisation, and whose consciousness of their own strength has been consequently weakened. But the paradox disappears if the present movement is considered as a stage in a process leading towards a definite goal, which is in accordance with the characteristics of the historical period we are passing through and with the problems it poses. These problems are not posed arbitrarily, but are the result of the whole course of evolution of capitalist society in Italy. Their solution is inescapable, and there is only one class that can provide it – the working class.

The above error must be considered the most serious that can be committed at the present time, precisely because the objective circumstances tend to keep the masses on this level. If we are to make clear the basic lines of our Party's policy, our principal objective must be a precise definition of the concept of proletarian hegemony, and of its necessity in the struggle against fascism. Here the following should coincide:

(A) The analysis of fascism as a form of stabilisation of the capitalist regime, and of the unity of the Italian ruling class.

(B) The demonstration of the maturity of the revolutionary proletariat in Italy, i.e. the impossibility of solving the fundamental problems posed by the development of the productive relations and the relations between classes in Italy other than through the proletarian conquest of power.

All our economic, historical and political analyses show that it is not a second bourgeois revolution but the proletarian revolution that is on the agenda in Italy. While it is true that at present the forces of the proletariat are scattered and disorganised, it is also inconceivable that fascism should fall and be eliminated from Italian political life, if the proletariat does not succeed in reorganising its forces and taking control of the struggle during the course of the country's economic and political crisis. This process of reorganisation is itself the development of the proletarian revolution. One cannot talk of a bourgeois-democratic revolutionary process which precedes the proletarian revolution. Much less can one talk of a development in which the working class has to content itself with falling in behind a liberal democracy and playing second fiddle to it. Our polemic against this deviation must be a continuous and determined one.

A viewpoint that is in a certain respect opposed to the preceding one, is that which contents itself with demonstrating the historical maturity of the proletarian revolution in Italy, and deduces from this that the process of concentrating those forces around the proletarian vanguard that will ensure victory for the proletarian revolution – the forces of the worker–peasant alliance – has already been accomplished.

It is worth remembering here, for example, the political line taken by our Party in the first two years of its existence, and particularly in 1922, before the March on Rome. Our Party had made the basis of its political approach the proposition that the different methods employed by the bourgeoisie to keep the proletariat submissive are substantially the same. Bourgeois dictatorship and democracy are two forms of one and the same power; the difference between them is insignificant. From a broad historical point of view this proposition is correct, but from the standpoint of actual politics it is mistaken, because – leaving aside all other considerations – the transition from one to the other, from the regime of formal bourgeois democracy to an open dictatorship or tyranny, never takes place without a decided shift in the balance of forces. If the party of the working class assumes their identity without qualification, even before the transformation has taken place, it closes its eyes to a whole series of developments, to a whole period which is normally full of uncertainties, of conflicts and contradictions, and so it renounces any opportunity for action or political influence – any chance of intervening in these uncertainties and conflicts, either by modifying the course of events, or at least of getting the greatest possible profit from them.

Our Party, during 1921–2, assumed the identity 'capitalism = fascism' as a fact, as an outcome already firmly assured, when it was at that time merely one tendency in Italy's political life. It did not see that, while it was true that the majority of objective factors inclined to make this the prevalent tendency other factors also worked against it, and it required a countervailing effort on the other side – a *coup d'état*, such as the march on Rome – to overcome them. Right up to the eve of the march on Rome, and even while it was taking place, the Communist Party was denying the possibility and the actuality of the *coup d'état*. Immediately after the march on Rome the Party's theoretical journal published an article which maintained that the advent of Mussolini to power would not substantially change the country's political situation, and that the parliamentary farce would simply continue in another form. It is impossible to read this article again today without a smile. In its assessment, the particularity of the political situation is submerged by an exclusive preoccupation with the broader historical dimension, which is correct, but cannot be substituted for the particular. The Party's line was decided on the basis of research which took into account only the general characteristics of the historical period and the objective conclusion of the process that was taking place, and ignored any examination of the stages of development in this process, and of the particular point at which the Party found itself.

We would be repeating the error of 1921–2 if, after having established that at the point of development which Italian society has reached, it is not a bourgeois democracy but a proletarian socialist revolution that is on the agenda, we then rejected any further research to determine what would be the likely course of such a revolution, given the situation already established in Italy by the fascist dictatorship, given the present disposition of class forces, and given the resistance they will encounter in achieving an alignment favourable to the success of a proletarian revolutionary movement . . .

People often speak about the problem of the 'popular revolution'; referring to an expression contained in the resolution approved by the Praesidium of the International in January 1927 on the situation in Italy. This problem is in fact simply one aspect of the general problem of the manner in which the proletarian revolution will develop in Italy. One could formulate this problem more precisely as follows: is it possible for the first surge of a mass anti-fascist movement to proceed directly to the setting up of a proletarian dictatorship, or should we expect a period of open mass struggle against fascism, in which the anti-fascist forces which are not Communist (democratic, Social Democratic) will succeed in assuming the leadership of the masses or part of them, and in offering serious resistance to the proletarian and communist direction of the movement? We think that the second supposition may also be likely. How probable we consider it depends on the manner in which we foresee the course of events unfolding, but we cannot rule it out altogether.

If such a hypothesis as the second were to be realised, it is certain that the function of the democratic and Social Democratic parties would be a counter-revolutionary one; but this does not mean that they would merge with fascism. The Aventine (sc. opposition) was a counter-revolution and a reaction, but it was not fascism. Turati and Salvemini, dedicated to resist by every means the development of a mass anti-fascist struggle up to the point of the institution of the proletarian dictatorship, would be a counter-revolution and a reaction, but they would not be fascism.

However, it is certain that such a situation would not be a stable or lasting one. It would have to develop rapidly, either towards openly declared reaction, or towards the establishment of the proletarian dictatorship. The instability of such a situation moreover corresponds to the character of the social strata of which it would be the expression – social strata of the rural and urban petty bourgeoisie, which can serve as the protagonists in a transient and uncertain situation, but which are unable to create a stable social order.

11 On the Question of Fascism, *Palmiro Togliatti*

This article, published in 1928 in *L'Internationale Communiste*, offered to the international Communist movement a definitive summary of the conclusions about fascism attained within the PCI in this period. It represents a scrupulous attempt to distinguish fascism from other forms of reaction, and to relate it to circumstances specific, though not unique, to Italy.

Fascism, its essence, origins and development, seems to be increasingly interesting as an object of study to the world of labour and the parties which constitute the Communist International. However, I do not believe that this desire for knowledge is always matched by a precise conception of the fascist phenomenon, considered under its various aspects; or that this curiosity is always accompanied by a determination to arrive at the truth by a careful study of the actual form in which fascism manifests itself in Italy and in the other countries. On the contrary, it seems to me instead that people allow themselves to substitute an exposition of quite abstract generalisations, which cannot correspond entirely to reality, for a thorough investigation of this phenomenon. Even so, the fault which consists in generalising *as nauseam* is still not the worst, since it is not uncommon when people talk of fascism for really crude errors of judgement, and of political and historical interpretation, to be committed. I do not propose to draw attention here to all these errors; I merely wish to emphasise certain aspects of the problem, and to draw some conclusions from them. I shall make use for this purpose of the results obtained through the analyses and researches carried out in this field by our own Party. In fact, some of these results can by now be considered definitively established.

I want to examine first of all the error of generalisation that is commonly made in the use of the term 'fascism'. It has become customary to use it to designate every form of reaction. A comrade is arrested, a workers' demonstration is brutally dispersed by the police, a court imposes a savage sentence on some militants of the labour movement, a Communist parliamentary fraction sees its rights infringed or abrogated, in short whenever the so-called democratic freedoms sanctified by bourgeois constitutions are attacked or violated, one hears the cry: 'Fascism is here, fascism has arrived'. It should be realised that this is not just a question of terminology. If someone thinks it reasonable to use the term 'fascism' to designate every form of reaction, so be it. But I do not see what advantage we gain, except perhaps an agitational one. The actuality is something different. Fascism is a particular, a specific type of reaction; and we must understand fully the precise nature of its particularity. We should not imagine that such an analysis is necessary merely for the purposes of objective, scientific differentiation. It is equally indispensable to the attainment of political ends, so as to be able to define the precise attitude to take towards fascism as it currently exists, and above all the measures to be adopted for the future, during the period of preparation and development of a fascist movement. We could actually work out in the course of this preparatory period a precise course of action intended to distract these preparations and hinder this development, but our actions could only be successful if we were able to assess exactly what was afoot in the opposition camp. If, in contrast, we took as our point of departure the well-known saying that 'all cats are grey at night', and inferred from this that all manifestations of reaction are fascist, we should never reach any firm political or tactical positions.

The first example I want to use to prove the correctness of my assertion will be drawn from the experience of our own Party. In 1921–2, when the Party had been in existence for no more than two years, and the fascist offensive had reached its highest point, without however having attained complete victory – i.e. the fascist conquest of power – we witnessed at the heart of our Central Committee the triumph of a doctrine that penetrated the whole policy of our organisation; the starting point of this doctrine was the assertion that fascism was purely and simply capitalist reaction. Obviously this assertion was not wholly mistaken. Indeed it expressed a truth, since in practice during the course of those years the activities developed by the fascist gangs to the detriment of the workers' and peasants' movement in Italy worked naturally to the advantage of industrial and financial capital. But fascism was not simply capitalist reaction. It embraced many other elements at the same time. It comprised a movement of the rural petty-bourgeois masses; it was also a political struggle waged by certain representatives of the small and middle bourgeoisie against a section of the traditional ruling classes; it was an attempt to create a comprehensive organisation, covering the whole country, to regroup a fraction of the urban petty bourgeoisie under the direction of *déclassé* elements (ex-officers, unemployed professionals); finally it was a military organisation which claimed the ability to take on the regular armed forces of the state with some probability of success. Embracing all these elements, besides capitalist reaction, fascism's development was bound to be complex. It was absolutely naïve to believe that capitalism would have used this movement as a tool intended to break the strength of the proletariat, except with the intention of subsequently casting it aside so that it could continue in power itself, reverting to its customary procedures and employing the same institutions, the same politicians, the same methods as before. Yet the complexity of the fascist phenomenon ensured that the evolution of the movement was not determined exclusively by the aims of the bourgeoisie and the landowners, but was also influenced by other motives of a quite different character, and by other impulses which arose from the very heart of the movement and which at certain moments even attempted to control it.

The over-simplification displayed by our Party had two consequences which did us great harm. First of all, we did not realise that it would have been possible to prevent fascism conquering certain elements of the petty bourgeoisie; more precisely, we could have helped accentuate the contradictions in this movement at the heart of the petty bourgeois masses. Besides, we had not taken account of the fact that the conquest of power by the fascists could not take place without a fairly violent struggle between them and a section of the old ruling classes. Right up until the eve of the event, and while it was actually taking place, we denied the possibility of a fascist *coup d'état*. As can be seen, these were consequences of considerable political importance.

Let us take another example. In 1924 people started to become clearly aware that the developments that had occurred in the economic structure of French capitalism demanded political changes in a reactionary direction. The political positions of the big industrial and financial bourgeoisie had to be strengthened, in order to assure them an undisputed hegemony. It was then that certain apparent militants of the French Communist Party launched the pronouncement: 'Fascism is here, fascism has arrived'. In fact the arrival of fascism has till now been delayed, and it only appears in France in a very weakened form. All the same the reaction is self-evident. In the course of this period a real political transformation had undoubtedly taken place, though not by a direct mobilisation of petty-bourgeois strata assembled around the more reactionary groups of the bourgeoisie. Nor has it even manifested itself in a struggle against the traditional ruling groups of the centre and right, or against parliament; nor has it taken the form of illegal violence directed against the workers' organisations, nor of a conquest of power by recourse to illegal extra-parliamentary methods that are characteristic of fascism. The reaction has been carried out quite differently, by means of an absorption of the left petty-bourgeois groups into a reactionary political bloc, led by members from the traditional ruling classes. This has led to the necessity of complicated manoeuvres, resulting in parliamentary compromises which include even the Socialists. Besides, the repression of the workers was arranged by the normal agencies of the bourgeois 'democratic' state. It is possible, and could even be considered certain, that the final outcome will be the same; but the methods employed, and the course of development are profoundly different. Now, it is impossible to carry out any serious policy, or even any 'policy' at all, by considering only the final outcome, and taking no account of the course of events and the different stages traversed. In the case that we have just examined, certain political errors committed by the PCF in the course of the past few years (among others its failure to recognise in time the development of a clear split between the vanguard of the working class and the political formations of the petty bourgeoisie) may well have been caused by a mistaken assessment of the course which French political life had taken in its development towards reaction.

Let us turn, then, to a critical examination of certain characteristic features of Italian fascism, the 'typical' fascism; we shall then see how far it is possible to generalise, and what conclusions can be drawn, from the Italian experience. In the first place we can say that fascism is the most thoroughgoing and systematic form of reaction that has so far emerged in the countries where capitalism has reached a certain level of development. This assertion is not based on the terrorist atrocities, nor on the large number of workers and peasants assassinated, nor on the cruelty of the methods of torture applied on a vast scale, nor on the severity of the sentences handed out. It is based on the systematic and total suppression of all forms of autonomous organisation on the part of the masses. It may be that other countries, especially those where reaction was installed after the checking of a revolutionary struggle at the point of insurrection, have witnessed a larger number of victims and a harsher terror. But no other country has seen such a radical suppression of any possibility for the masses of creating their own autonomous organisations, under whatever form, as has Italy. In no country has the struggle for the destruction of formal democratic liberties been waged in such a consistent manner, and with such effectiveness.

How are we to explain this side of Italian fascism that is so characteristic? It would be absurdly mistaken to look for the causes in the exceptional savagery of fascism's purposes and those of its most obvious militants, or to discover there that species of collective sickness which the feeble ideologists of pure democracy and idiotic pacifism have been pleased to designate by the term 'militaristic psychosis' and 'disease of violence', etc. The total suppression of democratic liberties, such as the freedom of assembly, of expression, of association, the right to strike, direct universal suffrage, etc., alongside the prohibition against setting up autonomous mass organisations, corresponds to a specific necessity of Italian capitalism and its stabilisation.

Italy is a very poor country. Capitalism there, although it has reached a considerable level of development, has been undermined by the contradictions inherent in imperialism, and has a wretchedly weak structure. During the whole period of the development of the bourgeois state prior to the world war, the ruling classes had been compelled to take account of the growing pressure exerted by the abundant working population of the towns (proletarians and artisans) and the countryside (agricultural labourers, poor and middle peasantry), a population that was continually on the increase. Only in the years immediately preceding the war was it possible for the bourgeoisie, thanks to a favourable economic situation, to corrupt a small fraction of the proletariat, which could consider itself privileged in comparison with the great mass of workers and above all the poor peasants, who were the most heavily oppressed and exploited. The crisis after the war drove the internal contradictions of Italian capitalism even deeper, and these found expression in violent conflicts. From that moment the conditions which had allowed the existence of a labour aristocracy ceased to hold. The profit margin reserved for the benefit of the capitalists was squeezed. The pressure of the masses on the apparatus of bourgeois power and of capitalist production broadened and intensified. The process of capitalist stabilisation was bound thereafter to lead rapidly to desperate economic and political pressures (more rapidly than in other European countries where the bourgeoisie, being richer and stronger, could afford the luxury of a greater room for manoeuvre). In the economic field, the stabilisation could take no other form than the one it took after the advent of fascism to power: penetration of finance capital into the whole economic life of the country, in an attempt to reduce the internal contradictions that obstructed a rapid stabilisation; a savage reduction of wages; hateful exploitation of consumers; unprecedented taxation of petty-bourgeois producers. This economic programme could not have been realised if the working population, and especially the proletariat, had not already been deprived of every possibility of collective action; this is the reason why fascism's victory was rapidly followed by a fundamentally reactionary transformation in the whole political life of the country.

The reactionary character of fascism in respect of its consequences is thus first of all the expression of an economic necessity and of a process whose causes must be traced in the sphere of the relations of production. The tendency of Italian capitalism not only to become reactionary (a tendency present in all countries in the imperialist epoch), but to make use of fascism from the outset, and subsequently to identify with it, derives directly from its distinctive structure and from the special features of the crisis which it underwent. It is impossible to predict if fascism, in the form it has taken in Italy, can become established in another country, unless one first takes the trouble to analyse carefully its capitalist system, and likewise its relations of production and those of its dominant classes.

This general observation gains a much sharper clarity when it is tested against two special features of the fascist regime – the suppression of parliament, and the fascist policy towards Social Democracy.

We shall see later the importance that fascist ideology attached to the abolition of parliament. For the moment it is necessary to grasp its essential importance from the standpoint of class relations. The parliamentary system is a way of organising political life that is well suited to the political requirements and ideology of the petty bourgeoisie. Politically speaking, the links between the small and middle bourgeoisie on one side, and the big bourgeoisie on the other, are mainly formed on the parliamentary level; they are realised here in the form of a political compromise concluded between the leading groups of the different parties. If one examines the basis of this compromise, one discovers that it is due in part to economic concessions, in part to an actual correspondence of economic interests. The closer the limit of these concessions is approached, the more the big bourgeoisie is led to infringe upon the interests of the middle classes, and the greater difficulty it experiences in manoeuvring between parliamentary compromises. But the more the crisis of the capitalist system deepens, the more the conflicts and the pacts between the different parties, which can all in the final reckoning claim to be essentially bourgeois, become a useless luxury which the bourgeoisie can no longer indulge in. The only road to salvation left to it is to establish a direct political unity, in which all its factions reach agreement in the interests of a reactionary victory. Italian fascism, once embarked on this road, quickly reached its extreme conclusions; and thus it discovered its incompatibility with parliamentarism.

The question of the relations between fascism and Social Democracy belongs to a similar context. On this point fascism is precisely different from all the reactionary regimes so far established in the modern capitalist world; It rejects every compromise with Social Democracy; it has persecuted it mercilessly; it has deprived it of all possibility of legal activity; it has forced it to emigrate. This has not happened in Hungary, nor in Poland, nor in Spain, nor in the Balkans. On the contrary, in all these countries Social Democracy collaborates more or less openly with the forces of reaction. While this fact has, as we shall see, certain connections with the social bases of fascism, it is to be explained by the situation of Italian capitalism, which does not allow it to support a labour aristocracy, or to make economic concessions to the petty-bourgeois strata in the towns, which constitute in part the social basis of Social Democracy in our time.

To sum up on this first point, I think it is possible to reach the following conclusions: on one side, one of the essential characteristics of fascism is that it is a reactionary regime driven to its logical extremes; on the other side, we must not forget that this characteristic derives from the special economic and class relations that exist in Italy. It is this particular situation that has determined the direction in which Italian fascism has developed. So if we wish to be prudent and anticipate the methods, the limits and the types of reactionary transformation that modern capitalist society can undergo, we should above all not lose sight of the economic situation.

The second important characteristic of fascism, besides its reactionary nature, is that it is closely bound up in its origins and evolution with a certain configuration of class relations; in saying this I am thinking not only of the major antagonistic classes of modern society, bourgeoisie and proletariat, but also of the relations that these two principal classes maintain with the intermediate classes which move about between the two. On this point, however, it would be particularly mistaken to be satisfied with general formulae. It is necessary to examine the class relations with great care, taking account of their development.

At the outset the social basis of fascism lay in certain strata of the rural and urban petty bourgeoisie. In more precise terms, its basis in the countryside was made up mainly from the middling peasants, farm managers and share-croppers, who were exasperated by the absurd policy of the Socialist organisations. The Socialists proclaimed the Maximalist programme in the countryside, including the socialisation of the land. In their practical activity they took no account of the existence or the interests of the intermediate strata of the rural petty bourgeoisie; they made no attempt to construct a political alliance between the proletariat and these strata; they did not even try to neutralise them. In the towns, as well, fascism rested at first on the petty bourgeoisie; these were partly artisans, skilled workers and shop-keepers, partly also elements displaced because of the war (ex-officers, the disabled, commandos, volunteers). If one considers on which side the aspirations of these social circles were directed, one can see that the interests of some drew them towards the anti-proletarian struggle, whereas the objective situation of others and even their rudimentary inclinations were anti-capitalist. It has already been shown elsewhere that historically the intermediate social groups can sometimes ally themselves with the bourgeoisie, and sometimes, depending on the precise circumstances, with the proletariat. It is true that among the strata which formed the basis of fascism at the outset there existed an anti-proletarian tendency; on the other hand they had no intention of fighting to establish the dictatorship of large industrial and financial capital. Which then was the element that prevailed, and decided the general orientation and development of the movement? As is well known, it was the anti-proletarian tendency that clearly had the upper hand. The big bourgeoisie and landowners succeeded in drawing fascism to their side for the attainment of a decisively reactionary objective. This did not happen, however, without opposition, hesitations and compromises. Only after passing through a whole series of stages were the big bourgeoisie and the landowners able to influence the movement in a decisive manner. And even when they succeeded in attaining their ends, they could not prevent fascism from developing and maintaining the character of a politically autonomous movement, and it was in this capacity that it set out on the conquest of power, dispossessing a section of the old ruling class.

On the basis of the whole period preceding the advent of fascism to power and, in general, of the whole history of its evolution, one can say that 'the factor that consistently determined the direction of fascism's development, and that ended with the major say in its administration was clearly the big bourgeoisie; while on the other hand the forms of its evolution were determined – apart from the particular historical context – by the petty-bourgeois social composition of the fascist movement'.

Such a conclusion should provoke us to considerable caution in generalising from the Italian experience, above all when it comes to extending the political implications that can be drawn from it. There is little likelihood of seeing a movement analogous to Italian fascism arising in a historical and social context that is quite different, especially in a country where capitalism is very strong. Certain aspects of the Italian phenomenon may reappear, and the general reactionary direction of the political transformation in bourgeois society may remain, but it will be difficult to find again the essential features characteristic of fascism. Above all it will be difficult to find again a situation like that in Italy, where we saw reaction take the form of a mass movement, thanks to a sudden and complete change in the attitude of the middle classes. A movement of the 'fascist' type, like the one in Italy, would have the greatest difficulty in conquering power elsewhere. Before announcing that a country is becoming fascist, therefore, it is always necessary to see if the situation of the country concerned allows for the repetition of the two fundamental factors that have been expounded above. Profound researches are hardly necessary to prove that in general these conditions only pertain in states with a weak economic structure, lacking political equilibrium, in which there is an abundance of middle- and petty-bourgeois strata. It is in fact countries of this type that, in the course of the last few years, have experienced developments of a truly fascist kind, or very similar to fascism (the Balkans, Lithuania, Poland).

If we now examine the period following the conquest of power, we see that the contradiction mentioned, between the social basis of fascism and its political results, does not disappear, but on the contrary becomes accentuated. The inescapable consequences of capitalist stabilisation impose themselves. Fascism finds itself obliged to carry out in brutal fashion, and without reservation, the policy of finance capital, of large industry and the banks, to the detriment of the majority of the working population. This creates a permanently unsettled state in the social base of fascism itself, and hence in turn the necessity of a reactionary pressure that operates with increasing intensity in certain directions. Some political elements could profit from an abandonment of fascism by discontented groups among the petty bourgeoisie. These groups mostly derive from the *productive* petty bourgeoisie (artisans, peasant farmers, share-croppers, farm managers, small traders), who resent in their distinctive way the consequences of the dictatorship of finance capital. Hence these political elements become the direct enemies of fascism, since they threaten to strike right at its foundations; and thus at certain moments the reaction becomes particularly infuriated against them. Thus fascism 'legally' dissolved the freemasons, for example, and the reformists in the same way, before it dissolved the Communist Party. This does not mean that the anti-fascist bourgeoisie and petty bourgeoisie have been persecuted more harshly than the revolutionary workers. Exactly the opposite has happened. But it shows that fascism needs to develop special measures against these organisations of the petty bourgeoisie, so as to impress them and prevent them from striking at its vulnerable point.

One of the most interesting facts to note, furthermore, is that fascism was obliged to become reactionary in its own internal organisation after the conquest of power; it was compelled to effect a quite rapid and far-reaching transformation in its structure and social composition. The principal forms of this process that we have been able to identify so far are the following:

(1) The supporters among the petty-bourgeois producers abandon fascism little by little. Henceforward the membership of the Party is predominantly composed of the non-producing petty and middle bourgeoisie (state functionaries, professional fascists, etc.) This fact is particularly important as it heralds a change in the balance of forces in the countryside.

(2) The fascist cadres are almost completely changed. In place of the former blackshirts, the 'fascists of the first hour', are the direct representatives of the big bourgeoisie (industrialists, bankers, landowners, and their agents), who occupy the leading posts in the Party.

(3) The Fascist Party gradually absorbs a part of the general staff of all the old parties of the bourgeoisie and petty bourgeoisie.

(4) At the same time democracy is completely eliminated at the centre of the Fascist Party, and replaced by a system of government from above.

In consequence of this process, fascism proves itself conclusively to be not only an instrument of reaction and repression, but also a centre of political unity for all the dominant classes: finance capital, large industry, the landowners. It identifies itself with Italian capitalism in the present period of its evolution. The Fascist Party thus tends to lose the character of an autonomous movement of certain intermediate social strata that it had to begin with, and becomes, along with its organisation, intimately fused with the economic and political system of the dominant classes.

Naturally this process is not yet completed. There are unknown factors, obstacles to be overcome. The whole complex problem of the relations between state and Party is not yet conclusively resolved; it is on this ground that the different tendencies within the fascist movement confront each other, and on this terrain that the fascist movement as a whole comes up against resistance from the established political apparatus and the traditional ruling classes. One proof of the difficulties that remain is the rumour currently circulating in Italy, according to which Mussolini would like in effect to dissolve the Fascist Party, while maintaining its parallel organisations and incorporating them into the state, thus uniting what is left of the mass base of the movement into a single whole. In conclusion, new conflicts can still take place, leading to new surprises; yet the general tendency remains as I have described . . .

All the considerations I have developed above, it should be understood, serve to establish the limits within which it is possible to generalise the conclusions derived from Italian fascism. There is no intention in this of underestimating the danger of fascism as a reactionary movement in general; nor is there any question of a lack of understanding of the reactionary tendencies that have triumphed up to now in almost all of the large capitalist states. But this account serves as a precaution against being satisfied with commonplaces, and as an exhortation to study fascism on the basis of the actual facts, according to the actual course and concrete forms of its development. This is to apply the differentiated method of analysis that lies at the root of all Marxist politics.

II The Communist International – from Social Fascism to Popular Front

12 The Victory of Fascism over the November Republic, *Communist Party of Germany (KPD)*

Under the state of emergency declared in Germany in October 1923, the coalition government, which included Social Democrats, and the Social Democratic president of the Republic, Ebert, granted wide-ranging powers to the army under General Seeckt to deal with the Hitler *putsch* in Bavaria and the threat of a Communist uprising in Saxony. An emergency regime was installed in Saxony by presidential decree, backed by the army, and the left SPD–KPD coalition there was dismissed from office. The following account is drawn from the resolutions adopted at a conference of the KPD held shortly afterwards.

The End of the November Republic

The November Republic has surrendered to fascism over the whole area of unoccupied Germany. Power is now in the hands of the military, which consciously sets itself the task of destroying the achievements of the working class, the eight-hour day and the works councils, so as to impose the final unlimited domination of the bourgeoisie on the backs of the defenceless proletariat. By surrendering power to the officer caste, and using the enabling act to destroy the social achievements of the November Republic at their root, the government of the November Republic has abolished its own historical *raison d'être*. This lay in the attempt to delude the working class, by means of a Social Democratic coalition, into believing that the restoration of capitalism in Germany was compatible with the maintenance of democracy, and an attentive regard for the workers' social interests. Now the bourgeoisie stands forward openly under the fascist banner. It is not democracy, but a white dictatorship, not concessions to the working class nor the phoney 'industrial partnership', but the open enslavement of the working class, that constitutes the government programme . . .

The victory of fascism over bourgeois democracy has taken place in a different manner from that expected by the working class, and for this reason was not immediately recognised. While the working class saw the centre of fascism in Bavaria, fascism established its centre in Berlin in the form of General Seeckt's dictatorship, behind which stood not only the army but decisive sections of the German bourgeoisie as well. While the working class, provoked by the threats of Ludendorff and Hitler, and the appointment of Kahn as dictator in Bavaria, gazed towards Munich as the place where the white dictatorship was expected to be proclaimed with flags and trumpets, the Social Democrat Ebert and the grand coalition cabinet appointed General Seeckt as dictator, ostensibly to combat the white dictatorship in Bavaria. General Seeckt proclaimed no Hohenzollern monarchy and no campaign against the traditional enemy, France. His first act was to outlaw the whole Communist press and its organisations; his second was to occupy proletarian Saxony, the focal position of the German proletariat between the fascist north and south; his third was to dismiss its democratically elected workers' government. General Seeckt's soldiers got their practice in Saxony in the dispersal of parliamentary institutions and governments. This dress rehearsal is intended to show the Stresemann–Sollmann government, which appointed Seeckt to power and instructed him to get rid of Zeigner's administration, that the moment they cease to be completely amenable to his wishes and those of his superiors in heavy industry, he can do just the same to the Reichstag and the national government.[9] The 400 parliamentary representatives in the beer restaurant of the Reichstag, the Reichs-chancellor with his magnificent speeches, the Social Democratic president of the Republic with his orders to the military, who treat him with disdain – all these fancies are still tolerated by General Seeckt. They cannot obscure the fact of the fascist seizure of power, although he allows the parliamentary-democratic diversion to continue as a screen to prevent any defensive action on the part of the masses.

Social Democracy as Accomplice of Fascism

The responsibility for fascism's victory over democracy, and for the absence of any proletarian resistance in face of it, must fall squarely upon the leaders of the SPD. By a series of concessions they have surrendered one proletarian position after another to fascism. Despite all the warnings of their Party comrades they allowed General Seeckt to carry on his preparations for the bloodless coup. As members of the coalition government they handed over power to him, and gave their blessing to the social aims of his dictatorship by approving the enabling act which allowed all the burdens of the disintegrating bourgeois state to be inflicted on the proletariat. They agreed to use the executive power of the Reich against proletarian Saxony, and they obstructed the general strike which was called there against the entry of the troops. Once all the strategic positions had been occupied by the army, the Social Democratic members of the national government approved the dismissal of their own Party comrades in Saxony, and the Social Democrat Ebert personally signed the orders for the expulsion of his own Party comrades by the Reichs-commissar Heinze . . .

There can only be a life and death struggle with these leaders of Social Democracy. A section of the Social Democratic masses seems to recognise this, to judge by their demand for Ebert's expulsion from the Party. But Ebert is not an isolated individual. He is the representative of the Social Democratic leadership, which has betrayed the German proletariat ever since 4 August 1914. Wels and Müller, Sollmann and Schmidt are the same flesh and blood as Ebert.[10] It is not a question of breaking with Ebert, of banishing one scapegoat to the wilderness, but of breaking with a ten-year policy of betrayal and with its representatives . . .

13 Resolution on Fascism, *Fifth Comintern Congress*

The resolution of July 1924 rejects the idea of 'the defeat of the November Republic', in the previous piece, though its reference to the fascist character of Social Democracy, and its optimism about the imminent demise of fascism proper, prefigure the Comintern line of 1928 and after.

Fascism is one of the classic forms of the counter-revolution in the epoch of capitalist decay, the epoch of proletarian revolution, particularly where the proletariat has taken up the struggle for power but where, through lack of revolutionary experience and a leading class party, it has been unable to organise the revolutionary struggle and to press the insurrection of the masses to the point of proletarian dictatorship.

Fascism is the instrument of the big bourgeoisie for fighting the proletariat, when the legal means available to the state have proved insufficient to subdue them. It is the extra-legal arm of the big bourgeoisie for establishing and consolidating its dictatorship. But in its social structure fascism is a petty-bourgeois movement. It has its roots in the middle classes, doomed to disappear as a result of the capitalist crisis, and in the elements declassed after the war (ex-officers, etc.), and partly also in the embittered proletarian elements whose revolutionary hopes have been disappointed.

The more bourgeois society decays, the more all the bourgeois parties, particularly Social Democracy, take on a more or less fascist character, using violent methods against the proletariat and themselves helping to undermine the social order which they were formed to preserve. Fascism and Social Democracy are the two sides of a single instrument of capitalist dictatorship. This is why Social Democracy can never be a reliable ally of the proletariat in its struggle against fascism.

Because of its internal contradictions (conflicts of interest between the big bourgeoisie on one side and the petty-bourgeois and proletarian elements on the other), fascism, after its victory, slides into political bankruptcy which leads to its internal disintegration (Italy). A similar crisis overtakes it where, without having won a formal victory, it is obliged openly to support and defend the bourgeois regime (Germany).

---

14 The Period of Bourgeois-Democratic Pacifism, *Joseph Stalin*

This article, written later in 1924, characterises Social Democracy as the 'moderate wing' of fascism, and contains the famous reference to them as 'twins'.

... Some people think that the bourgeoisie adopted 'pacifism' and 'democracy' not because it was compelled to do so, but voluntarily, of its own free choice, so to speak. And it is assumed that, having defeated the working class in decisive battles (Italy, Germany), the bourgeoisie felt that it was the victor and could not afford to adopt 'democracy'. In other words, while the decisive battles were in progress, the bourgeoisie needed a fighting organisation, needed fascism; but now that the proletariat is defeated, the bourgeoisie no longer needs fascism and can afford to use 'democracy' instead, as a better method of consolidating its victory. Hence the conclusion is drawn that the rule of the bourgeoisie has become consolidated, that the 'era of pacifism' will be a prolonged one, and that the revolution in Europe has been pigeonholed.

This assumption is absolutely wrong.

Firstly, it is not true that fascism is only the fighting organisation of the bourgeoisie. Fascism is not only a military–technical category. Fascism is the bourgeoisie's fighting organisation that relies on the active support of Social Democracy. Social Democracy is objectively the moderate wing of fascism. There is no ground for assuming that the fighting organisation of the bourgeoisie can achieve decisive successes in battles, or in governing the country, without the active support of Social-Democracy. There is just as little ground for thinking that Social-Democracy can achieve decisive successes in battles, or in governing the country, without the active support of the fighting organisation of the bourgeoisie. These organisations do not negate, but supplement each other. They are not antipodes, they are twins. Fascism is an informal political bloc of these two chief organisations; a bloc, which arose in the circumstances of the post-war crisis of imperialism, and which is intended for combating the proletarian revolution. The bourgeoisie cannot retain power without such a bloc. It would therefore be a mistake to think that 'pacifism' signifies the liquidation of fascism. In the present situation, 'pacifism' is the strengthening of fascism with its moderate, Social-Democratic wing pushed into the forefront.

Secondly, it is not true that the decisive battles have already been fought, that the proletariat was defeated in these battles, and that bourgeois rule has been consolidated as a consequence. There have been no decisive battles as yet, if only for the reason that there have not been any mass, genuinely Bolshevik parties, capable of leading the proletariat to dictatorship. Without such parties, decisive battles for dictatorship are impossible under the conditions of imperialism. The decisive battles in the West still lie ahead. There have been only the first serious attacks, which were repulsed by the bourgeoisie; the first serious trial of strength, which showed that the proletariat is not *yet* strong enough to overthrow the bourgeoisie, but that the bourgeoisie is *already* unable to discount the proletariat. And precisely because the bourgeoisie is already unable to force the working class to its knees, it was compelled to renounce frontal attacks, to make a detour, to agree to a compromise, to resort to 'democratic pacifism' . . .

15 Theses on the International Situation (1929), *Enlarged Executive of the Communist International (ECCI)*

The announcement made at the sixth World Congress of the Comintern in September 1928 that the period of post-war capitalist stabilisation was at an end, and a new period of economic crisis and revolutionary upheaval beginning ('third period'), was confirmed at the plenary meeting of the Executive the following July. The following theses, approved at the meeting, offer a typical characterisation of the role of Social Democracy in the crisis and of its relation to fascism.

Despite the prophecies made by the Social Democrats and echoed by the right wing and conciliatory elements, the stablisation of capitalism has not only become no firmer, but on the contrary, is becoming more and more undermined. The correctness of the estimation made by the Sixth Congress of the present third period of post-war capitalism is being ever more obviously demonstrated as a period of the increasing growth of the general crisis of capitalism and of the accelerated accentuation of the fundamental external and internal contradictions of imperialism leading inevitably to imperialist wars, to great class conflicts, to an era of development of a new upward swing of the revolutionary movement in the principal capitalist countries, to great anti-imperialist revolutions in colonial countries ...

In this situation of growing imperialist contradictions and sharpening of the class struggle, increasingly fascism becomes the dominant method of bourgeois rule. In countries where there are strong Social Democratic parties, fascism assumes the particular form of social-fascism, which to an ever-increasing extent serves the bourgeoisie as an instrument for the paralysing of the activity of the masses in the struggle against the regime of fascist dictatorship. By means of this monstrous system of political and economic oppression, the bourgeoisie, aided and abetted by international Social Democracy, have been attempting to crush the revolutionary class movement of the proletariat for many years. But here also their calculations have proved to be wrong. The increasing militant activity of the working class, the rise of a new tide of the revolutionary labour movement, signalise the inevitable breakdown of this regime of unexampled exploitation and outrage against the toilers, which international Social Democracy cynically declared to be the era of 'flourishing democracy' and of capitalism growing into 'socialism'. . . .

The impotence of the bourgeoisie to find a way out of the ever intensifying external and internal contradictions, the necessity to prepare for new imperialist wars, and to secure their rear by bringing the greatest possible pressure upon the working class as 'a means of extricating themselves' from the present situation; the inability of the bourgeoisie to carry out these tasks by their own efforts, without the aid of the Social Democratic parties, and finally, the need to screen this policy under the mask of democracy and pacifism have led to the need of open co-operation between the bourgeoisie and the parties affiliated to the Second International. Hence, the accession to government of the Social Democrats in Germany and of the Labour Party in Great Britain. The political mission of the governments of MacDonald and Müller is to carry out the policy laid down by the bourgeoisie in home politics (the utmost pressure upon the working class, the double enslavement of the working class of Germany in connexion with reparations, rationalisation in England) and in foreign politics (preparations for new wars and intensified oppression in the colonies).[11] In Germany we have a new experiment of the largest party in the Second International, the German Social Democratic Party, being in government. As a result of their own experiences the German workers are abandoning their illusions concerning the Social Democratic Party. The Social Democratic Party has revealed itself as the party which, on coming into office, has strangled the workers' strikes with the noose of compulsory arbitration, has helped the capitalists to declare lockouts and liquidate the gains of the working class (eight-hour day, social insurance, etc.). By the construction of cruisers and by the adoption of its new militaristic programme, breaking with all the remnants of pre-war traditions of socialism, Social Democracy is preparing the next war. The leading cadres of Social Democracy and of the reformist trade unions, fulfilling the orders of the bourgeoisie, are now, through the mouth of Wels, threatening the German working class with open fascist dictatorship. Social Democracry prohibits May Day demonstrations. It shoots down unarmed workers during May Day demonstrations. It is Social Democracy which suppresses the labour press (*Rote Fahne*) and mass labour organisations, prepares the suppression of the KPD and organises the crushing of the working class by fascist methods.

This is the road of the coalition policy of Social Democracy leading to social-fascism. These are the results of the governing activities of the biggest party of the Second International.

---

16 On Fascism, *Dmitrii Manuilski*

Manuilski was one of the leading exponents of the Comintern's theory of fascism in the 'third period'. The following extract is taken from his report to the eleventh ECCI plenum in April 1931.

The increase in the contradictions and the aggressiveness of imperialism in the sphere of international relations corresponds to a sharpening of class conflict in the internal class relations of the capitalist states, and to an intensification of bourgeois dictatorship, which increasingly switches to open fascist forms of suppression of the workers. Political reaction as a form of government has advanced continuously with the development of imperialism in all the capitalist states, and has become the counter-part to imperialist aggression. The fascist regime is not just any new type of state; it is one of the forms of bourgeois dictatorship characteristic of the imperialist epoch. Fascism grows organically out of bourgeois democracy. The process whereby bourgeois dictatorship switches to an open form of suppression of the workers thus also represents the essence of the fascisation of bourgeois democracy. A bourgeois democracy of the type characteristic of the age of bourgeois revolutions in the last century is nowhere to be found today. What we actually have is bourgeois-democratic forms of capitalist dictatorship belonging to the age of imperialism and the general crisis of capitalism – i.e. bourgeois democracies in the process of fascisation.

The totality of modern capitalist states constitutes a varied amalgam of fascist countries (Italy, Poland) and bourgeois democracies containing fascist elements, and standing at different stages of the fascisation process, such as France or England. Even countries which are only now carrying out bourgeois-democratic revolutions, such as Mexico and other countries of Latin America, because of imperialist encirclement reach the fascist forms of bourgeois democracy so rapidly that days and weeks correspond to whole years and decades in the history of the European bourgeois democracies which developed earlier. Marx said that bourgeois democracy as a political form had revolutionary rather than conservative consequences for the bourgeoisie. By means of it the bourgeoisie purchased the active co-operation and participation of the proletariat in the bourgeois-democratic revolutions. But as soon as the bourgeoisie had achieved political power, this political form evolved in a reactionary direction.

The first conclusion to be drawn from this is that only a bourgeois liberal can counterpose present-day bourgeois democracy and the fascist regimes as different forms of government in principle. By means of such a contrast, Social Democracy intentionally deceives the masses, obscuring from them the fact that the modern capitalist state constitutes a dictatorship of the bourgeoisie, whether this takes the form of a bourgeois democracy in the process of fascisation or of open fascism.

The second highly important conclusion, however, is that one should not ignore the stages of the development of fascisation of the capitalist state, and that one should carefully analyse and investigate the concrete circumstances and factors which bring about an acceleration in the fascisation of the bourgeois state. The mistakes that have occurred in particular Communist sections on the question of fascism have partly lain (Kostrzewa in Poland) in the direction of constructing a principled antithesis between bourgeois democracy and fascism, partly also (Austria and Finland) in effectively denying the stages in the development of fascist dictatorship. Both mistakes are connected with the absence of a concrete analysis of the level of intensification in the class struggle, of the level of crisis at the summit of society, and the consequent level of fascisation of the parties of the bourgeoisie. The opportunist error of the Kostrzewa group did not lie in its failure to identify social-fascism as fascism, but in its failure to recognise how far the fascisation of the Polish Socialist Party had gone in the concrete situation in Poland. The construction of a fascist dictatorship can take place in different ways: little by little, i.e. the so-called 'bloodless' route, where a strong Social Democratic party is available to disarm the proletariat by demanding that it stick to the law-abiding path, and so surrenders one position after another to fascism and leads the proletariat to capitulation (as in Austria). German Social Democracy is working to bring about the fascist dictatorship 'by the bloodless route', but because there is a strong Communist party there continuously mobilising the workers to struggle against the fascisation of the bourgeois dictatorship, the Austrian method for establishing the fascist dictatorship is not in prospect in Germany.

The fascist form of bourgeois dictatorship is not only a product of the 'objective' process at work in the ranks of the dominant class, but also a product of the relations between the classes. Its establishment is connected with either a retreat on the part of the proletariat (whether with or without a struggle) or its temporary defeat in the course of the contest. The other way of establishing a fascist dictatorship (Italy and Poland) is linked to the fascist *coup d'état*. Such *coups*, which have a distinctly comic-opera appearance when seen in the context of the internal squabbles among the bourgeois cliques, are exclusively directed against the proletariat, against the class of the oppressed which threatens capitalist society with the revolution. In both types of case, however, the establishment of the fascist dictatorship is equally preventive and counter-revolutionary in character.

Many people regard these co-called fascist 'revolutions' as marking the point of the establishment of the fascist dictatorship, or its definitive consolidation. This is mistaken. Italian fascism only accomplished a considerable portion of the tasks of fascisation after the 'march on Rome'. Social Democracy in particular makes great play with the spectre of the fascist 'revolution' so as to lull the workers to sleep in face of the fascisation 'by the bloodless route' promoted by

Social Democracy itself. There are even Communists who succumb to the hypnotic idea of the fascist 'revolution', and who believe that the struggle against fascism only begins at the point when it takes to the streets fully armed to carry out its *putsch*. The theory of 'fascism as *putsch*' is actually rooted in a purely formal, parliamentary conception of fascism. On this commonly-held view, the decisive feature of fascism is that it abolishes parliament and destroys the institutions of bourgeois democracy. In fact, however, fascism's essential characteristic is its open assault on the working class with every means of compulsion – of violence and of civil war directed against the work-force. The elimination of the remnants of bourgeois democracy is a secondary by-product of this decisive, overriding strategy of class offensive against the proletariat. In any case even the abolition of parliament is by no means inevitable in the course of the fascist dictatorship, as the example of Poland demonstrates.

In defining the nature of fascism reference is often made, even in our ranks, to those characteristics which the fascists themselves emphasise when speaking of their predatory regime – for example, the corporative character of the fascist state, the extreme nationalist ideology ('Great Italy', 'Third Reich'), or the whole medieval garb in which fascism appears, etc. But these features do not represent the essence of fascism. They are much more the ideological shell, which proves that the dominant classes in the period of capitalism's general crisis are incapable of producing any new influential ideas, and therefore have to invoke the past, much as Tsarism did on the eve of its demise when it invoked the age of Minin or Posharski or Ivan Kalita. Behind the appearance of the corporative state is concealed in actuality the establishment of the open dictatorship of the bourgeoisie over the working class. Under the garb of nationalist ideology is to be found in actuality the thoroughly modern imperialist aggression of the capitalist state.

Fascism is not a belated historical abortion from the middle ages, but a product of monopoly capital. It is based upon the concentration and centralisation of capital and the associated development of trusts and cartels, and leads to a massive centralisation of the whole apparatus of mass oppression – including the political parties, the Social Democratic apparatus, the reformist trade unions, the co-operatives, etc. Its stunted ideological forms stem from the fact that it represents the political superstructure of capitalism *in decay*. This retrograde ideology is mixed up with all the ideological features of bourgeois democracy in the epoch of monopoly capital, with the theory of 'organised capitalism', the theory of 'economic democracy', the idea of 'industrial harmony', the theory of state capitalism as the 'new era of social relations', the theory of 'the state standing above classes', and so on. Fascism without any ideas of its own to rub together, certainly did not discover these concepts either. It took them over from Social Democracy as going ideas, and decked them out in medieval forms. This community of ideology is the best proof of the affinity between fascism and social-fascism. Even Social Democracy admits as much through the mouth of Albert Thomas: 'Socialism and fascism differ only in their methods; both represent the interests of the workers'. Further proof is provided by the change in the social base of Social Democracy, which increasingly orientates itself towards the strata that provide the social base for fascism (petty bourgeoisie, white-collar workers). The main factor determining this similarity of ideology and of social base is that fascism and social-fascism alike consistently serve the interests of decaying capitalism in the epoch of its general crisis. Social Democracy is the apologist, not of capitalism as such, but of capitalism in decay. It takes over the responsibility for its existence along with all its contradictory effects . . .

17 The Revolutionary Way Out and the KPD, *Ernst Thälmann*

This speech by Ernst Thälmann, KPD leader, to the plenary meeting of the Party's Central Committee in February 1932, illustrates the practical implications of the Communist theory of fascism in this period. He identifies Social Democracy as providing the chief support for the fascisation process in Germany, through its toleration of the Brüning government, and he outlines the type of 'united front' policy that should be pursued.

The Fascist Course of the Brüning Government

... I come now to the question of fascisation. The process of development of the fascist dictatorship through the Brüning government, as we outlined it a year ago at the January 1931 plenum, has assumed the most intensified forms during the past twelve months. I will not mention details, since the whole range of oppressive measures used against the working class is sufficiently well-known: strike prohibitions, wage-robbery by the state, the dismantling of social welfare, the terror of Hitler-fascism, the fascisation of Social Democracy. No one today will any longer doubt that the direction taken by the Brüning–Groener government at national level, and its Braun–Severing branch in Prussia, is a fascist one; and that we were correct when we spoke in December 1930 of a maturing, though not yet fully matured, fascist dictatorship.[12]

In the course of this fascist development up to the present we find the policy of the German bourgeoisie distinguished by the peculiar system of reciprocal utilisation of Social Democracy and Hitler's Party, whereby the greater weight continues to rest on the SPD as the social bulwark of the bourgeoisie. The Centre Party is at present the party that finance capital has pushed into the foreground in order to maintain this reciprocal utilisation of the SPD and the Nazis. The Centre and Social Democrats together are at present carrying out the policy of finance capital in Germany ...

Nothing would be more disastrous than an opportunistic over-estimation of Hitler-fascism. If in face of the huge increase of the Hitler movement we were to allow ourselves to lose our correct class standard of assessment, and to be forced into a similar state of panic as Social Democracy is artificially seeking to arouse among the masses, that would necessarily lead to a mistaken orientation in our practical policy, above all in relation to the SPD as well as the Nazis. The National Socialist movement should rightly be seen as the mass base for Hugenberg and the German Nationals, while on the other side Social Democracy provides the strongest mass base for the Brüning government in its operation of the emergency dictatorship. We should recognise from our class analysis that the huge upsurge of Hitler-fascism derives mainly from the petty-bourgeois masses, and the corresponding strata of white-collar workers and officials, whereas it has generally failed to make any inroads into the industrial proletariat. Only if we recognise this shall we be able to attain complete clarity in the Party about the role of the SPD as the social bulwark for the bourgeoisie. Only then shall we be able to secure the necessary understanding among every Communist, and the broadest proletarian masses beyond, for our strategy, whose main thrust has to be directed against the Social Democrats. This is because it is Social Democracy, now as previously, that represents the most important mass base in the working class for the fascist development of bourgeois policy . . .

SPD and NSDAP are Twins

What then is the present relationship between the policy of the Hitler Party and that of Social Democracy? The eleventh (ECCI) plenum has already spoken of the conjunction of both elements in the service of finance capital. Comrade Stalin gave the clearest characterisation of the role of both these wings when as early as 1924 he spoke of them as 'twins' which 'complement each other'. This development is currently unmistakable in Germany. Social Democracy, the 'moderate wing of fascism', has in recent times partially adopted the nationalist phraseology of Hitler-fascism . . . In the matter of terror organisations as well the SPD increasingly copies Hitler-fascism. One has only to think of the *Reichsbanner* or more recently the so-called *Hammerschaften* of the 'iron front', which are to be made available in support of capital's dictatorship in its defence of the capitalist system against the revolutionary proletariat.[13] Above all it is the Prussian government of the SPD and the Federation of Labour (ADGB) that fully confirms the role of Social Democracy as the most active element in the fascisation of Germany, as the eleventh plenum established.

While Social Democracy in this way increasingly approaches Hitler-fascism, the latter in turn emphasises its legality and openly adopts the platform of Brüning's external policy as well. One has only to think of Hitler's various statements to the effect that any Nazi government would see that all 'private' financial obligations were met, and also that the question of the payment of public debts was only a problem of an ability to pay, not of our intentions. On all these points a far-reaching and reciprocal drawing-together is evident between the SPD and the National Socialists along the course of fascisation. The negotiations over the presidential elections in connection with Hindenburg's candidature have demonstrated most clearly how far this process of coalescence of the bourgeoisie around fascism has already gone . . .[14]

Our Struggle Against the SPD and NSDAP

Let us consider our struggle against the two most important counter-revolutionary mass parties, the Social Democrats and the National Socialists. Ahead of us stand the Prussian elections, to which the same considerations apply as to the presidential elections. The Social Democrats are attempting to persuade the masses that their policy and the Prussian government constitute a 'lesser evil' in comparison with the policy of the National Socialists and a possible future Hitler government. So for example the *Hamburg Echo* writes:

> Just as French Social Democracy has adopted that strategy for the approaching elections which will result in the defeat of the candidates of outright reaction, so German Social Democracy will choose the tactic that will defeat the reaction most decisively. In the contest between Hindenburg and a representative of the Harzburg Front, its attitude determines itself under present circumstances. The fact that the reaction is employing every possible means to torpedo Hindenburg's candidature is proof of its recognition that, despite his conservative convictions, he is just not available for *coups d'état* and suchlike.

We have to convince the broadest masses that this is a deception, we have to convince them that Hitler's party cannot be defeated until the mass influence of the SPD, especially among the proletariat, has been destroyed. We have to convince them that it will be impossible to resist a future Hitler government unless our main effort to win over the most important strata of the working class has been directed in good time against the SPD, since it is the SPD that keeps the broad masses of the working class captive to the bourgeoisie, and so prevents them from taking part in the class struggle or actually commits them against it.

Why Must Our main thrust be directed against Social Democracy?
Our strategy directs its main thrust against Social Democracy,
without thereby diminishing the struggle against Hitler-fascism. Our
strategy creates the necessary preconditions for an effective struggle
against Hitler-fascism precisely and only by directing its main thrust
against Social Democracy. Such a strategy is unintelligible without a
clear understanding of the role of the proletarian class as the only
thoroughgoing revolutionary class.

In the preface to his book *On the Road to October* Comrade Stalin
has provided a classic formulation of Leninist revolutionary strategy.
He defines the fundamental strategic principle of Leninism to consist
in the recognition that:

(1) the most dangerous support for the enemies of the revolution when
the period of revolutionary decision approaches is provided by the
parties of compromise;
(2) it is impossible to topple the enemy (Tsarism or the bourgeoisie)
without isolating these parties;
(3) consequently in the period of preparation for the revolution the
heaviest fire has to be directed towards isolating these parties, and
detaching the broad masses of the working population from them.

The practical application of this strategy in Germany demands the
main thrust to be directed against Social Democracy. Along with its
'left-wing' branches it constitutes the most dangerous support for the
enemies of the revolution. It is the social bulwark of the bourgeoisie,
the most active factor in the process of fascisation, as the eleventh
plenum so correctly declared, and also the most dangerous, as the
'moderate wing of fascism', in its understanding of the deceptions
necessary to capture the masses for the bourgeois dictatorship and its
fascist methods. To defeat Social Democracy is synonymous with
winning the majority of the proletariat, and creating the most
essential preconditions for the proletarian revolution.

Yet it is not enough for us to understand this. It is not enough for us
to have a theoretical understanding of the correct strategy. Rather we
must draw the necessary practical conclusions from it. That means,

above all other considerations, knowing how to resist correctly the deceptions of Social Democracy.

The Policy of Greatest Evil for the Working Class

The chief manoeuvre of Social Democracy over a whole period has been the fraud of the so-called 'lesser evil' ... We often speak ourselves of Social Democracy's policy of the 'lesser evil'. In my view this formulation of the concept is misleading and unhelpful. The policy which the SPD pursues is in reality not at all a policy of the 'lesser evil' but a policy of the greatest evil for the working class. This is what we have to convince the masses of. Social Democracy carries out at any given moment whatever schemes it is possible to carry out on behalf of the bourgeoisie against the proletariat and the working people, given the existing level of the fascisation process. If its counter-revolutionary actions sometimes fall short in one or two respects of the counter-revolutionary demands of the most extreme wing of fascism, of Hugenberg and Hitler, this is not because the SPD is somehow *better* than Hitler and Hugenberg nor because its policy is actually the 'lesser evil', but only because the given circumstances do not allow any greater degree of extortion and suppression of the workers to be attained . . .[15]

Our struggle to win the majority of the proletariat, our struggle to mobilise the decisive strata of the proletariat and their allies among the working people who follow their lead, against the capitalist route and for the revolutionary way out of the crisis – this primary strategic objective can only be attained when we understand how to defeat the fraudulent tactics of Social Democracy, when we understand how to tear the mask from its face, when we understand how to expose to the masses the true nature of Social Democracy's bourgeois, capitalist, fascist policy . . .

Revolutionary United Front from Below – The Cornerstone of our Policy

We say in our resolution that the revolutionary united front policy constitutes the cornerstone of proletarian politics in Germany . . . Revolutionary united front policy – that means relentless struggle against the social-fascists of every hue, above all against the most dangerous 'left' forms of social-fascism, against the SAP, the Brandler group and similar cliques and tendencies.[16] Revolutionary united front policy – that means effective mobilisation of the masses from below, in the factories and the offices. Revolutionary united front policy – that requires patient, systematic comradely persuasion of the Social Democratic, Christian and even National-Socialist workers, to convince them of the treachery of their leaders.

The united front cannot come about through negotiations in parliament, nor via arrangements with other parties or groups. It has to grow out of the mass movement, which alone can sustain a genuine, lively campaigning front. There must be no joint meetings held between the KPD and SPD, the SAP or the Brandler group! This naturally does not mean that we should renounce our previous tactic of challenging the opposing parties to public debate, in which we settle accounts with them decisively, item by item. We do not renounce this tactic. But it has nothing in common with opportunistic errors such as joint demonstrations without any denunciation of social-fascism or its 'left' variants, nothing in common with the setting up of parallel committees in place of the creation of united front organs of the masses from below on the basis of *our* campaigning slogans. If we really want to make the revolutionary united front policy the cornerstone of proletarian politics in Germany, we cannot allow it to become a lifeless formula; it has to be a really incisive weapon of the revolutionary class struggle.

Comrades, consider: six million unemployed in Germany! wages robbed, strikes banned, factory workers plundered! Tax profiteering, tariff robbery, increasing ruin for the middle classes! Are there not here all the preconditions for creating the broadest united front movement under our leadership, a veritable movement of millions? The party must take a mighty step to this end.

18 On the German Situation, *Palmiro Togliatti*

Togliatti, already established as a leading figure in the Comintern, examines the reasons for Hitler's victory in this article written in March 1933.

All that has happened in Germany can be simply defined as follows: the objective situation, by virtue of an unbroken series of intensifications in the crisis, has driven the ruling classes to liquidate the last remnants of their traditional system of government, to bring the fascisation of the state – a process begun and pursued for years – to its conclusion, and to set up an open fascist dictatorship. The working classes, on the other hand, have not succeeded with equal speed in concentrating their forces upon a revolutionary class front, and their determination to have done with the existing situation has been unable to find expression in a series of decisive struggles. Several questions arise from this. What are the causes of this situation? And, following from that, how will events unfold in the immediate future? What are our tasks?

In the first place we should consider the causes which have not merely allowed, but encouraged and even provoked a shift in mass support in favour of German fascism. These causes are to be found in the economic and political structure bequeathed to the capitalist world, and in particular to Europe, by the piratical terms of the Versailles Treaty, and by the policy pursued for fifteen years by Social Democracy. The double exploitation to which the German people has been subjected, the territorial dismemberment of Germany, the national oppression and humiliation that it has suffered, have created favourable conditions for mobilising the petty bourgeoisie and even sections of the workers under the leadership of the big bourgeoisie, and provoking them to armed mass struggle against the labour movement in the cause of an outraged nationalism. One of the essential conditions for the establishment of a fascist dictatorship (the creation of a mass base in its support) has thus been realised in

Germany to a far greater extent than in Italy, and with extreme rapidity. The difficulty encountered by the labour movement in opposing this alignment of reactionary forces, which has at certain points seemed like a veritable landslide, cannot be fully understood if this dimension is ignored . . .

In the second place, Hitler's accession to power represents not merely a temporary check or setback, but a sensational historical failure, *a new 4 August*, for international Social Democracy. It is the sudden outburst of a crisis of internal disintegration that will assume the proportions and have similar consequences to those produced by the crisis of 4 August 1914. On 4 August 1914 surprise played an important part; it brought to a head all at once all the elements of opportunism, of corruption, of betrayal, that had accumulated in the policy of the Second International. This time there has not even been the element of surprise. The collapse of the Second International represents the direct, logical and inexorable consequence of its *whole* policy over 14 years. It is thus a whole historical period that has come to a close . . .

Only the counter-revolutionary Trotsky, blinded by anti-Communist spite, was capable of believing and asserting that Social Democracy could have fought against fascism. The proposals for a united front, made repeatedly and in all sincerity by our Party to the Social Democratic leadership, the declarations of the Communist Party that it was ready to fight alongside any workers' organisations, could only be derided and rejected by the Social Democratic leaders, as indeed they were. Social Democracy was incapable of fighting fascism because it had penetrated too thoroughly the institutions of the reactionary capitalist state, because it had become integrated into it and into bourgeois society, because it was the twin sister of fascism, because it had become *social-fascism*.

The demonstration of Social Democracy's tranformation into social-fascism, made by the Communist International from 1929 onwards, has been attacked on all sides, and has produced a noisy reaction of anger and feigned outrage from the opportunists of the whole world. In an article of Trotsky of 14 March 1933 we read yet again that the doctrine of kinship ties uniting Social Democracy and fascism, and the doctrine of social-fascism itself are 'artificial, erroneous, charlatan theories'. On this occasion the charlatanry has not waited long to be exposed. A week earlier, on 7 March, in its commentary on Hitler's electoral victory, German Social Democracy had already offered its good services to fascism. And a week later, on 23 March, citizen Vandervelde, the president of the Second International, confirmed 'a susceptibility of part of the German working class . . . to fascist tendencies'. Citizen Vandervelde was being misleading. It is not a part of the German working class that is susceptible to fascist tendencies, but German Social Democracy and its allied union bureaucracy that has taken a fascist course, that has become *social-fascism* and reveals itself as such in the eyes of all . . .

Nor is the case of German Social Democracy an exception. Citizen Vandervelde, in the same work in which he denounces the fascist tendency of 'a part of the German working class', attacks German Social Democracy, not in the name of proletarian internationalism, but in the name of the imperialist interests of his own country and of France. The French Socialists hold the same position. The Italians, choking under our continuous pressure, have lamented a hundred times that they did not take the course the Germans are now taking, and allowed themselves to be driven to the dead-end solution of emigration. Austrian Social Democracy, on which Trotsky now stakes his cards, is not only united with the Germans in renouncing all international links in the struggle, but adopts the same course as the Germans over the whole range of its policy. The most recent speech of Otto Bauer to the (SDAP) Party faithful expounded the following line, with certain embellishments: postpone the struggle until the moment when the enemy has made it impossible for us to act effectively; then everyone do what he can! With this tactic Austrian Social Democracy will go from one defeat to the next and reach the same outcome as German Social Democracy, and for the same reasons. It is not this or that Social Democratic Party that fails or is found wanting; it is Social Democracy *as a whole*, that, at the moment when the stabilisation of capitalism has come to an end, and a new cycle of wars and revolutions approaches, collapses under the pressure of events, revealing its true social-fascist nature.

So the influence that Social Democracy has maintained within the German working class, and maintained up to the end in spite of everything, by means of its network of elaborate organisations, an influence that we succeeded in eroding but not destroying, has constituted a second condition for the victory of fascism.

The new profound crisis of the Second International confronts us not just urgently but in *quite a new way* with the problem of how to win the Social Democratic working masses for the revolutionary class struggle – the problem of the *united front*. The way in which the united front policy of the Communist International and its sections has developed in recent times corresponds to the new situation, and has indeed partly contributed to its creation. It is essential to hold this line, and campaign on it with all our powers. The more we understand how to make contact with the mass of socialist workers, and the more rapidly we succeed in establishing a united front with them to combat fascism and to defend the livelihood, the everyday interests and the freedoms of the working people, the quicker will be the transition to a new period of decisive revolutionary struggles, not only in Germany but in every country . . .

---

19 Resolution adopted by the National Conference, July 1934, *Communist Party of France (PCF)*

In July 1934 the PCF entered into negotiations with the leadership of the French Socialist Party for a programme of joint action in face of the fascist threat and the reactionary policies of the Doumergue government. This marked a break with the previous policy of united front 'from below', and was adopted as official Comintern policy the following year.

The Communist Party desires *at all costs* to achieve unity of action of the masses against the bourgeoisie and against fascism. With this aim the Communist Party employs the tactic of the united front sincerely and consistently. It gives priority to defending the demands of *all* the working masses. The orders-in-council attacking wages, salaries, benefits, allowances and pensions have aroused the condemnation of workers, officials and all working people. Money stolen from officials and ex-service men is used primarily to increase military expenditure (the recent vote of three billion extra war credits). The discontent in the countryside has never been so great. The peasant workers have been overcome by poverty. The economic crisis grows continually worse; unemployment persists and spreads.

Fascism, the Principal Danger
The fascists are making great efforts to increase their influence among the petty-bourgeois elements in the towns and the countryside, and to bring about a unification of their forces with a view to attaining power. At the present time fascism constitutes the chief danger. We must concentrate all the resources of mass proletarian action against it, and win all sections of the working population for such action.

The Struggle for Immediate Demands
The Communist Party gives priority to defending the demands of *all* the working masses. It is the task of each Party organ and union section to work out the demands appropriate to each industry, factory and section of the population: the unemployed, peasants, tradesmen, intellectuals, ex-service men, invalids, young people, women, the lower and junior ranks of the army which we should not neglect . . . The Communists should not overlook the existence of mass organisations (ex-service men, ratepayers, small traders, employees, etc.) which are often under reactionary influence, but the demands of whose members are not foreign to ourselves. We must know how to establish a united front with these groups of people, by defending the demands contained in the programme of their organisations, where these are not incompatible with the interests of the proletariat. We must establish fraternal relations with them, take the platform at their meetings, and expound our proposals and ideas about the joint struggle against capital and against fascism.

The victory or defeat of fascism in France depends in the last analysis on the attitude of the army. The Communists must link the defence of the immediate demands of the soldiers with the struggle of the working class, and must support their fight for political rights. A big campaign should be conducted to eliminate the chauvinist elements in the soldiers' hatred of Hitler, and direct this hatred against the Hitlerites in France, unmasking the fascists as enemies of the French people.

In its struggle for mass demands the Communist Party and its associates must have recourse to joint demonstrations, strikes and meetings, organised as far as possible jointly with the Socialists and affiliated organisations; it must make use of parliament in common with the Socialists to ensure that anti-fascist legislation is tabled; at the same time it must organise mass extra-parliamentary activity in defence of this legislation, in common with the Socialists and affiliated organisations, on the basis of the united front campaign.

The Defence of Democratic Freedoms
The fascists fight against bourgeois *democracy*, so as to destroy it. The Communists for their part fight against all forms of bourgeois *dictatorship*, even when this dictatorship assumes the form of bourgeois democracy. But the Communists are never unconcerned with the form assumed by the political system of the bourgeoisie. They expose in detail the process of reactionary degeneration of bourgeois democracy that opens the way to fascism. But they have always defended, and will continue to defend in future, all the democratic freedoms won by the masses themselves, especially all the rights of the working class. The Communists not only oppose with all their energy, now and in the future, every attempt on the part of fascism and the bourgeoisie in general to suppress or limit these freedoms; but they continually strive to extend their scope. There is a fundamental difference between the Communists and Socialists on this question: the Socialists, under the pretext of defending democracy and the Republic, succeed in defending the class dictatorship of the bourgeoisie; whereas the Communists defend the democtratic freedoms won by the masses, so as to mobilise and organise the latter against capital and the dictatorship of the bourgeoisie.

The Campaign of the Communists to set up the United Front
The Communist Party strives *sincerely* to set up the united front for the

anti-fascist struggle: it rejects those who treat the united front merely as a manoeuvre. Its desire for the united front, to support the demands of the working masses and bar the road to fascism, is a genuine one. People like Treint, for whom the united front tactic was a matter of 'fleecing the opposition', have been excluded from the Communist Party for a similar tendency, and have found refuge with the counter-revolutionary Trotsky before passing over to Social Democracy. The splitter Doriot takes the same route when he treats the united front simply as a manoeuvre, counting on a refusal by the Socialist Party which he can then use to 'fleece them'.[17]

The Communist Party has decided to renounce all propaganda attacks, both oral and written, against those organisations which loyally carry out any action that has been previously agreed. But it intends to campaign against all those who sabotage the united front in action, trying to destroy it and acting against the interests of the working class. By its attitude, its policy of unity and the devotion of its members to the cause of the united front, the Communist Party intends to prove to the broad masses that it is worthy and capable of leading the huge army of victims of the capitalist system to the conquest of power and the triumph of the proletarian revolution.

The Socialist Party, by dragging out the negotiations with the Communist Party instead of replying favourably and speedily to its proposals for joint action, restrains and slows down the pace of the united anti-fascist activity that has already been achieved by several important local and federal organisations. By acting in this way the Socialist Party restricts the revolutionary dimensions of the mass movement, a course that can only be profitable to fascism . . .

---

20 The Socialist–Communist pact, *Léon Blum*

Léon Blum, leader of the French Socialist Party, explains the reasons for the change of policy by the Communists, and the ambivalence with which their proposals for joint action were received in his own Party.

(1)

. . . The idea of 'united action' with the Communist Party, of a 'common front for action', whose first joint demonstrations we have so far supported, has aroused a mixture of enthusiasm, uncertainty and disquiet in our Party. The enthusiasm is an undeniable fact, and I note at once that it is not only in Paris and the surrounding region that it is to be found. The same electric current can be experienced in the most diverse places and at the furthest distance from each other. The desire for unity, the determination for unity, undoubtedly latent for many years, has suddenly appeared on the surface under the impact of the fascist assault of 6 February.

We can surely say, without too much presumption, that the political intelligence of the French population is quicker, keener and more independent than that of any other European proletariat. The popular masses felt instinctively, after 6 February, that the surest guarantee against the fascist threat, in France as elsewhere, lay in proletarian unity, in the possibility of a defence or a counter-offensive which brought together all the strength of the workers.[18] Moreover this reflex, the product of an instinct for self-preservation, corresponds to a more considered assessment of reality. We are in the presence of a powerful movement, the more powerful the more it is spontaneous, which no one can or should ignore. I should add that, among our ranks, despite the regular replacement of our personnel, there were many who had already experienced unity, who had never clearly supported the split of 1920, who were never reconciled to the idea that the division in the working class had to be eternal, and who hoped before they died to see a united party once more – or rather a single party, just as the social class of which it is the expression is a single class.

These, in short, are the reasons for the enthusiasm. The reasons for the uncertainty and disquiet are no less simple and no less obvious. First, it is impossible not to be astonished by the sudden precipitation of events and the rapidity of their tempo. One has the impression despite oneself of sliding down a steep slope, and being swept along by the laws of gravity much more than by one's own choice. Why is this? Because although the desire and the determination for unity have spread among the popular masses and aroused their enthusiasm for many months now, it is only a few days since they have prompted the actions of the Communist Party. Today the Communist Party is urgently repeating its proposals, and it is this sudden change of attitude that has precipitated matters and accelerated their tempo. Yet this sudden change has taken on a truly melodramatic quality, which still leaves us slightly 'dazed'.

There is another reason for disquiet. Our Party's Committee (C.A.P.) replied to the Communist proposals with considerable eagerness, sincerity and good sense. It asked – and asked earnestly – for guarantees of reciprocal good faith; it called for clarification about the latest number of *Cahier du Bolchevisme*, a document all the more disquieting in that it was exactly contemporaneous with the negotiations taking place. During this time a certain number of Federations, making use of the latitude granted them by the decision of the National Council, continued to organise joint activities, especially the Federation which attracts most attention in the Party, the Federation of the Seine. Our militants were thus subjected to a kind of hot and cold shower, reading in the *Populaire* one day the documents drawn up by the C.A.P., learning the next in the same *Populaire* about the massive joint demonstrations, such as those of Huyghens and Bullier, whose resonance was necessarily much stronger.[19]

The sensation of bewilderment is thus completely natural . . . However, these inevitable and perfectly understandable reactions on the part of many of our militants do not alter the basic outlines of the problem confronting the Party. Whatever its internal motivations or its after-thoughts, the Communist Party has confronted us with explicit proposals. Its determination to reach an agreement has been announced with a considerable stir. Is it possible in the present state of things to reply to it with a plea of rejection? Is is possible to ignore the spontaneous appeal for unity coming from the popular masses? In my view such an attitude is impossible. The task confronting our next Council will therefore be to define the terms of the agreement with sufficient clarity, frankness and discretion to secure the unanimous assent of the Party; to ensure its independence and 'security'; and to preserve its complete control over its own propaganda and activities . . .

(2)

In the article which he wrote yesterday in *l'Humanité* – a most interesting and important article in so many respects – Maurice Thorez endeavoured to prove that the current proposals of the Communist Party do not involve the surrender of a single one of its fundamental views.[20] I have no intention of entering into controversy with him on this point. I merely confine myself to recording a modification, or even a transformation, in its external behaviour. I myself remain convinced, though not on the basis of any privileged information, that this modification, or transformation, is the result of instructions emanating from Moscow. And I think I can understand the reasons why the Communist International is now leading the Communist Party in a different direction in its attitude towards ourselves.

The fascist uprising of 6 February and its repercussions on the popular masses in France have allowed the Communist International to execute a change of policy, whose necessity it must have foreseen after Hitler's accession to power in Germany. The Nazi victory has confronted the Russian revolution with the gravest danger it has faced in thirteen or fourteen years. The Soviet government was already threatened with Japanese aggression in the far east, and facing the prospect of imminent war, which it had managed to delay only with great difficulty by its courageous determination to maintain the peace. Now it discovers the menace of Hitler behind it as well. Hitler has always presented himself as the implacable enemy and predestined destroyer of communism. He has effected a rapprochement with Pilsudski's Poland that probably involves a solution to the question of the 'corridor', for which Soviet Russia will pay the price. On the day when Russia finds itself in action against Japan on its Asian front, it risks being attacked by a German–Polish coalition on its European front.

I have been informing the readers of *Populaire* of the seriousness of such a situation for a long time. The Soviet government is more aware and concerned about the danger than anyone. It is faced with a question of public safety, of revolutionary security, which explains all its external actions for over a year. We do not need to look for any further explanation of its new diplomatic policy, its conclusion of non-aggression pacts, the journeyings of Litvinov, or the impending entry of Russia to the League of Nations – a move which also represents, incidentally, a modification or transformation in attitude. The Soviet government seeks to guarantee the 'security' of its European front, if possible by a system of international agreements, if not, then with the support of individual powers. Nothing is more logical or more legitimate. But whether it is a matter of general agreements or of individual support, France has become the chief piece on the chessboard. It is France that contains the essential conditions of 'security' for Soviet Russia.

The same will to self-preservation, and I emphasise by peaceful means, has thus produced convergent results on both the levels of proletarian class action and of governmental and diplomatic policy respectively. At the same time as it effected a rapprochement with the French government, Soviet Russia was led to seek a point of support among the popular masses in France, which had come together around the idea of the anti-fascist or anti-racist struggle. It realised that one of its defences, and perhaps the most reliable of all, lay in the action of the proletarian parties, which would be the more powerful the more they were united.

This is how I myself see the course of recent events; this is how in my view they can be best explained. And while I completely reserve my judgement as a socialist on everything that concerns the internal condition of Russia, I scarcely need to add that in a choice between Hitler's racism on one side and Russian Communism on the other, international socialism does not remain neutral. If joint action in France could help defend the Russian revolution against racism, on the European level, at the same time as it barred the way to fascism at the national level, in my view it would be twice as valuable.

Yet on this point as on all the others it will be necessary to strive for frankness and clarity on both sides. The nub of the joint action that has been proposed to us is the struggle against fascism, and, following on from that, against the government of the national bloc which was brought to power by the fascist uprising. The Communist Party undoubtedly shares our intention that the struggle against the government of the national bloc will not be influenced at any point or in any way by the relations between Soviet Russia and this same government . . .

21 The Working Class against Fascism, *Georgi Dimitrov*

The seventh Congress of the Communist International in July–August 1935 confirmed the new 'people's front' policy. Dimitrov's speech was the leading contribution on the subject.

. . . The accession to power of fascism is not an *ordinary succession* of one bourgeois government by another, but a *substitution* for one state form of class domination of the bourgeoisie – bourgeois democracy – of another form – open terrorist dictatorship. It would be a serious mistake to ignore this distinction, a mistake which would prevent the revolutionary proletariat from mobilising the broadest strata of the toilers of town and country for the struggle against the menace of the seizure of power by the fascists, and from taking advantage of the contradictions which exist in the camp of the bourgeoisie itself. But it is a mistake no less serious and dangerous to *underrate* the importance, in establishing the fascist dictatorship, of the *reactionary measures of the bourgeoisie which are at present being increasingly initiated in bourgeois-democratic countries* – measures which are designed to destroy the democratic liberties of the toilers, to distort and curtail the rights of parliament and to intensify the repression of the revolutionary movement.

Comrades, the accession to power of fascism must not be conceived of in so simplified and smooth a form, as though some committee or other of finance capital decided on a certain date to set up a fascist dictatorship. In reality, fascism usually comes to power in the course of a mutual, and at times severe, struggle between the old bourgeois parties, or a definite section of these parties, in the course of a struggle even within the fascist camp itself – a struggle which at times leads to armed clashes, as we have witnessed in the case of Germany, Austria and other countries. All this, however, does not detract from the fact that before the establishment of a fascist dictatorship, bourgeois governments usually pass through a number of preliminary stages and institute a number of reactionary measures, which directly facilitate the accession to power of fascism. Whoever does not fight the reactionary measures of the bourgeoisie and the growth of fascism at these preparatory stages, *is not in a position to prevent the victory of fascism, but, on the contrary, facilitates that victory.*

The Social Democratic leaders glossed over and concealed from the masses the true class nature of fascism, and did not call them to the struggle against the increasingly reactionary measures of the bourgeoisie. They bear great *historical responsibility* for the fact that, at the decisive moment of the fascist offensive, a large section of the toiling masses of Germany and a number of other fascist countries failed to recognise in fascism the most bloodthirsty monster of finance, their most vicious enemy, and that these masses were not prepared to resist it.

What is the source of the influence enjoyed by fascism over the masses? Fascism is able to attract the masses because it makes a demagogic appeal to their *most urgent needs and demands.* Fascism not only inflames prejudices that are deeply ingrained in the masses, but also plays on the better sentiments of the masses, on their sense of justice, and sometimes even on their revolutionary traditions. Why do the German fascists, those lackeys of the big bourgeoisie and mortal enemies of Socialism, represent themselves to the masses as 'Socialists', and depict their accession to power as a 'revolution'? Because they try to exploit the faith in revolution, the urge towards Socialism, which live in the hearts of the broad masses of the toilers of Germany.

Fascism acts in the interests of the extreme imperialists, but it presents itself to the masses in the guise of champion of an ill-treated nation, and appeals to outraged national sentiments, as German fascism did, for instance, when it won the support of the masses by the slogan 'Against the Versailles Treaty!'

Fascism aims at the most unbridled exploitation of the masses, but it appeals to them with the most artful anti-capitalist demagogy, taking advantage of the profound hatred entertained by the toilers for the piratical bourgeoisie, the banks, trusts and the financial magnates, and advancing slogans which at the given moment are most alluring to the politically immature masses. In Germany – 'The general welfare is higher than the welfare of the individual'; in Italy – 'Our

State is not a capitalist, but a corporate State'; in Japan – 'For Japan, without exploitation'; in the United States – 'Share the wealth', and so forth.

Fascism delivers up the people to be devoured by the most corrupt, most venal elements, but comes before them with the demand for 'an honest and incorruptible government'. Speculating on the profound disillusionment of the masses in bourgeois-democratic governments, fascism hypocritically denounces corruption (for instance, the Barmat and Sklarek affairs in Germany, the Stavisky affair in France, and numerous others).

It is in the interests of the most reactionary circles of the bourgeoisie that fascism intercepts the disappointed masses as they leave the old bourgeois parties. But it makes an impression on these masses by the *severity of its attacks* on bourgeois governments and its irreconcilable attitude towards the old bourgeois parties.

Surpassing in its cynicism and hypocrisy all other varieties of bourgeois reaction, *fascism adapts* its demagogy to the national *peculiarities* of each country, and even to the peculiarities of the various social strata in one and the same country. And the petty-bourgeois masses, even a section of the workers, reduced to despair by want, unemployment and the insecurity of their existence, fall victim to the social and chauvinist demagogy of fascism.

Fascism comes to power as a *party of attack* on the revolutionary movement of the proletariat, on the masses of the people who are in a state of unrest; yet it stages its accession to power as a 'revolutionary' movement against the bourgeoisie on behalf of 'the whole nation' and for 'the salvation' of the nation. Let us recall Mussolini's 'march' on Rome, Pilsudski's 'march' on Warsaw, Hitler's National-Socialist 'revolution' in Germany, and so forth.

But whatever the masks which fascism adopts, whatever the forms in which it presents itself, whatever the ways by which it comes to power –

fascism is a most ferocious attack by capital on the toiling masses;
fascism is unbridled chauvinism and annexationist war;
fascism is rabid reaction and counter-revolution;
fascism is the most vicious enemy of the working class and of all the toilers . . .

182   The Communist International

Is the Victory of Fascism Inevitable?

Why was it that fascism could triumph and how?

Fascism is the most vicious enemy of the working class and the toilers. Fascism is the enemy of nine-tenths of the German people, nine-tenths of the Austrian people, nine-tenths of the other peoples in fascist countries. How, in what way, could this vicious enemy triumph?

Fascism was able to come to power *primarily* because the working class, owing to the policy of class collaboration with the bourgeoisie pursued by Social Democratic leaders, *proved to be split, politically and organisationally disarmed*, in face of the onslaught of the bourgeoisie. And the Communist Parties, on the other hand, were *not strong enough* to be able, apart from and in the teeth of the Social Democrats, to rouse the masses and to lead them in a decisive struggle against fascism.

And, indeed, let the millions of Social-Democratic workers, who, together with their Communist brothers, are now experiencing the horrors of fascist barbarism, seriously reflect on this. If in 1918, when revolution broke out in Germany and Austria, the Austrian and German proletariat had not followed the Social Democratic leadership of Otto Bauer, Friedrich Adler and Karl Renner in Austria, and Ebert and Scheidemann in Germany, but had followed the road of the Russian Bolsheviks, the road of Lenin and Stalin, there would now be no fascism in Austria or Germany, in Italy or Hungary, in Poland or in the Balkans. Not the bourgeoisie but the working class would long ago have been the master of the situation in Europe. Take, for example, the *Austrian* Social-Democratic Party. The revolution of 1918 raised it to a tremendous height. It held power in its hands, it held strong positions in the army and in the state apparatus. Relying on these positions, it could have nipped fascism in the bud. But it surrendered one position of the working class after another without resistance. It permitted the bourgeoisie to strengthen its power, annul the constitution, purge the state apparatus, army and police force of Social Democratic functionaries, and take the arsenals away from the workers. It allowed the fascist bandits to murder Social-Democratic workers with impunity and accepted the terms of the Hutenberg Pact, which gave the fascist elements entry to the factories. At the same time the Social Democratic leaders fooled the workers with the Linz Programme, in which the alternative was provided for the possibility of using armed force against the bourgeoisie and for the establishment of a proletarian dictatorship, assuring them that in the event of the ruling classes using force against the working class, the Party would reply by a call for a general strike and for armed struggle. As though the whole policy of preparation for a fascist attack on the working class were not one chain of acts of violence against the working class masked by constitutional forms. Even on the eve and in the course of the February battles the Austrian Social Democratic leaders left the heroically fighting *Schutzbund* isolated from the broad masses and doomed the Austrian proletariat to defeat.

Was the victory of fascism inevitable in *Germany?* No, the German working class could have prevented it.

But in order to do so, it should have compelled the establishment of a united anti-fascist proletarian front, forced the Social Democratic leaders to put a stop to their campaign against the Communists and to accept the repeated proposals of the Communist Party for united action against fascism.

When fascism was on the offensive and the bourgeois-democratic liberties were being progressively abolished by the bourgeoisie, it should not have contented itself with the verbal resolutions of the Social Democrats, but should have replied by a genuine mass struggle, which would have made the fulfilment of the fascist plans of the German bourgeoisie more difficult . . .

In this connection, we cannot avoid referring also to a number of *mistakes committed by the Communist Parties*, mistakes that hampered our struggle against fascism.

In our ranks there were people who intolerably underrated the fascist danger, a tendency which has not everywhere been overcome to this day. Of this nature was the opinion formerly to be met with in our Parties to the effect that 'Germany is not Italy', meaning that fascism may have succeeded in Italy, but that its success in Germany was out of the question, because the latter was an industrially and culturally highly developed country, with forty years of traditions of the working-class movement, in which fascism was impossible. Or the kind of opinion which is to be met with nowadays, to the effect that in countries of 'classical' bourgeois democracy the soil for fascism does not exist. Such opinions may serve and have served to weaken vigilance with regard to the fascist danger, and to render the mobilisation of the proletariat in the struggle against fascism more difficult.

One might also cite a number of instances in which Communists were caught unawares by the fascist *coup*. Remember Bulgaria, where the leadership of our Party took up a 'neutral', but in fact opportunist, position with regard to the *coup d'état* of June 9, 1923: Poland, where in May, 1926, the leadership of the Communist Party, making a wrong estimate of the motive forces of the Polish revolution, did not realise the fascist nature of Pilsudski's *coup*, and trailed in the rear of events; Finland, where our Party based itself on a false conception of slow and gradual fascisation and overlooked the fascist *coup* which was being prepared by the leading group of the bourgeoisie and which caught the Party and the working class unawares.

When National Socialism had already become a menacing mass movement in Germany, certain comrades, like Heinz Neumann, who regarded the Brüning government as already a government of fascist dictatorship, boastfully declared: 'If Hitler's "Third Empire" ever comes about, it will only be one and a half metres underground, and above it will be the victorious power of the workers'.

Our comrades in Germany for a long time failed to reckon with the wounded national sentiments and indignation of the masses at the Versailles Treaty; they treated as of little account the vacillations of the peasantry and the petty bourgeoisie; they were late in drawing up their programme of social and national emancipation, and when they did put it forward they were unable to adapt it to the concrete demands and the level of the masses. They were even unable to popularise it widely among the masses.

In a number of countries the necessary development of a mass fight against fascism was replaced by sterile hair splitting as to the nature of fascism 'in general' and by a *narrow sectarian attitude* in presenting and solving the actual political problems of the Party.

Comrades, it is not simply because we want to dig up the past that we speak of the causes of the victory of fascism, that we point to the historical responsibility of the Social Democrats for the defeat of the working class, and that we also point out our own mistakes in the fight against fascism. We are not historians divorced from living reality; we, active fighters of the working class, are obliged to answer the question that is tormenting millions of workers: *Can the victory of fascism be prevented, and how?* And we reply to these millions of workers: Yes, comrades, the road in the way of fascism can be blocked. It is quite possible. It depends on ourselves – on the workers, the peasants and all the toilers!

Whether the victory of fascism can be prevented depends *in the first place* on the militant activity displayed by the working class itself, on whether its forces are welded into a single militant army combating the offensive of capitalism and fascism. Having established its fighting unity, the proletariat would paralyse the influence of fascism over the peasantry, the petty bourgeoisie of the towns, the youth and the intelligentsia, and would be able to neutralise one section and win over another section.

Second, it depends on the existence of a strong revolutionary party, correctly leading the struggle of the toilers against fascism. A party which systematically calls on the workers to retreat in the face of fascism and permits the fascist bourgeoisie to strengthen its positions will inevitably lead the workers to defeat.

Third, it depends on whether a correct policy is pursued by the working class towards the peasantry and the petty-bourgeois masses of the towns. These masses must be taken as they are, and not as we should like to have them. It is only in the process of the struggle that they will overcome their doubts and vacillations. It is only provided we adopt a patient attitude towards their inevitable vacillations, it is only with the political help of the proletariat, that they will be able to rise to a higher level of revolutionary consciousness and activity.

Fourth, it depends on whether the revolutionary proletariat exercises vigilance and takes action at the proper time. It must not allow fascism to catch it unawares, it must not surrender the initiative to fascism, it must inflict decisive blows on the latter before it can gather its forces, it must not allow fascism to consolidate its position, it must repel fascism wherever and whenever it manifests itself, it must not allow fascism to gain new positions – all of which the French proletariat is doing so successfully.

These are the main conditions for preventing the growth of fascism and its accession to power.

The powerful urge towards the united front in all the capitalist countries shows that the lessons of defeat have not been in vain. The working class is beginning to act in a *new way*. The initiative shown by the Communist Party in the organisation of the united front and the supreme self-sacrifice displayed by the Communists, by the revolutionary workers in the struggle against fascism have resulted in an unprecedented increase in the prestige of the Communist International. At the same time, within the Second International, a profound crisis has been developing, which has manifested itself with particular clarity and has become particularly accentuated since the bankruptcy of German Social Democracy.

The Social-Democratic workers are able to convince themselves ever more forcibly that fascist Germany, with all its horrors and barbarities, is in the final analysis *the result of the Social-Democratic policy of class collaboration with the bourgeoisie.* These masses are coming ever more clearly to realise that the path along which the German Social-Democratic leaders led the proletariat must not again be traversed. Never has there been such ideological dissension in the camp of the Second International as at the present time. A process of differentiation is taking place in all the Social-Democratic parties. Within their ranks *two principal* camps are forming: side by side with the existing camp of reactionary elements, who are trying in every way to preserve the *bloc* between the Social Democrats and the bourgeoisie, and who furiously reject a united front with the Communists, *there is beginning to form a camp of revolutionary elements who entertain doubts as to the correctness of the policy of class collaboration with the bourgeoisie, who are in favour of the creation of a united front with the Communists and who are increasingly coming to adopt the position of the revolutionary class struggle.*

Thus fascism, which appeared as the result of the decline of the capitalist system, in the long run acts as a factor of *its further disintegration.* Thus fascism, which has undertaken to bury Marxism, the revolutionary movement of the working class, is, as a result of the dialectics of life and the class struggle, itself leading to the further *development of those forces* which are bound to serve as its grave-diggers, the grave-diggers of capitalism.

III Communists in Opposition, 1928–37

22 On Fascism, *August Thalheimer*[21]

Thalheimer's article comparing fascism with Bonapartism was originally written in 1928 as a policy document for the Comintern, shortly before he was expelled for 'rightist' deviation. He subsequently became the leading theoretician of the right Communist opposition in Germany, KPO.

The best starting point for an enquiry into fascism seems to me Marx and Engels' analysis of Bonapartism (Louis Bonaparte). Certainly I do not equate fascism with Bonapartism. But they are related phenomena, having common as well as differentiating characteristics, both of which require elaboration.

I shall start with a quotation from Marx's preface to the *Eighteenth Brumaire*, which runs as follows: 'Finally I hope that my work will contribute to the elimination of the school phrase 'Caesarism' which is currently in vogue, especially in Germany'. Marx then points to the fundamental difference between the ancient and modern proletariat, from which it follows that the Caesarism of antiquity and modern Bonapartism are, in terms of their class situation, fundamentally different things. Marx is underlining the necessity of a specific class analysis. But not only that. The result of a class analysis of the social and historical roots of Bonapartism is to demonstrate, not only the presence of particular classes in a given society, but also a specific relationship between them, as something historically produced and hence subject to historical dissolution. Marx also investigates meticulously the political manifestations of Bonapartism, its ideological roots and forms of expression, its state and party organisation. He shows in detail how the French bourgeoisie after 1848–9, in face of the uprising of the working class in the June massacre, surrendered itself to the dictatorship of an adventurer and his gang, abandoning its political position in order to save its social existence.

> Thus, he writes, by now stigmatising as 'socialistic' what it had previously extolled as 'liberal', the bourgeoisie confesses that its own interests dictate that it should be delivered from the danger of its *own rule*; that to restore tranquillity in the country its bourgeois parliament must, first of all, be given its quietus; that in order to preserve its social power intact, its political power must be broken; that the individual bourgeois can continue to exploit the other classes and to enjoy undisturbed property, family, religion and order, only on condition that their class be condemned along with the other classes to like political nullity; that in order to save its purse, it must forfeit the crown, and the sword that is to safeguard it must at the same time be hung over its own head as a sword of Damocles.

The bourgeoisie thus forms one of the social bases of Bonapartism; but in order to save its social existence in a specific historical situation, it surrenders its political power — it subordinates itself to the 'executive that has made itself an independent power'. The other major social base for this 'autonomisation of the executive power', for the dictatorship of Bonaparte and his gang, is the small-holding peasantry; not, that is to say, the revolutionary peasantry, which is in revolt against bourgeois property relations, but the conservative peasantry which wants to see its private small-holdings maintained and defended against the threatening proletarian revolution. Because of its economic and social fragmentation, and the lack of any economic and social organisation of its own, the peasant class cannot undertake such a defence by itself.

> In so far as there is merely a local interconnection among these small-holding peasants, and the identity of their interests begets no community, no national bond and no political organisation among them, they do not form a class. They are consequently incapable of enforcing their class interest in their own name, whether through a parliament or a convention. They cannot represent themselves, they must be represented. Their representative must at the same time appear as their master, as an authority over them, as an unlimited governmental power that protects

them against the other classes and sends them rain and sunshine from above. The political influence of the small-holding peasants, therefore, finds its final expression in the executive power subordinating society to itself.

As for the working class, it contributes to the emergence of Bonapartism inasmuch as it has attempted a revolutionary assault on bourgeois society and has thrown that society into a state of panic, without however proving mature enough to seize and maintain a hold on power by itself. A severe defeat of the proletariat in a deep social crisis is thus one of the prerequisites of Bonapartism. On the other hand Bonapartism is divided into various groupings and parties, as the bourgeoisie becomes split into its own warring factions following the defeat of the working class (and subsequently of the petty bourgeoisie). The executive power now appears as the longed-for representative of the common interest of its various fractions, which are no longer able to generate this unity for themselves . . .

The decisive element in Bonapartism is the totality of class relations of a given country, of a given society. Bonapartism, the autonomisation of the executive power, is the 'ultimate' and also the most rotten form of bourgeois state power in that period when bourgeois society has been most severely threatened by the onslaught of the proletarian revolution, and when the bourgeoisie has exhausted itself in its defence against this onslaught. In such a period all classes are played out and lie exhausted on the ground, and the bourgeoisie looks around for the strongest protection to defend its social domination. Bonapartism is thus a form of bourgeois state power in a period of defence, retrenchment and re-fortification against the proletarian revolution. It is one form of the open dictatorship of capital; the other, closely related, form is fascism. Their common denomination is 'the open dictatorship of capital'. Their external characteristics are: the autonomisation of the executive power, the destruction of the political rule of the bourgeoisie and the subordination of all remaining social classes under the executive. Their social or class content, however, is the dominance of the bourgeoisie and of property owners in general over the working class and all the other strata which are exploited by capital.

Bonapartism is the 'ultimate' form of bourgeois state power inasmuch as it is a form of open capitalist dictatorship and inasmuch as the open capitalist dictatorship appeared at the point when bourgeois society had reached the brink of the grave, mortally threatened by the proletarian revolution. Fascism is essentially the same: it is a form of the open capitalist dictatorship. An important correction is necessary here, consisting of one small word. Instead of saying that fascism is *the* open dictatorship of the bourgeoisie, we must say instead that it is *a* form . . .

We come now to the contemporary form of the open dictatorship of the bourgeoisie in Italy, the fascist state. There is no mistaking certain essential characteristics it has in common with the Bonapartist form of dictatorship. Once more there is the 'autonomisation of the executive power', and the political subordination of the masses, including the bourgeoisie itself, to the fascist state power. At the same time the social domination of the big bourgeoisie and large landowners is preserved. Fascism, like Bonapartism, seeks to be the benefactor of all classes; hence it continually plays one class off against another, and engages in contradictory manoeuvres internally. The fascist apparatus shows similar features. The Fascist Party is a counterpart to the December gang of Louis Bonaparte. Its social composition consists of socially uprooted elements from every class, from the aristocracy, the bourgeoisie, the urban petty bourgeoisie, the peasantry, the workers. As far as the working class is concerned, it brings together *déclassé* elements from two opposite extremes: from below the lumpen proletariat, and from above sections of the labour aristocracy and bureaucracy, of the reformist unions and parties. The similarity holds good for its military force as well. The fascist militia is socially the counterpart to the Bonapartist army, and like it provides a source of livelihood for the socially uprooted. In Italy, however, there stands alongside it the army formed by universal conscription, which has no parallel in Bonapartist France. Its existence alongside the fascist militia corresponds to the organisational requirements of an army under imperialist conditions, for which a professional or mercenary army on its own is manifestly insufficient, and which demand a mass army with the widest possible extension of military service.

A further parallel lies in the situation of class conflict out of which the Bonapartist and fascist forms of the state respectively arose. In the case of Italian fascism as with Bonapartism an unsuccessful proletarian onslaught ended with the demoralisation of the working class, while the bourgeoisie, exhausted, distraught and dispirited, cast around for a saviour to protect its social power. There is a correspondence in ideology as well, its chief elements being the idea of the 'nation', the token campaign against parliamentary and bureaucratic corruption, theatrical denunciations of capital, and so on. There are points of similarity, finally, with the 'hero' of the *coup d'état*.

Friedrich Engels emphasises the following characteristics which fit the hero of the *coup d'état* for his role: 'Ready for anything – a conspirator with the *carbonari* in Italy, an artillery officer in Switzerland, a debt-ridden aristocratic vagabond and special constable in England. Always and everywhere a Pretender'. The bourgeoisie, Engels continues, sees in him its 'great statesman'; flesh of their flesh, he is a parvenu like them. So is Mussolini, the bricklayer's son. In accordance with the changed times a parvenu from the working class is now more appropriate than one from the minor aristocracy, whence Bonaparte originated. Mussolini's period of activity with the Social Democrats in Italy corresponds to Louis Bonaparte's with the Italian *carbonari*. In recent times the passage through Social Democracy has become obligatory for the 'great statesmen' and 'saviours' of bourgeois society; more recently still the passage through communism, witness China. Mussolini, like Louis Bonaparte, endured the misery of long years in exile, an experience which in certain natures accentuates the hunger for power and wealth, sharpens the insight, toughens the will, and develops the necessary resilience. Under certain objective and subjective conditions this produces hardened and experienced revolutionaries, under others the cynical, counter-revolutionary putschist, ready for any eventuality.

Again, there are the internal contradictions between the social and material strengthening of the bourgeoisie, and its political subordination. There is the appearance of protection for the material interests of the proletariat while they are effectively surrendered to the interests of capital. There is the fascist state as 'intermediary' between the bourgeoisie and working class, a position which involves it continually in practical contradictions. The same holds in relation to the peasants and petty bourgeoisie. Fascism and Bonapartism both promised bourgeoisie society 'peace and security'. But in order to prove their indispensability as 'saviours of society', they have to make out that society is constantly under threat; hence proceeds perpetual restlessness and uncertainty. The material interests of the bourgeoisie and peasantry alike demand stringent economy in the state budget, a 'regime of austerity', whereas the material interests of the host of parasites who comprise the Fascist Party's organisation, the fascist state and local officialdom, and the fascist militia, in contrast, demand continual expansion of the fascist state and Party machines. Each of these conflicting interests has to be surrendered in turn. Every move to curb the fascist gang in the interests of bourgeois 'law and order' and sound economy, has to be compensated immediately by a new licence for terrorist excess and plunder.

These internal conflicts, combined with the nationalist imperialist ideology, push the dictator to external violations of the peace, and finally to war. Here the Italian counterpart to Louis Bonaparte confronts not only the same old contradictions – that its instrument of internal rule, in this case the national militia, is unsuited both by its internal function and its social composition to be an instrument of imperial conquest against states which have not yet been forced to encumber themselves with the most 'prostituted' of all forms of bourgeois power. To this is added a more extensive contradiction, between the privileged fascist troops and the regular army.

What are the essential differences between Bonapartism and fascism? These are in part locally determined, by national variations in class relations, historical traditions, and so on. They are also partly rooted in the general change that has taken place in the character of bourgeois society and the capitalist system. It is of course a matter of national historical tradition that the dictator in France should pose as 'Caesar' on the basis of the Napoleonic legend and its role among the peasantry. In Italy he had to content himself with the role of 'Leader', and allow the throne to exist alongside him. Instead of the Napoleonic masquerade, was the Sullan and Caesarist one of ancient Rome, which is nevertheless more artificial than the other.

Such differences are, however, insignificant in comparison with the differences which stem from changes in the general character of capitalism. Napoleon III still operated in the era of free capitalist competition, the era of incomplete bourgeois revolutions in Italy and Germany. The revolutionary claims, which had worked for a certain time to the advantage of Napoleon I, and which he sought to exploit, now proved counter-productive. In the Italian war he attracted the support of the Italian freedom movement, only to alienate it shortly afterwards when he left it in the lurch in the interests of his dynastic conquests. In the Franco-Prussian war he came into collision with Germany's revolutionary interests in national unification, which proved his undoing. The dynastic war of conquest that he was compelled to fight under the combined pressure of the Napoleonic legend and the internal contradictions of his system, was anachronistic: too late for someone who no longer represented any revolutionary principle, too early to represent the imperialist principle in its modern sense, in absence of the appropriate economic basis. Mussolini's foreign policy, in contrast, has been imperialist in the modern sense of the word from the outset. It wears the guise of antiquity, but is in fact 'up-to-date', and has been openly reactionary from the start. It is bound to be ruined by its own internal contradictions: on the one hand between the exaggerated aims it sets itself and the limited means for their execution; on the other hand the contradiction between the style and social structure of a military organisation appropriate for subjugating all the classes of society and living at their expense, and one appropriate to the very different requirements of an imperialist war.

A further difference, conditioned by the general development of bourgeois society and the state of the international class struggle, is to be found in the organisational bases and instruments of fascist political power. The 'December gang' of Louis Napoleon was the counterpart of the small secret revolutionary organisation of the French working class of the time, whereas the Fascist Party is the counter-revolutionary equivalent of the Communist Party of Soviet Russia. In contrast to the Napoleonic movement, therefore, it has been from the outset a broad mass organisation. This makes it stronger in certain respects, but also intensifies the internal contradictions between the social interests of this mass following and the interests of the dominant classes which it has to serve . . .

. . . The open dictatorship of capital can take diverse forms in different countries. Certain features will be the same, others will be different. It is impossible to construct them theoretically in advance. However the forms of the open dictatorship of the bourgeoisie are not arbitrary; they cannot occur in just any situation of class struggle or just any configuration of class relations. They are bound up with very specific class relations and situations of class struggle, which have been outlined above.

There is a fairly widespread endeavour today among the bourgeoisie of the developed capitalist countries to dismantle and constrict the parliamentary system, and to construct stronger political guarantees for bourgeois domination. Such tendencies are particularly apparent in such advanced capitalist countries as England, Germany and France which have experienced social and economic convulsions to a greater or lesser degree as a consequence of the war. Their movement is in the direction of fascism, and can lead in critical situations to forms of the open dictatorship of capital. But these are not necessarily identical with fascism.

In this context it is necessary to make a further clarification. The undermining of the bourgeois parliamentary regime takes place step by step, and its chief agent is the bourgeoisie itself. Marx's *Eighteenth Brumaire* delineates this process in its individual stages. But the establishment of the open dictatorship itself can take place only through a decisive leap, a *putsch* or a *coup d'état*, in which the bourgeoisie itself is the passive element. Its part is to create the condition for its own social 'salvation' and political violation, whereas the violation itself is effected by the hero of the putsch or coup d'état. The individual or organisation necessary for the purpose is always found when the need arises, and it is the bourgeoisie that promotes the appropriate organisation either actively or passively itself.

The Noske regime in Germany was undoubtedly a regime of open counter-revolutionary violence, but the form of the state was not a fascist one. The Noske experiment was no 'autonomisation of the executive'. Nevertheless, in establishing a regime of the sword, it led to an attempt in this direction. This attempt on the part of the military executive power, the Kapp *putsch*, in fact failed.

23 So-called Social-fascism, *August Thalheimer*

In this piece written in 1929 for the KPO journal *Gegen den Strom*, Thalheimer uses the categories developed in his analysis of Bonapartism to provide a critique of 'social-fascism'.

For weeks now the cry of 'social-fascism' has been running wild in the official Party press and Party speeches. At first it could be understood merely as a mindless exaggeration, appropriate to the new line whereby an intensified campaign was initiated against reformism, in the form simply of coining and giving currency to more extreme slogans. In time, however, people experienced an abnormal urge to make the word actually mean something. And so there developed that silly analysis according to Heinz Neumann and Hermann Remmele, a theory or philosophy of 'social-fascism', which is a perfect example of the complete incapacity of our puny theoreticians to understand even the ABC of actual class relations in Germany and their line of development.[22]

In the chatter about 'social-fascism' only the phrase is new. The substance is merely a rekindling of the old ultra-left embers of Social Democracy as the 'right' (or was it 'left'?) 'wing of fascism', which the fifth World Congress of the Communist International put into circulation under the patronage of Zinoviev and Stalin, and which Maslow and Ruth Fischer then seized on as the basis of their ultra-left tactic.[23] The Italian Communist Party, on the other hand, which had to cope with the real fascism, and which knew from the plain facts that it is absurd to equate fascism and reformism in practice, especially fascism in its fully developed form as a ruling power, ignored this nonsense altogether . . .

The role of the bourgeois parties, including Social Democracy, in preparing the way for fascism, does not consist in transforming themselves into elements of the fascist party, but in bringing parliament and themselves into discredit. This creates the favourable circumstances for the emergence of a fascist party, which carries out the verdict that they have pronounced on themselves – their own strangulation. You need only read Marx's account in the *Eighteenth Brumaire* to understand this process. The Bonapartist or fascist dictatorship is the dictatorship of large capital in terms of its *social content*. But in terms of its *political form*, it is a dictatorship *over* the big bourgeoisie and its parties. The big bourgeoisie indicates thereby, as Marx says, that its political rule is no longer compatible with its social domination.

Our 'official theoreticians' have the bourgeoisie politically abdicating and not abdicating simultaneously! They portray fascism as the *antithesis* of bourgeois-democratic parliamentarism and as its *substitute*, that is its *continuation* in a somewhat different form. This is the heart of the absurdity. Once more the long donkey's ears of parliamentary cretinism show themselves. This nonsense is duly expressed in its crudest form by the famous theoretician, Hermann Remmele . . . What is social-fascism according to Remmele? The fact that Grzesinski forbids demonstrations, and Severing uses section 48 when necessary?[24] Strange, then, that we have not heard of social-fascism any earlier. Ebert and Noske both made vigorous use of bayonets against the workers and also of section 48.[25] That was counter-revolutionary, but was no more fascism than it was Bonapartism when in June 1848 the French National Assembly under Caraignac had the Paris workers mown down with grapeshot.

What absurd confusion! The bayonet directed against the workers by a bourgeois parliament is undoubtedly a preparation for Bonapartism or fascism. But fascism only begins at the point when and where the bayonet becomes independent and turns its point against bourgeois parliamentarians as well. This is no gradual 'transition', whereby parliament transforms itself into its opposite; it is a sudden leap, in effect a *coup d'état*, whereby the previous owners of the bayonets are thrown to the ground by the new ones. These new owners, wherever they come from, cannot support themselves by a parliamentary-democratic ideology and its corresponding organisational forms; they have to fight this ideology and destroy the old political and economic mass organisations by means of a new one.

What practical consequences follow from this absurdity? The same as from social democracy as the 'left wing of fascism': it becomes impossible to mobilise the social-democratic workers, who still remain on the terrain of bourgeois democracy, against their leaders or against fascism; or to convince them that the workers' councils represent the real revolutionary counterpart to bourgeois parliamentarism. In the end it means complete isolation from the broad proletarian masses . . .

---

24 The Development of Fascism in Germany, *August Thalheimer*

The following piece, written after the resignation of the Social Democrats from the 'grand coalition' in March 1930 and the installation of Brüning's regime of 'emergency decrees', but before the first Nazi successes in the national elections of September, provides the framework for Thalheimer's subsequent analyses up to 1933.

(1) Foundations and Directions

. . . Our critic disputes the assertion that objective considerations are leading the German bourgeoisie from bourgeois democracy to fascist dictatorship. We contend that this transition is conditioned by the fact that parliamentary democracy rests on a situation in which the bourgeoisie combines the exploitation of the working class with specific concessions to them; and that the transition to fascist dictatorship depends upon its breaking with this system of concessions.

What are the objections of our critic? First, that even under a parliamentary democracy the bourgeoisie takes back concessions it has already made. Secondly, that even under a system of parliamentary democracy the German bourgeoisie still has abundant room for manoeuvre. Thirdly, that the bourgeoisie, which considers bourgeois democracy to be the most developed as well as the 'cheapest' political system, would only abandon it when it had no alternative left, since (and this is the real point here) it would never surrender voluntarily the political power of its own that it would thereby lose.

The following has to be said in answer:

(1) The German bourgeoisie has certainly dismantled a series of concessions that it was forced to make to the working class in the full flood of revolution, and done this under a parliamentary democracy as well. But it does not follow from this that it can continue the process indefinitely, and still maintain parliamentary democracy intact. At a certain point this becomes no longer possible. What is this point? It is precisely the point at which the democratic rights of the working class, which are also a concession granted to them, have to be revoked by the bourgeoisie, because their maintenance is no longer compatible with the rate of increase in economic exploitation that has become necessary. These rights include not only the conventional democratic rights of universal suffrage, freedom of the press and of assembly, but above all the right to form combinations and to withdraw labour, which is the very basis of the trade unions, the associations and the political organisations of the working class.

The question therefore presents itself, are the conditions at hand to induce the German bourgeoisie to do away with the democratic rights of the working class? The answer is that they are. The destruction of welfare policies and a 10–15 per cent reduction in general wage levels would indeed be incompatible with the continuance of the organisations and institutions of the working class in their present form. At the same time there can be no doubt that with the existing situation of the world economy and the role of German capital within it, the present taxation and tariff policy of the bourgeoisie is only a beginning, a prelude to the main act to follow, which will bring the destruction of welfare policies and a sweeping reduction of wage levels across the board.

World prices are falling. In German industry there is increasing support for strengthening its competitiveness on the world market by a general reduction in wage levels and internal costs, and at the same time closing off the home market more securely for itself by raising the tariff barrier. Increased agricultural tariffs, which could never have been pushed through without the approval of the industrialists, serve as a trailer for increased industrial tariffs, and are at the same time the willing price for the support of the *junkers* and large landowners against the working class. But to present the *junkers* with hundreds of millions and simultaneously to lighten the bourgeois tax burden by hundreds of millions is a sum far beyond the capacity of tax increases on the working masses alone to recoup. Welfare policies have to be dismantled and left in ruins. A further reason for dismantling them is to impose the planned wage reductions on the working class to their full extent.

These are the objective considerations which determine the bourgeois course towards fascism, and require the destruction of even those concessions to the working class without which bourgeois democracy cannot function, and of which bourgeois democracy itself is a part.

(2) The Social Democrats and the bourgeois-democratic press calculate that bourgeois democracy in general, and the grand coalition in particular, is much 'cheaper' than a fascist dictatorship or even a stage towards it such as the Brüning government. This calculation is a perfect example of vulgar economics. The fascist state apparatus will certainly be 'dearer' than the bourgeois-democratic one: the apparatus of repression has to be enlarged, the ruling fascist party has to be accommodated within the state, the *junkers* have to be fully paid off for their political help, and so on. Only the basic fact is overlooked that, despite the increase in the relative proportion of the cost of the state apparatus, the bourgeoisie can still emerge on the credit side of the total calculation if the stock of surplus value extracted from the working class, from which these costs are defrayed, increases still further. That is the whole point of the exercise.

Some figures will serve by way of illustration. Suppose the bourgeoisie 'saves' one billion marks on welfare policies, and increases its profits through wage reductions by a billion and a half. That is already $2\frac{1}{2}$ billion. Suppose at the same time it increases the cost of the state apparatus by a billion a year. It is still $1\frac{1}{2}$ billion to the good. And in addition the bourgeoisie will know how to secure for itself and its dependents an appropriate share of the increased spoils from the state. Thus the question of cost is a very superficial and quite inadequate argument on the side of bourgeois democracy.

(3) The bourgeoisie, so it will be said, never *voluntarily* surrenders its own political power to fascism. However, it is not a question of what it wants to do, but of what it is compelled to do under specific conditions — i.e. a question of where its own aims, and the consequences of the actions it undertakes to carry out these aims, lead it by virtue of their own internal logic. This does not necessarily correspond with the original subjective intention, and in fact mostly does not do so. The last thing the Italian bourgeoisie wanted when it encouraged the terrorist campaigns against the workers by the fascist bands was the rule of Mussolini and his fascists. It wanted the workers to be intimidated and subdued, and their organisations destroyed, not the rule of fascism. But to break the workers' organisations by systematic terror, it had to accept the creation, the arming and the militarisation of the fascist organisations as part of the bargain, as well as the acquiescence and support given to their activities by the civil and military authorities. The fascist march on Rome merely drew the accumulated credit from the account, and the logical consequences from the altered balance of power. This end result was never intended originally by the Italian bourgeoisie, but it was the inevitable consequences of its actions.

The last thing the SPD leadership wanted when it invoked Hindenburg's support to get the Young plan through parliament was a Hindenburg dictatorship. Yet this was its natural consequence. It hardly intended the strengthening of the fascist organisations when it was engaged in its systematic suppression of the Communist Party, but this was also the inevitable consequence.

Has the 'grand coalition' now become completely impossible? If no fundamental shift occurs in the balance of forces, it still remains possible, but only as an *interlude*. It is not merely a matter of theoretical interest, but of vital practical importance to make clear to the working class that, *if* it now fails to intervene decisively in the struggle for power, the logical development must run its course from the Brüning regime to the open, complete fascist dictatorship . . .

Our critic poses the question, whether the Communists should themselves abandon parliamentary democracy, refuse to defend it and devote themselves exclusively to the preparation of the proletarian dictatorship. To put the question in this way is mistaken. In the Kapp *putsch* the Communists defended bourgeois democracy against the Kapp putschists. In Russia in 1917 they defended the Kerensky Republic against Kornilov with weapons in their hands. In a conflict between fascists and the bourgeois Republic the Communists will not be neutral; in defending themselves against fascism they must also defend the bourgeois-democratic Republic against it. But it all depends *how* this is to be done.

Bourgeois democracy just cannot be defended by parliamentary means. Its defence requires the most energetic extra-parliamentary action by the working class as a class. It requires the working class to reinforce its own class position. It requires the working class itself to be armed, in order to be able to ward off the armed attacks of fascism against bourgeois democracy, seeing that the armed power of the state is today even less reliable as a defence against fascism than it was in the days of the Kapp *putsch*. It requires the working class to have an independent broad-based class leadership in the form of workers' councils, in order to employ its weapons against fascism purposefully and systematically, and with the necessary energy.

The question therefore is not: defence of bourgeois democracy *or* struggle for the proletarian dictatorship, but: the conquest of positions of strength for the struggle for the proletarian dictatorship, *as a result of* the defence of bourgeois parliamentary democracy against fascism. It is clear that, once bourgeois democracy, in the course of its own development, has produced forces which are willing to put an end to it by counter-revolutionary means, it can only be defended by forces which are ready to go beyond the existing situation, beyond bourgeois democracy itself. What is crucial is that the working class, in its struggle against fascism, should take the field as an independent class power, not as a subordinate appendage to the bourgeois democrats. It is for circumstances to determine in what forms and over what timescale the defence of bourgeois democracy actually passes over to the struggle for the proletarian dictatorship; this cannot be decided in advance . . .

Fascism's forward march objectively poses the alternative: fascist dictatorship or proletarian dictatorship? It puts the responsibility on the working class to create the subjective conditions for the struggle towards the proletarian dictatorship, and at an accelerated pace. But this is not yet to say whether the working class will actually succeed in creating these conditions effectively and in time. This crucially depends on the correct tactical and strategic leadership of the working class by its revolutionary party. Of course not everything depends on this, since there are objective as well as subjective factors involved. The only difference is that we can *influence* the subjective ones. It is therefore the task of the revolutionary party, while also taking an accurate account of the objective conditions at every point, to give special attention to the subjective conditions, to its own tactical and strategic line.

(2) Economic Preconditions and Political Consequences

... Fascism means the *destruction* of the democratic rights of the workers, their *complete* elimination, and the supremacy of the executive power. The *partial* elimination of the democratic rights of the workers, the *piecemeal* construction of the power of the executive is related to fascism as part is to whole, as preparation is to completion. How can anyone overlook this connection?

Not every reaction is fascism. The kind of reaction which leaves the bourgeois-parliamentary foundation unaltered is no fascism. This is what took place from 1926–8 and also in earlier years, namely the suppression of the working class with the means and on the basis of bourgeois democracy. This has already been demonstrated in our critique of the phrase 'social-fascism'. What we have now, however, is precisely the piecemeal and progressive demolition of this bourgeois-parliamentary foundation. This is not reaction pure and simple, this is not the familiar bourgeois-democratic reaction, but a very specific reaction in the direction of fascism.

Underlying Ernst Becker's position is apparently the unspoken assumption that the partial destruction of bourgeois democracy and of parliament cannot continue to the point of their complete destruction.[26] And underlying this is the further assumption that the bourgeoisie has both sufficient interest and enough power to keep this process within the confines of a partial destruction only. Here we come up against another fallacy. One of the necessary conditions for the full development of fascism is, according to Ernst Becker, 'the economic and political weakness of the bourgeoisie'. The mistake lies in the 'and', in the linking of the economic with the political strength and weakness of the bourgeoisie. It is precisely bourgeois economic strength, and the need to make this more secure, that has driven the class in a series of historical periods to renounce the direct exercise of political power in the form of bourgeois democracy, and to exercise its dictatorship *indirectly*. This is just what fascism is: one of the forms of the *open* but *indirect* dictatorship of the bourgeoisie.

Let me remind readers of two periods in the history of the German bourgeoisie. The first was after the revolution of 1848–9, when the German bourgeoisie devoted all its powers to the goal of material construction, but left the direct control of policy to the Hohenzollerns and their attendant *junkers* and bureaucracy. The second was the period from 1890–1914, a veritable period of *Sturm und Drang* for capitalism, which encompassed a colossal increase in the material power of the German bourgeoisie, but in which it likewise contented itself with handing over the government to the Hohenzollerns, the *junkers* and the bureaucracy, exercising its domination *indirectly*, by exerting influence on these elements 'from behind the scenes'. This system collapsed in the world war, and the German bourgeoisie got rid of it under the pressure of the defeat and the assaults of the working class.

A simple return to this system of abandoning the government to the *junkers* and their monarchical head, is no longer possible today. Hence the innovation that fascism provides: the counter-revolutionary yet outwardly revolutionary fascist *mass* organisation as an instrument of government. The counter revolutionary mass organisations are necessary as a counterweight to the mass organisations of the working class, which developed earlier on the soil of bourgeois democracy. They serve as an instrument for *smashing* the working class organisations, and replacing them with a counter-revolutionary formation . . .

As regards the tactical implications, it is my view that it would be opportunistic fatalism to wait passively for the development towards fascism; on the other hand it would be adventurism to attempt to create a revolutionary uprising against fascism by means of pistol shots. It is a matter simply of taking the first steps of extra-parliamentary mass action against the growing strength of fascism and fascist tendencies. To drive these tendencies back will depend entirely on the extent of such action and on the time scale within which it is successful. But it would be really dangerous fatalism to rely on forces from the bourgeoisie to stem the development towards fascism successfully. Instead we must recognise clearly that it is precisely the bourgeoisie which is assisting the development towards fascism, in part directly, in part indirectly, in part intentionally, in part against its own intentions.

Our analysis of the forces which are driving Germany towards fascism provides the strongest stimulus to action by the working class, because it shows that *only* the working class can be considered as providing any serious opposition to them. It would, however, really be childish to fix a date now for an anti-fascist uprising; that would be like taking a leap into mid-air. But to raise the question now of the first steps of extra-parliamentary mass action is absolutely essential; only when such action has emerged can the next stage develop. Yet these first steps of extra-parliamentary mass action can only be taken if the fascist danger and the forces promoting its development are recognised as *actual* and *immediate*, not if they are imagined as a vague possibility in the indefinite future . . .

---

25 The Danger of Fascism in Germany, *Leon Trotsky*

This extract, written immediately after the Nazi success in the elections of September 1930, sounds an urgent note of warning against the fascist danger.

. . . With every turn of the historic road, with every social crisis, we must over and over again examine the question of the mutual relations of the three classes in modern society: the big bourgeoisie, led by finance capital; the petty bourgeoisie, vacillating between the basic camps; and finally, the proletariat.

The big bourgeoisie, making up a negligible part of the nation, cannot hold power without the support of the petty bourgeoisie of the city and the village, that is, of the remnants of the old, and the masses of the new, middle classes. In the present epoch, this support acquires two basic forms, politically antagonistic to each other but historically supplementary: Social Democracy and fascism. In the person of the Social Democracy, the petty bourgeoisie, which follows finance capital, leads behind it millions of workers.

The *big German bourgeoisie* is vacillating at present; it is split up. Its disagreements are confined to the question: 'Which of the two methods of cure for the social crisis shall be applied at present?' The Social Democratic therapy repels one part of the big bourgeoisie by the uncertainty of its results, and by the danger of two large levies (taxes, social legislation, wages). The surgical intervention of fascism seems to the other part to be uncalled for by the situation and too risky. In other words, the finance bourgeoisie as a whole vacillates in the evaluation of the situation, not seeing sufficient basis as yet to proclaim an offensive of its own 'third period', when the Social Democracy is unconditionally replaced by fascism when, generally speaking, it undergoes a general annihilation for its services rendered. The vacillations of the big bourgeoisie — with the weakening of its basic parties — between the Social Democracy and fascism are an extraordinarily clear symptom of a pre-revolutionary situation. With the approach of a real revolutionary situation, these vacillations will of course immediately come to an end.

For the social crisis to bring about the proletarian revolution, it is necessary that, besides other conditions, a decisive shift of the petty-bourgeois classes occur in the direction of the proletariat. This will give the proletariat a chance to put itself at the head of the nation as its leader.

The last election revealed — and this is its principal symptomatic significance — a shift in the opposite direction. Under the impact of the crisis, the petty bourgeoisie swung, not in the direction of the proletarian revolution, but in the direction of the most extreme imperialist reaction, pulling behind it considerable sections of the proletariat.

The gigantic growth of National Socialism is an expression of two factors: a deep social crisis, throwing the petty-bourgeois masses off balance, and the lack of a revolutionary party that would today be regarded by the popular masses as the acknowledged revolutionary leader. If the Communist Party is the *party of revolutionary hope*, then fascism, as a mass movement, is the *party of counter-revolutionary despair*. When revolutionary hope embraces the whole proletarian mass, it inevitably pulls behind it on the road of revolution considerable and growing sections of the petty bourgeoisie. Precisely in this sphere, the election revealed the opposite picture: counter-revolutionary despair embraced the petty-bourgeois mass with such force that it drew behind it many sections of the proletariat.

How is this to be explained? In the past, we have observed (Italy, Germany) a sharp strengthening of fascism, victorious, or at least threatening, as the result of a spent or missed revolutionary situation, at the conclusion of a revolutionary crisis in which the proletarian vanguard revealed its inability to put itself at the head of the nation and change the fate of all its classes, the petty bourgeoisie included. This is precisely what gave fascism its peculiar strength in Italy. But at present, the problem in Germany does not arise at the conclusion of a revolutionary crisis, but just at its approach. From this, the leading Communist Party officials, optimists *ex officio*, draw the conclusion that fascism, having come 'too late', is doomed to inevitable and speedy defeat (*Die Rote Fahne*). These people do not want to learn anything. Fascism comes 'too late' in relation to old revolutionary crises. But it appears sufficiently early – at the dawn – in relation to the new revolutionary crisis. The fact that it gained the possibility of taking up such a powerful starting position *on the eve* of a revolutionary period and not at its conclusion, is not the weak side of fascism but the weak side of Communism. The petty bourgeoisie does not wait, consequently, for new disappointments in the ability of the Party to improve its fate; it bases itself upon the experience of the past, remembering the lesson of 1923, the capricious leaps of the ultra-left course of Maslow-Thälmann, the opportunist impotence of the same Thälmann, the clatter of the 'third period', etc.[27] Finally –

and this is the most important – its lack of faith in the proletarian revolution is nourished by the lack of faith in the Communist Party on the part of millions of Social Democratic workers. The petty bourgeoisie, even when completely thrown off the conservative road by circumstances, can turn to social revolution only when the sympathies of the majority of the working class are for a social revolution. Precisely this most important condition is still lacking in Germany, and not by accident.

The programmatic declaration of the German Communist Party before the elections was completely and exclusively devoted to fascism as the main enemy. Nevertheless, fascism came out the victor, gathering not only millions of semi-proletarian elements, but also many hundreds of thousands of industrial workers. This is an expression of the fact that in spite of the parliamentary victory of the Communist Party, the proletarian revolution as a whole suffered a serious defeat in this election – to be sure, of a preliminary, warning, and not decisive character. It can become decisive and will inevitably become decisive, if the Communist Party is unable to evaluate its partial parliamentary victory in connection with this 'preliminary' character of the defeat of the revolution as a whole, and draw from this all the necessary conclusions.

Fascism in Germany has become a real danger, as an acute expression of the helpless position of the bourgeois regime, the conservative role of the Social Democracy in this regime, and the accumulated powerlessness of the Communist Party to abolish it. Whoever denies this is either blind or a braggart.

In 1923, Brandler, in spite of all our warnings, monstrously exaggerated the forces of fascism. From the wrong evaluation of the relationship of forces grew a hesitating, evasive, defensive, cowardly policy. This destroyed the revolution. Such events do not pass without leaving traces in the consciousness of all the classes of the nation. The over-estimation of fascism by the Communist leadership created one of the conditions for its further strengthening. The contrary mistake, this very under-estimation of fascism by the present leadership of the Communist Party, may lead the revolution to a more severe crash for many years to come.

The danger becomes especially acute in connection with the

question of the *tempo* of development, which does not depend upon us alone. The malarial character of the political curve revealed by the election speaks for the fact that the tempo of development of the national crisis may turn out to be very speedy. In other words, the course of events in the very near future may resurrect in Germany, on a new historical plane, the old tragic contradiction between the maturity of a revolutionary situation on the one hand and the weakness and strategical impotence of the revolutionary party on the other. This must be said clearly, openly, and above all, in time.

---

26 For a Workers' United Front against Fascism, *Leon Trotsky*

In this piece, written in December 1931, Trotsky explains the kind of relationship Communists should enter into with Social Democrats in a united front.

. . . The thousands upon thousands of Noskes, Welses, and Hilferdings prefer, *in the last analysis*, fascism to Communism. But for that they must once and for all tear themselves loose from the workers. Today this is not yet the case. Today the Social Democracy as a whole, with all its internal antagonisms, is forced into sharp conflict with the fascists. It is our task to take advantage of this conflict and not to unite the antagonists against us.

The front must now be directed against fascism. And this common front of direct struggle against fascism, embracing the entire proletariat, must be utilized in the struggle against the Social Democracy, directed as a flank attack, but no less effective for all that.

It is necessary to show by deeds a complete readiness to make a bloc with the Social Democrats against the fascists in all cases in which they will accept a bloc. To say to the Social Democratic workers: 'Cast your leaders aside and join our "non-party" united front', means to add just one more hollow phrase to a thousand others. We must understand how to tear the workers away from their leaders in reality. But reality today is – the struggle against fascism. There are and doubtless will be Social Democratic workers who are prepared to fight hand in hand with the Communist workers against the fascists, regardless of the desires or even against the desires of the Social Democratic organizations. With such progressive elements it is obviously necessary to establish the closest possible contact. At the present time, however, they are not great in number. The German worker has been raised in the spirit of organization and of disclipline. This has its strong as well as its weak sides. The overwhelming majority of the Social Democratic workers will fight against the fascists, but – for the present at least – only together with their organizations. This stage cannot be skipped. We must help the Social Democratic workers in action – in this new and extraordinary situation – to test the value of their organizations and leaders at this time, when it is a matter of life and death for the working class.

The trouble is that in the Central Committee of the Communist Party there are many frightened opportunists. They have heard that opportunism consists of a love for blocs, and that is why they are against blocs. They do not understand the difference between, let us say, a parliamentary agreement and an ever-so-modest agreement for struggle in a strike or in defence of workers' print-shops against fascist bands.

Election agreements, parliamentary compromises concluded between the revolutionary party and the Social Democracy serve, as a rule, to the advantage of the Social Democracy. Practical agreements for mass action, for purposes of struggle, are always useful to the revolutionary party. The Anglo-Russian Committee was an impermissible type of bloc of two leaderships on one common political platform, vague, deceptive, binding no one to any action at all. The maintenance of this bloc at the time of the British General Strike, when the General Council assumed the role of strike-breaker, signified, on the part of the Stalinists, a policy of betrayal.

No common platform with the Social Democracy, or with the leaders of the German trade unions, no common publications, banners, placards! March separately, but strike together! Agree only how to strike, whom to strike, and when to strike! Such an agreement can be concluded even with the devil himself, with his grandmother, and even with Noske and Grzesinski. On one condition, not to bind one's hands.

It is necessary, without any delay, finally to elaborate a practical system of measures – not with the aim of merely 'exposing' the Social Democracy (before the Communists), but with the aim of actual struggle against fascism. The question of factory defence organizations and institutions, the question of arsenals that may be seized by the fascists, the question of measures in the case of an emergency, that is, of the coordination of the actions of the Communist and the Social Democratic divisions in the struggle, etc., etc., must be dealt with in this programme.

In the struggle against fascism, the factory councils occupy a tremendously important position. Here a particularly precise programme of action is necessary. Every factory must become an anti-fascist bulwark, with its own commandants and its own battalions. It is necessary to have a map of the fascist barracks and all other fascist strongholds, in every city and in every district. The fascists are attempting to encircle the revolutionary strongholds. The encirclers must be encircled. On this basis, an agreement with the Social Democratic and trade-union organizations is not only permissible, but a duty. To reject this for reasons of 'principle' (in reality because of bureaucratic stupidity, or what is still worse, because of cowardice) is to give direct and immediate aid to fascism.

A practical programme of agreements with the Social Democratic workers was proposed by us as far back as September 1930 (*The Turn in the Comintern and the German Situation*), that is, a year and a quarter ago. What has the leadership undertaken in this direction? Next to nothing. The Central Committee of the Communist Party has taken up everything except that which constitutes its direct task. How much valuable, irretrievable time has been lost! As a matter of fact, not much time is left. The programme of action must be strictly practical, strictly objective, to the point, without any of those artificial 'claims', without any reservations, so that every average Social Democratic worker can say to himself: what the Communists propose is completely indispensable for the struggle against fascism. On this basis, we must pull the Social Democratic workers along with us by our example, and criticize their leaders who will inevitably serve as a check and a brake. Only in this way is victory possible . . .

But it is necessary to *desire* this victory. In the meantime, there are among the Communist officials not a few cowardly careerists and fakers whose little posts, whose incomes, and more than that, whose hides, are dear to them. These creatures are very much inclined to spout ultra-radical phrases beneath which is concealed a wretched and contemptible fatalism. 'Without a victory over the Social Democracy, we cannot battle against fascism!' say such terrible revolutionists, and for this reason . . . they get their passports ready.

Worker-Communists, you are hundreds of thousands, millions; you cannot leave for anywhere; there are not enough passports for you. Should fascism come to power, it will ride over your skulls and spines like a terrific tank. Your salvation lies in merciless struggle. And only a fighting unity with the Social Democratic workers can bring victory. Make haste, worker-Communists, you have very little time left!

---

27 Lessons of the Italian Experience, *Leon Trotsky*

Trotsky here explores the theoretical errors which contributed to the victory of fascism in Italy, and shows them being repeated in Germany.

Italian fascism was the immediate outgrowth of the betrayal by the reformists of the uprising of the Italian proletariat. From the time the war ended, there was an upward trend in the revolutionary movement in Italy, and in September 1920, it resulted in the seizure of factories and industries by the workers. The dictatorship of the proletariat was an actual fact; all that was lacking was to organize it, and to draw from it all the necessary conclusions. The Social Democracy took fright, and sprang back. After its bold and heroic exertions, the proletariat was left facing the void. The disruption of the revolutionary movement became the most important factor in the growth of fascism. In September, the revolutionary advance came to a standstill; and November already witnessed the first major demonstration of the fascists (the seizure of Bologna).

True, the proletariat, even after the September catastrophe, was capable of waging defensive battles. But the Social Democracy was concerned with only one thing: to withdraw the workers from under fire at the cost of one concession after the other. The Social Democracy hoped that the docile conduct of the workers would restore the 'public opinion' of the bourgeoisie against the fascists. Moreover, the reformists even banked strongly upon the help of Victor Emmanuel. To the last hour, they restrained the workers with might and main from giving battle to Mussolini's bands. It availed them nothing. The Crown, along with the upper crust of the bourgeoisie, swung over to the side of fascism. Convinced at the last moment that fascism was not to be checked by obedience, the Social Democrats issued a call to the workers for a general strike. But their proclamation suffered a fiasco. The reformists had dampened the powder so long, in their fear lest it should explode, that when they finally and with a trembling hand applied a burning fuse to it, the powder did not catch . . .

In its politics as regards Hitler, the German Social Democracy has not been able to add a single word: all it does is repeat more ponderously whatever the Italian reformists in their own time performed with greater flights of temperament. The latter explained fascism as a postwar psychosis; the German Social Democracy sees in it a 'Versailles' or crisis psychosis. In both instances, the reformists shut their eyes to the organic character of fascism as a mass movement growing out of the collapse of capitalism.

Fearful of the revolutionary mobilization of the workers, the Italian reformists banked all their hopes on 'the state'. Their slogan was, 'Victor Emmanuel! Help! Intervene!' The German Social Democracy lacks such a democratic bulwark as a monarch loyal to the constitution. So they must be content with a president. 'Hindenburg! Help! Intervene!'

While waging battle against Mussolini, that is, while retreating before him, Turati let loose his dazzling motto, 'One must have the manhood to be a coward'. The German reformists are less frisky with their slogans. They demand, 'Courage under unpopularity (*Mut zur Unpopularität*)'. Which amounts to the same thing. One must not be afraid of the unpopularity which has been aroused by one's own cowardly temporizing with the enemy.

Identical causes produce identical effects. Were the march of events dependent upon the Social Democratic Party leadership, Hitler's career would be assured.

One must admit, however, that the German Communist Party has also learned little from the Italian experience.

The Italian Communist Party came into being almost simultaneously with fascism. But the same conditions of revolutionary ebb tide which carried the fascists to power served to deter the development of the Communist Party. It did not take account of the full sweep of the fascist danger; it lulled itself with revolutionary illusions; it was irreconcilably antagonistic to the policy of the united front; in short, it ailed from all the infantile diseases. Small wonder! It was only two years old. In its eyes fascism appeared to be only 'capitalist reaction'. The *particular* traits of fascism which spring from the mobilization of the petty bourgeoisie against the proletariat, the Communist Party was unable to discern. Italian comrades inform me that with the sole exception of Gramsci, the Communist Party wouldn't even allow of the possibility of the fascists seizing power. Once the proletarian revolution had suffered defeat, and capitalism had kept its ground, and the counter-revolution had triumphed, how could there be any further kind of counter-revolutionary upheaval? The bourgeoisie cannot rise up against itself! Such was the gist of the political orientation of the Italian Communist Party. Moreover, one must not let out of sight the fact that Italian fascism was then a new phenomenon, and only in the process of formation; it wouldn't have been an easy task even for a more experienced party to distinguish its specific traits.

The leadership of the German Communist Party reproduces today almost literally the position from which the Italian Communists took their point of departure: fascism is nothing else but capitalist reaction; from the point of view of the proletariat, the differences between diverse types of capitalist reaction are meaningless. This vulgar radicalism is the less excusable because the German party is much older than the Italian was at a corresponding period; and in addition, Marxism has been enriched now by the tragic experience in Italy. To insist that fascism is already here, or to deny the very possibility of its coming to power, amounts politically to one and the same thing. By ignoring the specific nature of fascism, the will to fight against it becomes inevitably paralysed.

The brunt of the blame must be borne, of course, by the leadership of the Comintern. Italian Communists above all others were duty-bound to raise their voices in alarm. But Stalin, with Manuilski, compelled them to disavow the most important lessons of their own annihilation.[28] We have already observed with what diligent alacrity Ercoli switched over to the position of passively waiting for the fascist victory in Germany . . .[29]

---

28 Bonapartism and Fascism, *Leon Trotsky*

This article, written in 1934, defines Bonapartism as a transitional regime, distinct from, though connected to, fascism.

The vast practical importance of a correct theoretical orientation is most strikingly manifested in a period of acute social conflict, of rapid political shifts, of abrupt changes in the situation. In such periods, political *conceptions* and *generalizations* are rapidly used up and require either a complete replacement (which is easier) or their concretization, precision or partial rectification (which is harder). It is in just such periods that all sorts of *transitional, intermediate* situations and combinations arise, as a matter of necessity, which upset the customary patterns and doubly require a sustained theoretical attention. In a word, if in the pacific and 'organic' period (before the war) one could still live on the revenue from a few ready-made abstractions, in our time each new event forcefully brings home the most important law of the dialectic: *the truth is always concrete.*

The Stalinist theory of fascism indubitably represents one of the most tragic examples of the injurious practical consequences that can follow from the substitution of the dialectical analysis of reality, in its every concrete phase, in all its transitional stages, that is, in its gradual changes as well as in its revolutionary (or counterrevolutionary) leaps, by abstract categories formulated upon the basis of a partial and insufficient historical experience (or a narrow and insufficient view of the whole). The Stalinists adopted the idea that in the contemporary period, finance capital cannot accommodate itself to parliamentary democracy and is obliged to resort to fascism. From this idea, absolutely correct within certain limits, they draw in a purely deductive, formally logical manner the same conclusions for all the countries and for all stages of development. To them, Primo de Rivera, Mussolini, Chiang Kai-shek, Masaryk, Brüning, Dollfuss, Pilsudski, the Serbian King Alexander, Severing, MacDonald, etc., were the representatives of fascism. In doing this, they forgot:

(A) That in the past, too, capitalism never accommodated itself to 'pure' democracy, always adding to it and sometimes replacing it with a regime of open repression:

(B) That 'pure' finance capitalism nowhere exists;

(C) That even while occupying a dominant position finance capital does not act within a void and is obliged to reckon with the other strata of the bourgeoisie and with the resistance of the oppressed classes;

(D) That, finally, between parliamentary democracy and the fascist regime a series of transitional forms, one after another, inevitably interposes itself, now 'peaceable', now by civil war.

And each one of these transitional forms, if we want to go forward and not be flung to the rear, demands a correct theoretical appraisal and a corresponding policy of the proletariat.

On the basis of the German experience, the Bolshevik–Leninists recorded for the first time the transitional governmental form (even though it could and should already have been established on the basis of Italy) that we called Bonapartism (the Brüning, Papen, Schleicher governments). In a more precise and more developed form, we subsequently observed the Bonapartist regime in Austria. The determinism of this transitional form has become patent, naturally not in the fatalistic but in the dialectical sense, that is, for the countries and periods where fascism, with growing success, without encountering a victorious resistance of the proletariat, attacked the positions of parliamentary democracy in order thereupon to strangle the proletariat.

During the period of Brüning–Schleicher, Manuilski–Kuusinen proclaimed: 'Fascism is already here'; the theory of the intermediate, Bonapartist stage they declared to be an attempt to paint over and mask fascism in order to make easier for the Social Democracy the policy of the 'lesser evil'. At that time the Social Democrats were called social fascists, and the 'left' Social Democrats of the Zyromsky–Marceau Pivert–Just type passed – after the 'Trotskyists' – for the most dangerous social fascists. All this has changed now. With regard to present-day France, the Stalinists do not dare to repeat: 'Fascism is already here'; on the contrary, they have accepted the policy of the united front, which they rejected yesterday, in order to prevent the victory of fascism in France. They have found themselves compelled to distinguish the Doumergue regime from the fascist regime. But they have arrived at this distinction as empiricists and not as Marxists. They do not even attempt to give a scientific definition of the Doumergue regime. He who operates in the domain of theory with abstract categories is condemned to capitulate blindly to facts.

And yet it is precisely in France that the passage from parliamentarism to Bonapartism (or more exactly, the first stage of this passage) has taken on a particularly striking and demonstrative character. It suffices to recall that the Doumergue government appeared on the scene between the rehearsal of the civil war by the fascists (February 6) and the general strike of the proletariat (February 12).[30] As soon as the irreconcilable camps had taken up their fighting positions at the poles of capitalist society, it wasn't long before it became clear that the adding machine of parliamentarism lost all importance. It is true that the Doumergue government, like the Brüning–Schleicher governments in their day, appears at first glance to govern with the assent of parliament. But it is a parliament that has abdicated, a parliament that knows that in case of resistance the government would dispense with it. Thanks to the relative equilibrium between the camp of counterrevolution that attacks and the camp of the revolution that defends itself, thanks to their temporary mutual neutralization, the axis of power has been raised above the classes and above their parliamentary representation. It was necessary to seek the head of the government outside of parliament and 'outside the parties'. The head of the government has called two generals to his aid. This trinity has supported itself on its right and its left by symmetrically arranged parliamentary hostages. The government appears not as an executive organ of the parliamentary majority, but as a judge-arbiter between two camps in struggle.

A government that raises itself above the nation is not, however, suspended in air. The true axis of the present government passes through the police, the bureaucracy, the military clique. It is a military-police dictatorship with which we are confronted, barely concealed with the decorations of parliamentarism. But a government of the sabre as the judge-arbiter of the nation – that's just what *Bonapartism* is.

The sabre by itself has no independent programme. It is the instrument of 'order'. It is summoned to safeguard what exists. Raising itself *politically* above the classes, Bonapartism, like its predecessor Caesarism, for that matter, represents *in the social sense*, always and at all epochs, the government of the strongest and firmest part of the exploiters; consequently, present-day Bonapartism can be nothing else than the government of finance capital, which directs, inspires and corrupts the summits of the bureaucracy, the police, the officers' caste and the press.

The 'constitutional reform', about which so much has been said in the course of recent months, has as its sole task the adaptation of the state institutions to the exigencies and conveniences of the Bonapartist government. Finance capital is seeking legal paths that would give it the possibility of each time imposing upon the nation the most suitable judge-arbiter with the forced assent of the quasi-parliament. It is evident that the Doumergue government is not the ideal of a 'strong government'. More suitable candidates for a Bonaparte exist in reserve. New experiences and combinations are possible in this domain if the future course of the class struggle is to leave them enough time.

In prognosticating, we are obliged to repeat what the

Bolshevik–Leninists said at one time about Germany: the political chances of present French Bonapartism are not great; its stability is determined by the temporary and, at bottom, unsteady equilibrium between the camps of the proletariat and fascism. The relation of forces of these two camps must change rapidly, in part under the influence of the economic conjuncture, principally in dependence upon the quality of the proletarian vanguard's policy. The collision between these two camps is inevitable. The measuring time of the process will be calculated in months and not in years. A stable regime could be established only after the collision, depending upon the results.

Fascism in power, like Bonapartism, can only be the government of finance capital. In this *social* sense, it is indistinguishable not only from Bonapartism but even from parliamentary democracy. Each time, the Stalinists made this discovery all over again, forgetting that *social* questions resolve themselves in the domain of the *political*. The strength of finance capital does not reside in its ability to establish a government of any kind and at any time, according to its wish; it does not possess this faculty. Its strength resides in the fact that every nonproletarian government is forced to serve finance capital, or better yet, that finance capital possesses the possibility of substituting for each one of its systems of domination that decays, another system corresponding better to the changed conditions. However, the passage from one system to another signifies the *political crisis* that, with the concourse of the activity of the revolutionary proletariat, may be transformed into a social danger to the bourgeoisie. The passage of parliamentary democracy to Bonapartism itself was accompanied in France by an effervescence of civil war. The perspective of the passage from Bonapartism to fascism is pregnant with infinitely more formidable disturbances and consequently also revolutionary possibilities.

Up to yesterday, the Stalinists considered that our 'main mistake' was to see in fascism the petty bourgeoisie and not finance capital. In this case too they put abstract categories in place of the dialectics of the classes. Fascism is a specific means of mobilizing and organizing the petty bourgeoisie in the social interests of finance capital. During the democratic regime, capital inevitably attempted to inoculate the workers with confidence in the reformist and pacifist petty bourgeoisie. The passage to fascism, on the contrary, is inconceivable without the preceding permeation of the petty bourgeoisie with hatred of the proletariat. The domination of one and the same superclass, finance capital, rests in these two systems upon directly opposite relations of oppressed classes.

The political mobilization of the petty bourgeoisie against the proletariat, however, is inconceivable without that social demagogy, which means playing with fire for the big bourgeoisie. The danger to 'order' of the unleashed petty-bourgeois reaction has just been confirmed by the recent events in Germany. That is why, while supporting and actively financing reactionary banditry, in the form of one of its wings, the French bourgeoisie seeks not to push matters to the point of the political victory of fascism, but rather only to establish a 'strong' power, which, in the last analysis, is to discipline the two extreme camps.

What has been said sufficiently demonstrates how important it is to distinguish the Bonapartist form of power from the fascist form. Yet, it would be unpardonable to fall into the opposite extreme, that is, to convert Bonapartism and fascism into two logically incompatible categories. Just as Bonapartism begins by combining the parliamentary regime with fascism, so triumphant fascism finds itself forced not only to enter into a bloc with the Bonapartists but, what is more, to draw closer internally to the Bonapartist system. The prolonged domination of finance capital by means of reactionary social demagogy and petty-bourgeois terror is impossible. Having arrived in power, the fascist chiefs are forced to muzzle the masses who follow them by means of the state apparatus. By the same token, they lose the support of broad masses of the petty bourgeoisie. A small part of it is assimilated by the bureaucratic apparatus. Another sinks into indifference. A third, under various banners, passes into opposition. But while losing its social mass base, by resting upon the bureaucratic apparatus and oscillating between the classes, fascism is regenerated into Bonapartism. Here, too, the gradual evolution is cut into by violent and sanguinary episodes. Differing from prefascist or *preventive Bonapartism* (Giolitti, Brüning–Schleicher, Doumergue, etc.), which reflects the extremely unstable and short-lived equilibrium between the belligerent camps, *Bonapartism of fascist origin* (Mussolini, Hitler, etc.), which grew out of the destruction, the disillusionment and the demoralization of the two camps of the masses, distinguishes itself by its much greater stability.

The question 'fascism or Bonapartism?' engendered certain differences on the subject of the Pilsudski regime among our Polish comrades. The very possibility of such differences testifies best to the fact that we are dealing not with inflexible logical categories but with living social formations that represent extremely pronounced peculiarities in different countries and at different stages.

Pilsudski came to power at the end of an insurrection based upon a mass movement of the petty bourgeoisie and aimed *directly* at the domination of the traditional bourgeois parties in the name of the 'strong state'; this is a fascist trait characteristic of the movement and of the regime. But the specific political weight, that is, the mass of Polish fascism, was much weaker than that of Italian fascism in its time and still more so than that of German fascism; to a much greater degree, Pilsudski had to make use of the methods of military conspiracy and to put the question of the workers' organizations in a much more circumspect manner. If suffices to recall that Pilsudski's coup d'état took place with the sympathy and the support of the Polish party of the Stalinists. The growing hostility of the Ukrainian and Jewish petty bourgeoisie towards the Pilsudski regime made it, in turn, more difficult for him to launch a general attack upon the working class.

As a result of such a situation, the oscillation between the classes and the national parts of the classes occupied and still occupies with Pilsudski a much greater place, and mass terror a much smaller place, than in the corresponding periods with Mussolini or Hitler; there is the Bonapartist element in the Pilsudski regime. Nevertheless, it would be patently false to compare Pilsudski to Giolitti or to Schleicher and to look forward to his being relieved by a new Polish Mussolini or Hitler. It is methodologically false to form an image of some 'ideal' fascism and to oppose it to this real fascist regime that has grown up, with all its peculiarities and contradictions, upon the terrain of the relationship of classes and nationalities in the Polish state. Will Pilsudski be able to lead the action of destruction of the proletarian organizations to the very end? The logic of the situation drives him inevitably on this path, but the answer depends not upon the formal definition of 'fascism' as such but upon the true relationship of forces, the dynamics of the political processes taking place in the masses, the strategy of the proletarian vanguard and, finally, the course of events in Western Europe and, above all, in France.

History may successfully inscribe the fact that Polish fascism was overthrown and reduced to dust before it succeeded in finding for itself a 'totalitarian' form of expression.

We said above that Bonapartism of fascist origin is incomparably more stable than the preventive–Bonapartist experiments to which the big bourgeoisie resorts in the hope of avoiding fascist bloodletting. Nevertheless, it is still more important – from the theoretical and practical point of view – to emphasize that *the very fact of the regeneration of fascism into Bonapartism signifies the beginning of its end.* How long a time the withering away of fascism will last, and at what moment its malady will turn into agony, depends upon many internal and external causes. But the fact that the counter-revolutionary activity of the petty bourgeoisie is quenched, that it is disillusioned, that it is disintegrating, and that its attack upon the proletariat is weakening opens up new revolutionary possibilities. All history shows that it is impossible to keep the proletariat enchained with the aid merely of the police apparatus. It is true that the experience of Italy shows that the psychological heritage of the enormous catastrophe experienced maintains itself among the working class much longer than the relationship between the forces that engendered the catastrophe. But the psychological inertia of the defeat is but a precarious prop. It can crumble at a single blow under the impact of a powerful convulsion. Such a convulsion – for Italy, Germany, Austria and other countries – could be the success of the struggle of the French proletariat.

The revolutionary key to the situation in Europe and in the entire world is now, above all, in France!

29 Against the 'People's Front', *Leon Trotsky*

Trotsky denounces the Popular Front in France and the French–Soviet
non-aggression pact of 1935 as a betrayal of the working class to the
interests of French imperialism.

... Today, as everybody knows, these gentlemen have made an
antifascist 'People's Front; with the 'fascist' Daladier. The Stalinists,
who call themselves Communists, have stopped talking altogether
about the intervention of French imperialism into the USSR. On the
contrary, at present they perceive the guarantee of peace in the
military alliance between French capital and the Soviet bureaucracy.
Upon Stalin's order, Cachin, Thorez and Co. are summoning the
French workers today to support their national militarism, i.e. the
instrument of class oppression and of colonial enslavement. These
calumniators have exposed themselves quickly and mercilessly.
Yesterday they branded me as the ally of Daladier and the agent of
the French bourgeoisie, but today they themselves have actually
concluded an alliance with Daladier–Herriot and Laval and have
harnessed themselves to the chariot of French imperialism...[31]

To justify their social-patriotic turn, these gentlemen invoke the
necessity to 'defend the USSR'. This argument is utterly false. As is
very well known, even the idea of 'national defence' is only a mask by
means of which the exploiters cover up their predatory appetites and
bloody brawls for booty, turning, besides, their own nation into mere
cannon fodder. But if we Marxists have always maintained that the
imperialist bourgeoisie never can and never will defend the actual
interests of its own people, how, then, can we suddenly believe that it
is capable of defending the genuine interests of the USSR? Can
anyone for a moment doubt that at the first favorable opportunity,
French imperialism will set in motion all its forces in order to
overthrow socialized property in the USSR and restore private
property there? And if that is the case, then only traitors to the
working class are capable of painting up their own militarism, giving
direct or indirect, open or masked support to the French bourgeoisie

and its diplomacy. Stalin and his French flunkeys are precisely such traitors . . .

It would be absurd, of course, to deny the Soviet government the right to utilize the antagonisms in the camp of the imperialists or, if need be, to make this or that concession to the imperialists. The workers on strike also make use of the competition between capitalist enterprises and make concessions to the capitalists, even capitulate to them, when they are unable to gain victory. But does there follow from this the right of the trade-union leaders to cooperate amicably with the capitalists, to paint them up and to turn into their hirelings? No one will label as traitors the strikers who are forced to surrender. But Jouhaux, who paralyzes the class struggle of the proletariat in the name of peace and amity with the capitalists, we have not only the right but the duty to proclaim as a traitor to the working class. Between the Brest–Litovsk policy of Lenin and the Franco-Soviet policy of Stalin, there is the same difference as between the policy of a revolutionary trade unionist, who after a partial defeat is compelled to make concessions to the class enemy, and the policy of the opportunist, who voluntarily becomes the ally and flunkey of the class enemy . . .

The betrayal of Stalin and of the leadership of the Communist International is explained by the character of the present ruling stratum in the USSR; it is a privileged and an uncontrolled bureaucracy, which has raised itself above the people and which oppresses the people. Marxism teaches us that *existence determines consciousness*. The Soviet bureaucracy, above all, fears criticism, movement and risk; it is conservative; it greedily defends its own privileges. Having strangled the working class in the USSR, it has long since lost faith in the world revolution. It promises to build 'socialism in one country', if the toilers shut up, endure and obey.

To defend the USSR, the bureaucracy pins its hopes upon its political agility, upon Litvinov's diplomacy, the military alliance with France and Czechoslovakia, but not upon the revolutionary proletariat. On the contrary, it is afraid lest the French or Czech workers frighten the new allies by their careless actions. It sets as its task to put a brake upon the class struggle of the proletariat in the 'allied' countries. Thus, the source of Stalin's betrayal is the national conservatism of the Soviet bureaucracy, its outright hostility to the world proletarian revolution.

The consequences of Stalin's betrayal manifested themselves immediately in the cynical change in the policy of the French Communist Party, which is led not by the leaders elected by the workers but by agents of Stalin. Yesterday these gentlemen babbled about 'revolutionary defeatism' in event of war. Today they have assumed the standpoint of 'national defence' . . . in the interests of securing peace. They repeat word for word the formulas of capitalist diplomacy. The imperialist vultures, of course, have always stood for 'peace'; they all conclude alliances, increase armies, manufacture poison gases, cultivate bacteria – only and solely 'in the interests of peace'. He who says that 'the Franco-Soviet pact is the guarantee of peace' assumes the responsibility not only for the Soviet government but also for the French stock market, its general staff and the gases and bacteria of this staff.

L'Humanité writes that the French government will find itself 'under the *control* of the French workers'. But that is only a hollow phrase of miserable demagogues. Where and when has an oppressed proletariat 'controlled' the foreign policy of the bourgeoisie and the activities of its army? How can it achieve this when the entire power is in the hands of the bourgeoisie? In order to lead the army, it is necessary to overthrow the bourgeoisie and seize power. There is no other road. But the new policy of the Communist International implies the renunciation of this only road.

When a working-class party proclaims that in the event of war it is prepared to 'control' (i.e., to support) its national militarism and not to overthrow it, it transforms itself by this very thing into the domestic beast of capital. There is not the slightest ground for fearing such a party; it is not a revolutionary tiger but a trained donkey. It may be kept in starvation, flogged, spat upon – it will nevertheless carry the cargo of patriotism. Perhaps only from time to time it will piteously bray: 'For God's sake, disarm the fascist leagues'. In reply to its braying, it will receive an additional blow of the whip. And deservedly so!

30 The Spanish Revolution, the Communist Party and the Opposition, *Andrés Nin*

In this article, written in 1932, Nin criticises the irrelevance of Comintern strategy to Spanish conditions. He looks to a period of bourgeois democracy following Primo de Rivera's dictatorship, during which the immature revolutionary movement could grow in strength.

The fundamental error of the International and its 'executants' in Spain during Primo de Rivera's dictatorship lay in considering this to be a purely fascist regime which could be brought down only by the insurrection of the working classes and peasants. This erroneous conception distorted all the political views of the Party (as far as one can talk of views in referring to this Party since the lack of them was its distinguishing feature) and determined the tactics which isolated it completely from the masses.

The Party, loyal to the abstract schematism which in recent years has come to replace Marxist dialectics in the management of the International and its branches, confused all the harsh forms of bourgeois dictatorship with fascism, forgetting that the latter constituted something new which had risen up after the imperialist war and which was characterised by the utilisation of the petty bourgeoisie by capital as a mass movement for the destruction of the workers' organisations. Primo de Rivera's *coup d'état* was a typical *pronunciamiento* which was not based on the active collaboration of the petty bourgeoisie but rather on their indifference and weariness. And the regime was set up, a military dictatorship of which several examples can be found in nineteenth-century Spanish history. Obviously, deep down, *generally speaking*, both military dictatorships and fascist dictatorships – and parliamentary regimes too – strive after the same goal: to secure the domination of the bourgeoisie; but there are differences in the relationships and combinations of class which the revolutionary strategist must take into account if he wishes to prepare an effective policy based on the study of reality and not on the abstract.

These are the extremely important differences which the International's unfortunate theorists failed to take into consideration and which were the source of all their constant tactical errors. The plan could not have been simpler: on the one side the bourgeois dictatorship in all its forms (military dictatorship, fascism, parliamentary rule, 'social-fascism'); on the other, the revolutionary proletariat. The immediate consequence of this false position was the absolute impossibility for manoevre, the impossibility of neutralising the petty bourgeois masses and even gaining their sympathy, of using the democratic slogans to their own benefit, of assembling the popular masses for the revolution. The possibility of a bourgeois democratic regime succeeding Primo de Rivera's dictatorship was completely rejected. Primo de Rivera – the International said, and its Spanish followers repeated it parrot-fashion – can only be brought down by the working class and peasant masses. This erroneous concept was joined by the famous theory of the 'third period', which occurred to the unhappy Molotov (in the post-Leninist International 'hitting on an idea' has taken the place of Marxist analysis), according to which Europe had entered a period of immediate battles by the proletariat for power, when, on the contrary, capitalism was going through a stage of relative stabilisation and the working classes found themselves on the defensive. Assuming such a premise, could one conceivably consider the possibility of a democratic phase in Spain before the proletariat found itself in a position to seize power? Clearly, a mistaken appraisal of the situation was to lead to the wrong tactics; but what did it matter as long as the 'principles' were saved? A plan is drawn up, an abstract formula launched and the facts have to adapt themselves to this plan and to this formula. And if this is not the case, so much the worse for the facts. Naturally, history follows its course and reality shows the unsoundness of the plan at every step; but this does not silence the International's bureaucrats. When the catastrophe is imminent the zealous 'executants' of the 'general line' will get the blame.

Under these circumstances it is not surprising that Primo de Rivera's fall – easy to foresee in the preceding months – should catch the Party completely unawares. Things were not happening as they had been laid down in the International's plan. Primo de Rivera, ignoring the wise forecasts of Stalinist augurs, had decided to leave without waiting for the insurrection of the working classes and the peasants to throw him out. The Party's bureaucrats were taken completely by surprise. If they had been revolutionary Marxists and not poor civil servants with no other desire than to serve and please their superiors, they would have corrected the error which was staring them in the face, and fitted their tactics to objective reality. But Moscow stuck to its guns; Manuilski, the official on duty for affairs in the Latin countries, said that the political developments in Spain were less important than any strike in a European country, and the Spanish Stalinists, instead of surrendering to reality, declared that nothing had happened and that the only news was that one general had replaced another.

It was obvious, however, that 'something' had happened, and something very important. Primo de Rivera's fall, and his replacement by a regime such as that represented by Berenguer's government was easily foreseeable by anyone who did not have their political vision blurred by bureaucratic schematism. The reader will allow me to quote a lengthy extract from my booklet *El proletariado español ante la revolución*, as incontestable proof that the Communist opposition of the left had seen this fundamental question far more clearly than the Party.

Here is what I said:

Primo de Rivera was replaced by General Berenguer. Some members of the revolutionary camp, who unfortunately have abandoned the Marxist methods of analysis of objective situations declared that in Spain 'nothing had happened', that the situation remained the same as before. This conclusion was erroneous, a logical consequence of a completely incorrect conception which had taken hold in certain sectors of the Communist movement and which consisted in maintaining that the military dictatorship could not be brought down except by the violent action of the working masses, who would in turn destroy bourgeois rule. Since the facts turned against this plan there was no alternative but to say that *nothing had happened*.

Experience has shown how profoundly mistaken this conception was. As Lenin used to say, 'In reality there are no hopeless situations for the bourgeoisie'. Capitalism is still strong and can still fall back on infinite resources. It is obvious that if the workers' movement had not been in the disorganised state of ideological confusion in which it found itself at the time of Primo de Rivera's fall, that if at that moment a big Communist party had existed capable of leading and guiding the actions of the masses, the bourgeoisie would have been denied the possibility of operating, and the working classes would have seized power. But these factors were missing, and because of the circumstances set out above the possibility of a new attempt at democracy arose. This question is extremely important, because it is found in analogous if not identical form in other countries, principally in Italy. There are Communists in Italy who maintain that there is no possibility of a new bourgeois democracy in that country. If this is true as a general view in the sense that democratic forms of bourgeois domination cannot resolve the internal contradictions of capitalist rule it is certainly not true with respect to the immediate outlook. Whether Mussolini's fascist regime is replaced by a bourgeois-democratic regime or by a proletarian dictatorship, depends on the correlation of social forces at the time that fascism crumbles. If at that moment the Italian Communist Party has not won the hegemony in the upheaval of the large popular masses in the country, the possiblity arises of a new period, whether it be brief or lengthy, of bourgeois-democratic rule, supported by the petty bourgeoisie and the democratic illusions of the proletariat.

Spanish experience has shown the possibility of this variant. At the time of Primo de Rivera's fall, the petty-bourgeois masses, called upon to play an extraordinarily important role, were unable to follow the working-class revolutionary party simply because this, in reality, did not exist. Because of this, big opportunities arose for the development of the democratic demagogy. The situation was, however, so confused that the direct step to democratic rule was dangerous and impossible. The reader will allow me to quote a passage from an article published by me on the eve of the fall of the military dictatorship in a foreign magazine. In this article I said:

'When the time comes for the dictatorship to prepare to leave and look for a successor, there are neither parties nor men, and – as Cambó rightly observes in his book on dictatorships – organised parties and disciplined forces to govern are lacking, and along with the dictatorship political parties or forces have either disappeared altogether or have become greatly reduced in size'.

The industrial bourgeoisie, of which Cambó is the visible head, does not constitute an exception in this sense. The Regionalist League, so strong in former days, hardly exists as an organisation. But even if, by taking advantage of the constitutional regime, it managed to reconstitute its forces, which is not impossible, it would not be in a position to take on the full responsibility of power . . . Objectively the necessary premises for a revolution exist. But at the present moment there is no organised political force in Spain, neither among the industrial bourgeoisie, nor among the working classes, capable of taking the power into its hands.

---

31 The Political Situation and the Tasks of the Proletariat, *Andrés Nin*

Nin's critique of the popular front strategy in Spain, and the Communist Party's role in it, was intended to provide the basis for a discussion on political strategy at the POUM national conference in June 1937. The Party was outlawed before it could take place.

(I)

The events which have taken place in Spain since the POUM's constitutional congress which was held in Barcelona on the 29 September 1935 have confirmed that the fundamental position of our Party, in declaring that the battle is not between bourgeois-democracy and fascism but between fascism and socialism, and in classifying our revolution as social-democratic, was completely accurate.

The 1931–5 experience had more than shown the inability of the bourgeoisie to resolve the fundamental problems of the bourgeois-democratic revolution and the need for the working classes to put themselves resolutely at the head of the emancipation movement to carry out the democratic revolution and to start the socialist revolution. The persistence of democratic illusions and of the organic alliance with the republican parties, was to lead fatally to the reinforcement of the reactionary positions and, in the near future, to the triumph of fascism as the only escape from a capitalist regime incapable of resolving its internal contradictions within the frame of bourgeois-democratic institutions.

The lesson from Asturias, where the proletariat, on resolutely taking over the leadership of the movement in October 1934 delivered a mortal blow to the reaction, and that from Catalonia, where at the same time the incapacity and irresponsibility of the petty-bourgeois parties was evident once again, was not made the most of, as a result of the absence of a large revolutionary party. The Socialist and Communist parties, instead of taking advantage of the October lesson by pushing the workers' alliance, which had given such splendid results in Asturias, and channelling all the forces towards securing the hegemony of the working classes, subjected the proletariat again, through the popular front, to the bourgeois republican parties, which after their resounding failure in October had virtually disappeared from the political scene.

The period immediately preceding the elections of 16 February was characterised by the galvanisation of the republican parties, thanks to the efforts of Socialists and official Communists, and by a certain rebirth of democratic illusions among the masses, who however, seemed to be moved more by the vehement desire of obtaining amnesty for the prisoners and convicts of October than through confidence in the republican parties. This wish was so unanimous, and the movement so overpowering, that our Party had no choice but to join it, while retaining its personality and independence intact, and exercising a harsh and pitiless criticism of the republican parties. This tactic, which saved us from isolation, allowed us to get closer to the broad masses, until then out of our reach, and disseminate our principles among them.

The conduct of the leftist republicans in power, after 16 February, was absolute confirmation of our forecasts. From the beginning, a deep split was established between the government and the powerful drive of the masses who forced it to issue the amnesty decree and started a vast and profound movement of strikes. From below rapid and energetic action was demanded together with a policy of revolutionary achievements and of rigorous measures against the reaction, which was growing more insolent every day. From above a policy of passivity, of fatal leniency was carried out, a policy whose motto seemed to be not to change anything, not to startle anybody nor to damage the interests of the exploiting classes. The result of this policy was the military–fascist uprising of 19 July 1936. On that early morning in July the explosions of cannons and the crackle of machine guns woke the workers who still harboured illusions of democracy from their sleep. The electoral victory of 16 February had not cleared up the problem created in our country. The fascist reaction resorted to more forceful arguments than the ballot paper. Making use of the privileged position granted them by the republican government itself by keeping them in the most important strategic positions, the vast majority of army officers, at the service of the reactionary classes, started the Civil War.

(II)

The military–fascist uprising provoked a formidable reaction among the working classes, who threw themselves resolutely into battle and, in spite of passivity, in some cases, and betrayal, in others, of the republican parties, whose official representatives refused to hand over arms to the workers, they crushed the insurrection in the most important industrial centres of the country.

This resolute intervention by the workers had enormous political consequences. The bourgeois organs of power were, in reality, destroyed. Revolutionary committees were set up everywhere. The permanent army collapsed and was replaced by the militias. The workers took possession of the factories. The peasants took over the land. Convents and churches were destroyed by the purifying fires of the revolution. In a few hours, or at most in a few days, the workers and peasants, by direct revolutionary action solved the problems which the republican bourgeoisie had not been able to solve in five years – that is to say, the problems of the democratic revolution – and they started the socialist revolution with the expropriation of the bourgeoisie.

For a certain length of time the organs of bourgeois power were no more than a shadow. The revolutionary committees exercised the real power, forming a dense network in all the regions not occupied by the rebels.

However, in this initial period the revolutionary drive was much stronger in Catalonia than in Spain. Catalonia went undoubtedly to the head of the revolution because thanks to the influence of the POUM, the CNT, and the FAI who did not join up with the popular front, democratic republican opportunism had penetrated less into the working masses.

The fascist insurrection then, destined principally to suffocate the working class revolutionary movement, accelerated it very rapidly, giving the class struggle an unheard-of violence, and squarely posing the problem of power: either fascism or socialism. What was intended as a preventitive counter-revolution became a proletarian revolution, with all the distinguishing features of the same: slackening of bourgeois state mechanism, decline of the army, of the coercive forces of the state, and of the judicial institutions, arming of the working classes, who attacked and damaged the right to private property; direct intervention by the peasants who expropriated the landowners, and finally the conviction, on the part of the exploiting classes, that their domination had ended.

In the first weeks following 19 July, the conviction that the past could not return, that the democratic Republic had been overcome, was widespread. And the drive of the revolution was so strong that the petty-bourgeois parties themselves proclaimed the end of capitalist rule and the necessity of undertaking the socialist transformation of Spanish society.

The only immediate way out of the situation was to co-ordinate the thrust of the masses into creating a strong power, based on the organisms which had come out of the entrails of the revolution, as a direct expression of the wishes of those who had played the leading roles in the fight against fascism. This strong power could be none other than a government of the workers and peasants. This position, supported by the POUM from the moment at which the character of the fight became clear, ran up against opposition from all the popular front parties, and above all from the Communist Party, and against the indecision of the CNT, whose anarchist ideology prevented it realising the fundamental and decisive importance of the power problem.

Meanwhile, with the help of a tenacious and systematic campaign two ideas with unfortunate consequences for the victorious development of the working-class struggle, were breaking through. The first of these ideas was expressed in these terms: 'First win the war, then the revolution will look after itself'. According to the second, which is a direct consequence of the first, the workers and peasants are fighting the present war to maintain the parliamentary democratic Republic, and therefore, one cannot talk of a proletarian revolution. Later this idea underwent an unsuspected change: the dramatic battle which caused great bloodshed and ruined the country, became 'a war for national independence and the defence of the homeland'.

From the very first, our Party adopted a stance of resolute opposition in the face of these counter-revolutionary ideas.

(III)

The formula 'First win the war, then the revolution will look after itself' is basically incorrect. In the battle which is developing in Spain at the present moment, war and revolution are not only two inseparable terms, but synonyms. Civil war, a more or less prolonged state of the direct conflict between two or more classes of society, is one of the manifestations, the sharpest, of the fight between the proletariat, on the one hand, and the grande bourgeoisie and the landowners on the other, who, frightened by the revolutionary advance of the proletariat, are trying to establish a regime of bloody dictatorship, which will consolidate the privileges of their classes. The fight on the front lines of battles is no more than an extension of the fighting at the rear. War is a form of politics. This politics is what guides war in every case. The armies always defend the interests of a particular class. It is a case of knowing whether the workers and peasants at the front are fighting for the bourgeois order or for a socialist society. War and revolution are as inseparable at the present moment in Spain as they were in France in the eighteenth century and in Russia in 1917–20. How can we separate war from revolution, when war is no more than the violent culmination of the revolutionary process which has been developing in our country from 1930 to the present day?

In reality, the formula: 'First win the war . . .' conceals the effective intention of frustrating the revolution. Revolutions have to be carried out when the circumstances are favourable, and these circumstances are rarely offered to us by history. If we do not take advantage of the times of greatest revolutionary tension, the class enemy will gradually reconquer positions and will end up by strangling the revolution. Nineteenth century history, and the more recent post-war history (Germany, Austria, Italy, China, etc.) offers us numerous examples in this sense. Putting off the revolution until after the war is won is equivalent to leaving the hands of the bourgeoisie free so that, by taking advantage of the decrease in revolutionary tension, they can re-establish their mechanism of oppression in order to systematically and progressively prepare for the restoration of capitalist rule. War – we have already said – is a form of politics. Political regimes always serve a particular class of which they are the expression and the instrument. While the war goes on policies must be made: to serve whom; which class interests? This is the whole question. And the guarantee of a sure and rapid victory at the front lies in strong revolutionary policies at the rear, capable of inspiring the fighters with the necessary spirit and confidence for the battle; capable too, of promoting the revolutionary solidarity of the international proletariat, the only one on which we can rely, to create a solid war industry to rebuild the economy, upset by the civil war, on socialist foundations, to form an efficient army at the service of the proletarian cause, which is that of civilised humanity. The instrument of these revolutionary policies can be none other than a workers' and peasants' government.

(IV)

In the whole of Europe since the imperialist war just as in Russia in 1917, the biggest obstacle opposing the victorious advance of the proletarian revolution is reformism, a bourgeois agent in the working-class movement. But paradoxically it happens that the most characteristic exponent of castrating reformism in our country is the Communist Party of Spain itself and its subsidiary the Unified Socialist Party of Catalonia, both affiliated to an international one, the Communist International which sprang up as a consequence of the ideological and organic rupture with reformism. A prisoner of Soviet bureaucracy, which has turned its back on the international proletarian revolution to place all its hopes on the 'democratic' countries and the League of Nations, official communism has definitively abandoned the revolutionary policies of class to turn towards an alliance with the bourgeois-democratic parties (popular front) and to prepare the masses psychologically for the next world war. Hence the slogan: 'Fight for national independence', which translated into the language of international politics means 'subordination of revolutionary Spain to the interests of the Franco-British imperialist bloc', of which the USSR is also a member. The fateful consequences of these policies have not taken long to make themselves felt: speculating with the difficulties of the war and the possible international complications, reformism, efficiently supported by the representatives of Stalinist bureaucracy, who in their turn, have speculated with the support of the USSR, has managed to systematically undermine the revolutionary conquests, preparing the ground for the counter-revolution. Our elimination from the *Generalidad* government, the attempts at forming a popular 'democratic' and 'neutral' army, the suppression of the rearguard militias and the restoration of law and order on the basis of re-establishment of the old mechanism, and the censorship of the press, are the most important stages of this counter-revolutionary process, which will continue inflexibly until the revolutionary movement is totally crushed if the Spanish working classes do not decide to react quickly and vigorously, reconquering the positions taken in the days of July and advancing the socialist revolution.

In the present, unequivocally revolutionary situation the slogan 'fight for the parliamentary-democratic Republic' can serve no other interests than those of the bourgeois counter-revolution. Today more than ever, 'the word *democracy* is no more than a cover with which to stop the revolutionary people from rising up and attacking, freely, intrepidly, and on its own, the construction of the new society' (Lenin). As revolutionary Marxism has shown us, the democratic Republic is no more than a camouflaged form of bourgeois dictatorship. At the height of capitalism, when this represented a progressive factor, the bourgeoisie could allow itself the luxury of conceding a series of 'democratic' liberties – considerably limited and full of conditions, because of its economical and political domination – to the working classes. Today in the imperialist era, 'the final stage of capitalism', the bourgeoisie, in order to overcome its internal contradictions, is forced to resort to the establishment of regimes of brutal dictatorship (fascism) which destroy even the paltry democratic liberties. Under these circumstances, the world finds itself facing a fatal dilemma: either socialism or fascism. The 'democratic' regimes must inevitably be transient and inconsistent, with the added difficulty that by calming the workers and stripping them of their dreams, they are effectively preparing the ground for the fascist reaction.

In order to justify their monstrous betrayal of revolutionary Marxism, Stalinists argue that the democratic Republic that they propose will be a democratic Republic different from the rest, a 'popular' Republic from which the material base of fascism will have disappeared. That is to say, that they scandalously leave to one side the Marxist theory of the state as an instrument of domination of one class to fall into the Utopia of the democratic state which is 'above classes', at the service of the people, with the aim of deceiving the masses, and preparing the pure and simple consolidation of the bourgeois regime. A Republic from which the material base of fascism has disappeared, can be no more than a socialist Republic, since the material base of fascism is capitalism.

---

32 What is Fascism? *Ignazio Silone*

In this final chapter of his book, *Fascism*, published in 1934, Silone is concerned to distinguish fascism from other forms of reaction.

... It can seldom have happened that the opinions of contemporaries about a historical occurrence have been so diverse and mutually inconsistent as has been true of opinions about fascism over the past ten years or so, and that not only in respect of its political role, but its external characteristics as well. If we had only books, newspapers and journals to instruct us, we would not know whether we were concerned with a movement of large capitalists or petty bourgeois, of soldiers or workers, a reactionary or revolutionary movement, a transient or a permanent one. And all this in spite of the fact that fascism is no secret society, and does not inhabit the coast of Zanzibar.

These false opinions about fascism that are current, these misleading characterisations and interpretations, are to be explained first of all by the rapid development of fascism and by the contradictions that fascism itself embodies. Even when these views are mistaken and inadequate, they at least contain an element of truth, in so far as they relate to a particular stage of fascist development, or to fascism in a particular region, or only to the social composition of the fascist organisations, to its methods of struggle, or its ideology – whereas a genuinely historical judgement on fascism should take account of all these elements in their totality and in the contradictory rhythm of their mutual interconnectedness.

A further explanation for the conceptual confusion that prevails on the subject of fascism is undoubtedly to be found in the fact that the political commentators in the final analysis treat fascism simply from the standpoint of their own party. And in those countries experiencing a deep crisis the sphere of party organisation has been taken over by the bureaucratic apparatus at the expense of the political one. Tactical problems have crowded out the discussion of party programmes, and in their press and literature the requirements of agitation, which seeks immediate results, have replaced the critical activity of analysis, which seeks nothing if not the truth. *A la guerre comme à la guerre*. Even Marxism has not always escaped this degeneration in its own critical–analytical method. Agitation requires simplified concepts by its very nature, and such concepts become blunted very quickly. A political movement which seeks to grapple seriously with reality always therefore needs the check of a truly critical analysis. But thanks to this simplified way of thinking fascism has now become what Caesarism became in Marx's time: 'a dark night in which all cats are grey'. Just as Marx's contemporaries called every reactionary movement 'Caesarist', many of our contemporaries similarly treat fascism and reaction as mutually interchangeable concepts. Certainly the meaning of words is always a convention; and just as we could agree to call all fruit trees cherry trees, we could as easily call all the political formations of past, present and future by the name of fascism – absolutism and liberalism, parliamentarism and syndicalism, Social Democracy and communism. Yet even the laziest and least analytical of intellects will readily appreciate that a verbal confusion of this sort must lead directly to a confusion of understanding; or else that, once the word fascism has been deprived of its particular significance, it has to be accompanied by a specifying adjective in order to designate and make intelligible any form of political power that is different from true fascism. The differentiation of language is thus merely the product of the differences between things. Of course you can call the same thing by different names – that is the poet's style. But you cannot for long call two different things by the same name.

Fascism is not the only form that reaction takes at the present time. The tendency to dismantle democratic institutions, to restrict popular control of government and to make the preservation of the dominant class increasingly secure – this is the universal tendency in every capitalist country, including the expressly democratic ones. Underneath this general tendency, however, are to be found the most varied configurations of social forces, a fact that is fully explained by the Marxist theory of the uneven development of society.

The forms which reaction assumes are never arbitrary. In the last analysis they are always determined by the historical situation and by class relationships. We can divide the very different historical phenomena that are currently classified as fascist into three basic types:
(A) Military dictatorships.
(B) The reactionary consolidation of ancient state-forms, without the suppression of parliament or the abolition of the traditional party system.
(C) Fascist dictatorships.
Military dictatorship should not be confused with fascism.

Pronunciamentos and military dictatorships are to be found in all periods, even among pre-capitalist forms of government, whereas fascism is a phenomenon typical of our own time. Military dictatorships tends not to occur in an advanced capitalist country, in which there are strong political organisations and a numerous petty bourgeoisie, but rather in a backward country, in which the modern bourgeoisie is still weak, unorganised and divided into numerous individualist circles, and where the feudal elements are still strong and the army is the most powerful political organisation. In general a military dictatorship does not alter the social status quo, but performs a purely conservative function. It also shows itself incapable of establishing an organic equilibrium between the various branches of production, between industry and agriculture, between the feudal elements and the modern bourgeoisie, between foreign and domestic capital. In contrast, fascism is able to develop new forms of industrial and financial organisation under the direction of large scale capital, and thereby to push the concentration of capital to its very limits.

In backward countries the army forms the strongest line of defence against the so-called 'anarchy' of the popular masses and the 'corruption' of the ruling politicians. It can easily seize supreme power. The only difficulty that the authors of a *pronunciamento* have to fear is always the internal conflicts within the army, or more precisely within the officer corps. They have nothing to fear from the ruling political parties; a telephone call to the nearest barracks is sufficient to render them amenable. The route that fascism has to travel to win power is very much harder. Fascism arises from the dissolution of the established system of traditional parties, against which it is forced to wage a highly energetic political struggle. At the same time it fights with the most modern weapons of civil war against the workers' organisations for months, often for years before the issue is decided.

This is not to deny that there is also a militarist element in fascism, but it is not its basic one. The entire institutions of the established constitutional state (the army, police, judiciary, educational institutions) find themselves naturally driven to take part in the struggle for the fascist reorganisation of the state. But the character of fascist reorganisation is such that its basic features cannot be supplied by any of the institutions of the established constitutional state. Otherwise fascism would be superfluous, and superfluous also the subversion of the whole existing party system and the civil war that is long, hard, bloody and of uncertain outcome.

Another consideration is that in the major economically advanced countries, where universal military service is the norm, it is not so easy to use the army for political purposes as it is in more backward countries. There too, political life is not the privilege of a few cliques of politicians, but is a matter of mass involvement which immediately reflects itself in the army as well, in which not only the soldiers but often their officers belong to opposing political camps. This may also explain why, ever since the march on Rome, Mussolini has opposed too active an involvement of his officers in political life, and why he has prevented military demonstrations in support of fascism, repeating the old refrain about 'the army above parties'.

It is equally mistaken to confuse fascism with the reactionary consolidation of established institutions in the context of parliamentarism and under the leadership of the traditional conservative parties. The reactionary consolidation of established state forms is a general tendency of all bourgeois states, even those that are in no immediate danger because of the weakness of their workers' movement. Even in such countries, which are still hardly affected by the economic, social and political crisis, exceptional legislation has been passed against the workers' organisations, and antiquated laws that have fallen into disuse have been resurrected. Even here the authorities have little hesitation in employing the most brutal measures to suppress the political and economic movement of the working class. They have little hesitation either in abandoning legality when it comes to depriving the workers of the weapon of street demonstrations, or blocking the expansion of the Socialist or Communist press, or when necessary disbanding the workers' parties altogether and driving them into illegality. These have become the established methods in all the capitalist countries, even those where the crisis is not yet dangerous. What we have here is certainly a tendency towards fascism, but not yet fascism itself. Fascism comes later. In Italy Giolitti was responsible for an unprecedentedly ruthless suppression of the labour movement, without bothering himself in the slightest about legality. This was a preparation for fascism, but not yet fascism itself.

In Poland the representative of the large landowners, Witos, subjected the labour movement to a real reign of terror. For this reason his government was considered a fascist dictatorship. And it was this mistaken assessment that enabled the real fascism to develop and come to power under the slogan 'down with fascism'. It was not till a few years later that people realised Witos had prepared the way to fascism, but that he was not himself fascist. The Poles had to pay a very heavy price for this mistaken analysis with the *coup d'état* of Pilsudski. A similar error can occur in any country where the crisis has not yet reached the favourable point for the development of fascism, where the old system of traditional parties still keeps the petty-bourgeois masses in check, and the disruption of the workers does not yet threaten capitalist profit.

Events sufficiently prove that fascism is not a specifically Italian phenomenon, but an international one. Once we have demolished the view of those who see fascism everywhere, we have to combat even more decisively the view of those who regard fascism as a privilege of certain 'inferior' peoples.

The first aspect of any attempt to define fascism is the *chronological* one, involving an answer to the question: *when* did fascism first appear? Fascism originated in a few capitalist countries with relatively weak economies, where a unified national state was still a recent creation and lacked any rooted tradition among the masses; it originated immediately after the war, when the pressure from the proletarian movement was very strong, the whole social edifice was shaken to its foundations, the established system of historical parties was in disarray and broad strata of the small and middle bourgeoisie were in a state of panic. German fascism proves, however, that economic advance is insufficient to render a country immune from the fascist threat.

Without doubt the uneven development of different countries tells against any simultaneous occurrence of political phenomena across the whole globe. This fact has always encouraged the fanatical exponents of national particularity to regard every new political phenomenon as uniquely determined by the circumstances of a single country . . . In Hungary fascism occurred after the overthrow of the government of workers' councils. In Italy, Poland and Finland fascism developed after an unsuccessful onslaught by the revolutionary proletariat. In Germany and Austria fascism came after an abortive revolution and in the course of a crisis that convulsed all parties, including the workers' parties, to the core.

From the chronological point of view we arrive at the following two conclusions: (i) the only countries to escape a genuine fascist movement are those where capitalism is not yet seriously endangered; (ii) the prospect of an extension and aggravation of the capitalist crisis, together with the disintegration of the traditional bourgeois parties, and a prolongation sufficient to render the workers' parties impotent, contains all the ingredients for a further extension of fascism.

The second aspect of the attempt to define fascism is the *morphological* one, in answer to the question: 'In what *form* did fascism emerge?'

In its first phase fascism always presents itself as a patriotic movement. In Italy the first fascist recruits came on the one hand from the middle strata who saw themselves doomed to extinction by the capitalist crisis and rose against their traditional parties and institutions, on the other hand from strata of the working class who were disappointed in their revolutionary hopes and rose against the proletarian parties. This is a fact that can no longer be denied . . .

'The petty-bourgeoisie is an integral component of all revolutions in the making', Marx wrote in the *Eighteenth Brumaire*. Today we can add that it is also an integral component of all fascist movements. Yet one cannot explain this by reference to ideological factors, by the presence of some reactionary spirit 'inherent' in the middle strata – a myth that has definitely had its day. An explanation has to be sought instead in the class position of the petty bourgeoisie.

In the most advanced societies, Marx wrote to Annekov in respect of Proudhon, the situation of the petty bourgeois predisposes him towards both socialism and capitalism, i.e. he is dazzled by the expansion of power of the big bourgeoisie on the one side, yet he shares in the suffering of the people on the other. He is bourgeois and people simultaneously. At heart he prides himself on being neutral, on having found the true balance, albeit without falling into mediocrity. This petty bourgeois is the glorification of antithesis, since antithesis is the basis of his existence. He himself is nothing other than the personification of social contradiction.

In every social crisis the petty bourgeoisie is a potential supporter of both warring parties, reaction and revolution, without being conscious of the fact. When the two fundamental classes of society come into conflict, the petty bourgeois plunges into the fray as champion of the fatherland, of order, of civilisation, of the general interest 'standing above all' . . . for this reason he is easy prey for big capital. Yet it would be mistaken to imagine that the petty bourgeoisie is historically condemned to a condition of permanent opposition to the working classes, and that it could never become an ally of the socialist movement. This mistake was made in Italy in 1919. Of all the mistakes committed then it was the most fateful, and the one which helped fascism the most to its success.

First conclusion: the Fascist Party should not be confused with the traditional conservative parties, despite the fact that it arises from their dissolution. Its manner of emergence, its social foundations, its organisation, methods, ideology and leadership all make of it a new and characteristically contemporary kind of party. Second conclusion: fascism is not only and not primarily a movement of armed mercenaries; it is not only and not primarily a movement of white-guardists. It is a broad political movement of the masses. At its inception the majority of its supporters were unaware that it acted in the service of capitalism.

The third aspect to the definition of fascism is the *dialectical* one, in answer to the question; how does fascism develop and change? The historical conclusion that is demonstrated from this standpoint by every fascist party is this: nowadays it is impossible to fight the revolutionary workers' movement without falling prey to high finance. All fascist movements that have achieved power have confirmed this law. There is not one fascist party so far that has been able to avoid this fate. The support of high finance for the fascist cause inevitably brings in its wake the support of the whole traditional superstructure of society – all the established political parties and institutions, from the general staff to the church, from the judiciary to the universities . . .

First conclusion: the petty bourgeoisie can certainly provide the political leadership for any type of government, but it is unable as a class to shape any government decisively. Even fascism, the strongest movement that has ever emerged from the petty bourgeoisie, results in the open dictatorship of high finance and in an unprecedented repression of the petty bourgeoisie as a class. Second conclusion: there are no other historical possibilities available to the petty bourgeoisie than either the support of fascism or the support of the socialist movement.

The political immaturity of the labour movement has driven the petty bourgeoisie into the arms of capitalism in the post-war period, and helped fascism to victory. Those readers who have succeeded along with us in grasping the significance of the historical possibility of fascism, will have no difficulty in understanding on their own the necessity of its downfall, and the manner in which this will take place. It may take years. It may even take decades. But the triumph of capital over labour cannot last for ever. The future belongs to socialism. The future belongs to freedom.

IV Social Democracy and Fascism

33 Force and Democracy, *Karl Kautsky*

This extract from Kautsky's major post-war theoretical work, *The Materialist Conception of History*, published in 1927, considers fascism in the context of a possible bourgeois reaction to a socialist parliamentary majority.

... There is no doubt that the plentiful resources available to the capitalists to purchase the organs of democratic opinion in one form or another, constitute a major obstacle to the strengthening of the workers' parties. Yet the results show that this obstacle is not insuperable. Democracy enables the political strength of the working classes to grow in step with the widening of their political experience, the extension of the means of their political enlightenment, and the growth and increased determination of their parties. It is not only the number of their votes, but their understanding also that increases. Some of the workers' parties already stand on the threshold of the conquest of political power by democratic means.

But will the capitalists calmly accept this? This is the question posed by those socialist opponents of democratic methods, who see armed civil war as the only means of bringing the class struggle to a decisive conclusion. There is no doubt that the capitalists will put up the bitterest fight to resist their political dispossession by a democracy, knowing that this must ultimately lead to their economic dispossession as well. They will use every means to prevent the victory of democracy, even military ones, if these are available to them in sufficient measure.

We have seen how the military superiority of a conquering group created the State and the means of exploitation, and how the military might of the aristocracy sustained both against a defenceless peasantry. Anyone who only knows about this is likely to see military force as crucial to the internal developments of modern democracy as well. But we have also seen how, with the development of industrial capital, and its offspring the industrial proletariat, an entirely new economic and political factor emerged: from now on exploitation and class domination depended less and less on military force for its maintenance. The further industrial development proceeds, the more it is economic, not military power that becomes decisive in the state.

The capitalists are the dominant class not, as the warrior aristocracy, because of their own military superiority over the masses, whom they are much inferior to in number as well. They have achieved their supremacy up to now by means of their wealth and the importance of their economic function in the contemporary process of production. Their supremacy will continue as long as the masses whom they dominate and exploit do not understand how to replace the capitalists and their institutions with institutions of the working class which can perform these functions as well if not better. It is the weapon of economic indispensability, not of military superiority, that the capitalists can hold against a democratic regime of the working classes; if they believe themselves threatened by the development of democracy, they will sabotage it by making industry idle, as they predominantly did for a period in the Russian revolution from 1917 onwards.

Whether this capitalist weapon is successful – indeed, whether it is used at all – will depend above all on the political and economic sophistication of the workers who come to power. It will depend on whether they can keep production going, by operating their own organisations in decisive branches of production. It will further depend on whether, in those branches of production where such methods are not yet possible, they have enough good sense and moderation to allow the capitalists to continue under conditions which will make it seem worthwhile for them to keep their operations going. If such a solution fails, if a workers' government does not understand how to socialise some branches of production immediately and allow the capitalists to continue production in the rest, the consequences will be either a simple capitulation of the workers to the capitalists – naturally not forever, but for a period at any rate – or else a resort by the workers to senseless acts of violence, to occupation of all the factories and the expulsion of their owners and managers, as in 1917 in Russia. Such a course cannot under existing conditions lead to socialist production but only to chaos, which will not necessarily be immediately resolved by a return to private capitalism. Under certain circumstances this restoration can take place via a detour through a form of state capitalism. There is just no way that this method can achieve the introduction of a system of social production run by free associations of workers.

The economic means of struggle – i.e. production stoppages – are thus the most inherently appropriate means for capital to use against any development of democracy which threatens it. The countermeasures to be taken by a workers' regime against this weapon, supposing it is indeed used, which is by no means certain, will have to vary according to the maturity of the proletariat and the level of production.

There is nothing here to alter our attitude to democracy, or our expectations of the possibilities which it offers. The anti-democratic socialists, however, usually view the matter differently. According to them it is not economic but military resistance that is to be expected from the capitalists, as soon as democracy threatens them. They expect democracy to be overthrown by force, and civil war and a dictatorship based on military power to be unavoidable as a consequence. It may indeed come to this here and there . . . However, an armed attack on democracy by the capitalists is by no means inevitable. We have already indicated that they constitute a small minority which has no superiority over the majority through any special military competence. Where the capitalists achieved military success, it could only occur through the agency of military units paid for or directed by themselves from among the exploited classes.

The question whether the capitalists will undertake an armed attack on democracy therefore reduces itself to the question whether they will be able to find a sufficient armed force at their disposal for this purpose. This is a question which cannot be determined in advance. It depends entirely on the circumstances in which the workers' party comes to power. This will only take place in a democracy when it has a majority of the population behind it. If a system of universal conscription exists, especially with short periods of military service, then a majority of the army will also support the new regime. Furthermore, it is not only the socialists who support democracy. Democracy is important for all popular elements, including those who are neither proletarian nor socialist inclined. In a modern industrial country, and it is only these we are concerned about, the totality of the working people, the huge majority of the population, will support the maintenance of democratic rights. Given these conditions, an appeal by the capitalists to a conscript army to overthrow democracy would prove more dangerous for the instigators themselves than for anyone else.

Are conditions any more favourable with an army recruited from volunteers? Depending on the selection of recruits such an army can have either proletarian or capitalist sympathies. But even in the latter case, it will be too small to disrupt democracy seriously against the opposition of the great majority of the nation. It could no doubt create a good deal of mischief, but this would not restore the political and social position of its masters.

There is still a third possibility: the capitalists may recruit hired agents to arm and use in the fight against troublesome movements of the working class. The American capitalists were the first to use such mercenaries in the class war, the so-called Pinkertons, whose special task is strike-breaking. Nowadays it is the fascists who have become the paid executioners of popular liberty. They are certainly dangerous, but fortunately only under certain conditions, which cannot be conjured up at will by our noble capitalists.

For the fascists to have a political impact, they have to be available in large numbers — in Italy around half a million out of 39 million inhabitants. To reach this proportion in Germany they would have to be almost a million strong. In an industrial country such a large number of lumpen elements in the prime of life, ready to serve capitalist ends, just cannot be dredged up. In Italy the conditions for fascism were especially favourable. First of all from olden time — a glorious tradition — its number of *déclassé* elements was exceptionally large. The *déclassé* peasants and petty-bourgeoisie became bandits, especially in the Church lands and the kingdom of Naples. The numerous unemployed intellectuals attempted throughout the nineteenth century to win positions for themselves by *putsch* and similar political activity.

In his book entitled *A Conspiracy against the International*, Marx cites the following statement of Bakunin: 'In Italy there exists, as nowhere else, an ardent and energetic young generation, without position, career or future, which despite its bourgeois origins is not morally and intellectually exhausted, as is the bourgeois youth of other countries'. Marx adds the comment: 'All the self-styled sections of the Italian International are led by lawyers without clients, doctors without patients or professional skills, billiard room students, commercial travellers and other salesmen, and above all by small-time journalists of more or less ambiguous reputation'. Fifty years ago these elements became Bakunin's supporters. Now they flock to Mussolini with the same enthusiasm, though better success, since now they enjoy the blessing of big business.

The industrial development of the last half-century has reduced the number of these elements somewhat, as well as putting an end to banditry. But the world war tore many otherwise industrious individuals off the rails, made them unaccustomed to work, and introduced them once more to the traditions of the earlier lumpen proletariat which had never entirely died out. If we add to this that fascism occurred at a time when Communist influences had split and completely disrupted the Italian proletariat, and provoked it to senseless experiments which on the one side frightened capital into the arms of fascism, on the other side exhausted and demoralised the proletariat with their failure, then we have the conditions for the rise of the fascists. They are confined to a particular country at a particular point in time, and will not recur so easily.

Capital will not experience much joy from them. These half million bandits, accustomed to rob and plunder with impunity, will eventually not stop short of their original protectors. Capitalist production and accumulation is in the long run only possible under conditions of complete security for property and person. In Italy today these capitalist foundations have already been completely undermined. The 'Duce' will be amazed at what happens when he tries to restore them.

The rise of fascism provides no evidence that it will be the universal answer of capital to the workers' victory in a democracy. All it shows is that capital is already scared of the coming victory, and that already in certain countries, where a favourable opportunity exists, reckless and short-sighted capitalist elements will take advantage of it to engineer an armed suppression of democracy. If this does not happen everywhere, it is because the opportunity is not universally available – but also because the more far-sighted statesmen of the ruling classes realise that this method of saving capitalism is in effect to cast out Satan by Beelzebub.

There is no reason to expect that the situation in the future, when the proletariat achieves political power, will be any more favourable to attempts to overthrow democracy by force than it is now. On the contrary. With every passing year that separates us from the world war, and the attitude of military adventurism it created, with every year in which production returns to its normal channels, and the number of the unemployed and the hopeless diminishes, so too the prospect progressively disappears for the terrorists of capitalism to halt the democratic advance of the workers, or to abolish democracy itself, by unleashing a civil war.

But even if this were to happen in one country or another, under exceptional conditions, the victory would be a Pyrrhic one. This is because in the long run the progress of democracy just cannot be prevented in a modern state. And where it is temporarily retarded, this can only be achieved by means which are immensely damaging to economic life, and which depress the state which uses them to a lower level within the family of nations.

34 Speech to the SPD Conference 1927, *Rudolf Hilferding*

These two brief extracts from Hilferding's speech summarise his views on the character of the post-war economy and the task of socialism, and emphasise the centrality of the defence of the Republic for the Party's programme.

Socialism, the Task of our Time

... Nowadays we all have the feeling that even the private enterprise
and the economic management of the individual entrepreneur have
ceased to be his private concern. Society has understood that it is in its
own interest if the productivity of each individual enterprise is
increased, that is, if the relevant manager actually fulfils his technical
and organisational duty as entrepreneur to increase production. I
remind you that institutions such as the Board for Economic
Efficiency, and all officially sponsored attempts at rationalisation,
which seek to persuade the entrepreneur to improve the performance
of his business, amount in effect to a pronouncement by society that
the management of an enterprise is no longer a private matter, but a
social responsibility. The most important aspect is the following: the
creation of industrial combines, the concentration of ever more
undertakings under the control of a single administrative head,
signifies the end of free competition for the individual concern.
Capitalist theory has always argued that only the pressure of free
competition can generate the technical innovations necessary for
economic progress. The chief argument against socialism has always
been: remove the private initiative of free competition, and you have
nothing to put in its place. Your economy will consequently fail,
because it takes no account of the ambition and self-interest of the
private owner of the means of production. So it is very interesting to
see how, in the development of modern management science, means
are being sought for replacing this free competition of private self-
interest by the methods of scientific planning. It is quite clear: the
head of the combine has the greatest interest in being able to establish
at any moment whether the maximum utility is being achieved in the
individual enterprise which forms part of his undertaking, even
though it is not competing with similar concerns in the same combine.
Very precise methods have been evolved for replacing the stimulus of
self-interest by a scientific method of competition. This is precisely
our socialist principle of economic management. So capitalism itself
surrenders its main anti-socialist argument, and with it the final
psychological objection to socialism disappears. Organised capitalism
thus means in effect the replacement of the capitalist principle of free
competition by the socialist principle of planned production. This

planned, deliberately managed form of economy is much more susceptible to the conscious influence of society, which means to the influence of the sole institution capable of the conscious, compulsory organisation of the whole society, the state.

This being so, we see confronting each other the capitalist organisation of the economy on the one side and the state organisation on the other; and the problem is what kind of reciprocal inter-relationship we wish to create. This means that our generation confronts the problem of using the state and its means of conscious social regulation to transform the present capitalist controlled and organised economy into an economy subject to the control of the democratic state. It follows that the problem confronting our generation can be nothing other than the problem of socialism. Previously we campaigned as Social Democrats for political rights, for the inauguration and expansion of social policy. Now it is economic development itself that has posed the question of socialism . . .

Democracy and the Working Class

From a historical point of view, democracy has always been the concern of the proletariat. I have never ceased to be amazed by the assertion, which occurs even now in some resolutions, that democracy has historically been a matter for the bourgeoisie. That reveals an ignorance of the history of democracy, and a pallid intellectualist tendency to deduce its history from the writings of a few theoreticians. In fact there is no more bitter political struggle than the struggle waged by the proletariat for democracy against the bourgeoisie. To refuse to recognise that this struggle belongs among the great exploits of the proletarian class struggle, and that it is false and historically misleading to talk of 'bourgeois democracy', is to renounce the whole of socialist history from the moment when Marx made his famous remark about raising the working class to the level of a political party. Democracy is *our* affair. We have had to wrest it from the bourgeoisie by dogged struggle. Remember the campaigns for the suffrage. How much proletarian blood has flowed for the achievement of universal suffrage!

The term 'bourgeois democracy' is misconceived not only

historically, but from the standpoint of social analysis as well. Democracy signifies a quite distinct method of determining state policy. In the authoritarian state we were confronted by powerful social organisations which stood outside the electoral process and the popular will that it expressed. The point needs no amplification. The truism about the will of parliament being a mere bagatelle in face of the top brass, the top officials and the monarch is sufficient for us Germans. Now, however, the determinants of state policy are nothing other than the political views of its individual citizens. Parliament is no longer confronted by exclusive organisations of the rulers; they must now appeal to the electorate and have their authority repeatedly ratified by a majority in the struggle of ideas with ourselves. If they fail, then their power comes to an end on the terrain of democracy itself.

But what if the rulers have no respect for democracy? Is that a problem for us? Surely it is a self-evident proposition not only for every Social Democrat, but – and I say this deliberately – for any republican, that the moment an attempt is made to destroy the basis of democracy, every means will be used to preserve it. This is where the question of the use of force comes in. Our experience in Germany in 1918, and especially the experience of Russia, shows that the use of force in the class struggle – I am talking about serious violence, stabbing, shooting, killing – does not mean a momentary *putsch*, but a very bitter, long drawn-out and exceedingly bloody *civil war*. If the basis of democracy is destroyed, we are forced on to the defensive and have no choice. Then every means must be used. But no Socialist – and I say this particularly from the standpoint of a Socialist – will say: 'I do not want socialism if I cannot use force to bring it about'. I am quoting here the words of Otto Bauer. We will not take that view, because we know that there is no greater obstacle to the realisation of socialism than a civil war, and because our position as Socialists is almost impossible if it is through civil war that the proletariat achieves political power. For this reason we as a proletariat have an absolute interest in the preservation of democracy. We intend to defend it – that has to be said continually – and for that reason we thank the *Reichsbanner* for its work.[32] We hope the *Reichsbanner* is imbued with the republican sentiment, that no sacrifice is too great, even in the interests of the working class, to preserve the Republic and democracy. If you do not understand that the preservation of democracy and the republic is the most essential interest of the Party, you have not learnt your political ABC.

---

35 In the Danger Zone, *Rudolf Hilferding*

This article, written for the theoretical journal of the SPD soon after the Nazi success in the elections of September 1930, justifies the policy of 'toleration' of the Brüning regime in order to keep the Nazis out of power.

The economic crisis has turned things completely upside down since 1928. The history of economic crises in England shows how the crises of earlier times radicalised the masses, and had politically progressive consequences. The first great political and social reforms in England in the nineteenth century came about under the pressure of mass movements which had been provoked by the crises. This changed as the workforce became organised and the trades unions grew in influence. Unemployment weakens union militancy; the longer it lasts, the heavier is the pressure exerted by the industrial reserve army on those still in work. The workers are forced on the defensive, while the employers' eagerness and capacity for confrontation intensifies. The difficult position of the unions in turn affects the workers' political outlook. While the unorganised mass movements of earlier times received a strong impetus precisely during periods of crisis, now in the era of organised economic and political struggle, it is during the periods of prosperity that the working class develops its strongest offensive capacity and achieves its successes.

Since the war, conditions have altered again, at least in Germany. War and inflation forced millions of the economically independent into employment, or rendered them completely *déclassé*, while the standard of living of others was seriously depressed. These strata are full of bitterness; lacking any union education, and divided between their original petty-bourgeois outlook and ideals and their new-found economic situation, they desperately seek a way out. The hard methodical struggle of the organised workers is not their way; they must have instantaneous salvation. Their misery was a consequence of the revolution, and democracy has failed to restore them to their orginal status; so a new revolution is necessary, and the Third Reich that they will establish and control will surely bring their salvation. Women, children, the despairing, receive this message gladly.

Today the state plays a quite different role in the economy than previously. Taxes comprise more than a quarter of the national income. Through its social policy and arbitration system the state intervenes in the labour contract in a way previously unknown. It thus seems as never before to be directly responsible for the condition of the economy, and for the economic fate of every individual. The economic crisis appears no longer as the product of economic causes, as a periodical accompaniment of capitalist development; it is rather a failure of the state and its policy. The state has therefore to be seized, the old parties driven out, policy fundamentally changed, if the people are to be saved and their distress eliminated. Democracy has brought these strata an increased awareness of their power; but they now turn against the democratic state from which their power derives . . .

No less significant is the change in the political psychology which the crisis has brought about in the higher reaches of capitalist society. The crisis threatens profit margins, already squeezed by the high levels of taxation. At the same time it intensifies the tax burden still further because of the rapid increase in expenditure on support for the unemployed. Profitability has to be restored by diminishing the tax burden, and this in turn presupposes a reduction in social expenditure. It must be restored by reducing wage levels, and the opposition of a democratic government which can resist such a reduction through its arbitration system, has to be broken. In periods of crisis the co-operation of Social Democracy in government becomes increasingly intolerable for the employers.

The Social Democrats championed the democratic system, because they knew that it had to be imbued with a social content. In advanced industrial states, democracy and social reform are one and the same, and the theoretical distinction between political form and social content is a lifeless abstraction. By the same token, the struggle to restrict the sphere of social policy, in particular the institutions of unemployment insurance and state arbitration, which regulate the labour market directly, has escalated into a struggle against democracy and the democratic parliament. Where in 1928 a parliamentary policy was taken for granted, now opinion is turning increasingly towards outright opposition to parliament. Order at any price, financial recovery, renunciation of the existing system, strong government, which will take its orders from 'business' and where necessary execute them independently of parliament and even against its wishes – this is the solution of the most economically influential strata.

This reaction at the top and bottom of society already decided the fate of the last parliament and its Grand Coalition. It dictated the attitude of the *Volkspartei* towards the government of Hermann Müller, which resulted in the fall of this government, the only parliamentary government possible.[33] It led the government of Brüning to embark on a policy which began with the rape of parliament and has its destruction as the logical conclusion. It induced the right-wing groups among the parties of government to frustrate all attempts to resolve the parliamentary crisis by parliamentary means, and to obstruct any serious negotiations with Social Democracy which might lead to a resolution of the *impasse*; the intention of their policy was to exclude Social Democracy for the duration of the economic crisis. If a more lasting breakdown of parliament resulted as well, so much the better . . .

In order to justify the exclusion of Social Democracy and secure their own position in the future Reichstag, the bourgeois parties declared all previous governments to be failures. They demanded, not a set of specific measures, which the electors would have had to make a clear decision about, but a break with the past, a new era, to save Germany from the abyss. Since 1918 in Germany a major work of construction has in fact been achieved in the field of home and foreign policy, under the most difficult circumstances and in spite of everything. But instead of emphasising the positive achievement, the bourgeois parties united to foment a mood of despair, which was bound in the end to react against themselves. They were after all themselves the supporters of the governments which had supposedly been such failures. To call now for deliverance was in effect to frame the accusation against themselves. The response of the voters could only be to call for new agents of deliverance. And these already stood at the door.

The National Socialists are an all-embracing party; their present following ranges from generals, princes, aristocrats, landowners, industrialists, through the middle classes, the peasantry and government officials, to the working class and declassed elements – supporters from all social strata. This ability to overcome the divisive barriers of class distinction that exist in present-day Germany is no small achievement. At the same time the participation of princes, generals, industrialists and landowners seems to offer the bourgeois classes a sure guarantee for the behaviour of the Party's following, should it ever achieve power. It gives them the impression that the essence of National Socialism is its hostility towards Social Democracy and the democratic parliament, not its ambiguous, pseudo-socialist programme. The anti-parliamentary, anti-democratic tendencies among the industrialists and landowners thus coincide with the direction of a party that has suddenly become a major force both inside and outside parliament. The Party appears as the instrument for generating the mass following that can be mobilised by the anti-parliamentary strata of large industrial and agrarian capital, and used to paralyse the struggle of the democratic masses.

It is the conjunction of these tendencies that makes the situation for democracy so threatening ... The expectation that the rise of the National Socialists would produce a bloc for the defence of parliament, a 'coalition of moderates', has been disappointed from the outset. The coalition of moderates for the moment commands no majority in the Reichstag. The government's hopes for a right-wing loyal to the state have melted away. Those who split off from Hugenberg's party are now making overtures to it and to the National Socialists, while the *Volkspartei* and the *Wirtschaftspartei* want to continue in its ambit. The constitutional parties – the Social Democrats, Centre, *Staatspartei* – are in a minority, even if you include the Bavarian *Volkspartei*. *The majority of parliament is now opposed to parliament*, and only the divisions between them prevent them from operating as an effective parliamentary force. But this would change as soon as the desire of the groups on the right to form a government with the National Socialists and Hugenberg were realised. Such an attempt just cannot be assessed according to the rules of the parliamentary game. The admission of the National Socialists into government would be seen by them merely as an opportunity to build up their power, a chance to use the organs of the state for their own purposes, and to infiltrate the army and the police. It is an illusion to believe that their bourgeois partners, united with them in hostility to parliament and to democracy, either could or would prevent them. Once such a government were formed, it would prove difficult to remove from any parliamentary basis . . .

One thing can be said with absolute certainty: if we cannot hold the parliamentary ground intact, there will be even less chance of preserving the social policy and advancing it later, since social policy and democracy are one and the same. The reverse also holds: if we succeed in maintaining the Reichstag in operation, the defence against the deterioration of social conditions becomes possible, provided the National Socialists do not defect to the camp of open social reaction, which they can hardly afford to immediately.

To support a government of the centre that has moved so decisively to the right means a heavy sacrifice for Social Democracy. It only makes sense as the necessary price for the defence of democracy in a parliament with an anti-parliamentary majority, and in an extra-parliamentary situation in which the economic crisis has led not only the employers but also broad masses of the people into opposition to parliament. Yet even in this situation there is a clear limit to Social Democratic toleration. Even in an election when everyone attacked Social Democracy, the Party has proved itself to be the secure bulwark against the destructive radicalism of both left and right. Its support should not be expected for any policy which destroys this bulwark, and breaks up the surest defence against civil war and counter-revolution. The other side must recognise this, if any agreement for the preservation of parliament is to take place.

If this agreement succeeds, and parliament is preserved, we can expect the resolution of the political crisis . . . If parliament is preserved, the Reichstag will be confronted with the most urgent concrete tasks, and the pressure will lead to a coalition of the 'moderates' perhaps more rapidly than appears likely just now. This will then allow time for the abatement of the economic crisis to help resolve the political crisis as well. If the attempt fails, however, we will stand on the threshold of a conflict, whose course and outcome are uncertain, but whose cost in terms of welfare, however unforeseeable, can only be high.

---

36 Between the Decisions, *Rudolf Hilferding*

In this article, written in January 1933, Hilferding looks back over the policy of 'toleration' and pronounces it a success, in view of the decline in the Nazi vote in the December elections of 1932.

In the mighty power struggle which Social Democracy has been waging in Germany since the start of the world economic crisis, to maintain its own viability, to secure and re-establish democracy in the area of Central and Eastern Europe, and to defeat the forces of social, political and cultural counter-revolution, the year 1932 saw a series of crucial decisions, which have far reaching consequences for the eventual outcome. The year saw the culmination of German fascism, which was reached on 13 August, the day when the Reich-president refused Hitler's demand for the transfer of state power, and Hitler capitulated to the supreme commander of the German army. So the plot unfolds, and this year will see the *dénouement*.

The presidential elections had taken place earlier. They had not brought Hitler to power, but his success was impressive and the political issue was undecided. After all, Hitler had only been defeated because Hindenburg was his opponent, Hindenburg – that was no unambiguous political decision for Republic and democracy, nor yet a decision against fascism. Hindenburg's supporters were not united: only the Social Democrats and the majority of the Centre voted out of purely political considerations, while the remainder, whose support was indispensible to prevent a fascist victory, voted from personal sentiment. These were no unconditional opponents of fascism; in so far as political considerations played a part, they merely wanted to deny Hitler sole power, and ensure that his participation in government was under their control.

The fascist movement had not yet attained complete victory, but its ascent remained unchecked, as the regional elections in Prussia and the first Reichstag elections demonstrated. Another factor was, however, important. The National Socialists had openly made full preparations, in the event of Hitler's election to the presidency, to complete their apparently democratic victory with an immediate violent revolutionary act, correctly supposing that the fascist seizure of power would have to be consolidated immediately by the destruction of the opposing organisations and their leaders. The 'march on Rome' would have to be laid on subsequently, as it were, after the legal title to power had been won according to the rules of the democratic game. Since the strength and determination of the German workers' organisations had prevented German fascism from achieving what the Italian fascists were able to before their conquest of the state – the terrorisation, immobilisation or destruction of the organisations opposed to them – they were compelled to adopt the tactic of legality, which is incompatible with the essence of fascism and brings them repeated setbacks . . .

Hitler was set on the sole possession of power. Brüning's ministry was the first obstacle that had to be removed. The ministry that followed was to be transitional. New elections were to bring the National Socialists decisive power by legal means, while the removal of the ban on the fascist militia would restore its revolutionary instrument, and the unification of the Prussian police and administration with that of the Reich would create the essential precondition for the operation of the total state. On these conditions Hitler gave his agreement. He approved the support of the Papen government, which only came into existence because of it. The most reactionary wing of the counter-revolutionary camp now held power on its own. Hitler had allowed this for one purpose, to organise electoral victory and to strengthen his storm troops in full legality.

But legality kills him – *la légalité le tue*.[34] Hitler now controlled the largest party in the Reichstag, over a third of all representatives.

Further, the Reichstag was rendered impotent by its three parties of dictatorship – National Socialists, Nationalists and Communists; the 'system' was destroyed and the constitution unworkable. Herr von Papen declared as much, and the new authoritarian leadership of the state waited for its fascist partner. On 13 August Hitler stood in front of Hindenburg, as ten years earlier Mussolini had stood in front of the king. The German plays the same card as the Italian: surrender of state power into the hands of fascism. After the Italian tragedy comes the German farce. Hitler descends the palace steps empty-handed – it marks the downfall of fascism.[35]

Hitler himself had helped Papen's ministry into the saddle, and made his own followers into the pedestal to support the old reaction. Was it now to capitulate before him? Were the Prussian *junkers*, so long accustomed to power, and the higher echelons of the bureaucracy and military to abandon the field voluntarily and unconditionally to a plebeian mass movement? Mussolini appeared before the king after the destruction of the opposing organisations and after the march on Rome. And the king surrendered to Mussolini because the Italian general staff demanded it. But the power of the German state remained undisturbed, not least thanks to the tactics of Hitler himself. To demand the fruits of revolution without the revolution – such a political design could only evolve in the brain of a German politician.

The defeated Hitler sought to save himself once more by legal means. But legality now meant the struggle against authoritarian power, against dictatorship, against nationalism – the struggle against fascist ideology in the name of democracy. Legality is his undoing. In the second elections to the Reichstag, Hitler lost two million votes; the aura of invincibility was broken; his decline had begun . . .

The political problem is not exhausted, however, with our opposition to the presidential regime. The position now is not as simple as when the bourgeois liberals were engaged in their struggle against absolutism on behalf of the parliamentary system. The presidential regimes are only possible in Germany because parliament has been rendered unworkable by the parties of dictatorship – the National Socialists, the Nationalists and the Communists. The struggle against the presidential regimes must therefore be linked with the struggle for a viable parliament, and that means struggle against the parties of dictatorship. The presidential regimes are the secondary phenomenon; the primary is the paralysing of parliament.

For Social Democracy this question is a matter of fundamental disagreement with the Communists. This means that the slogan of a united front, which made some sense in the immediate post-war years of Social Democratic superiority, when the authority of the trades unions was undiminished, is now a dead letter, and can only cause confusion. The Communists seek to create a unity of the labour movement on the basis of a programme for immediate revolutionary action and the direct seizure of power. For this they need to subordinate the workers to the leadership of the revolutionary vanguard – i.e. to Communist leadership. Unity thus presupposes the subordination of the Social Democratic masses to their leadership, and the destruction of the organisation, independence and the very essence of Social Democracy. When we Social Democrats speak of unity, we are thinking of the unity of a labour movement that is struggling for its own goals, goals that are established by a process of democratic self-determination. The same words thus have totally different meanings. To let oneself in for pseudo-revolutionary actions in the present situation would throw fascism into the hands of the state and help it to certain victory – a gambit that we must reject from the outset, since its conclusion is not revolution but counter-revolution.

Our task is not an easy one. It goes against the worker's nature to fight his own class comrades, especially in view of the fascist danger, which demands the unity of proletarian action more urgently than anything. Yet the fulfilment of the task is indispensable, since the tactics of the Communist leadership damage the effectiveness of the working class on both the parliamentary and the extra-parliamentary levels. Their continually repeated attempt to exploit the 'united front' to unmask the Social Democratic leadership, and detach our following from us; the repeated contrast they make between the 'truly revolutionary posture' of the Communists and the 'betrayal of the Social Democrats', inevitably transforms every extra-parliamentary action into a putschist adventure. That is why the uncompromising struggle against the Communist leadership, and to win the support of the Communist workers, is only the other side of the fight against the presidential regime, the fight for the re-establishment of democracy. Only democracy, re-established on a secure foundation, can provide the terrain on which the working class can attain its goals.

In the meantime the political situation remains fluid and uncertain. The economic crisis confronts the Schleicher government with problems, in attempting to solve which it can lose its position in just the same way as did its predecessor, the Papen government, and revive the same danger that salvation will be sought in a surrender of power to fascism. It is indeed the characteristic feature of the time that a kind of race is taking place between the developing economic crisis on the one side, and the political rebellion that it has generated on the other, and it remains uncertain whether the crisis will come to an end before the rebellion has run its full course.

So we stand between the decisions. Although the fascist movement appeared on the point of seizing power in Germany, it has been kept from doing so thanks to the tactic of the Social Democrats, whose policy of 'toleration' prevented the bourgeoisie from uniting in a reactionary mass under fascist leadership, and so obstructed the entry of the fascists into the government during the period of their ascent. The same tactic kept the Centre firm in its opposition to a (monarchist) restoration government, and so deprived the latter of the support of the only bourgeois party with a secure basis. The National Socialists are now confined within the bounds of legality, and have only the choice of either participating in a bourgeois coalition and so accelerating their recent decline, or achieving the same fate by remaining in opposition, a course which can only disappoint the impatient hopes for salvation of their followers. It is this beginning of decline that reduces the danger of compromise between Hitler and Schleicher, since a party in decline has progressively less chance than one in the ascendant of displacing its partner in government, and so achieving sole power.

This is how the verdicts have gone so far against both fascism and restoration. The final shape of political developments will, however, be determined by events in the economy.

37 No to 'Toleration', *Max Seydewitz*

Max Seydewitz, a spokesman for the left opposition within the SPD through the journal *Der Klassenkampf*, which he edited, wrote a number of articles in the autumn of 1930 denouncing the policy of 'toleration' of the Bruning government.

(1) Warning Before the Agreement

Those who toy with the idea that Social Democracy should 'tolerate' the government, start from the consideration that a government in which the Nazis participate should on no account be allowed to come into existence. Even supposing a government under the influence of the National Socialists were such a terrible thing, we cannot prevent this terror by the unconditional capitulation of Social Democracy to the Brüning government. The capitulation involved in agreeing to the Brüning government and its emergency decrees would undermine the effectiveness of Social Democracy as a fighting force. Once the first step was taken, the bourgeois parties would immediately impose more wide-ranging demands and continually formulate more stringent conditions, each time on the understanding that they would otherwise take the National Socialists into government. One day the Social Democrats would have to call a halt; but the opportunity for the entry of the Nazis into government, which we are now trying to stop, would still exist. The only difference, and it is a decisive one, is that the entry of the National Socialists into government would take place after the decline or defeat of working-class militancy, whereas now this militancy is unimpaired, as the election campaign proved. The march on Rome was undertaken after the militancy of the Italian workers had been broken; we can prevent the march on Berlin, provided the morale and effectiveness of the German workers remains intact . . .

The Social Democrats who toy with the idea of capitulation to Brüning and the toleration of his regime in order to avoid a government with Nazi participation, raise the objection against us that we can demonstrate no other means of avoiding a Nazi government. Indeed we cannot, since the Nazi government can at present only be prevented by unconditional capitulation to Brüning. This fact, is, however, no objection against us, but the most serious criticism of the previous coalition policy of our Party, which has brought us to such a constricted and apparently impossible position. We certainly see no other means at present to prevent a Nazi government than the unacceptable capitulation of Social Democracy, but we do see the way to overcoming the Nazis and the fascist danger by a radical alteration of the previous course of the Party. This would mean a policy which pays no heed to coalitions, but campaigns directly for the proletarian demands, as the only means to overcome the crisis and unite the masses around the banner of Social Democracy. This is the way to mobilise them for the victory of a true Social Democracy and for socialism.

(2) After the decision

After the Reichstag decision of 18 October, comrades from the majority breathed a sigh of relief believing that they had attained their goal, and had saved the parliament from the Nazi onslaught.[36] Yet that decision has in fact not lessened the fascist danger the slightest. The most serious aspect in the present situation is that the decision on whether and when the National Socialists enter the government does not rest with the Social Democrats, but depends much more on the right-of-centre parties of the government, which work tirelessly for the incorporation of the Nazis into the government, and are ready to dissolve Brüning's regime despite the Social Democrats' toleration at a moment that seems most convenient to themselves and most unfavourable to Social Democracy. Nothing is more illusory than the hope that the proletariat can unite with a section of the bourgeoisie to suppress or destroy fascism. The bourgeoisie does not see fascism as its enemy, but as the ultimate weapon for use in emergency to defend its power against the advancing proletariat. The big bourgeoisie only regards fascism as an inappropriate instrument as long as it is able to maintain its position intact with the help of democracy. If the failure of the capitalist system and the intensification of the terrible economic crisis increases the disaffection of the masses so that democracy no longer provides any security for the rule of the big bourgeoisie, the latter will play the fascist card as its last trump . . .

For as long as the reduction of social benefits can be undertaken by a bourgeois regime with the toleration of Social Democracy, the dominant class does not need to mobilise fascism to achieve its goals. But as soon as Social Democracy is compelled to renounce responsibility for the policy of reduction, it will become clear that the fascist movement is not an independent entity between the contending class forces of bourgeoisie and proletariat, but that in the present phase of the class struggle it constitutes a weapon, perhaps the most decisive weapon, in the hands of the dominant class of the big bourgeoisie for the prosecution of its socially reactionary demands. Fascism already tends indirectly to this result under the Brüning government, in so far as the majority of the Social Democratic Party in the Reichstag view the National Socialist movement from their own political standpoint as an independent danger standing between the class forces; they fail to recognise clearly enough the inner connection of fascism with the economic crisis, and the attempts of the dominant bourgeois class to resolve the crisis to its own advantage. The socially reactionary demands of the bourgeoisie will grow with every intensification of the economic crisis, and with every concession made by the Social Democrats under the threat of the fascist danger, until one day the limit will be reached and Social Democracy will have to say – thus far and no further. The greater the number and the more significant the concessions made on the way to this point, the more compromised will be the fighting spirit of the working class at the inevitable moment when it is forced to bring its defensive struggle into the open.

Party and trade unions are calling for action against fascism, and this call finds a welcome response among the class-conscious proletariat. But successful action in the mobilisation against fascism can only be sustained and intensified if it is set in motion and stimulated by manifest and evident activity in parliament, on both the political and economic fronts. During the present political struggles in parliament we should never forget that the parliamentary and extra-parliamentary arenas are inseparably linked to each other. After a certain time the offensive mobilisation will be jeopardised, if at the same time we shrink from the economic contests and political struggles in parliament to overcome the oppressive and daily intensifying crisis, and retreat on to the *defensive*.

---

38 The Mission of the Socialist Workers' Party, *Max Seydewitz*

This call to action in June 1932 was addressed to the members of the SAP, formed from a small group of left deputies and their followers who broke away from the SPD at the end of the previous year.

Political events follow each other thick and fast. The failure of both the established working-class parties in the present historical situation accelerates the speed of the development towards fascism in Germany. The presidential election, the elections in Prussia, the ejection of the Communist fraction from the Prussian assembly at the hands of the Nazis, the collapse of Groener and of Brüning's government shortly afterwards – these are the external signs of this development. The new government of Hindenburg's, a coalition of the powers which rule behind the scenes in Germany, the generals, the major landowners and big business, is openly and unmistakably the form of dictatorship which prepares the way for the harshest fascist dictatorship.[37] It will employ without restraint even harsher political and economic pressures against the working class than before, in order to impose the cost of the capitalist solution of the crisis on the lower and middle classes.

A situation so increasingly threatening for the German working class should have led the Social Democrats and the KPD at the eleventh hour to overcome all the obstacles and difficulties which stood in the way of a united front against fascism. There is still time even now for this last rescue attempt. But if the direction of both parties is not at once radically altered, with the daring the historical situation demands, everything can be lost. Certainly there are some among both the Social Democratic and Communist leadership who see the full size of the danger, some who appreciate what is needed even now to remove the danger, but apparently no one has the courage openly to admit the mistakes of the past year, to demand their immediate correction and insist on a common front of all workers' organisations.

The collapse of Brüning's government, and above all the circumstances which led to its collapse, provide a clear proof of the false policy pursued by the Social Democrats in recent years. Since 14 September 1930, the date when the mistaken 'toleration policy' of Social Democracy began, we have repeatedly pointed out in the pages of this journal that the policy of acquiescence in and support for a capitalist solution to the crisis, at a time when the growing crisis was intensifying mass suffering, did not serve to check the fascist movement, but only gave it lasting strength. We have repeatedly pointed out that all the sacrifices that Social Democracy has made at the expense of the working class, in order to keep the Brüning government in being, have been made in vain, since the fate of the government when it came to the point did not depend on Social Democracy, but on big business and other unaccountable powers working behind the scenes, and ready to take the initiative in removing the government at a moment which would be most inconvenient for Social Democracy and the working class.

Unfortunately our prediction has proved only too accurate. As *Vorwärts* itself is now compelled indirectly to recognise, Hindenburg prepared the downfall of Brüning and arranged his new cabinet at the very time when the SPD leadership was leading the social-democratic workers into battle for Hindenburg's re-election, and announcing to them that Hindenburg was their guarantor against fascism, and that his re-election would signify the defeat of fascism in Germany. Now that Hindenburg has contrived the downfall of the Brüning government without regard for the rules of the constitution, and shown his friendly disposition towards the fascists, the bubble of the Social Democrats' pretentions about the president has burst, exposed as a massive error, just as its whole policy in recent years has been a massive error, not least responsible for the present dangerous and apparently hopeless situation of the German working class.

Brüning's new dictatorship, or the fascist regime which will shortly follow it, will have the particular task of bringing sharper economic pressure to bear against the working class, so as to mitigate the effects of the daily intensifying crisis for the ruling class. These measures of the new government, and the increasingly dominant nationalist tendencies associated with them, will intensify the economic crisis in Germany far beyond its present level, and increase the sufferings of the masses. The German fascists, who in the last few years have promised every single stratum of the population everything they wanted, will not only be unable to fulfil any of their promises, but will only increase the burden carried by the lower and middle classes. Increasing mass dissatisfaction and desperation will force these future governments to measures of extreme terror internally, to the suppression of the workers' organisations, and to the stifling of every freedom enjoyed by the class conscious working class. To distract attention from their inability to solve the ever-worsening crisis, the future governments will commit the German people to foreign adventures, whose results will be not only a new war against Poland, but a new world war as well. The danger of renewed warfare is closer than it ever was; and if the class-conscious German working class does not take decisive action at the eleventh hour to stop the fascist *coup*, it will find itself driven into the worst of all catastrophes.

We hope that the Social Democrats and the Communists also recognise these dangers. Unfortunately, there is no evidence that either of them draw the necessary conclusion from this recognition, or that they are ready to bury the past for the sake of the future, and to establish a united front of workers' organisations on an honest basis under the pressure of the common threat. In view of this failure of the two established working-class parties, it is the historical mission of the Socialist Workers' Party, born in a moment of peril for the working class, by its insistent warnings to urge on the task of their salvation . . .

39 Some Causes and Consequences of German National Socialism, *Karl Kautsky*

In this article, written after the Nazi seizure of power in 1933, Kautsky argues that the defeat of Social Democracy was the result of the 'irresistible' progress of the Nazis, due to a combination of the Versailles settlement and the economic crisis, not the result of any mistaken strategy.

Just now the view is frequently propounded that the working classes of Germany are paralysed in the face of dictatorship. Many attribute the cause of this above all to the fact that the opponents of fascism did not stand their ground, but deserted the field without a fight. Yet the representatives of this opinion cannot claim that we would have been victorious had we joined battle. What they mean is that defeat in battle would have been infinitely preferable to capitulation without a fight. This is, as I said, at present a common view. Even comrades, not just in Austria but throughout the world, who viewed the tactic of German Social Democracy with complete approval, now confess with anguish that the passivity of German Social Democracy has deeply hurt and disappointed them.

Is this condemnation justified? In answer I should like to make just one observation first of all: the condemnation applies not only to Social Democracy but to the Communist Party as well, which is far stronger in Germany than it is here (sc. in Austria). The Communist Party was for a time almost as strong as the Social Democrats (in November last year almost six million votes compared with a little over seven million for our Party). In the face of such numbers it is not a question of identifying the *guilty*, but of discovering the *causes*: how did it happen that thirteen million proletarian combatants could allow themselves to be deprived of their rights without a blow in resistance?

This behaviour is particularly remarkable when compared with the resistance evoked by a previous attempt to set up a dictatorship in Germany – the Kapp *putsch* of March 1920. The occupation of Berlin by counter-revolutionary troops was immediately answered by a general strike of such momentum that it brought the counter-revolutionary *coup* to its knees within a few days. These were the same parties, even in many cases the same leaders, who behaved so differently in 1933 from 1920. This itself indicates that we should seek the causes of the different attitudes then and now, not in persons, but in the *difference between the two situations*. This difference is not hard to discover. The Kapp rebels of 1920 were soon forced to recognise that they were completely isolated among the population. They wanted to restore to supremacy the class that had led the German people into the bloodiest war and the most terrible defeat. People had not yet forgotten that in 1920; hence the unanimous resistance which found its energetic expression in the great general strike. The Communists felt themselves so strong at that point that they attempted armed uprisings in the Ruhr and the Vogtland, which nevertheless quickly collapsed. Yet the Social Democrats could say with justice that the great majority of the German people supported them in their resistance to dictatorship.

Hitler and his followers are in a quite different position today from those around Kapp. They owe their advance not to the *putsch* of a few brigades, but to the constant increase of mass support. Till 1928 they were an insignificant band (in the Reichstag elections of 1928 they won only twelve seats); but then their numbers shot up so abruptly that in July last year they were already by far the strongest party with 230 seats. Since then their ascent has continued to gather momentum, as the elections of 5 March this year revealed, when the National Socialists alone won almost half the votes, and more than half with their allies.

This points to a deep-seated change in general popular attitudes. Such a change affects all parties, and none that are not small sects, but whose strength is rooted in the broad masses, can escape its influence. Revolutionary parties of the working classes are strong and often successful when they oppose a government which is universally hated. On the other hand their strongest weapons, whether barricades or general strikes, are useless when they have not only the power of government but the majority of the population against them as well. In such cases it is simply a misreading of the situation to launch a decisive struggle regardless . . .

40 Methods and Aims of the Struggle against Fascism, *Karl Kautsky*

The following pieces offer differing definitions of the task confronting
Social Democracy following the Nazi seizure of power in 1933.
Kautsky, writing later that year, argued that the goal should be the re-
establishment of parliamentary democracy, within which the Social
Democrats could resume their progress towards socialism.

The struggle against fascism unquestionably requires illegal, secret
organisations. If these are to serve not merely for propaganda, but to
prepare uprisings against the dictatorship, they must become
conspiratorial. Just as in war, including here civil war, that means
dictatorial powers for the leaders. War and conspiracy have always
been unfavourable to democracy. Of course this is regrettable, but it
should not prevent us from employing every effective means in the
fight against fascism, even when it can only be waged by dictatorial
and undemocratic ones. It would be quite impractical to reject any
form of dictatorship in advance. On this point all of us in the Party are
agreed. But that leaves open the question of the political goal that we
seek to promote and secure in the struggle against fascism. Is it to be
the conquest of democracy, or the replacement of Hitler's
dictatorship by a 'Marxist' one?

There are two very different questions here: that of the *means* by
which the struggle against Hitler is waged, and that of the political
goal on whose behalf it is fought. The two should be kept clearly
separate. It is perfectly possible to admit that democratic methods are
out of place, indeed impossible, in the struggle against Hitler, and yet
insist on the necessity of democracy as its goal. Not a little confusion
is caused in discussion by the failure to keep the two questions
separate, and by the assumption that, if democracy is no longer an
effective weapon against fascism once it has won power, it must
therefore also be ineffective once fascism has been defeated.

It is quite self-evident that we cannot use democratic methods of
struggle where these are no longer available. An antithesis has
increasingly been posed recently, including at the Paris Conference,

between democratic and revolutionary methods, as if some of us in principle favoured only democratic, and some only revolutionary ones (by which is apparently meant insurrection and general strike). But this antithesis between democrats and revolutionaries is no less mistaken than that between reformists and revolutionaries. Our goal is a socialist—revolutionary one. Whether we work for this goal by reformist or revolutionary means is not a question of our consciousness, but always a practical matter of the situation pertaining at any given time in society and state, and of the relation of class forces, which we cannot determine according to our pleasure. On this depends also whether we employ democratic or 'revolutionary' methods . . .

Naturally it is stupid to say we should only employ democratic methods in all circumstances. We should commit ourselves to them in a democracy, and against opponents using the same methods. Acts of violence, on the other hand, cannot be prevented by votes and editorials, or by protest meetings. Yet even where we are compelled to meet force by force, we must strive above all to win the support of a majority of the population. This is the first prerequisite for any victory on our part, whatever the means we may use, violent or democratic. Further, we must keep in mind that the terrain of democracy is always the most favourable for a workers' party; where it is lacking, no task can be more urgent for such a party than the conquest of political freedom. It is quite wrong to suppose that the workers must first achieve economic freedom, and that only then can 'real' democracy be possible.

Whether a vigorous system of popular representation, chosen by equal, universal suffrage, whether the freedoms of the press, of assembly and association, are regarded as 'really' or merely 'formally' democratic, is irrelevant to the fact that without these arrangements the proletariat cannot achieve its economic liberation. Of course these democratic rights will take on a different character when we have organised society on socialist lines. For the present they are indispensable means of *struggle* for the proletariat. Under socialism they will be just one more means of social *self-management*. That is the difference between democracy in the present and democracy under socialism, not that between a 'real' and a 'formal' democracy . . .

41 Revolutionary Socialism, *Rudolf Hilferding*

This article was written in February 1934, shortly after the publication of the 'Prague Manifesto' by the SPD in exile. In this extract Hilferding argues that the result of the workers' struggle against Hitler cannot simply be a return to democracy as it was before he came to power.

. . . It has to be made clear first of all that the victory of fascism has placed the German labour movement – and the same goes for the Italian as well – in a radically new position. Its methods of combat are dictated to it by its opponents, and the political struggle of the German socialists is as different from that of the Socialist parties in other countries as the dictatorship of Hitler and Mussolini is from the governmental methods of France, England and Denmark. There is simply no further place for reformism of any kind, since reformism presupposes the possibility of legal activity at the very least. The German struggle can only be a revolutionary one in the most straightforward and precise meaning of that term: the employment of every possible means to achieve a revolutionary seizure of power and the total distruction of fascism. All other goals whatever the circumstance – whether in war or peace – are simply subordinate to this end, since only in this way can the freedom of the German workers be realised . . .

The dictatorship, by suppressing the workers' organisations, has delivered them over to the arbitrary power of capital. This one-sided alteration of power relations threatens the workers with a progressive deterioration in their standard of living, and compels them to fight to protect and improve their material existence. Yet all wage agitation is forbidden, and every strike becomes a political rebellion. Such a situation must necessarily generate the demand for free collective bargaining to be restored, and new workers' organisations to be formed to protect their social interests. But the freedom of collective bargaining is impossible without the freedoms of assembly, association and expression. Thus the imperative needs of the workers generate the demand for political rights and a struggle for democratic freedoms, whose attainment is the indispensable condition for the labour movement to become a mass movement once more. Yet any democratic right is a threat to dictatorship. Hence the struggle for democracy broadens into a struggle for the overthrow of National Socialism, and for the *conquest of state power*.

Democracy won in this way is not the basis, the 'most favourable terrain' on which to resume once more the class struggle between capital and labour, and the political struggle between Social Democracy and the bourgeois parties, in much the same form as it was carried on in the Weimar Republic before the victory of fascism. The victory of democracy is only possible after the bitter contest of a civil war, in which the opponents of fascism have won the upper hand and overthrown the Nazi dictatorship. This manner of achieving power determines the manner of its use. Democracy won in a victorious revolution undergoes a *complete change* in its functioning. Control of the state passes to a powerful revolutionary government which, supported and controlled by the successful revolutionary mass party, has the task of securing state power for the successful revolution and of transforming its institutions into an instrument of rule by the popular masses.

It is a remarkable fact that most people regard political arrangements quite independently of their development and of the social circumstances from which they grew. Yet it is a matter of simple experience that universal suffrage, for example, has different effects when it is won as the product of drawn-out struggle, from when it is imposed by an established reactionary regime. Many people are now seized by the fear that democracy, which has failed to prevent the victory of fascism, could deprive the workers of the fruits of their victory a second time, if they return to democracy.

This plausible simplification ignores entirely the complete transformation that democracy undergoes in its functioning as a result of a successful revolution. The political transformation of 1918 took place at the culmination of a counter-revolutionary development. The Kaiser's regime was eliminated, not by the organised, self-conscious revolutionary struggle of the working class, but as a result of defeat on the battlefield.

Social Democracy took over the government without any opposition, and from the outset shared power with the bourgeois parties, the old bureaucracy and even with the reorganised military apparatus. The fact that it took over the old state apparatus virtually unchanged was a major historical error on the part of the German labour movement, disoriented as it was by the war.

So runs our manifesto.

Can anyone imagine that the repetition of such a situation is possible? Would that not represent a total ignorance of the dynamic necessary to a true revolution? The tasks of a revolutionary regime that has emerged from a civil war are dictated by the same historical compulsion that has brought it to power in the first place: destruction of the opponents' power base in the state; trial of state criminals by revolutionary courts; purging the civil service, the judiciary and the military, and filling all important posts with supporters of the regime; securing the revolution against the social agents of reaction; expropriating the large estates and heavy industry without compensation; and the transfer of the Reichsbank and the other major banks to the ownership and administration of the state – such will be the minimum programme of this government. Such will be its first measures, which will not require legitimation at the hands of the electorate, since the regime's existence itself will prove that it has the support of the vast majority of the active, committed and combative elements of the population that has won the victory.

---

42 Revolutionary Social Democracy, *Alexander Schifrin*

Schifrin, one of the leading writers for the SPD's theoretical journal in exile, argues in these two extracts that the new situation requires a complete break with the theory and strategy of the Party under the Weimar Republic.

(I)

A necessary contribution to securing the revolutionary future of German Social Democracy is the conscious political liquidation of the epoch that lies between 4 August 1914 and 5 March 1933. It is not the experience, nor the education, nor the determination to achieve what we fought for in this period that must be liquidated, but the political methods and political ideology of the epoch. German Social Democracy has to choose between its past and its future. To cling to *this* past means to reject the future. This does not mean that the Party must reject its past altogether. It depends on *which* tradition of its past it chooses to link its struggle with. German Social Democracy has two traditions: one originates with Marx and Engels, and passes via Wilhelm Liebknecht and August Bebel to Luxemburg and the Hilferding of Finance Capital and thence to the USP. The other originates with Lassalle and Schweizer, and passes via Vollmar and David to Ebert and Leipart. The first tradition is vigorous, but the second is exhausted. Political parties are able to reconstruct their own history: i.e. they can themselves determine which moment in their history shall serve as their rallying point, and they test the value of that history in the present. It is no accident that the history of Bolshevism, and the interpretation of its significance, is the object of such intra-party conflict.

The spiritual continuity of Social Democracy implies nothing else than a return to its own revolutionary Marxist tradition in the situation of unparalleled difficulty which it now tragically confronts. The victory of counter-revolution has destroyed the efforts and the tradition of German reformism, but it cannot obliterate German Marxism. It was on the shoulders of this German Marxism that the revolutionary Russian Social Democracy was constituted 35 years ago, and from it the left wing of French socialism also drew its support in that period. But Marxism in the German labour movement became a revolutionary ideology without a revolutionary praxis. Now, hardened by the blows of counter-revolution it is becoming a revolutionary ideology founded on a revolutionary praxis . . .

The end of reformism does not signify the end of Social Democracy, nor yet of democratic socialism. The way in which the Weimar Republic met its downfall has severely compromised the ideas of democracy and of democratic socialism in the eyes of millions of the socialist working class in Germany. Nothing damaged the future of democratic socialism more than the statement of a previous Social Democratic Chancellor: 'Social Democracy is the National Liberal Party of the Weimar state'. If that were true Social Democracy would have to perish along with the Weimar state. In fact it will outlast it. But the idea of democratic socialism has to be purified of the dross of the previous reformist period. Democratic socialism is not the opposite of revolutionary Marxist socialism, but a component part of it; it does not contradict the revolutionary liberation struggle, but is its specific political ideology. Revolutionary democracy does not exclude the concentration of power and its underpinning of revolutionary violence. The French Jacobins were excellent democrats. So was the Bolshevik wing of Russian Social Democracy until the October revolution of 1917. The socialist liberation struggle presupposes democratic socialism. The anti-fascist proletarian revolution can only triumph when it assumes the leadership of all the impulses and striving for freedom that exist among the people, and when it becomes synonymous for the majority with liberation from the fascist yoke. The political antithesis of fascism is not Bolshevism, from which fascism has simply taken over its political methods and its contempt for personal rights and intellectual freedom; the antithesis is revolutionary democratic socialism . . .

(2)

All Socialist programmes of the past had a common characteristic: they presupposed that the realisation of socialism would take place in the context of a democratic evolution. All German Party programmes from Gotha to Heidelberg, the Linz Programme of the Austrian Social Democrats, the programme of the French Workers' Party (Guesdists), the programme of Russian Social Democracy of 1903 – all expounded the same point of view: the preparation of the working class for the attainment of power and the realisation of socialism could only take place in the context of a democratic order . . .

The distinctive feature of the Prague Manifesto is that it has broken with this by now traditional historical sequence: first the attainment of democracy, and only then the struggle for socialism on democratic foundations.[38] The liberation struggle against fascist dictatorship is now to be directly connected with the socialist struggle against the capitalist order. The downfall of the fascist dictatorship is only possible by means of the proletarian conquest of power. When the party of revolutionary socialism comes to power, it will immediately resort to the most decisive socialist measures. The restoration of democracy in Germany is now only possible in the form of the proletarian exercise of power, and on the basis of a developing socialist economic system.

This view – unfortunately not clearly enough formulated in the Manifesto – is no wishful thinking. Fascism accentuates the social crisis of capitalism to the point of political disaster for bourgeois society. *It makes the return to bourgeois democracy impossible.* Just as Tsarism prevented any possibility of a political stabilisation of Russian capitalism by its denial of rights to the peasantry and its obstruction of political self-determination for the bourgeoisie, so fascism prepares the political destruction of bourgeois society by its elimination of all the political forces which have sustained bourgeois democracy in Germany: reformist socialism, political Catholicism, the liberal bourgeoisie . . .

The Prague Manifesto sets as goals for the revolutionary socialist movement the complete destruction of fascist dictatorship and the assumption of total power by the revolutionary government. Its practical demands, however, are not sufficiently clear or consistent with this purpose: e.g. the demand for the complete renewal of the officer corps, as if the rank and file were not to be replaced; e.g. the demand for the reform of the judiciary by a strengthening of the lay element, as if this were the decisive point for ensuring the political control of the judicial system. The destruction of counter-revolution requires the concentration of the *total* state power in the hands of the revolutionary government. The term 'dictatorship' remains an empty noise until its institutional form is clarified – i.e. as a totality of concrete arrangements. Power – that means the army, the police, the administration, the judiciary, the education system. The term 'dictatorship of the proletariat' in its original sense signified merely the breaking of opposition on the part of the possessing classes; it had merely a negative character, and indicated nothing about how the socialist revolutionary state was to be organised, or how the political power of the proletariat was to be exercised.

The means of revolutionary stabilisation to be employed by a government that is brought to power by the successful anti-fascist proletarian revolution involve political power, economic transformation, mass-psychological influence and cultural production. The re-establishment of the state on a socialist foundation is itself part of the social revolution, in that the wholesale advancement of proletarian cadres to positions of power and their enrolment in the state machine signifies a massive social upheaval. The newly constructed state apparatus in turn provides the support for the socialised economy. Socialisation is not just a matter of the *content*, but also of the *agents* of socialism; not just the material, but the instrument as well. On the other hand, socialisation is itself a means to the political consolidation of the revolutionary state; thus power, politics and the economy are all intimately intertwined in the course of the socialist revolution. The first phase of socialisation is the political one, socialisation for the purpose of rendering the counter-revolution and large-scale property socially powerless, and so strengthening the revolutionary state. The expropriation of the large landowners and the socialisation of the key industries signify not merely the creation of the material foundation for a collective economy, but economic sanctions against the forces of counter-revolution. The socialist revolution disposes of a fearsome weapon of destruction that the fascist counter-revolution does not have: it can bring about the social dissolution of its enemies, by depriving them of the economic basis of their power and their very social existence. The whole feudal complex of society will be eradicated by the expropriation of the large landholdings, and the social and political power of the big bourgeoisie will be broken by the socialisation of the key industries and the nationalisation of the major banks.

The transformation to be carried through by this combination of revolutionary power politics and socialist economic policy must be consolidated by establishing a favourable influence over the mass consciousness, and completed by the production of a socialist culture. German fascism has brought about an unprecedented mobilisation and agitation of mass consciousness, using psychical manipulation for political ends to an unprecedented degree. Its strongest weapon has been to popularise the cause of counter-revolution. The cause of the anti-fascist proletarian revolution has to be made even more popular. Socialism has to be able to win the struggle for the people's allegiance before and after the seizure of power. But where mass influence, which can only be counted on for relatively short periods, finds its limit, the more lasting effects of socialist culture take over, in the creation of a cultural foundation for society. Fascism has politicised culture and made it into a state monopoly. The proletarian revolution will liberate it from the shackles of fascist barbarism, and will find in socialist culture a powerful weapon for the historical stabilisation of socialism in power. Why is a relapse of the socialist order back to capitalism impossible? Not only because, in the transition period, the socialist state concentrates significant means of power into its hands, and because the changed economic structure and the new balance of social forces allow for no return to capitalist economic anarchy; but also because the new culture transforms society through its educative influence, creating a new consciousness, new values, and a whole new imaginative outlook. The reproduction of socialist society takes place through the agency of socialist culture.

43 The Only Route to Power, *Max Seydewitz*

Von Seydewitz, who had rejoined the SPD in exile, offers a more Leninist conception of the revolutionary struggle against fascism.

In the programme of the new movement there must be clarity above all about the central problem of *democracy and dictatorship*. The decision about the route to the seizure of power will determine in every detail the organisational structure, and the internal and external features of the new battlefront. Whoever nurses the hope that there may perhaps still be the eventual possibility of the working class attaining power through the ballot box and a growing into socialism by peaceful means, will also reach different conclusions about the form of its organisational reconstruction than someone who starts from the assumption that the working class, whatever the situation, will *only* succeed in opening the way to socialism by a *revolutionary struggle for power*.

With the progress of capitalism's crisis, the acceptance of a democratic system by the dominant capitalist powers has in every country for a long time now been no longer a question of principled conviction but of expediency. They make use of parliamentary democracy for as long as it appears useful and adequate for securing their domination. As soon as this ceases to be the case, they desert the democratic arena without hesitation, mobilise fascistic means of violence, or fascism itself, destroy democracy and establish the open and most brutal dictatorship, as in Germany.

That is why the working class cannot adopt the position of regarding the democratic route as a possible means to the attainment of power provided its class enemies accept the democratic arena, and only resort to dictatorial methods when its class enemies turn to other means of struggle to secure their power. Such a strategy lands the working class in the disastrous defensive position that we experienced in the Weimar Republic; it renders it incapable of fighting on the new terrain dictated by its class enemies, and leaves it the alternative of defeat or surrender without a fight.

The working class must recognise that it has no choice between a democratic and a dictatorial route to socialism. Even the democratic arena and the rights of the working class can only be preserved, defended and re-established against its class enemies when the proletariat is strong and capable enough to prosecute the struggle with every means, and to break the power of the dominant classes by *dictatorship*. There is therefore only one route to socialism, the *revolutionary* one ... Once the working class has achieved political power, it must use every means to consolidate and extend this power. It should not hand it over again into the hands of a national assembly representing parliamentary democracy, but must rest its exercise of power on the class organs of the workers, on the soviets of the working class and of all employed classes, which become the instruments of executive as well as legislative power, of administrative as well as political control. The task of this revolutionary socialist dictatorship is the complete victory over bourgeois class rule. Its goal is not to establish a new system of class domination to exploit whatever social groups, but to abolish all class rule and every form of exploitation in the classless community of the socialist order.

---

44 The Struggle for State Power, *Social Democratic Workers' Party of Austria* (*Linz Programme*)

Austrian Social Democrats were better prepared than their German counterparts for a counter-revolutionary coup against the democratic state. This section from the Party's Linz programme of 1926 outlines a strategy of working-class defence.

In the democratic Republic (i.e. Austria) the political dominance of the bourgeoisie no longer rests on political privileges, but on its ability to keep the majority of the population under its ideological influence by means of its economic power, the weight of tradition, and the power of the press, school and church. If the Social Democratic Workers' Party could only overcome their influence, unite the manual and white-collar workers in town and country, and win as its allies the adjoining strata of the peasantry, the petty bourgeoisie and the intelligentsia, it would then have the majority of the population on its side. By the decision of universal suffrage it would then acquire state power ...

The SDAP seeks to acquire power in the democratic Republic, not in order to abolish democracy, but so as to put it at the service of the working class, and to adapt the state apparatus to working class needs. It seeks to use it as an instrument to wrest the means of production and exchange from the ownership of big capital and landed property, where it is concentrated, and transfer it to the common property of the whole people.

The bourgeoisie will not voluntarily surrender its position of power. It resigns itself to the democratic Republic which the working class forced upon it, for as long as it is able to control it. But as soon as the decision of universal suffrage threatens to hand over power to the working class, or once it has already done so, the bourgeoisie will attempt to destroy the democratic Republic and set up a monarchist or fascist dictatorship.

Only if the working class has the fighting capacity to defend the democratic Republic against every monarchist or fascist counter-revolution; only if the army and the other militarised state corps are willing to defend the Republic even when the decision of universal suffrage hands political power to the working class; only then will the bourgeoisie not dare to rebel against the Republic, and only then will the working class be able to win and exercise state power by democratic means.

The SDAP must therefore keep the working class in a constant state of organised mental and physical readiness to defend the Republic; it must cultivate the closest sense of solidarity between the working class and the soldiers in the army; and it must inculcate in all the armed forces of the state an allegiance to the Republic. This is the way that the working class will maintain the possibility of breaking the class power of the bourgeoisie by democratic means.

But if, despite all these efforts on the part of the SDAP, a bourgeois counter-revolution should succeed in breaking the democratic system apart, in that eventuality the working class could only win state power through civil war . . .

45 Austrian Democracy under Fire, *Otto Bauer*

The attack on democracy in Austria came under different circumstances from those anticipated in the Linz Programme. Here Bauer, a major participator in the events he describes, outlines the stages between Dollfuss' assumption of dictatorial powers in March 1933 and the abortive workers' uprising in February 1934.

The Dictatorship of Dollfuss

Under the immediate impression of Hitler's electoral victory on 5 March 1933, Dollfuss decided to carry out a *coup d'etat*.[39] A Parliamentary incident, which, under other circumstances, would have been liquidated inside of twenty-four hours, was seized upon as a pretext for cutting out Parliament altogether. Dollfuss established a Government dictatorship. An Emergency Powers Act, dating from 1917, which empowered the war-time Governments to take the necessary economic measures for carrying on the war by issuing Orders, was interpreted as empowering the Government even today to impose its will by decree without consulting Parliament. The Court of the Constitution was broken up so as to prevent it from declaring the Orders issued by the Government in this way invalid. The Constitution of the Republic was thus overthrown, and an unrestrained dictatorship of the Dollfuss–Fey Government established.

The dictatorship immediately opened hostilities on two fronts: against the National-Socialists and against the Social-Democrats. Dollfuss dissolved the National-Socialist Party, put its leaders in concentration camps, and banned its press. But at the same time he began his campaign against the Social-Democrats, considering that the moment at which the great Social-Democratic movement of Germany lay smashed beneath the blows of German National-Fascism was also the most favourable opportunity for annihilating Social-Democracy in Austria as well.

The dictatorship began by destroying the rights and liberties guaranteed to the people of Austria by the Constitution. The freedom of the press was abolished; it was made impossible to print a word in opposition to the regime. The right of assembly continued in existence solely for the Government parties. The trial of political offences was transferred to the police; Social-Democrats and National-Socialists alike were sentenced by the police to terms of imprisonment ranging up to six months, without any proper judicial trial, for a word of opposition to the Government, expressed publicly or privately, or for handing on a leaflet. The jury courts were rendered impotent, as the Public Prosecutor can appeal against any acquittal by a jury to a higher court, composed solely of professional judges.

Simultaneously, the Dollfuss dictatorship started a drive against the rights acquired by the workers and employees in the social field. Collective agreements legally concluded between Trade Unions and employers were annulled by Government Order, and the Government decreed that wages should be cut. Unemployment relief was considerably reduced, and, for whole categories of unemployed persons, completely abolished. Important labour laws were amended, considerably for the worse. Strikes were prohibited by Order in a number of industries, under pain of imprisonment. The Chambers of Labour, elected by the votes of the workers, and the Works Councils elected by the workers in the State undertakings, were dissolved, and replaced by bodies consisting of representatives of the Government parties, nominated by the Government.

Against the municipality of Vienna, administered by the Social-Democrats, the Government launched a campaign of financial annihilation. More than one-third of the municipality's revenues were withdrawn by Government Orders, so that the municipality was reduced to the verge of bankruptcy and the continuation of its constructive work in the social and economic fields was rendered impossible . . .

The workers looked to their Party for help and protection. They could not understand how it was that the Party, previously so powerful, could have been rendered impotent at a single blow. They demanded that the dictatorship should be resisted.

But how, and by what means, was the dictatorship to be resisted, seeing that there were no longer any legal means of defence?

The Austrian workers, in common with the workers throughout the world, had heard with feelings of shame how in Germany both the powerful Social-Democratic Party and also the great Communist Party had collapsed before Fascism without fighting. They had learnt at their own expense how greatly this unresisting collapse of the German working class had encouraged the reaction in other countries. They vowed that in Austria things should happen differently. They felt that freedom was as good as lost unless men were prepared to defend it at the risk of their lives. They said to themselves that a band of men, relying on the use of violent methods, and supported only by a small minority of the population, was waging war on Social Democracy and National-Socialism alike – i.e., on at least 70 per cent of the nation as a whole. Regardless of the sanctity of oaths, this gang had abolished the Constitution, and was daily trampling underfoot the rights guaranteed by the Constitution to the people and to the individual citizen. They themselves, as citizens, were entitled to repel this gang of lawbreakers and to fight for the restoration of the democratic Constitution. Thus the feeling in favour of revolution against the dictatorship spread to wider and wider circles of the working class.

The Party was fully conscious of the dangers involved in a revolutionary rising. We knew how difficult it would be for a general strike to succeed at a time when more than a third of all the workers were unemployed, when many of the unemployed had been crushed and demoralised by the terrible misery of three, four or five years of continued unemployment, and when every worker still in work trembled for fear of losing his job. We knew that the dictatorship would try to break any strike by force, and that therefore a general strike would necessarily degenerate within a few hours into an armed struggle. We knew that in such a struggle our opponents would possess the terrible superiority conferred by modern military technique. We therefore made every possible effort to avoid a violent issue . . .

Again and again we seized every opportunity of warning bourgeois politicians, and through them the Government, of the growth of revolutionary feeling among the workers and of the increasing danger that some incident might lead – even against the will of the Party – to a violent outbreak of the pent-up wrath against the dictatorship. Again and again Dollfuss arrogantly rejected these warnings.

We offered greater and greater concessions with a view to making a peaceful solution possible. We let Dollfuss know that we would be prepared to grant extraordinary powers to the Government, in a constitutional manner, for two years, provided that these powers should only be exercised subject to the collaboration of a small Parliamentary Commission and under the supervision of the Court of the Constitution, and that in return all that we demanded for our Party was a certain freedom of action – the restoration of the legal right of assembly and of freedom of the press, within the limits imposed by the law. We declared that we would be prepared even to make concessions to the notion of a 'corporative' organisation of society and of the State, in order to make any understanding possible. It was all in vain – Dollfuss refused to enter into any negotiations . . .

But, unsparing though our efforts for the maintenance of peace were, right up to the last, we had still to reckon with the possibility that we might not be spared the final decisive struggle; for ever since 7 March we had been resolutely determined that we would not let the democratic Constitution, which we had helped to draft, and which we had defended for fifteen years, be violently destroyed, nor abandon the working class to the Fascist dictatorship, or let a Party which was the outstanding work of three generations of workers be wrecked without a struggle, without a manful attempt at resistance.

We knew that we could only emerge victorious from the unequal fight against the overpowering forces of the State if the whole body of workers, even in the most insignificant industrial centres, genuinely joined in the rising. Accordingly, we did not want to give the signal for battle until the dictatorship committed acts calculated to arouse popular indignation and popular passion to the highest pitch. During the autumn an extraordinary Party Conference decided that a general strike might be called in any of the four following cases:

(1) If the Government, in defiance of the law and the Constitution, introduced a Fascist Constitution.

(2) If the Government illegally and unconstitutionally deposed the municipal and Provincial authorities of Red Vienna and handed over the administration of Vienna to a Government Commissioner.

(3) If the Government dissolved the Party.

(4) If the Trade Unions were dissolved or 'brought into line'.

In any of these four cases the Labour Movement was to reply with a general strike.

This decision of the Party Conference was communicated and broadcast among the masses. At first the 'four points' met with their approval. But the longer the dictatorship continued, the harder the Labour Movement was hit by its decrees, the more clearly the workers realised that in the meanwhile the State machine was increasing its military force, whilst at the same time endeavouring to destroy the fighting strength of the Labour Movement, the greater became the number of those who, in the factories and the Party branches, gave voice to their impatience, their longing to fight. 'Why wait?' they said. 'By the time that one of the four points materialises, we shall no longer be in a condition to fight. Let us strike now, while we are still ready for battle. Otherwise, we shall share the fate of our comrades in Germany'.

Our Mistakes

We have been defeated; and each of us is turning over in his mind the question whether we brought the bloody disaster on ourselves by our own political mistakes.[40]

Some of us are saying: For years past our policy has been too doctrinaire, too radical, too uncompromising, too much to the left; others are saying, on the contrary, our policy was too timid, too hesitant, it lacked revolutionary *élan* such as could alone have carried the vast majority of the masses with us, it put off the fight until too late, and so was responsible for our defeat – it was too much on the right.

Where does the truth lie? Undoubtedly, we made mistakes; only those who remain inactive make none. It is useful that we should frankly confess our mistakes, for those who follow after us may learn important lessons from our experience. It is all the easier for me personally to confess our mistakes, for I can do so without throwing the blame on anyone else; since I am more responsible than anybody else for the mistakes that were committed.

In April 1932, the elections to the Provincial Diets and the municipal councils showed a bound upwards in the strength of National-Socialism in Austria. The Greater German Party – which had been in opposition since Schober's enforced resignation – and the National-Socialists demanded that fresh elections should be held for the National Council. The Christian-Social Party was terrified of fresh elections. If at that time we had shown ourselves ready to vote in the National Council against the ordering of fresh elections and if we had at the same time assured the Buresch Government, which was still in office, that we were prepared to 'tolerate' it in the same way as the German Social-Democrats had tolerated the Brüning Government, we might, perhaps, have succeeded in preventing the formation of a coalition Government between the Christian-Social Party, the *Landbund*, and the *Heimwehr*. We did not do so. We considered that fresh elections would be useful because they would bring the National-Socialists into Parliament, and because their demagogy would be unmasked when they were forced to take up a position with regard to concrete economic and political questions. In view of the experience of the German Social-Democrats, we were afraid of lapsing into a 'policy of toleration'. We believed that only the maintenance of a frankly opposition policy by the Social-Democratic Party could prevent the masses, impoverished and embittered by the economic crisis, from flocking over to the National-Socialists. The consequence of our attitude was that the Christian-Social Party formed a coalition with the *Heimwehr*, and that Dollfuss formed his Government with Fey as a member of it. In the elections held in the autumn of 1930, we had been successful against the first coalition Government of the Christian-Social Party with the *Heimwehr* – the Vaugoin–Starhemberg Government; and in 1932, misled by this experience, we failed to perceive that at a time when Fascism in Germany was carrying all before it the participation of the Fascists in the Government of Austria must necessarily be far more dangerous. Our attitude, after the 1932 elections, was thus perhaps mistaken – a 'left deviation' . . .

Parliament was eliminated. The dictatorship established itself. The attempt made on 15 March to carry on the work of Parliament was forcibly prevented by Dollfuss. We could have responded on 15 March by calling a general strike. Never were the conditions for a successful strike so favourable as on that day. The counter-revolution which was just then reaching its full development in Germany had aroused the Austrian masses. The masses of the workers were waiting the signal for battle. The railwaymen were not yet so crushed as they were eleven months later. The Government's military organisation was far weaker than in February, 1934. At that time we might have won. But we shrank back dismayed from the battle. We still believed that we should be able to reach a peaceful settlement by negotiation. Dollfuss had promised to negotiate with us at an early date – by the end of March or the beginning of April – concerning a reform of the Constitution and of the Parliamentary agenda, and we were still fools enough to trust a promise of Dollfuss. We postponed the fight, because we wanted to spare the country the disaster of a bloody civil war. The civil war, nevertheless, broke out eleven months later, but under conditions that were considerably less favourable to ourselves. It was a mistake – the most fatal of all our mistakes. And this time it was a case of 'right deviation'.

Was our policy too much on the left or too much on the right? There is no such thing as a doctrine of strategy that lays down that victory can be secured under all circumstances by aggressive or under all circumstances by defensive tactics, or that a decisive issue can always be forced on the left or always on the right wing. The problems of working class tactics in a period of rapid change are too complicated to be reduced to the simple division – 'right' or 'left'. Our mistakes were in some cases 'left' and in others 'right' deviations from the path which now, looking backwards and in the light of subsequent knowledge, we may suppose to have been the correct one.

But, though we have no desire to deny our mistakes, the question remains: after the victory of Fascism in Germany, would it in any case have been possible to prevent the Austrian counter-revolution? Could it have been prevented by another policy or by other tactics? If, after the elections of April 1932, we had decided to adopt a policy of 'toleration' towards the Buresch Government, should we not have simply followed in the footsteps of the German Social-Democrats and shared their fate? If, on 4 March 1933, Renner had not resigned the Presidency of the National Council, would the Government, terrified by the revolution in Germany, not have found some other pretext for eliminating Parliament? And if we had forced the issue on 15 March 1933, would the civil war not have brought about a coalition between the black and the brown forces, which, at the time were not so hostile to each other as they have since become, and thus made Hitler master of Austria?

The Hungarian Social-Democrats in 1919, and the Italians down to 1922, pursued a 'left' revolutionary policy, closely akin to Communism – and in both countries their policy ended disastrously. Conversely, the German Social-Democrats adopted a very 'statesmanlike', nationalist, 'right' line of policy – and they too, have been laid low. We in Austria tried to tread a path midway between the Italo-Hungarian and German extremes – and we, too, have been defeated. The causes of the defeat of the working class clearly lie deeper than in the tactics of its parties or than in this or that tactical mistake.

The Reasons for our Disaster

On the day that our rising was crushed a bourgeois democrat said: 'It was Breitner who brought bad luck to the Austrian Social-Democratic Party'. To have built magnificent dwellings for the workers out of the proceeds of taxation so that they could be let cheap to workers, both employed and unemployed, since there was no burden of interest to be paid on loans raised for building them; to have taxed wealth, luxury and enjoyment in order to build cheap dwellings for the poor, to make provision for their welfare and to provide modern education for their children – these were the activities that the propertied classes found insupportable. To say that our offence consisted in Breitner's fiscal policy is equivalent to saying that our offence consisted in being Socialists.[41]

On the day that our rising was crushed a capitalist paper wrote that Social-Democracy had been smashed because it had stood in the way of acquiescence in the dictates of economic necessity – in other words, because it had offered such obstinate resistance to the abolition of tenants' protection. Economic necessity, forsooth! – necessity of producing rent and profit for the capitalist would be a truer description. Our offence consisted in the fact that we attached more importance to the human necessity of keeping a roof over the heads of ill-paid workers, of unemployed members of the proletariat, of impoverished artisans, than to the 'economic necessity' of rent and profit.

Even before we were defeated we often heard it said on the side of the bourgeoisie that a dictatorship had become necessary because the Social-Democratic Party in Parliament was standing in the way of cutting down a code of social protective legislation which had become an intolerable burden in a time of economic crisis. In other words, democracy had to be destroyed and Socialism overthrown amid bloodshed so that the employers might whittle down the laws for the protection of the workers, free themselves from 'social charges', and break up the Trade Unions which imposed restrictions on the possibilities of exploitation.

The economic crisis had intensified class conflicts. Undoubtedly, the Austrian bourgeoisie had been impoverished as a result of the crisis. But the impoverished employer is a more malignant opponent of the working class than the rich employer whose business is prospering. The latter is prepared to let a few crumbs fall from his well garnished table for the workers; the former sees no other means of saving himself from imminent bankruptcy than wage-cuts and the 'reduction of social charges'.

The economic crisis had involved the proletarisation of the lower middle class and the peasants; bourgeois democracy has proved incapable of protecting the masses from the crisis. It was unable to protect them from the crisis not because it was a democracy, but because it was a *bourgeois* democracy – a democracy founded on the conditions inherent in capitalist property and capitalist production. But the masses of the peasants and the *petite-bourgeoisie* did not understand this. Impoverished and embittered, they turned against democracy in general, and sought for something new, something fresh, something unspoiled by compromise, that might spell their salvation. They thus became ripe for Fascism, and the sons of the peasants and the *petits-bourgeois* turned a ready ear to the appeals of the *Heimwehr* recruiting agents. And so they have fallen in behind the aristocratic landlords and the generals of the old Imperial army who are in command of the *Heimwehr* battalions – behind the classes that the 1918 revolution stripped of its privileges.

And at the very time when the capitalist bourgeoisie was turning against democracy in order to break the power of the Trade Unions and cut down the social reforms that the workers had succeeded in obtaining; at the very time when the aristocrats and generals had assembled an army of sons of impoverished peasants and *petits-bourgeois* in order to overthrow the democracy that they detested, and restore their own State — the authoritarian State, the pre-war State, the State in which they had been the masters — at this very time the workers' capacity for resistance was weakened to a terrible degree, more than one-third of the workers having been thrown out of work and the remainder trembling for their jobs . . .

And now they have won in their class struggle against the working class. Now they are proclaiming: 'There must be no more class struggle!' It does, indeed, appear questionable whether, when the working class is defenceless, impotent, deprived of all rights, and forced to support the class domination of the capitalists and big landlords, of the ex-generals and the Catholic Hierarchy, without any possibility of revolt, a class struggle can still be said to exist. The reconciliation of classes which they are now proclaiming, having slaughtered the men, women and children of the working class, hanged wounded prisoners, and shot to pieces the workers' dwellings, means in reality the complete subjection of the working class beneath the dictatorship of the ruling classes. But these gentry are making a mistake. They will soon learn by experience that their victory in a single class battle is very far from signifying the end of the class struggle.

46 Fascism,[42] *Otto Bauer*

Bauer's analysis of fascism, written in 1936, explores the relationship between its three social bases of support: the *déclassé* ex-combatants, the impoverished petty bourgeoisie, and the capitalist class (cf. Zibordi above pp. 88–96). This brief extract emphasises the role of fascism in undermining the achievements of reformist socialism.

. . . Fascism likes to justify itself to the bourgeoisie in terms of having saved it from the proletarian revolution, from Bolshevism. And it did actually use the spectre of Bolshevism by way of propaganda to strike terror into members of the intelligentsia, petty bourgeoisie and peasantry. In reality, however, fascism did not triumph at a moment when the bourgeoisie was threatened by the proletarian revolution, but rather when the proletariat had for long been weakened and forced on to the defensive, and the revolutionary flood had already subsided. The capitalists and large landowners did not surrender state power to the violent hordes of fascism in order to protect themselves from the threats of proletarian revolution, but with the aim of depressing wage levels, reversing the social achievements of the working class, and destroying their unions and their political power. Their aim, in other words, was not so much to suppress revolutionary socialism as to smash the achievements of reformist socialism. 'The verbal revolutionism of the maximalists', writes Silone, 'endangers only the street lamps and occasionally the bones of a few police agents. But reformism with its co-operatives, its pay increases in times of crisis, and its unemployment insurance, threatens something much more sacred: capitalist profit . . .'

In bourgeois democracy the capitalist class rules, but it does so under continuous pressure from the working class. It is obliged to make repeated and increasingly extensive concessions to the working class. The constant struggle waged by reformist socialism and the trades unions for higher wages, shorter working hours and the extension of law and administration in the social field certainly does nothing to disturb capitalism in the period of its expansion; on the contrary, it raises it to a higher technical, social and cultural level. But in the periods of severe economic crisis which have followed the world war, the achievements of reformist socialism appear to the capitalist class as obstacles to the 'normal' process of production and circulation as determined by the movements of the profit rate. It is then determined to refuse all further concessions, and to retract those already made. Democratic institutions prevent it from doing this; so it turns against them. The democratic legal order prevents the state authorities from using the official means of coercion against a reformist socialism that employs legal means of struggle; so the capitalist class makes use of the illegal, private coercive force of the fascist gangs alongside its legal state apparatus. But when it unleashes the fascist gangs against the proletariat, it makes itself their prisoner. Once the fascist bands are mobilised against the proletariat, it can no longer suppress them without exposing itself to the danger of proletarian revenge. Consequently it is itself obliged to submit to the dictatorship of the fascist gangs, and to sacrifice its own parties and organisations to fascist violence.

The fascist dictatorship thus comes into existence as the result of a unique balance of class forces. On one side stands the bourgeoisie, controlling the means of production and circulation, and also state power. But the economic crisis has destroyed its profits, and democratic institutions prevent it from imposing its will on the proletariat to the extent that seems necessary to restore the loss. The bourgeoisie is too weak to enforce its will any longer through the use of those cultural and ideological means by which it controls the mass electorate in a bourgeois democracy. Constrained by the democratic legal order, it is too weak to crush the proletariat by legal means, through the use of its legal state apparatus. But it is strong enough to equip a lawless and illegal private army, and to unleash it on the working class.

On the other side stands a working class led by reformist socialism and the trade unions, both of them stronger than the bourgeoisie can tolerate. Its resistance to any intensification of the rate of exploitation is an obstacle to deflation, which can only be broken by force. Yet if reformist socialism is too strong, its achievements too considerable and its capacity to resist too great to be attacked except by force, it is at the same time too weak to resist that force. Operating on the terrain of the existing bourgeois democracy, and holding fast to democracy as the position which provides its chief source of strength, it appears to the broad masses of the petty-bourgeois, peasant and proletarian strata as an 'establishment party', as participant and beneficiary of that very bourgeois democracy which is unable to protect them from the impoverishment brought about by the economic crisis. It is consequently unable to attract the masses who have become revolutionised by the crisis, and who flock instead to its deadly enemy, fascism. The result of this balance of forces, or rather of the weakness of both classes, is the triumph of fascism, which serves the capitalists by crushing the working class, and yet, despite being in their pay, so far outgrows them that they cannot help making it the undisputed master over the whole people, themselves included . . .

However the process of stabilisation of the fascist dictatorship destroys the balance of class forces from which it originally arose. When the capitalist class surrendered power to fascism, it had to sacrifice to fascism its own governments, parties, institutions, organs, traditions, a whole massive retinue of followers who had given it service and enjoyed its confidence. But once the fascist dictatorship was established, the leading stratum of the bourgeoisie, the big capitalists and landowners, succeeded extremely quickly in transforming even this new system of rule into an instrument of its own class domination, and the new rulers into its servants.

Of course, the fascist dictatorship seems at the outset to be quite autonomous and independent even of the capitalist class, and more decisively opposed to it than the governments of bourgeois democracy. The fascist terror threatens the capitalist class along with everyone else, and its dictatorship dissolves capitalist organisations as well, or at least subjects them to its tutelage. It reduces the capitalist press to submission, by transforming its publications into the mouthpiece of the government, and so denies capital any independent access to the most important means of influencing the mass of the people. Yet at the moment when it achieves supremacy even over the capitalist class, the fascist dictatorship becomes unavoidably the executive organ of the needs, the interests, the purpose of that same class . . .

---

47 The Unification of Socialism, *Otto Bauer*

Here Bauer sees the struggle against fascism in power as providing the opportunity and necessity for uniting the reformist and revolutionary traditions of socialism in a way that does justice to both.

Reformism is not a bourgeois ideology, not the 'ideological enslavement of the workers by the bourgeoisie'. It is the ideology of the working class at a particular stage of its development. The Marxist, who has understood that the reformist ideology and tactic is an unavoidable phase in the development of proletarian class consciousness at a specific stage of its development, and under specific circumstances, cannot believe that he can overcome the reformist ideology of the masses or prevent the reformist tactic of the mass parties, as long as the developmental circumstances, from which this ideology originates and to which the tactic conforms, have not themselves been overcome. He will not therefore see his task within the mass working-class parties to be that of forming cells to capture the leadership of these parties or create splits within them, nor of opposing demands required by the struggle for democracy and social reform within capitalist society, nor yet of deluding the working class into a tactic of 'revolutionary gymnastics' which will lead to their defeat and consequent demoralisation. But he does have 'over the great mass of the proletariat the advantage of clearly understanding the line of march, the conditions and the ultimate general results of the proletarian movement'. In other words, he knows that every temporary economic conjuncture, which offers the workers the possibility of successful struggle, will be followed by crisis, which once more destroys the achievements won in the struggle.

The Marxist knows that it is precisely the successes which the working class wins on the terrain of democracy, that drive the capitalist class towards fascism. He knows that it is when the proletariat is poised to win power on the terrain of democracy, that democracy is itself in the greatest danger of being destroyed by capitalist reaction. He knows that the way to achieve a thoroughgoing democracy, that is no longer dominated by capital nor endangered by class conflicts, is through the dictatorship of the proletariat – i.e. through a concentration of proletarian power, that, whatever form it may take, is strong and durable enough to accomplish the transformation from capitalist to socialist society. He knows that only the dictatorship of the proletariat, not the reforms of bourgeois democracy, can liberate the working class from exploitation and unemployment, free society from fascist barbarism, the nation from foreign domination and mankind from war. In other words, he shares none of the illusions which arise in the mass parties of the working class as a result of their successful struggles. Yet he has 'no interests separate from those of the proletariat as a whole'. This means that he engages all his energies in the struggle of the reformist parties to achieve every possible reform, however small, within capitalist society. He does not presume to 'set up any sectarian principles, by which to mould the proletarian movement' – i.e. he acknowledges the tactical requirements of the struggle for reforms within capitalist society, and does not oppose the tactical measures which this struggle demands. But 'in the various stages of development, which the struggle of the working class against the bourgeoisie has to pass through, he always represents the interests of the movements as a whole' – i.e. while he takes part in the struggles of the reformist mass parties, and conforms to the necessities of the reformist stage of development, he is immediately aware of its limitations, and sees the development in some countries already breaking the bounds of this stage, and in others being about to do so; he sees the conditions of struggle being revolutionised, and compelling a breach with reformist ideologies, illusions and methods. He instructs the working class of the democratic countries, where the movement still remains in the reformist stage of development, in the revolutionary necessities of the movement in the fascist countries and the revolutionary achievements of the country of the dictatorship of the proletariat. He warns the working class, where its conditions of life and activity still ensure the dominance of reformism, that tomorrow or the day after historical circumstances will force even them on to a different track, that of revolutionary struggle. In this way he transcends the limitations of both time and space.

Such is the task that Marxism has of asserting revolutionary ideas and training revolutionary cadres within the reformist parties of the working class and within an International dominated by them. By this means it transcends the one-sided and narrow-minded conceptions that have arisen as a result of the split of the working class into two hostile camps, conceptions which have become undialectically opposed to one another as if they were mutually incompatible and irreconcilable antitheses. Marxism conceives of reformism as the accommodation of the workers' movement to a particular stage of development, as the product and necessary result of a particular stage of development. But precisely because it so understands it, it recognises that its necessity is only a temporary, only a transitory one, which has to be transcended as soon as the developmental stage to which it corresponds has itself been transcended. Here Marxism sets itself the task, while the reformist period is still in being, of developing and disseminating those revolutionary ideas, and training the revolutionary cadres, that will enable the movement to pass beyond it. Such a conception, rising as it does above the antitheses of both the reformist workers' movement and of revolutionary socialism, and transcending their opposing ideas, leads Marxism to a reintegration of socialism, and makes it a force capable of reuniting the broken halves of the workers' movement.

Marxism has, then, to transmit to *revolutionary* socialism the great inheritance of the struggles for democracy, and the high estimation of the idea of democratic socialism and its irreplaceable values: security for individual rights, intellectual freedom, collective self-determination and a shared humanity – ideas which constitute the achievement of the bourgeois epoch, but which are threatened with destruction by the development of class conflicts, and whose preservation and restoration is socialism's supreme responsibility. Marxism has equally to transmit to *reformist* socialism the great inheritance of the proletarian revolutions: the realisation that it is not a matter of patching up capitalist society, but only its overthrow, only the proletarian revolution and the consequent dictatorship of the proletariat that can free humanity from exploitation, unemployment, crises, fascism and war. Marxism must therefore acknowledge the full historical, social and cultural significance of bourgeois democracy, as the product of decades of successful class struggles by the working class and the fertile soil for its economic, social and intellectual development. At the same time it must also understand that, in spite of all, bourgeois democracy remains only one form, albeit the highest form, of the class rule of the capitalist-led bourgeoisie. Marxism has to teach the working masses that only a temporary dictatorship of the proletariat can finally destroy the economic power and ideological domination of the capitalist bourgeoisie, and so re-establish democracy at a higher level and in a more complete form as the foundation of a new social order. This is the only way to make secure those great cultural achievements of the bourgeois epoch as a permanent possession. It is in this conception of history, then, that Marxism must bring together the moral sense of democratic socialism and the urgency of revolutionary socialism in a higher unity.

---

48 The Origins of Fascism,[43] *Richard Löwenthal*

In 1935 Richard Löwenthal published a systematic article-series on fascism in the theoretical journal of the SPD in exile. In this extract he thematises the nature of the political crisis that brought fascism to power.

The Mechanism of 'Interest Democracy'

... The parliamentary state, whose parties are interest parties based on class organisations, represents a characteristic final form of democracy. It has the character of a huge market place of interests, in which class compromises are worked out. The formation of political decisions here is every bit as much the consequence of particular interests as is the formation of prices on the economic market, though their significance is a correspondingly much more general one: once mediated by the state, the division of the social product becomes increasingly determined not by the direct economic power of the individual classes, but according to their social importance as reflected in the political sphere. This applies as much to the 'political wage' as to state support for East Prussian agriculture.

The fact that state policy within a 'democracy of interests' (*Interessendemokratie*) is not determined exclusively by the dominant class, but is the outcome of compromise, has itself frequently given rise to misconceptions about the class nature of this form of state. When German Social Democracy spoke of the Weimar Republic as 'its state', and sections of the bourgeoisie described it as 'Marxist', it was precisely this processual character that was responsible. By virtue of the political rights they enjoyed in this form of state the workers' parties were able to push through partial demands, which were felt by the bourgeoisie to be antithetical to their own interests and hence to the functioning of the capitalist economy. The political elite was formed not only from the bourgeoisie and its syndicates, but also from the leadership of all interest parties including those of the working class. The necessity of deciding all measures by means of class compromise seemed to make the concept of the political class rule of the bourgeoisie meaningless in this phase of democracy.

In fact, however, the democratic nature of this state-form abolishes its character as a structure of domination as little as the contractual nature of the wage relationship abolishes its character as a system of exploitation. The compromises which are at issue in this form of democratic state are compromises of sectional interests seeking to pursue their competing interests within the framework of bourgeois society. The greatest partial success of reformism can certainly disturb the capitalist mechanism, but not abolish it. No bourgeois regime can get along without some concessions to the dominated and exploited classes. In an 'interest democracy' the system of concessions enjoys legal guarantees, and is therefore both more visible in its operation and in material terms qualitatively more substantial than under dictatorial forms of rule. Nevertheless it remains a system of concessions within the capitalist framework.

The decisive guarantee of class domination resides in the system of 'interest-democracy' itself – i.e. in the self-evident limitation of all interests to the framework of bourgeois society. This limitation normally takes place without the use of exceptional pressure, through the automatic operation of bourgeois ideology, which prevents more far-reaching demands from becoming current within the subordinate classes. Because of the nature of bourgeois relations in which these classes are enmeshed, every attempt to go beyond this framework is experienced as a disturbance of the normal order. These are the only grounds on which the power of the executive state machine, created for maintaining order, can be used against them. The bureaucracy and the executive do not see themselves as agents of capital, but as professional guardians of order, which in practice can only mean bourgeois order. Only in this sense is it true to say that the class character of the democratic state is guaranteed by the independence of the executive power from the legislature.

There is, however, another function to the independence of the executive in this system. We said that the system of 'interest democracy' develops in parallel with the economic tasks of the state and the politicisation of class conflicts. It therefore also develops in parallel with the growth in the size and power of the bureaucracy. A developed system of 'interest democracy' and a powerful bureaucracy belong historically together. The connection also finds expression in the bureaucratisation of interest-parties themselves, in their leadership by routine officials, etc. But while the development of the whole system of 'interest democracy' reflects both the intensification of class antagonisms and the organising, centralising tendency of the capitalist economy, it becomes increasingly the task of parliament to represent the class antagonisms and of the bureaucracy and executive to represent the necessity for a unified central decision-making authority. It is in this divergence of functions that the system's line of fracture becomes visible.

'Interests' in the Crisis

All the tendencies specific to the most recent phase of capitalist development, especially as regards the shift in class- and interest-positions indicated in my first article, occur in an accentuated form in the crisis, in two senses: they become exaggerated by the conjuncture, even to the extent that some of the changes become reversed; and the shift is concentrated into a short space of time. In the space of a few years during the recent crisis unemployment became multiplied many times over. At the same time there was no (or no corresponding) reduction in the apparatus of distribution or administration, so that the cost of the decline in employment was borne almost exclusively by those productively engaged. At the same time the stratum of ruined but non-proletarianised middle classes grew rapidly, while the number of people not productively employed increased to an above average level at a rapid tempo. Of necessity there followed a decline in the productive role of that 'miscellaneous' stratum of officials and white collar workers. At the same time the proportion of stagnating branches of production urgently in need of subsidy increased, so intensifying the opposition between them and the remaining healthy ones. This opposition came to a head in the question: either a speedy resolution of the crisis on free market principles, with the destruction of millions of jobs, or a protracted resolution in which subsidies would be used to avoid an open catastrophe. The question: 'Pay the debts or cancel them?' formed one part of this problem. Another consequence was that the cross-fracturing of classes in the crisis, mentioned earlier, reached an exceptional intensity.

These contradictions are reproduced in the relations between national economies and hence between nation states. The debtor nations become insolvent. The disruption of international credit leads to an abnormal contraction of foreign trade, and hence to an intensification of protectionist tendencies and of nationalism, especially in the debtor countries which largely coincide with those least competitive in world markets and most encumbered with 'lame-duck' industries.

An additional factor in the strengthening of nationalism is contributed by the contrast in crisis intensity between countries with colonial and other imperialist outlets for shifting the burden of crisis, and those lacking these. In those countries that arrived too late in the partition of the globe, the pressure for an imperialist solution to the crisis intensifies, especially as the whole development of the expansionist, imperialist industries in such countries is still at an early stage that makes their every step dependent upon state support. In addition the proportion of the population whose primary interest directly or indirectly demands an effective state grows larger both because of the increasing number of the unproductive whose livelihood depends on state employment (leaving aside those who live off state securities) and because of the growing need of industrial production for subsidisation. This interest cuts rights across the classes, and during the crisis it comes to displace the interests determined by general class position in the process of production as the foremost consideration. It combines with the tendencies towards economic isolation on the part of the debtor nations and towards imperialist expansion to create an increasing requirement for a strong national state. Just as the shift in the basis of economic interests itself, this requirement merely expresses in momentarily exaggerated and concentrated form a general tendency typical of the period. The dynamic concentration of general tendencies of development into a brief but intense moment is the hallmark of all revolutionary situations.

The Party System in the Crisis

The first effect of the crisis on the system of interest parties is to exaggerate its character. The parties of the big bourgeoisie become revealed for what they are with a clarity that rapidly deprives them of their mass base. Because of the internal differentiation of the bourgeoisie into the profitable and the subsidised, the creditors and the debtors, its parties and coalitions are subjected to new splits. The various groups of small producers desert the old bourgeois parties to create new splinter parties (peasant parties, middle class parties, etc.), in so far as they have not already done so. Heightened conflicts occur within the working class on the basis of the sharp differentiation between the employed and the unemployed, the mobilised and the demoralised, those interested primarily in the level of wages and those in preserving a job at all – contrasts which deepen existing divisions, threaten united organisations with disintegration and generate conflicts between parties and trades unions. The overall result is to make any balance between the multitude of parties increasingly unstable, any compromise increasingly difficult, in the absence of a power strong enough to subordinate all the others.

Following the increasing politicisation of class organisations and the corresponding increase in the number of interest parties, there soon occurs a weakening of class organisations which in turn has a debilitating effect upon the interest parties themselves. The effectiveness of all classes declines with the decline in production, and with it the significance of organisations devoted to class action. The capacity of the unions to sustain strikes is weakened, the cartels break their pricing agreements, the rural credit associations can no longer support their members. This leads to a loss of confidence in such organisations and a decline in their membership. The only collective economic actions whose incidence increases during the crisis are those of consumers and debtors: rent strikes, strikes of tax payers, refusals to auction property. The crisis of interest associations and parties, which are thus simultaneously split and weakened, produces a tendency to place all hopes on the state and on purely political organisations, corresponding to the shift in the basis of economic interests described above. Parallel to the decline in economic effectiveness goes an insistence on military activity, and parallel to the decline of class organisations the rise of defence leagues. The organisations of the employed for economic struggle decline, while the organisations of the unemployed for the struggle over power increase (the defence leagues are also a form of job creation). In all periods the development of private armies from the unemployed has been a symptom of social disintegration.

'Interest Democracy' in the Crisis

The more the party system fragments the harder it becomes to achieve a compromise within the system of 'interest democracy'. The decline in the effectiveness of class organisations accentuates rather than alleviates the difficulty; the less their capacity to act directly in the economic sphere, the more insistent become the attempts of the parties to achieve their aims through pressure on the state, and so maintain their supporters' waning confidence. The viability of the parliamentary system is thus brought further into question. This is especially so from the standpoint of the bourgeoisie, whose parties lose their mass base fastest, and consequently are increasingly unable to realise their demands by parliamentary means – demands which also constitute the sole means of resolving the crisis within the framework of capitalism. It becomes increasingly difficult for the weakened bourgeois parties, which are also progressively split by the internal conflict between the subsidised and subsidising sectors to hold the balance between the large opposing mass blocks; and the role of the executive power in achieving the balance becomes ever greater.

The instability of this system renders impossible any consistency in the state's overall economic policy just at the moment when it is becoming a vital concern for increasingly large numbers. The crisis in state finances, which is an inevitable reflection of the economic crisis within the subventionist state itself, is exacerbated by the political instability, and has the immediate consequence of lowering the standard of living of all those economically dependent on the state. In other words the state fails just when the dependence of the masses on its performance is at its greatest, and it fails precisely because it is an 'economically democratic' state, because it comprises a mass of competing interests incapable of decisive action. So the economic necessity for a strong state suddenly turns into the cry for the abolition of parliament.

At this point the system of 'interest democracy' enters its decisive crisis. The contradiction between the functional requirements of the subventionist state and the mode of its political operation becomes manifest, and drives the masses into active opposition. Where a socialist transformation of the crisis does not succeed, the unavoidable centralisation of economic power takes place within the framework of the existing state – i.e. the bourgeois nation state. The mass base for this transformation is provided by a coalition of the unproductive and subsidy-dependent strata from all classes, who have a direct interest in the continued functioning of the subventionist state. The beneficiaries are the dependent sectors of the bourgeoisie and large landowners, who assume the leadership of the dominant class, along with those who have a direct interest in a state-sponsored expansion: the arms industries and the state executive itself. The closer the traditional relationship between these groups – e.g. through the recruitment of the state executive from the ranks of the indebted landowning class, and the more powerful therefore the means available to them from the outset – the more likely they will be to favour an overturn of the existing system.

The Labour Movement as Object of the Crisis
The development described above takes place where a socialist transformation of the crisis of 'interest democracy' does not succeed. The question why the latter does not necessarily happen can be answered first by the fact that the crisis leads of its own accord not to a strengthening but to a weakening of the working class and its organisations. The labour movement not only forms a part of bourgeois society; it especially constitutes a part of the system of democratic class organisations. As such it is also affected by the crisis of the system, at first helplessly, as it is exposed to the same divisive tendencies, the same reduction in effectiveness, the same loss of confidence as affects the other elements of the system. The dilemma of its position is expressed above all by the fact that any effective resistance to the attacks of the bourgeoisie only makes a capitalist resolution of the crisis more difficult; it intensifies the crisis and contributes to the further undermining of democracy. On the other

hand, to make concessions directly benefits its opponents by weakening its own basis of support. All discussion about effective class politics, or coalition politics with the middle strata, remains a dead end so long as class politics means purely negative resistance, and coalition politics means retreating on class issues. The conscious co-ordination of all oppositional elements behind the proletarian class struggle can only take place in a struggle for power on the basis of a Marxist understanding of the situation, and with a leadership united in the pursuit of this goal. Only such a combination can produce a socialist resolution of the crisis. To date no labour movement in any democratic country has produced a leadership equal to such tasks.

By way of contrast, the resolution of the crisis of 'interest democracy' within the framework of bourgeois society, and through the mobilisation of groups that have nothing to lose by the collapse of democracy, requires no conscious organisation; it is in this sense the natural outcome. Democratic rights have a real significance for the different social classes so long as they guarantee freedom for the independent representation of their interests. Such rights are valueless to groups that carry no real weight at the point of production, or whose importance is in continuous decline. Driven to despair by the failure of the state on which they rely, and freed from the inhibitions that accompany the defence of worth-while rights, they seize on the idea of dictatorship with enthusiasm. The democratic rights of the various interests necessarily appear to them as an obstacle to their own livelihood; this is especially true of the rights of the working class, the effective defence of whose interests within bourgeois society inevitably produces disruptive consequences. The more the labour movement becomes the passive victim of the democratic crisis, without the capacity to transform it, the more the mere continuation of its existence is widely seen as itself the cause of the crisis, or at least of its perpetuation. The less it is able to exercise a Marxist dominance over the situation, the more the dominance of Marxism is made responsible for every misfortune. Such a view has this much substance, that in the hour of crisis every exercise of working class power, however restrained, constitutes a threat to order and to the necessities of capitalism. This is precisely what the fascists understand by 'Marxism'.

V The Fascist State, The Economy, and War

49 The Proletariat, Fascism and the Italian Economy, *Angelo Tasca*

Tasca, one of the leaders of the PCI until his expulsion from the Party in 1928, is best known for his book on the rise of fascism, in which he argued that fascism can only be understood in terms of its history.[44] This article, written in 1927, traces the continuity between Mussolini's economic policy and that of previous bourgeois governments.

... Now is the time to pose the question: does fascism offer an original solution to the problems of the Italian economy? To this question corresponds another: what are the characteristics of Italian imperialism?

There is undoubtedly a certain process of concentration taking place in the Italian economy, an increase in the number of large firms and in the weight of their contribution to overall production. Fascist policy has favoured such a concentration, but not yet in a way that is distinctive to it. Only the hydro-electric industry has experienced a real 'trustification', brought about particularly by the need to ensure a distribution of energy that overcomes the seasonal and regional disparities. Interconnections in the financial and industrial world have multiplied, and collaboration has been much more frequent between the large credit institutions, yet without profound effect or organic change ... Italy has not experienced anything like the German rationalisation. Its industrial topography has undergone no perceptible changes in accordance with any kind of plan. The Italian bourgeoisie has no other plan than that of 'holding out'. Not for nothing is this the motto of the fascist regime. For a country like Italy that has to import its raw materials and grain, where the productive capacity has grown markedly and the home market has little capacity to absorb its products, the process of capitalist concentration should have been carried out with a view to ensuring the maximum development of exports.

The National Export Bureau was set up with the blessing of one of the more flamboyant speeches of the Duce. But what can it achieve, when the whole policy of the regime is opposed to the goals for which it was created? The export battle involves much more, for Italy, than a tariff war, to which it has been effectively reduced. Seriously pursued by a bourgeoisie which still maintained a progressive function in the process of capitalist development, it would have meant the reorganisation of industry and agriculture on a new basis, with a view to providing at competitive prices the goods and products that the foreign markets could absorb, and that would correspond more closely to the national resources and capacities of the Italian economy. It would have involved a redistribution of agricultural capital from one form of cultivation to another according to a general plan; it would have required a reconstruction of Italy's economic system, profound changes within the various strata of the bourgeoisie, and radical modifications in the relations between the latter and the other social classes.

Fascism never confronted this problem, and could never do so. We stress this point because of the important consequence that follows from it: 'Italy's industrial and agrarian revolution, which could have been carried out by the bourgeoisie in the last phase of capitalism, will have to be accomplished instead by the proletariat, in alliance with the peasants and the non-capitalist classes'.

In the post-war period the Italian bourgeoisie, having first immobilised and overcome the workers, entrusted itself after some hesitation to protectionism as its sole source of salvation. Whoever writes Italy's post-war history should pay the closest attention to the Alesso law of 1921, which marked a decisive turning point in the fate of the bourgeois dictatorship. It signified the collapse of the whole democratic economic policy, so coveted by the reformist collaborators. The bourgeoisie plucked up its courage (the factories had already been returned to the industrialists, and no one was frightened any more by trade-union control), and prepared the economic basis for its own political power by means of new tariffs.

What was lacking from the structure of 1921 was an agreement with the landowners, which was only effected under fascist auspices in 1925 with the restoration of the grain tariff. In this way the new government adhered closely to preceding tradition, reinforcing the Alesso tariff and restoring that bond between the protectionism of large industry and agriculture that provided the basis for more than a decade of Giolittian politics.

The home market has thus become the sole horizon of fascist economic policy, until a victorious war opens up new ones. Not that the fascist bourgeoisie has intentionally or willingly renounced the conquest of foreign markets. But once having turned back to protectionism in 1921 to retrieve the easy profits of the wartime period, it was in no position to face the ultimate consequences of the export problem: a reduction in heavy industry and in the cultivation of grain . . . The fact that the Italian bourgeoisie strives to establish a closed economy, based on the intensive exploitation of the labour force and of the home market (the consequence both of circumstances and of the intrinsic logic of the whole preceding development of capitalism), is the underlying fact of the Italian situation and of its characteristic crisis. Such a line of development, if so it can be called, is in flat contradiction with the basic features of the Italian economy: (A) absence of the most important raw materials; (B) inability of Italian agriculture to keep step with the increase of population; (C) growing demographic pressure.

While the reduction of wages lowers the cost of production, it has no effect on prices, because the protectionist policy of the dominant class keeps them at a very high level. The home market is thus impoverished on one side by the cut in wages, and on the other by the policy of high prices, which is even resistant to the pressure of monetary revaluation. Here lies the conservative and reactionary character of the economic policy of the fascist bourgeoisie, despite the progress achieved in this or that branch of industry. It assimilates the most modern technical processes, but within the framework of an economy dominated by a kind of agrarian and industrial feudalism. Individual features are modern but the overall framework is reactionary, in the sense that the dominance of this framework (which means the dominance of the bourgeoisie in the historical form it took after political unification) has become the most serious obstacle to the development of Italy's productive forces. To break this framework means to wrest power from the Italian bourgeoisie, and from the fascist bourgeoisie which is its substitute, since the latter could not have an economic programme different from the one which now prevails, and which, as we have seen, perpetuates in turn that of various preceding governments . . .

If we pass from the industrial to the agricultural sphere, we find that the efforts of fascism have been even more negative. There has been no process of industrialisation of agriculture; no noticeable flow of new investment has enabled the necessary improvements to be made. The problem of agricultural credit has not even been broached. The recent 'wheat battle' with its negligible if not actually damaging results, shows clearly that fascism has followed a regressive policy for the agrarian economy. Under pressure from the landowners and from the necessity to ensure a united protectionist front with the industrialists as already indicated, it has developed measures leading in precisely the opposite direction from that required by a progressive economy. The substantial cuts in agricultural wages have served to increase the price of land, thus reducing proportionally the amount of capital actually employed in the course of business. The backward conditions of our agriculture in the whole of central and almost all southern Italy have thus experienced a further deterioration from the fiscal, tariff and credit policies of the fascist government.

The problem of Italian agriculture is above all the problem of what can be termed 'southern' agriculture, giving the term a considerably broader geographical reference than the word itself implies. The problem of 'industrialisation' here is quite different from that of the large scale farming in the Po valley, and would require the widespread establishment of processing industries alongside specialised types of cultivation (grass for silage, vines, olives, fruit, vegetables, industrial crops). But this is impossible without the expropriation of the large landowners, and that means the overthrow of the government for which they provide the support. There can be no agrarian transformation without the corresponding changes in land-tenure, that is without a revolution that gives first place to the land problem and is ready to face radical solutions. A modern agriculture in southern Italy is impossible without a profound change in existing property relations, without the application of vast amounts of capital, without a radical alteration in tariff policies. Such conditions can only be attained by a worker–peasant government, founded on an alliance between the working masses of the north and the peasant masses of the south. The institution of such a government, following the defeat of the existing ruling classes, would open the way for the progressive economy that is presently being sacrificed to the requirements and contradictions of the fascist regime . . .

In the situation in which it finds itself, the fascist bourgeoisie is compelled to seek by military adventure the solutions that it has been unable to find to its economic problems, either at home or abroad. This is the basic cause of Italian imperialism, even more than the immediate pressure of capitalist development. Italy's warlike policy is not the result of the bellicose tendencies of the fascist strata; its essential elements can be traced to the policy followed by the Italian bourgeoisie as a whole for several years, and whose development is marked by the workers' defeat in 1920, by the Alesso tariff of 1921, by the 'productivism' whose common formula for both Nitti and Volpe has been to 'produce more and consume less'.

The balance sheet of fascist economic policy thus reduces itself entirely to the following three main elements: (A) suppression of the working class and its increasing immiseration; (B) uncompromising protectionism and a high cost of living; (C) preparation for war. There is nothing revolutionary in all this. There has been a certain group-displacement at the heart of the ruling class; certain institutions have been put in suspense; the five years of concentrated power continue . . . But the intensive exploitation of the workers is not a 'discovery' of the fascist government. All Italian industrialists and landowners follow a policy of low wages and slavish discipline. This policy is at the same time the corner-stone of the regime and the biggest contribution to the balance sheets of all Italian agricultural and industrial concerns. Fascism upholds it, and maintains the apparatus that makes it possible, but it has not itself invented starvation wages. When the workers take steps to improve them, the first thing they find is the resistance of the employers, and it is this that is the most decisive. The intervention of the fascist unions and of the aggressive power of the state is a direct function of the owners' purposes and attitudes. The violence employed by the *squadrista* or the policeman against the workers simply provides a measure of the determination and the intransigence with which the employer seeks to defend his profits. We can be certain that the fascist attacks would never have become so systematic, and that terrorism would never have become state policy, if it had not had workers' wages as its sphere of operation. No successor government to fascism will improve the economic condition of the workers, since none will be in a position to replace the extreme exploitation of labour as the chief source of capitalist profits, which cannot be renounced.

For this reason our Party considers the struggle for economic demands to be the fundamental struggle against fascism at the present time, both because of the actual situation of the masses, and because it strikes at the very heart of all the regime's activity. One should therefore recognise that such a struggle is at the same time an anti-fascist and an anti-capitalist one, and that the fall of fascism will give it new opportunities and a more extensive development.

By common agreement fascism and the bourgeoisie have reduced large sections of the population of Italy 'to the limit of physiological malnutrition' as it is called. By common agreement they are erecting customs barriers and preparing for war. *No* economic progress, *no* improvement in the condition of the working class, *no* peaceful policy is possible in Italy without the overthrow of fascism and the social classes whose interest has been served by the emergence, and continues to be served by the perpetuation, of the present regime.

---

50 Fascist Italy, Hotbed of War, *Palmiro Togliatti*

Writing contemporaneously with Tasca, Togliatti explains the distinctive form of Italian imperialism as a product of internal contradictions, including those within fascism itself.

From a purely theoretical point of view we can strictly question whether there yet exist in Italy at the present time all the typical factors necessary to the development of the capitalist economy in the period of imperialism. At first sight it appears that some of these factors are not yet present, and in actual fact they do not exist in the characteristically marked form typical to other countries. Is fascist Italy, for example, now an exporter of capital? It is open to doubt. The capital which Italy exports, especially to the Balkan countries, does not represent a substantial amount either relatively or absolutely. Italy cannot be considered among the great 'colonial' powers, that is the states in the forefront of the chase to exploit colonial markets. The conquest of markets as outlets for the products of Italian industry is still only an aspiration, a goal to be striven for, rather than one actually realised on any large scale. There is a sense in which it can be said that the factors still lacking from the 'imperialist' development of Italian capitalism are precisely those which give the imperialist countries in general their strength. But this would merely be to say that Italian imperialism has its own specific characteristics which distinguish it from the others. When we talk of the 'imperialist' development of a country's economy, we do not generally mean by this that its economy is growing stronger, but only that it is experiencing the development and intensification of certain characteristic contradictions. It was in this sense, and with particular reference to Italy, that Lenin spoke before the war of an imperialism 'in rags'.

Italy does not export capital to any great extent. But it is a country which every year produces a considerable surplus population, a country which every year has to find the means to feed a huge number of hungry mouths, and find work for a huge number of new hands. Naturally Italian capitalism cannot afford to lose them. It seeks to keep them in the internal labour market as a reserve industrial army to hold down wages, or at least to employ them in a labour market abroad in a way which will ensure that the profit realised from their labour will not be completely lost to Italian capital. The first of these solutions is dangerous because it requires a continuous intensification of the economic and political pressure on the working class, while the realisation of the second brings capitalist Italy up against barriers which it cannot surmount by peaceful means. There is no labour market today in any part of the world which capitalist Italy can use to export its excess labour and set it to work for its own profit. Even those labour markets where so far the emigrant Italian workers have been exploited by foreign capitalists are now beginning to be closed. France is about to expel hundreds of thousands of Italian workers from its industries in order to solve its own crisis. Other countries which could have provided outlets for emigration are already closed. Italian capitalism has no other choice but to attempt the conquest – by force of arms – of countries where Italian labour can be employed and exploited by Italian capitalism.

Italy does not have any colonies. Its development as a great capitalist power came too late, when the distribution of colonial markets had already taken place. Its participation in the world war, while having had terrible consequences for the country, was only considered a secondary factor by the large imperialist states, and failed to secure for Italy a portion of the booty when the German colonies came to be shared out. The triumphant revival of Turkish nationalism has deprived Italy of the possibility of making good its still unsatisfied claims in Asia Minor. The few miserable colonies which Italy possesses in Africa are now considered more of a liability than an advantage to the country's balance sheet. Yet it is precisely for this reason that Italian aspirations to a colonial empire now assume a directly threatening form. Italy cannot launch itself into colonial conquest in any direction without coming up against the economic, territorial and political network of interests that constitutes the sphere of influence of the great European imperialist powers. It has no alternative but to try any manoeuvre to break this network. This is why Italy is now being actively drawn into all the contradictions and conflicts that exist at an international level; this is why its foreign policy does not follow a single course, but a variety of directions, all of which seek in their different ways to make use of the existing conflicts and rivalries of capitalist Europe, to exaggerate and intensify them, and so create a favourable opportunity for fulfilling the aspirations of Italian capitalism . . .

Italy certainly does not yet possess a large export industry; but it is precisely here that lies the heart of the problem. An examination of

Italy's post-war economic development, and a comparison between it and that of the other capitalist countries, reveals that Italy stands at the forefront in terms of the 'pace' of its development, leaving countries far behind which in absolute terms may well be economically more sound. This means that there has grown up between Italy and these other countries one of those 'breakdowns of equilibrium' which are a law of development of the capitalist economy and the source of its profound crises. Italy's productive base has expanded enormously and in a quite unexpected manner. This expansion reached its peak at the point of fascism's seizure of power and as a result of its oppressive policy towards the working class, which sought to bring a renewed confidence and mobility to capital. Yet this expansion of the productive base was followed almost immediately by a restriction of export markets, thus creating a contradiction which Italian capitalism is wrestling with in vain at the present moment, and whose immediate consequence is the beginning of a profound crisis. Every possible effort is being made to find a foothold in those markets which still offer the chance of a sale (the Balkans, Near East, Egypt etc.) while other markets are being sought which, because of their exceptional circumstances can now be opened to Italian goods (Far East, China). The decisive overall result, however, is that the Italian economy is obliged to orientate itself towards an internal market that is poor, restricted, and sluggish, and to do this can only mean in the last analysis to orientate itself towards war. What is the significance of a programme of import restrictions for a country that has few raw materials? What is the significance of the huge efforts made by heavy industry, an industry that is artificial and parasitic? What is the significance of the propaganda for a massive campaign to grow wheat at the expense of more profitable crops? What is the significance of an autonomous economic policy based on the principle of 'going it alone', of becoming economically independent of other countries? What does all this signify if not an orientation towards war? What solution is possible to the situation brought about by the basic principles that have guided the development of the Italian capitalist economy? What other way out than that of war?

If the classical form of imperialist development cannot yet be seen in present-day Italy, nevertheless Italy reveals itself even more clearly, in every way, as a capitalist country which exerts all its powers to resolve its internal contradictions by means of war. And not only its own internal contradictions. On the level of political contradictions the chief problem, underlying all the others, is that of fascism itself, its social origins, its policies, its prospects. Fascism's seizure of power, as we have already said, was the immediate cause of the distinctive pattern of development taken by Italy's capitalist economy in the post-war period. The policy of the fascist government has been directed principally towards satisfying the interests of the highest strata of capitalist society: the big industrialists, the large landowners, the bankers. The fascist government has intentionally encouraged the concentration of finance capital and its dominant position in the direction of the country's economic affairs. The consequences of the bloody campaign waged for five years to silence the working class and peasantry and to reduce them to a condition of slavery, have only worked to the advantage of this limited group of the ruling oligarchy. Yet was this the social base on which fascism was originally formed? No! It arose from a mass movement, which brought together elements of the petty and middle bourgeoisie, *déclassé* elements and even proletarian ones, demoralised and hopeless, behind an instinctive ideology of 'struggle and conquest'. Conquest of what? First of all the conquest of wealth and power at home, following the defeat of the working class and the removal of the old ruling classes from power; then conquest by the routes of nationalism and imperialism, in a struggle against the whole world.

The first part of this programme has failed, lamentably failed, in face of the inexorable historical laws of capitalist society in the imperialist era, which exclude the possibility of any intermediate solution between the dictatorship of the proletariat and the dictatorship of the big bourgeoisie, and also in face of the inability of the petty bourgeoisie to play a role of its own, or direct the capitalist state independently. The members of the old ruling class have disappeared. The working class offensive has been repulsed by force of arms and by terror. Yet it is not the petty bourgeoisie, which provided the framework for the fascist movement, that now governs, but the forces of big business and finance. Fascism has to content itself with being an instrument in their hands for oppressing the great mass of the population – the proletariat, the peasants and the petty bourgeoisie. Will this instrument be able to resist? In order to ensure that it does, war and the desire for conquest must now move into first place, so as to maintain that unity and agreement in fascism's ranks that is necessary as a second basic element in the fascist ideology. This is why war assumes such a prominence and decisive significance in all fascism's activity. All its activity has necessarily to be directed towards war . . .

---

51 The Corporations and State Capitalism, *Ignazio Silone*

Silone's chapter offers a later perspective on Italy's economic development under fascism, and one which singles out the active role of the state as its most distinctive feature.

The Transformation of Italy's Economic Structure
Under the hegemony of fascist large-scale capital, Italy's economic and industrial structure has undergone significant changes. Agricultural production is still quantitatively greater than industrial production, but this superiority has diminished; the pace of agricultural development does not match that of industry, and its inability to satisfy the additional demand generated by the increase of population has not been rectified. We mention this for the benefit of those who insist on the agrarian character of the fascist dictatorship. The different branches of Italian farming have either stood still at their existing level of development, or regressed, or else have made quite insignificant progress at the expense of other branches. The development of agriculture could not keep pace with the process of industrialisation, with the result that under fascism the relative weight of Italian industry as compared to that of agriculture has further increased. This is even more obvious at the political level. The dominance of landowners over the central government, which still

made itself felt when occasion demanded, has completely disappeared since the attempt on King Umberto's life. It revived when the urban bourgeoisie was in a state of extreme confusion (the 'truce' of 1921), only to be brought to an end by the industrial orientation of the Commercial Bank in 1922, and the sudden change in Giolitti's policy as well as the policy of the crown.

Under fascism the industrialisation of the country advanced by leaps and bounds. The factors which made this possible were the following: (A) the capitalist super-profits, which derived from the 30–40 per cent lowering of wages; (B) fascism's tariff policy; (C) the import of foreign and particularly American capital to a sum of 1.5 billion lire. In the rubber industry, in ship building, in the manufacture of artificial silk, synthetic fibres and the generation of hydro-electric power, Italy is at present at the forefront of the whole world. The same is not true for the key industries in which raw materials are of greater importance than wages, since Italy possesses neither coal, nor iron, nor petroleum. The absence of heavy industry has not prevented the creation of a productive system that has seized a monopoly position in the home market with the help of the state, and very quickly disturbed the balance between production and consumption (imbalance between production and consumption – that is also the basis of the present world economic crisis).

In 1925 the character of the fascist state as governmental form of finance capital showed itself in a quite brutal manner. Fascism worked consciously and openly for the centralisation of capital and of production. In 1928 and 1929 it took the final steps along this road that still remained available. The amalgamation of the investment banks with the Commercial Bank, the participation of the state in certain private industrial concerns, the grants and subsidies allowed to firms involved in mergers, and the tax concessions guaranteed them, the subordination of banking and governmental credit policy to the same ends – all this led to the creation of huge monopolies in all the main branches of Italian production.

In this way the fascists believed that they could overcome the difficulties caused by production developing anarchically – i.e. by a concentration of production developing on the basis of free competition. By means of state intervention, Italy's capitalist system skipped several natural stages of capital concentration and reached the stage of monopoly immediately. Using Soviet terminology, fascism portrays the Italian economy as a 'planned economy'. It may well be possible, in a certain sense, to talk of an Italian economic plan, which gives a certain unity not only to the economy but to the whole of Italian life. It is a plan that aligns economic monopoly with political monopoly, and makes each of them the basis of the other: it is a plan for the preparation of war. But this plan contains all the contradictions of production to be found in the system of free competition: low wages, depressed demand, increase in the cost of production, decline in exports, etc. For this reason one finds once more the *old* contradictions exacerbated by *new* ones, the contradictions of free competition exacerbated by the contradictions of monopoly.

Italian industry is not sufficiently equipped to overcome the competition from the Americans, Germans, English or French, in spite of the low wages it pays. Even in the industry for which Italy provides its own raw materials (natural silk) it is on the way to being overtaken by Japan. The drama of Italian industry remains entwined in a dilemma: if industry pays wages proportionate to the cost of living, the increased costs of production lose it the few foreign markets still remaining; if it sticks to its policy of low wages it produces a further narrowing of the market at home.

State Capitalism

State capitalism has arisen in Italy as a means to strengthen the concentration and centralisation of capital. This concentration is closely bound up with the currency reform. Italian industry, having expanded considerably during the period of inflation, now had to slim down and find a new method of organisation which would still ensure profits in the new situation. The firms whose organisation was weak or inadequate had to be weeded out, and above all the various levels of operation, which could no longer develop independently, had to be co-ordinated. At the same time the currency reform necessitated a measure of credit restriction, which both required and enabled pressure to be put on the individual enterprises to ensure their amalgamation.

Fascist state capitalism has striven to mobilise economic sources of support to sustain the government in power (a problem which continues to exercise the dominant class). With its help the government has secured a breathing space, and postponed for a while the disintegration of the Italian economy and the panic reaction of the bourgeoisie to the ever-increasing difficulties the economy faces. Without state capitalism the policy of strongly protective tariffs and monopolistic price increases would have compelled Italian industry to concentrate on the home market. This has partly happened. But monopolisation has led to a progressive weakening of internal trade. For this reason the controlling hand of state capitalism turned Italy's industrial concentration towards the creation of an artificial market: the defence industry and public works, both a charge on the state. The state became the largest, and for some sectors of industry the only, customer. The state took the place of the banks in financing industry, i.e. it placed the combined resources of the country at the disposal of the banks and of industry, and set up special organisations to carry this out . . .

Savings and the proceeds from taxation were fed into these new state organisations, which held them at the disposal of industry. However the state does not help just any manufacturer. Thousands upon thousands of them have gone bankrupt because they have failed in their approach to the state for help. Who then disposes of the national wealth in a country where there is no parliament, no freedom of the press, and no public control? Who administers it, without having to render any account to anyone? It is a small group, the leaders of the big banks and the trusts. Behind the majestic stage show of fascism, this small group is master of Italy.

The consequences of this capitalist dictatorship have been very serious. The economic crisis, which began everywhere in the years 1929 and 1930, dates from as early as 1927 in Italy. In 1928 national wealth had dropped by a third in comparison with 1925. The state finances are also in poor shape. The fiscal year 1932–3 ended with a state deficit of 10,171 million, in comparison with a figure of 1,472 million in January 1926 . . . A further symptom is the steep rise in taxes. In 1913–14 Italy's state taxes absorbed 12.5 per cent of personal income. In 1925–26 the proportion rose to 20 per cent and in 1927–8 to 23.3 per cent. In no other country has central taxation reached such a level. The impoverishment of the masses is enormous. The statistics relating to consumption give an even more striking impression of the conditions under which the economic 'progress' of the Italian bourgeoisie has taken place . . .

The fascist system has thus made no contribution to eliminating the crisis of Italian finance capital which was started by the war. It has only intensified it, and handed over the great mass of the population to a veritable slavery. It has depressed their standard of living to the borders of starvation. The new phase of Italy's economic crisis dates from 1927 and it still continues today. It cannot be resolved within the confines of the capitalist system. Its resolution requires: the removal of the parasitic sectors of the economy; a redistribution of capital in accordance with the country's needs and natural resources; a reorganisation of Italy's economic relations with the rest of the world, which at present are geared towards nationalism and military preparation; a radical alteration of the colonial style relations between the north and south of the country, and an improvement in the living conditions of the masses, i.e. an increase in their spending power. All this, however, is incompatible with capitalist profit, and can only be realised in a state that is governed in opposition to capitalist profit . . .

The Corporations

. . . After eleven years of fascist dictatorship in Italy the fascist leaders are still debating about the structure and functions of the corporations – but the corporations do not exist. Mussolini has himself announced that they cannot be created for two or three years. Despite this there is considerable talk abroad about the 'success of the Italian corporations', great admiration is expressed for these corporations 'that have so brilliantly proved themselves in Italy', and widespread proposals are made for adopting this Italian corporative system. And all the time the corporations do not actually exist at all in Italy. I cannot pronounce judgement on them, I cannot even inform the reader about them – they simply do not exist.

What does exist in Italy is the corporatist ideology ('corporatism'). We shall concern ourselves briefly with this great mystification. Corporatism is hailed by many as the vehicle for socialism, as a way out of the contradictions which the socialist critique has revealed in existing society. In reality corporatism is quite the opposite. Socialism opposes the fiction of freedom in the capitalist system; under corporatism freedom disappears, but capitalism remains. Socialism attacks bourgeois democracy; under corporatism democracy disappears, but the bourgeoisie remains. Socialism first pointed out and then explained the disappearance of economic liberalism; under corporatism liberalism is abolished, the monopolies remain. Only the massive intellectual impoverishment that mankind experienced as a result of the war can explain the sympathy with which even certain socialists, democrats and liberals follow the corporatist system. Corporatism is not a transcendence of capitalism, but an attempt to solidify its external features, an attempt to destroy those forces maturing in the womb of capitalism that tend towards socialism.

Consider socialism's ABC. The aim of socialism is to transform private property into collective property. Fascism effects the opposite, by putting all the resources of the state (of the collective property) at the disposal of the large capitalists. The initiative and the profits remain a private affair; but when bankruptcy comes, the corporatist principles come into play, whereby production is a national concern and consequently the losses of private initiative become a charge on the state. The alleged superiority of corporatism over socialism should have shown itself on the other side, in the problem of the class struggle. Remember that the goal of socialism is not class struggle but its abolition, through the elimination of classes themselves and the capitalist system that engenders them. The aim of corporatism, in contrast, is to fossilise society at its current stage of development and perpetuate the present state of things whereby a small minority controls the majority of the population. The corporatist regime bans the class struggle of the workers, which is considered high treason. The only class struggle that is tolerated is the struggle of the capitalists against the popular masses. Corporatism helps large capital in its attempt to conceal its hegemony over the life and wealth of the country. The essential superiority of corporatism over democracy in the sight of capitalism lies in the fact that, whereas under democracy capitalism's harsh exploitation of the workers is continually exposed by the freedom of criticism and public accountability, in the corporatist system the worker loses all his rights as a citizen and sees his person fused with his profession. The horizon of his activity can no longer be the state and society in its totality, but may only extend to the problems of his profession. So the state is now ruled by large capital without any resistance. War and peace, trade agreements, taxation, public order, the operation of the law – everything eludes the control of the people. In essence corporatism marks a return to feudal forms of organisation.

A new type of state has thus emerged, the corporatist state, constructed on the economic relations of state capitalism. The economy is merged with the polity. The lie about formal democracy is replaced by the lie about the corporatist economy. Philology has already been pressed into its service. The capitalists and the workers are no longer called capitalists and workers, but *producers*. Private property is from now on called *national wealth*. Capitalist theft from the public treasury is called *national solidarity*. Wage reductions are termed *patriotic sacrifices*. Violent suppression of all critical and socialist opinion is termed *national discipline*. All this is perfect on paper. And because it only exists on paper it can be deemed perfect. 'This is the greatest revolution', proclaimed Mussolini. The greatest revolution on paper. For the moment, however, the corporations just do not exist . . .

---

52 The Fascist State and Monopoly Capitalism, *Richard Löwenthal*

The first part of this article series, written in 1935, analyses the complexity and contradictory character of state intervention under monopoly capitalism, and shows the inherent limits to policies of economic autarky. This prepares the ground for an analysis in the second part of the structure of the fascist state, the contradictions of its economic policy and the sources of its imperialism.

(1) Changes in Capitalism: the Double Character of State Interventionism

... In our investigation of monopoly capitalism we repeatedly referred to its connection with the increasing economic activity of the state. If we now examine the state's role in economic development, it should be said at the outset that we are concerned here only with the economic function of the interventionist state in its various modes of activity, not with the social dynamic which leads to this form of state and determines the general course of its actions. It is obvious that in reality these two sides are inextricably linked, but in our view it is more useful to examine the social dynamic aspects and the context of class conflict in which the transformation of the state takes place, in a separate survey devoted to the overall socio-political development, and to confine ourselves here to an analysis of the economic trends which result in interventionism.

State intervention in the capitalist economy takes the form on the one hand of the regulation of economic policy, on the other of direct economic activity by the state through its own independent investment. We must examine the economic functions of both forms of activity. In both we shall find measures of quite different content. On the one hand the state takes over requirements of the whole society that cannot be fulfilled, at least not rationally, by private capitalism. Here it is undoubtedly, under monopoly conditions even more than before, a question of basic social organisation. On the other hand we find governmental measures in the direct interest of specific capitalist interest groups, and here again we should distinguish between those on the economic upgrade which make use of the state to reinforce their momentum, and those which can no longer survive without the state's crutches. In both these instances the state's economic activity is a function of monopoly capitalist development, in the one case as assistant to 'progressive' monopolies (without however their reaching a qualitatively more advanced form of development through their involvement with the state), on the other as assistant to the downright reactionary monopolistic tendencies. We should always bear in mind here as well, that in the actual world of monopoly both aspects usually occur together. Finally, parallel to the growth of capital's contradictions, in particular the destruction of capital, we find the state in situations where it becomes quite independent in its performance of this negative function for society as a whole ...

These various functions of the state that we have distinguished in our analysis are frequently intertwined with one another in the real world. Often they are combined in a single measure, and regularly occur together in one and the same period; however, it is undoubtedly possible to observe a variation in the importance of the different functions at different stages of the state's development. Under early capitalism progressive subsidy predominates, under mature capitalism the fulfilment of requirements for the whole society, and under pre-war imperialism the promotion of monopoly expansion. Since the war, however, it is the support of economic dead-weights and in general the organised destruction of capital that comes increasingly to the forefront of the state's activity in the older countries, although certainly the other functions do not cease to be of significance in the total picture.

During the course of this development there occurs a continuous expansion in the overall scope of the state's economic activity, alongside the qualitative change in its content. This expansion is an expression partly of the growing necessity of society-wide regulation, partly of the increasing intensity of the class conflicts and competitive struggles that break out over the content of such regulation. In so far as the state's organisation of society becomes a pre-condition for the attainment of specific economic goals, to that extent class conflict and competitive struggle turn into a conflict over the state. One form this development takes is the politicisation of conflicts of economic interest, and the emergence of a system of parties tied to particular interests. The other is the increasing importance of the state bureaucracy. Bureaucracy in general is of growing importance as a result of the increasingly scientific character of production, the growth of social organisation and the expansion of bureaucratic structures from the sphere of production to all areas of life (e.g. the army). The development outlined above necessarily leads also, at each stage, to a strengthening of the state bureaucracy, the bureaucracy 'par excellence'. It produces a chronic contradiction, whereby the expansion of its tasks requires increasing uniformity and independence on the part of the bureaucracy, whereas the growing importance of its activity for the economic fate of all classes and groups intensifies the pressure exerted upon it and threatens the same uniformity and independence. The respective strength of these tendencies varies with the different stages of development of the state's economic activity, and with the different types of state. Where the tasks are essentially those of societal organisation as a whole, the bureaucracy's independence and room for manoeuvre are strengthened. Where the particular interests of special groups come to the fore, as under imperialism and subventionist policies, the opposite is more likely to be true. Where the state takes on the independent organisation of capital destruction, as in the latest phase, the bureaucracy's autonomy increases once more. Among the different forms of state, it is those where the head of the executive is either a monarch or president independent of parliament which are most favourable to the autonomy of the bureaucracy. The apparatus is dependent only on the head of state, and the latter's supremacy removes it to a certain extent from the direct pressure of interests. While no form of state can fundamentally abolish this pressure or the resulting contradiction mentioned above, it is only in respect of the state's *function* that this form reveals the fundamental contradiction between increasing social organisation on the one hand, and growing class conflict and competitive struggle on the other – i.e. the growth of organisation on an antagonistic basis.

The further the bureaucracy goes in its attempts to achieve uniformity in its economic policy, the greater the resistance it meets from the autonomous spheres of social life, which it strives to control. The more essential it is for the subventionist state to engage all the nation's energies together towards a particular goal, the more emphatically will the autonomy of the law, of religion, of scientific discussion, of literature and art be perceived as a hindrance. The guarantee of a system of law which was independent of political influence and operated according to predictable rules, was a precondition for the expansion of world trade and rational competition under the free market system. The more that economic development comes to depend upon the regulation of power struggles between the big monopolies, rather than on the guarantee of free scope for the individual, the more the standpoint of formal legality loses its point and becomes an obstacle to the development of a co-ordinated policy. The same could be shown for the other 'spheres' as well.

The end result of the trends towards the overall organisation of society within the confines of capitalist antagonism, is thus the tendency to subordinate all spheres of life to the requirements of a bureaucratically co-ordinated state economic policy. This tendency, which may find expression in the most varied kinds of political reform, legal reform, etc., always marks a significant advance from the standpoint of formal organisation. The *content* of the state's economic policy in the capitalist countries, however, as the preceding survey has shown, increasingly develops in a reactionary direction.

The USA is currently catching up the European states in the performance of society-wide functions, which they have long undertaken; in Japan the imperialist expansion is in full bloom; in Central Europe it is almost impossible to find a sound economic concern in face of all the subsidisation and destruction of capital that is taking place; and in the British Empire the pressure of dead-weights has once again been relieved by an exceptionally favourable position in the world economic conjuncture, though this cannot contain their increasingly damaging effects indefinitely. In other words the state in these countries is becoming a reactionary obstructive force, as it attempts to reconcile the contradiction between productive forces and productive relations beneath it, and the later it becomes involved, the more this is so. This does not necessarily mean that all development beneath must come to an end, or that the state can bring the economic force of productive development to a halt; only that it generates its own tendencies in that direction. It does so as the executor, not of some economic necessity, but of an expanding social group of reactionary character: the non-producing classes and those producers who require subsidisation.

We have now all the elements assembled to pose the question: does the pattern of development point unambiguously towards a resolution of the contradictions, either through the necessity of socialism or of some reactionary stagnation? The previous survey shows that both the technical and the organisational requirements for a socialist solution – i.e. those to be found in the state of the productive forces –

have advanced and are continually advancing further. The course of development certainly shows an increase in capitalist contradictions, but no decline in the sense of a lessening maturity for socialisation. Every new development in productive capacity, and every new-found method of organisation and planning, even if for the most reactionary purposes, signifies a further precondition for the possibility of a socialist solution. Technology itself, in so far as it leads to concentration and organisation, generates new forms of co-operation and society-wide integration between different complementary branches of production; such forms are no longer a function of the market, but a deliberate creation.

On the other side we have seen the growth of social and political opposition to any national planning, in proportion to the number of old industries and the increasing role of the national state. The obstacles to accumulation, which can only be effectively overcome by international planning and a reapportionment agreed at an international level, find their economic expression in national-based policies of state subsidy and in the organised destruction of capital by both monopolies and states. These obstacles produce the paradox of a growth in socio-economic irrationality, although the means of rational control have increased. The logical conclusion of the one tendency, if pursued in isolation, would be the development of socialism; of the other, the disintegration of the world economy into stagnating, autarkic, bureaucratic nation states.

To assess the relative weight of these tendencies is to pose the question of the limits of state intervention in the capitalist economy. It has already been suggested that it is impossible to halt the technical dynamism of capital. Here the power of the state finds its limit in the fact that the subsidisation of backward branches of production requires the existence of economically healthy ones, whose profits can supply the subsidies. It finds its limit in the persistence of international competition, precisely in the healthiest branches of production, and in the military necessity for each individual state to stay at the forefront of technology, which is ultimately the consequence of this competition. The result is that the tendencies towards autarky and stagnation are repeatedly interrupted, and every stabilisation of power relations is continually subject to alteration. The vulnerability of those artificial monopolies which depend on the support of governmental compulsion rather than on any genuine, technically based logic of amalgamation, is a clear example of this . . .

The international trustification of the expanding industries and the banks despite every law against foreign ownership shows clearly how far these tendencies escape the control of state power in peacetime. War itself is nothing other than one of those explosions of competitive conflict between giants which prepares the way for new amalgamations. The monopolies make corresponding use of the state as a weapon in their competitive struggles, internally as well as externally, but the state does not play any independent role in this, and is unable to transcend the competitive process. The ruthlessness of the competition between the giant monopolies and its tendency towards trustification, ultimately signifies a trend towards the legendary 'general trust' embracing all branches of production in all countries. The conflicts that will take place on the way will lead mankind through an abyss of economic destruction, war, mass poverty and social disintegration, whose extent is still unforeseen. At the end of this process a situation could well be reached in which production would lose its commodity character, and private property would become merely a source of rent without any productive function. At the same time the complete organisation of production would prefigure the arrival of socialism – only in antagonistic forms – and the proletarian revolution would thereby become unavoidable. Yet this situation, whose arrival was so self-evident once the bourgeois revolution had taken place, would only come as the final culmination of a development in which mankind would be repeatedly subjected to all manner of barbarism, so that it is idle to speculate about this kind of 'necessity'.

In practice we are confronted with the first stages of this process, with the simultaneous development of both the preconditions for socialism and the obstacles and contradictions which stem from private property and express themselves in the politics of the bourgeois states. To grasp both sides of this development in which we find ourselves, and to recognise the impossibility of its standing still, provides the basis for an analysis of the likely course of development in class structure, social organisation and political systems, and therewith also an understanding of political possibilities and their associated consequences.

(2) System and Contradictions: the Fascist State

The fascist state must essentially be understood as an exceptional historical form of the bourgeois state. It shares with all bourgeois states the class content and function characteristic of bourgeois class rule; it shares with many others the dictatorial form; but it is distinguished from all other forms of the bourgeois state, both in the character of the economic group that has won the leadership within the ruling bourgeoisie and in the mode of political operation of the power structure composed from the bureaucracy and the party. This determines a particular relationship between the state and the natural forms of organisation of social forces, and a particular manner in which it seeks to maintain its mass base. An investigation of these distinctive features of the fascist system will at the same time reveal its specific contradictions, and thereby also the starting point for revolutionary anti-fascist politics.

The apparatus The dictatorship of the fascist party, the amalgamation of its own bureaucracy with the state's, and the destruction of all independent social organisations, facilitate a huge modernisation and expansion in the power of the state apparatus, and a maximum degree of uniformity, centralisation and autonomy of the bureaucracy. The subordination of independent powers under the central bureaucracy is being carried out right down to the level of communal self-government. The various branches of state activity are being reorganised in such a way that all departments can be committed together to carrying out overall policy directives. The evident dependence of sections of the bureaucracy on the central apparatus renders them less amenable to pressure from special interests, and creates a level of independence which in principle requires such interests to go over the head of the apparatus to attain their goals. This is not how the fascist state necessarily operates in practice, but is the principle which affects its practice to a far-reaching extent.

The process described above, whether it involves the abolition of limited powers or special competences, whether it is the Bavarians or southern Italians, lawyers or mayors, teachers or priests who are subordinated to the uniform direction of the apparatus, represents in principle an advance in terms of the rational organisation of tasks for the whole society. It creates the technical—organisational *capacity* for the co-ordinated, scientific direction of the whole state's activity, particularly in the economic sphere, and so makes possible the rational performance of the greatly expanded economic functions of the state. In practice, however, this rational performance does *not* take place, because the struggle of interests to influence the content of policy continues, and because one of the most reactionary interest groups occupies the political leadership. However, the creation of an apparatus for the national control of the economy is itself an advance.

The contradiction between the progressive form and the reactionary content expresses itself in important conflicts within the apparatus itself. The removal of political opposition deriving from the special agencies responsible for the various aspects of social life, and the subordination of all social organisations to the state, makes the bureaucracy appear all-powerful. Its control of every means of propaganda – press, education, culture, etc. – seems to give it the ability to 'determine' the ideology of the people, and to direct all the nation's energies to its own goals. In fact, however, persisting class antagonisms and realignments of social forces ensure a continuing autonomy in the depths of society, which repeatedly frustrates the attempted co-ordination of the nation's energies. The illusion of total power of the state apparatus, which is necessarily bound up with its function in the fascist system, creates a distinctive bureaucratic subjectivism that stamps its influence on the whole of public life.

A further important conflict stems from the opposition between party and professional civil service that belongs to the essence of fascism. The principle of hierarchical centralism, on which the fascist party is organised, is certainly well suited to the task of controlling the state apparatus, and facilitates the amalgamation of the two bodies, and the build-up of the party's power. The party's composition, however, drawn as it is from the most parasitic and reactionary strata, and representing a form of negative selection, is incompatible with the qualities required for controlling a state with wide-ranging powers of intervention in the economy. The fascist party is thus necessarily involved in a change of its personnel, by expelling lumpen-proletarian elements and recruiting members of the bourgeoisie, the civil service and technical intelligentsia in their place. Yet this attempted transformation is limited by the rigidity with which the founding ideology of the party has become dogmatised and permanently embodied in aspects of its organisation. To fashion a party of qualified functionaries, capable of directing the modern subventionist state and the fascist mass organisations, is unthinkable without a system of rational training. But rational training is incompatible with the prohibition of discussion and the general anti-rationalist outlook of the fascist party. To remove the ban on discussion for the sake of adaptation to the new requirements is not only impossible on grounds of tradition, but implies a process of democratisation which would inevitably make the party the plaything of the continuing class antagonisms. Apart from its irrationalism, the party's ideologically-based principles of selection (e.g. the racial theory in Germany) also restrict the creation of a suitably qualified professional administration. The transformation of the party thus takes place only slowly, and only at its upper levels, in the form of the assimilation of professional personnel educated outside the party. The antagonism between specialised administrators and the party's rank and file thus persists as an antagonism between qualitative principles, irrespective of whether the specialists are formally party members; and this gives the professional administrators as such an influence that runs counter to the totalitarian aspirations of the party. Whenever the party's ideological predispositions prove an obstacle to rational policies demanded by the interests of the fascist state itself, and particularly of its dominant bourgeois factions, this antagonism becomes acute, and aligns the professional bureaucracy, including the military and technical intelligentsia, on the side of the 'oppositional' bourgeoisie. This is an unalterable aspect of the fascist political system, and can contribute in critical situations to an intensification of the crisis; yet in itself it represents only an antagonism between the personnel of the fascist system, and hence no independent cause of crisis.

State and society A state whose essential goal from the moment of its origin is the perpetuation of class rule through the retardation of economic development, and whose aim is to preserve the balance of class forces that existed at the time of its own institution, is bound to break radically with the movement of social forces embodied in democratic institutions. The fascists themselves regard this requirement as a condition for preserving their party monopoly. The origin of parties is to be found in class organisations, and only the destruction of these can produce a fully totalitarian state. A regime which comes to power with the support of a mass movement, however, has the advantage over a pure military–bureaucratic dictatorship of a certain insight into the importance of maintaining contact with the masses and the means of influencing them. The fascist state therefore seeks not simply to abolish class organisations, but to replace them with quite different organisations comprising the same groups of people arranged along status lines. The class organisations generated spontaneously by the process of capitalist development are democratic associations, based upon a voluntary struggle for common interests, and acting freely in opposition to one another. The status organisations that fascism creates are compulsory organisations, constructed in a centralised fashion from the top down, and integrated into the higher unity of the party. People belong to them not from their own choice but by virtue of the state's decree . . .

The fascist mass organisations are thus specifically reactionary in form. Their task is not to give expression to class forces, but to stifle them. In this they represent the essentially reactionary character of the strata that helped fascism to power. Their existence stands in perpetual contradiction to the realignments of forces that are brought about by the actual process of economic development, and to which adjustments have to be made after the event by roundabout means, since there is no way of coping with them directly. These realignments, for which no democratic barometer exists, assert themselves even in the fascist system, in the form of departmental conflicts, struggles between cliques, and intrigues behind the scenes.

What all this means is that the fascist system of mass organisations does not encapsulate social reality, nor create a unity between state and society; assertions to this effect are simply a bureaucratic illusion. The actual character of the fascist mass organisations is decidedly negative. So long as the monopoly of organisation and propaganda persists, it prevents the creation of new voluntary class organisations corresponding to the natural movement of social forces. The effect of the status organisations on social classes is to atomise, not organise them. Herein lies the particular difficulty of revolutionary struggle under fascism. But herein also lies the characteristic crisis of these organisations. They have no life of their own, no decisive influence on their members, no idea of the latters' views, as many painstaking enquiries show. Their cadres are not supported by the confidence of the membership, and this, together with their own lack of convictions, prevents them from carrying out their function of mediating between state and people. Frequent reorganisations precisely at this point prove that the crisis in the fascist mass organisations is chronic, and constitutes the weakest point of the fascist system.

The contradictions of fascist economic policy All the contradictions of the regime find their concentrated expression in an economic policy where nothing is permanent except change. The outward form, whereby all activity proceeds from a centralised all-powerful administration, contradicts the content, which reveals the apparatus as plaything of conflicting interests and object of their shifting power relations. Its tendencies towards nationalisation, autarchy, constriction on development of all kinds, contradict the economic and military necessity for further development. The fact that the power structure can neither do away with economic necessity nor shed the birthmarks that are indelibly printed on its programme and organisational structure, is what gives fascism's economic policy the unpredictable zigzag character that repeatedly contradicts the appearance of a co-ordinated plan . . . The same economic laws hold for the fascist state as for capitalism in general, and it makes use of them to stay at the forefront of development; yet in so far as it does so unwillingly, it falls behind. The tendencies of the reactionary regime to obstruct development can never be fully realised, but they leave their marks on all sections of the economy. Fascism is unable to impose stagnation against the imminent dynamic of the economy, but it can so obstruct this dynamic as to bring about a slowing of tempo at the expense of the nation's living standards.

Fascist economic policy confronts the task of encouraging those sectors that are important for economic vitality and for the military development of the state, despite its general retardation of development. It accomplishes this task in the only possible way: by an additional charge on the broad masses and particularly the working class in comparison with other countries. A greater degree of wasteful social expenditure and capital destruction can only take place without retarding the whole economy at vital points if the level of exploitation is intensified. A recovery of international competitiveness in spite of the subsidisation of high living costs is only possible by a substantial reduction in real wages. Even this downward pressure naturally finds its limit in the requirements of maintaining the quality and intensity of work, though these limits are relatively wide and impossible for anyone to predict exactly in advance, least of all for the fascist state.

The compulsion to resolve its contradictions at the expense of the working class is the crudest indication of the class character of a regime that has eliminated the direct rule of the bourgeoisie and its organisations to a greater extent than any previously. The disappearance of the bourgeois parties under fascism has put an end to the direct governmental function of the bourgeoisie, and the fascist party monopoly has removed the visible processes of political compromise. The regime's policies give the appearance of a party standing above classes, and accommodating itself directly to objective necessities. In fact, however, the ruling apparatus is neither classless nor independent of the balance of forces in society. The interest of every ruling apparatus in the maintenance of the existing social order, together with the character of the fascist party as a party created to defend the endangered rights of ownership and income within the framework of bourgeois society, compels the system's representatives to keep within the limits of capitalist society. Indeed, because of the inability of the oppressed classes to organise independently, the bourgeois content of policy is guaranteed much more effectively under this system of indirect rule than under the last phases of democracy. The power of the bourgeoisie rests on its economic position, which remains unaltered under fascism and can always make its weight felt *vis-à-vis* the head of the administration, as indeed it does. In this the professional civil service is always the natural ally of the capitalist class. The power of the working class, in contrast, can only be made effective by organisation, and is thus decisively diminished at the outset by the destruction of the proletarian mass organisations. The same also holds for the middle classes.

It would therefore be mistaken to interpret the zigzag course of fascist economic policy as a process of oscillation between the policy of the ruling class and pressure from its radicalised proletarian and middle class supporters. Such pressure only plays an important role when fascism is still not fully developed, and afterwards in situations of pronounced crisis. The oscillations are oscillations between different sections of the ruling class. The group requiring subsidies, which gained the ascendancy within finance capital with the victory of fascism, remains in persistent conflict with the healthier sectors of industry and finance. The military and defence interests, which are most intimately bound up with overall imperialist interests, play a balancing role, allied now with the one group and now with the other, a process which makes itself visible in the oscillations at the top. The compromises typical of every regime in class society are thus not done away with, but given the minimal concessions made to the working population, take the form primarily of compromises within the exploiting class itself. They are resolved along the line of least resistance, at the expense of the working class, and it is this that remains the most persistent feature of fascist politics behind all the adjustments it has to make (including the possible revival of the proletariat's social importance as unemployment declines).

Fascism and imperialism Fascism comes to power that much more easily in a country, the deeper its economic crisis and the smaller the reserves it has to alleviate it. It also comes to power that much more easily the fewer areas of imperialist influence, colonies, etc. the country has in relation to the needs of its capitalist class. It comes to power more easily in a country dependent on imported capital and with international debts, than in a capital-exporting country which can live off its revenues. It comes to power more easily in a country with a large number of economic dead-weights which reduce its international competitiveness, than in a country enjoying rapidly increasing production and an expanding world market. It is therefore an essential characteristic of fascism that it has to make the most vigorous assertion of its imperialist claims, precisely because the basis for such claims is relatively weak. Fascism exemplifies the imperialism of those who have arrived late at the partition of the world. Behind this imperialism lies a huge need for expansionary opportunities, but none of the traditional weapons for realising them. It is a form of imperialism which cannot operate by means of loans, since it is so much in debt, nor on the basis of technical superiority, since it is uncompetitive in so many areas. It is something novel in history – an imperialism of paupers and bankrupts.

Fascism seeks to overcome these disadvantages through maximum organisation, concentration of effort and exploitation. The single-minded aim, to which the centralised state subordinates all its powers, is the imperialist goal of expanded military capability. The policy of autarchy, the organisation of the economy, the propaganda apparatus of the ruling party are all pressed into service towards this end. Public investment is systematically directed to those branches of production essential to war, and foreign trade is controlled from the same standpoint. The finance for these undertakings is squeezed out of the workers by wage reductions, and from all the other sectors of the economy by government loans. The same means serve to force exports way above their natural level of competitiveness. Fascism thus operates on the level of world politics and the international economy according to the same principles that launched it on its career at home. Its original aim was the use of political power to enable the economically weaker sections of the capitalist economy to hold their own against the stronger. Its international ambition is to assist the imperialism of the weaker capitalist powers – the 'proletarian nations' as they are called – to triumph over the stronger. Fascism's external policy is the same as its internal: the planned, ruthless exercise of concentrated force, as its only hope of success.

However, the balance of forces in international capitalism is essentially different from that in the countries already subject to fascism. The first fascist countries are precisely the first because their proportion of unviable industries is higher than in the others. It is not within their power to hinder the process of uneven development in the world economy, or the rise of new industries and stronger imperialisms. The international formation of older, 'sated' imperialist powers and newly ascendant countries is both individually and collectively more than a match for the fascist powers. The latter's chance of success, therefore, depends on divisions or inertia among their opponents, or on making individual alliances with them. To this end they possess one great advantage: the much greater single-mindedness of policy compared with the democratic states. The fascist state can successfully play off one set of foreign interests against another, even in face of their own government's official policy, whereas the same tactic is necessarily ineffective against itself. Its manoeuvrability is greater than that of its opponents, as is also its determination to stake everything on success.

The more the internal contradictions of the fascist system come to a head, threatening its stability, and the more intolerable the economic pressure of systematic and concentrated military preparation becomes for the fascist country, with its poor capital provision, the more urgent becomes the attempt of fascist foreign policy to use every difference between the other powers to achieve an independent position for itself, or an aggressive alliance with others. Fascist imperialism, the imperialism of the bankrupt, is the most aggressive force for war among all the forms of imperialism. Only in a new division of the world into two great military camps, only in the massive realignment of a new world war can it hope to achieve its aim of shifting its own burdens onto foreign shoulders and effecting a new stabilisation of its power. In pursuit of this aim, however, it has to take the risk that its system will not withstand the massive shock involved in the trial of war . . .

---

53 The 'Controlled' Economy, *Otto Bauer*

Writing in 1936, Bauer explained the development of state-controlled economies, of which fascism constituted the most thoroughgoing type, as a new phase of capitalism in response to the severity of the international economic crisis.

In every deep depression there occurs a period of monetary fluidity once the initial acuteness of the credit crisis has been overcome. The idle factories, the restrictions in production and stockholding, set free large amounts of capital which stream to the banks in search of utilisation. In previous depressions, however, once this period of monetary fluidity set in, the interest rate fell, and once the interest rate fell, there occurred a revival of housing construction and agricultural improvement. This time such a result has just not taken place. The decline in mass incomes pushes rents down, and makes housing construction unprofitable, even with a low interest rate. Because of the crisis in agriculture a low interest rate cannot encourage the farmers to invest either. So the state intervenes to facilitate the realisation of the capital set free by the depression, and appropriates it in the form of loans for the purpose of 'labour procurement'. The return to productive utilisation of capital made idle in the crisis, which in previous depressions occurred spontaneously through the free play of market forces, is now mediated through a process of governmental 'labour procurement'. But once the state assumes control of this capital, it does so in a way consistent with its own power interests. It uses it to meet the expenses of rearmament. If state expenditure is needed to reactivate the economy, then it is through orders for bombers and tanks, for poison gas and warships that the reactivation takes place.

In Germany the state has gone much further. In order to secure the means for rearmament, it has restricted the flow of capital to private industry by setting a legal limit on the dividends that companies are allowed to pay out and putting an embargo on new share issues, thus compelling the capitalists to put their available capital at the disposal of the state. The expansion of the state in the economic sphere proceeds still further where, as a consequence of the crisis, large parts of the banking system and of industry have come into the hands of the state. In Germany and Austria the state restored the banks which had collapsed, acquiring a large part of their share capital in the process. In Italy the state bought up the shares of Italian industry from the banks which had lost their liquidity, and transferred them to state credit institutions. In each case the state makes use of its control of the banks and of industry in accordance with its power interests. In Germany Hitler uses his control over large sections of national capital in order to relocate essential war industries from threatened border areas further inland, and to develop industries which can produce substitute raw materials in the event of war. Once the state achieves control over capital, it utilises it to enlarge its military potential.

This system of state-managed economies has not been constructed according to any preconceived plan. The individual measures were decreed unsystematically under the pressure of emergency, the particular arrangements for defence against the immediate economic dangers were constructed piecemeal. The individual states adopted these measures and created these arrangements so as to protect their national economies against the disruptive effects of the world economic crisis, and to reorientate them towards rearmament and the supply of military necessities. But the crisis of the whole world economy was only intensified by this arrangement of enclosed, bureaucratically managed, national economies. The progressive barricading of individual territories against each other caused the collapse of world trade and intensified the downward pressure on world prices. The individual national economies promoted the development of branches of production which could only be developed at the cost of their own populations; on one side they depressed the living standards of the masses, on the other they increased world production in the sectors thus developed, with the result that the disproportion between the far too limited purchasing power of the masses and the far too sizeable world production was exacerbated. Those countries whose production was predominantly oriented towards satisfying their domestic needs could at least protect themselves to a certain extent from the effects of the world economic crisis by means of this national bureaucratic regulation of the capitalist economy. But the countries which were more fully integrated into the world market, and oriented more to the export of their own products and the import of foreign goods, were that much more severely affected by the intensification of the world crisis and the economic nationalism that it produced.

No doubt some of these measures will be allowed to lapse and some of these arrangements will be dismantled. An economic reaction against the new system may set in as soon as financial stability is restored, like the reaction after the war which forced the war economy to be dismantled ... . But undoubtedly much of the new system will remain. New branches of production have been developed under its protection, which would rapidly collapse if economic freedom were restored; the protectionist structures of the new system will be preserved to defend them. The new system simultaneously keeps internal prices high and depresses wages, thus shifting the distribution of the social product to the advantage of the possessing classes; the latter will not readily allow the new means for intensifying exploitation to be snatched from their grasp. The new system enlarges the state bureaucracy's sense of power; their new source of power will be defended. But above all it is the national military requirements that demand a succession of new interventions in the economy. The sanctions which the League of Nations employed for the first time in 1935 against Italy threaten every state with the risk of being excluded from the supply of essential raw materials. Fear of this drives governments to take steps to ensure that these raw materials are internally produced, or that they are replaced as far as possible by substitutes manufactured internally, and that extensive stocks of raw materials essential for war are held in the country. All these precautions in the event of war can only be enforced by far-reaching state regulation of economic life.

The new system has been developed to a different degree in the different countries, and further in the fascist than the democratic ones. In fact democracy hinders the bureaucratic regulation of the economy. Whenever the state regulates imports and exports, prices and wages, the conditions of labour and capital utilisation by decree, each of its decisions encroaches on the interests of class, of the different branches of production and of occupational groups. In a democracy, where all these elements seek to promote their interests publicly through their influence on public opinion and on parliament, the state is compelled in the preparation of every decision to make laborious compromises between the conflicting interests, which satisfy no one. In a fascist state these decisions are simply decreed by the autocratic power without the fuss of public controversy or the tedium of laborious negotiations in search of compromise. It is because the fascist state can therefore operate this system more easily that the groups which have a particularly decided interest in national protectionism turn to fascism, tired as they are of laborious negotiations with opposing interests and unsatisfying compromises.

Marx says in the Communist Manifesto: 'The ideas of freedom of conscience and religion merely expressed the supremacy of free competition in the realm of knowledge'. In fact broad sections of the bourgeoisie are ready to abandon free competition in the realm of knowledge, as soon as free competition in the market of goods, labour and capital no longer suffices. On the other side, however, the fact that the fascist dictators have to bear the sole responsibility for the daily regulation of economic life has far-reaching consequences. In a period when all the bureaucratic regulation conceivable is unable to halt the severe depression, but only modify its symptoms, the effect of such regulation is to provoke the dissatisfaction of one class or branch of production after another. This lowers the prestige of the fascist dictators and strengthens the opposition against them. It even brings classes which contributed to the rise of fascism into opposition against it.

The fascists justify their system to the anti-capitalist masses by saying that the state direction of the economy has overcome capitalism. In fact it is only liberal capitalism that has been abolished. Capitalism itself has no more been abolished by the present transition from liberalism to neo-mercantilism than it was by the transition from mercantalism to liberalism in the first place. The bureaucratically directed monopoly capitalism is one phase of capitalist development, just as the liberal capitalism of the era of free competition was only a phase. Bureaucratically managed monopoly capitalism is that phase of capitalist development which results from the most severe crisis of the capitalist world economy, which dissolves the world economy into a series of national economies in conflict with one another, and which subjects the populations within these national economies to the severest and most violent oppression.

The 'managed economy' commends itself as a 'planned economy'. It is supposed to abolish the anarchy of the capitalist mode of production. It is supposed to make possible the prevention of those disproportionalities which precipitate crises, because the state regulates the distribution of the social product and controls the direction of capital investment. In fact the bureaucratic regulation of the economy on the basis of capitalist ownership of the means of production cannot abolish the fundamental contradictions of the capitalist mode of production. If the state by its measures lowers the rate of surplus value, it depresses the profit rate and thereby renders capitalist prosperity, capitalist investment and any further autonomous development of the economy on a capitalist basis impossible. If, however, it raises the rate of surplus value, in order to lift the profit rate, and so revive the capitalist economy again, it only intensifies the disproportionality between productive capacity and the purchasing power of consumers. It can of course stimulate consumption again by increasing its own consumption of tanks, bombers and armour plating. But a planned economy, which would abolish the disproportionalities of the capitalist mode of production, is impossible on the basis of capitalist private property, since on this basis the rhythm of production remains dependent on the movement of the profit rate. In so far as a planned economy is possible at all on the basis of capitalist ownership, this depends on the extent to which economic development can also be subordinated to the plan for military production and the preparation for war.

The German fascists characterise their economic system as 'National Socialism'. In fact it has nothing at all to do with socialism. I does not abolish the concentration of capitalist private property in the means of production, but serves its interests. It does not abolish the exploitation of the working class, but intensifies it. Yet doesn't it subordinate all economic forces to the will of the state, all individual interests to the common interest? In fact it constrains all economic forces so as to bring them into line with the supreme national task of the economic struggle against the other national economies.

The world economic crisis has impoverished and embittered the broad masses of the population. To prevent their bitterness from being turned against their own ruling classes, it has to be directed against other nations. To prevent the masses from becoming a danger to the social system of capitalism, they have to be taught that the other nations are responsible for their misery, and that they must therefore suspend the class struggle for the sake of a fusion of all national forces for the struggle of their own nation against the others. Since fascism won state power in the first place by unleashing national animosities against other nations, it can now only assert its prestige, increasingly precarious because of its responsibility for the state managed economy in a period of severe economic crisis, through its success in the struggle against other nations, and only justify the state's fettering of all social forces by such success. Thus the system of the managed economy becomes in its hands a means of external struggle, an instrument of rearmament and preparation for war.

54 Fascism and War *Otto Bauer*

This uncompleted pamphlet was the last piece Bauer wrote on fascism; he was still working on it the day before he died in 1938.

From World War to Fascism

In 1919 Great Britain and France, the victors in the World War, revised the map of Europe according to the requirements of French imperialism, and the global distribution of economic and political power according to the requirements of both their imperialist interests. Italy, which had only entered the war after bitter internal conflicts, and whose army and state had proved themselves inadequate during the course of the war, in which it had only been saved from defeat by the victory of its allies, felt itself disadvantaged by the division of world power made by the western powers in 1919, and cheated of its share in the spoils of victory. Germany suffered defeat in the war, and the new division of the world took place at its expense.

All the combatant countries experienced powerful mass disturbances following the war. In Great Britain and France, where the popular authority of the ruling bourgeoisie had been strengthened by victory in the war and by the size of the booty, the mass disturbances of 1918–20 were unable to unsettle the system of bourgeois democracy handed down from pre-war times. In Germany and Italy, in contrast, the world war was followed by revolutionary processes which, although unable to destroy the capitalist system, precisely because of that intensified class conflict enormously. Bourgeois democracy, of much more recent origin in these countries, succumbed to the succession of revolution and counter-revolution.

With the new division of power brought about by the treaties of 1919 British and French imperialism achieved their war aims, and since then they have successfully defended the position of power won by conquest in the war. The imperialism of Great Britain and France is the imperialism of the satisfied, of the satiated. For this reason it is conservative and peaceful. In Germany and Italy, in contrast, there developed an aggressive, warlike imperialism, which seeks to revise the global distribution of economic and political power. The opposition between the conservative imperialism of Great Britain and France on the one hand, and the aggressive imperialism of Germany and Italy on the other, is the opposition between those capitalist classes which actually exploit the worker and peasant masses of the colonial peoples, and those who would like to do so.

Wherein, then, lies the contrast between the 'authoritarian states' on one side and the 'western democracies' on the other? On the one hand it is the contrast between those states, in which the world war unleashed massive revolutionary processes, and which experienced the succession of revolution and counter-revolution, and those other states in which the organic development of ancient democracies, reinforced as they were by victory in the world war, was uninterrupted by any revolution and consequently any counter-revolution. On the other hand it is the contrast between the sated imperialist powers, which themselves dictated the global distribution of power after the world war and are now concerned to defend it, and the aggressive imperialism of the dissatisfied powers, which rebel against this distribution.

Fascism was victorious first in Italy and Germany. On one side it was the result of the intensified class conflicts which stemmed from the revolutionary processes of the post-war period and the counter-revolution that followed them. On the other side it is the instrument of an aggressive imperialism on the part of these states, seeking to fuse together the whole economic and cultural power of the people under a unified command, for the struggle over a new distribution of economic and political power in the world.

Wherever fascism is victorious, it establishes not only an essentially new political system, but an essentially new constitution for industry and labour as well. Its new political, industrial and labour system must be understood as a new phase in the overall development of capitalism . . .

Fascism's Economic Order

. . . In what way is fascist *étatisme* different from the earlier phases of capitalist development? All capitalist production is production for profit. The movement of the profit rate has therefore up to now regulated the capitalist economy. It is this that has determined the distribution of capital and hence also the distribution of labour between the different branches of production. Capital would avoid those branches of production with a lower profit rate and flock towards those where the rate was highest. The movement of the profit rate determined the changes in the economic conjuncture: when it rose, capitalists expanded their existing enterprises, and established new ones; the industries producing the means of production got under way quickly, and prosperity flowed out from them over the whole economy. When the profit rate sank, share prices plunged, and with the collapse of the stock market investment ceased, the producer goods industries came to a halt and the whole economy sank into a depression. Fascist *étatisme* has abolished this controlling function of the automatic movement in the profit rate. It is no longer the rate of profit in the individual branches of production but the decision of the state that determines in which branches of production the fresh accumulations of capital should be invested. It is no longer changes in the average rate of profit overall, but the decision of the state that determines the extent of new industrial investment and hence the economic conjuncture.

It was the greatest triumph of capitalism that the social forces of production enjoyed their unprecedented development in a society where their control was surrendered exclusively to the individual pursuit of profit. But now that capital seeks refuge in fascist *étatisme*, it is an admission that the capitalist economy can no longer be regulated by the automatic movement of the profit rate, and can no longer remain the province of the individual pursuit of profit, but requires social regulation at the hands of the state. It is an admission that the development of the social forces of production has come into glaring contradiction with the social system based upon private ownership of the means of production and the individual pursuit of profit.

In fact the development of the fascist states demonstrates the superiority of the social organisation of the economy over capitalist anarchy, which allows the development of production to be determined by the profit motive. The rapid abolition of unemployment in the Third Reich, the impetuous development of new branches of production under the orders of the fascist dictatorship, the sheer speed of Germany's economic, and hence also military and political, recovery, the shift in the balance of power in favour of the fascist states – all demonstrate nothing else than the superiority of planned social organisation over private capitalist anarchy.

Yet however effective the increased capacity of fascist *étatisme* may prove, it is a capacity which is devoted exclusively to the service of military and economic preparation for war. Fascist *étatisme* cuts off food imports from abroad, so as to use the foreign currency to import raw materials necessary for war. It restricts the development of the consumer goods industries through its prohibitions on investment and capital accumulation, and its regulation of raw material imports, so as to concentrate the whole power of society on the development of the industries essential for war. As a result it throws society into crises of an exceptional kind. The normal crises of the capitalist economy are crises of over-production: the purchasing power of the masses, lagging behind the development of production, is insufficient to purchase the increasing mass of products of their own labour. Fascist *étatisme*, in contrast, produces crises of scarcity. Although all the workforce is employed and feverishly active, although the means of production are being used to the full, there is a scarcity of essential food and raw materials. As the number of employed workers and their productive output increases, so a rapidly increasing proportion of their labour is devoted, not to the production of consumer goods for their own needs, but to the expansion of the war industries and the production of military equipment. In other words, the share that the working class enjoys of the products of its own labour declines. The exploitation of the working class is intensified. This intensification of exploitation is enforced by the distinctive fascist system of labour legislation . . .

The fascist labour system constitutes the basis of its *étatiste* economic order. It is only because fascism abolishes the freedom of the labour contract, and refuses to allow wages to be settled by free agreement between employers and workers, but fixes them along with the price of goods through its own institutions, that the fascist state is able to regulate the distribution of the social product between capital and labour. The fascist labour system presupposes fascism's 'totalitarian' political structure of suppression and domination; it requires the terror of the totalitarian power structure to intimidate the working class to the point where it endures without opposition this system of exploitation so antagonistic to its fundamental interests. The fascist labour system serves the aggressive imperialism of the fascist states; it is only the substantially intensified exploitation of the work-force that enables the fascist state to build up its armaments and develop its war industries with such extreme rapidity and thereby mightily strengthen its political power in relation to the other states.

Fascism and War

German fascism has succeeded in rearming a German Reich that was defeated in the world war and disarmed by the Versailles Treaty. It has reintroduced universal conscription. Its state control of the economy was directed first of all to the task of equipping a modern mass army in the space of a few years. Fascism has completed massive works of fortification; it has rapidly expanded the essential war industries and re-sited them from the border areas further inland; it has built the motorways necessary for war. Its aim now is to make Germany immune from blockade by exploiting Germany's own natural resources, by the more intensive cultivation of agriculture, by the construction of huge plants for producing substitute materials, and by stockpiling the raw materials essential to war.

Hand in hand with the economic goes the political rearmament: the suppression of all parties, social organisations and intellectual currents that could offer resistance to the preparation and conduct of war; the organisation of a terrifying apparatus of violence to destroy all opposition to war once it has started; the indoctrination of the whole people with national-imperialist sentiments through the ruling party's monopoly of propaganda, and the national-imperialist education of youth. Strengthened in this way, German fascism was able to force the democratic powers on to the defensive, occupy and fortify the Rhineland, intervene in Spain, annex Austria, threaten Czechoslovakia, exert pressure on the whole of south-eastern Europe and demand the return of the colonies lost in the world war.

These huge successes are undoubtedly the product of the fascist system of state, economy and labour. Only the totalitarian dictatorship has made it possible to concentrate the whole of society's powers on the goal of a reinforced national imperialism. Only the fascist economic order has made it possible to strengthen Germany's armaments and war potential at such an alarming rate. Only the fascist system of labour legislation has provided the necessary intensification of working class exploitation to generate the huge quantity of surplus value that has enabled the enormous expansion of its war machine to proceed so rapidly. Yet however stupendous these achievements of fascism may be, they are circumscribed within insuperable limits.

The equipment of a huge modern army, the building of fortifications and motorways, the switch-over of industry to military production, the creation of new industries to manufacture substitute materials, all these involve an essentially non-recurring use of labour. Once they are effectively complete, the fascist dictatorship will confront the following choice: *either* to consign the working masses employed on these activities to unemployment, and plunge the whole economy into a severe crisis, in which the contradiction between fascist policies for a huge state-induced expansion of the apparatus of social production on the one hand, and for a savage limitation of mass purchasing power through its system of labour legislation on the other, would become so evident and so damaging that fascism's political supremacy would be severely convulsed; *or* to set in motion the product of all this immense labour, and direct its military machine on to the path of war.

The economic and military rise of the fascist states has overturned the existing power relations in the world, so that they no longer conform with the political order and balance of power dictated by the victors at the end of the world war. The contradiction between this twenty-year-old political order and the new power relations points forcibly to a violent revision of state borders in a new war. The powers which are threatened by the aggressive imperialism of the fascist states are forced into equally feverish rearmament to counter the military preparations of the other side. The world has been thrust into a feverish arms race and a perpetual state of war scare.

In order to minimise the dangers of a coastal blockade in wartime the fascist states construct their own raw materials production regardless of cost. They produce raw materials at home which they could import far cheaper from abroad, and so raise the general price level in their countries. So as still to remain competitive on the world market, they guarantee their industries export premiums at state expense, which enable them to dump their exports in foreign markets. On the other side the raw materials producers overseas lose part of their market and are thrown into crisis because of the development of such production on the part of the fascist countries. The latter also manipulate the financial system so as to defraud their overseas creditors and use the resulting funds for export subsidies, so compelling foreign states to assume payment of the interest owed to their own contractors. In this way the whole world economy is substantially disrupted because of the policy of the fascist states. The international division of labour evolved during the course of capitalist development is set back. World trade collapses. The crises of the international economy are exacerbated. The arms race leads everywhere to significant increases in the burden of taxation. War scare deters productive investment. The antagonisms between the capitalist classes of each country intensify. Imperialist tendencies are strengthened everywhere by the severe convulsions in the world economy.

So fascism plunges the world into an impasse from which it can find no outlet except through war. Since fascism has forced major nations to devote their social life to the service of military preparation, and so revolutionised the relations of political and economic power across the globe, it brings war inexorably onwards . . .

The Internal Contradictions of Fascism
Fascism concentrates the power of the state into an unlimited totalitarian force. It keeps all opposition of the exploited classes

against capitalism violently suppressed. It intensifies capitalist exploitation to the highest degree. By subordinating the process of capitalist production to the compulsion of its decrees it raises it to the supreme pitch of achievement. Fascism seems to represent the most complete victory of capitalism over proletarian socialism. And yet it is a product of capitalism in decline. It only arises when the capitalist bourgeoisie is no longer able to maintain its cultural hegemony over the popular masses, and when their obedience can consequently no longer be secured by democratic forms, but only by a terrorist dictatorship. Fascism only arises when the economy can no longer be effectively regulated by the individual capitalist's pursuit of profit, but requires social control by the state.

The socially planned control of economic life proves its effectiveness, its superiority over the anarchy of private capitalism even within the constraints of fascism. Yet under the fascist dictatorship the state's regulation of the economy takes place on the basis of capitalist property relations and is devoted exclusively to rearmament, military preparation and the imperialist power struggles of the state. It thereby subordinates the working class to an unbearable slavery to the state, intensifying its exploitation. It can only be sustained by means of a terrorist dictatorship which comes into chronic antagonism with the vital interests of the working class. On the other side it leads to a retrogression in the international division of labour, and intensifies all the economic and political antagonisms between states, leading inevitably to war.

The social regulation of economic life takes place under the fascist dictatorship on the basis of the private ownership of the means of production and circulation. The state abandons the means of production to private owners who only produce for the sake of profit; yet it refuses to allow production to be determined by the rule of profit, but only by its own direct command. In so far as it subordinates all the particular interests of the various entrepreneurial strata to the spurious general interest of rearmament, the bureaucracy which controls economic life finds itself unavoidably in conflict with one sectional interest after another. These accumulating conflicts express the contradiction between the social regulation of the economic process and the private ownership of the means of production and the products of labour.

Fascism is the state form of a capitalism which fears the proletarian revolution at both national and international level, and seeks to overthrow it. But it produces a society whose organisation stands in utter contrast to the vital interests of the working class, a society whose ruling caste is necessarily drawn into continuous conflict with the particular interests of every individual group of the propertied classes, a society whose development can only culminate in a war that convulses all the power relations within the state – i.e. a society possessing more acute revolutionary tensions than any society before it.

The revolutionary tendencies inherent in fascist society, however, though masked by the fascist dictatorship, are themselves full of inner contradictions. The contradiction between the social regulation of the productive process and the private ownership of the means of production can be resolved in one of two different ways. Either private property can break the constraints imposed by the social control of production, in which case society would regress to the phase of liberal capitalism. Or the social regulation of the productive process can abolish the limitations of private ownership of the means of production, in which case society would progress from the state regulation of the capitalist economy in the interests of imperialism to a socialist organisation of the economy serving the needs of society as a whole. In other words, concealed within the revolutionary tendencies inherent in fascist society there lies the contradiction between liberal and socialist potentialities. This contradiction can only find its resolution in a historical revolutionary process, in the course of which the anti-fascist revolution through the defeat of fascist *étatisme* develops into the socialist revolution, which re-establishes the social organisation and control of economic life on a higher plane and for higher purposes . . .

The Propertied Classes and Fascist Etatisme

The fascist counter revolution delivers state power into the hands of the fascist party, which begets a new bureaucracy that coalesces with the bureaucracy of the state and subordinates it to itself. A massive bureaucratic apparatus takes command of society and all aspects of its life, controlling all its members with complete arbitrariness. The means of production and exchange remain the property of the capitalists. The fascist state protects capitalist property against every workers' revolt, and reduces the workers to an outlawed, demoralised 'retinue' in the service of capitalist management, thus facilitating their more intensive exploitation. On the other side the fascist state secures for its own capitalist class the fullest possible development of national forces in the struggle with the competing imperialisms of other countries. The fascist state, or rather the fascist bureaucracy, serves as the attorney for the class interests of the capitalist class against the working class at home and the other capitalist classes abroad. Although the fascist bureaucracy is the ruling caste, the capitalist class remains the dominant class, whose interests the ruling caste protects. Yet in making decisions about the price of goods, about the import of raw materials, about the use of the means of production, about the rate of profit in the individual branches of production, about the investment of accumulated capital, the fascist bureaucracy subordinates all the particular interests of individual capitalists, of capital sectors and branches of production, to the imperialist interests of the capitalist class as a whole. In doing so, however, its measures come into conflict with the particular interests of one capitalist group after another. The capitalist class is still the dominant class, but unavoidable conflicts and antagonisms develop between it and the ruling caste. Despite these the capitalist class cannot overturn the fascist power structure since to do so would unleash the class struggle of workers against capitalists once more, and jeopardise the imperialist interests of the capitalist class as a whole in its competitive struggle with the imperialism of other states. The result is that the antagonisms which develop between the dominant class and the ruling caste turn into conflicts within the ruling caste itself, within the upper echelons of the bureaucracy in party, state and economy that are closely allied with the capitalist class. This explains the continual disagreements, conflicts of interest, internal disputes, the vacillation and disorganisation that takes place within the bureaucracy.

Fascism had its origin in rebellions of the petty bourgeoisie, peasants and intellectuals. Having used these rebellions in the interests of preserving capitalist class domination fascism has been obliged even after its seizure of power to attempt to keep the support of the classes which originally assisted its rise. To this end it makes concessions to the petty-bourgeois trade associations, approving prices for peasant produce and assuring a plentiful supply of cheap labour. But its *étatisme* subjects the economy of petty bourgeoisie and peasants to a hateful compulsion, and its totalitarian dictatorship stifles the cultural life of the intellectuals. The peasants are deprived of the right to dispose of their own produce, which has to be brought to sales outlets and sold for prices determined by the bureaucracy. Fascism denies the craftsman the raw material which he needs for his work, and subjects the retailer to compulsory rationing and sales taxes. The harsher the regulation of economic life by the fascist bureaucracy, the more powerful is the opposition generated against it within the petty-bourgeois classes.

The most effective means employed by German fascism to mobilise and, after the seizure of power, to control the petty bourgeois classes was its anti-semitism. Wherever the proportion of Jews in the urban population, and consequently in the development of capitalism, was very large, opposition had frequently arisen between the 'Aryan' craftsman and the Jewish trader, between the 'Aryan' peasant and the Jewish moneylender, between the 'Aryan' shopkeeper and the Jewish department store, between the 'Aryan' worker or salaried employee and the Jewish employer, between the 'Aryan' intellectual and his Jewish rival. Fascism takes advantage of the widespread hatred of Jewish exploiters and competitors in its own struggle for power, and, once power has been seized, continues to exploit anti-semitism in consolidating its rule. It expropriates Jewish capitalists and transfers their businesses to its own supporters, thus creating a new bourgeoisie at the expense of Jewish capitalists from among the members of the ruling party, who become fascism's most dependable class support. By excluding the Jews from economic life fascism liberates the 'Aryan' shopkeepers, craftsmen, employees and intellectuals from Jewish competition, and gives them a corresponding interest in the continuation of its rule. But in realising its brutal implications, anti-semitism destroys its own social roots. The petty bourgeois, the peasant, the intellectual, the worker, all discover that there is no less exploitation and competition when the Jewish exploiter and the

Jewish competitor are displaced by their Nazi counterparts. The extermination of the Jews from economic life can therefore provide only temporary satisfaction for the petty-bourgeois classes; it can only briefly retard the development of their opposition to fascist *étatisme*.

Just as the conflicts of the individual factions of the capitalist bourgeoisie with the fascist bureaucracy are transposed to the summit of the fascist hierarchy, so also are the oppositional tendencies of the petty-bourgeois classes transposed to the masses inside the fascist party. Broad strata within the party become influenced by the petty-bourgeois opposition to fascism, and contrast the petty-bourgeois–socialist promises of fascism's ascendancy with the capitalist reality of its rule. Of course the petty-bourgeois classes are unable to assume the struggle against fascist state power by themselves. It is only when the working class has been set in motion, only when the fascist system of rule and *étatiste* economic compulsion have been convulsed by mass strikes that substantial numbers of petty bourgeois, of peasants and intellectuals, will rally round the working class, and make common cause to bring down the hated fascist bureaucracy together with its totalitarian rule and its dictatorship over economic life.

At the point when the dissatisfaction of broad strata of the propertied classes themselves has produced uncertainty and conflict at the summit of the fascist bureaucracy, and oppositionist sentiments among its supporters, and when the capacity of the fascist terror apparatus to resist a hostile popular movement has been consequently weakened . . .

(Here the manuscript breaks off.)

Biographical Notes

Bauer, Otto, 1881–1938. Made an early mark within the SDAP, publishing a major study of Marxism and the national question in 1907, and being appointed the Party's parliamentary secretary the same year. He was editor of the theoretical journal *Der Kampf,* which he helped to found. An officer in the world war, he was imprisoned in Russia for three years, but returned to serve briefly as under-secretary for external affairs in the new Austrian Republic from 1918–9. He accepted the Bolshevik revolutionary model as appropriate for the USSR, but not for Austria, for which he sought to work out a process of socialist transformation distinctive from both reformism and Bolshevism. This strategy was embodied in the Party's Linz Programme of 1926. He was a member of the National Assembly until 1934, when he was forced to leave Austria after the unsuccessful February insurrection. He spent his last years in exile in Czechoslovakia and then Paris.

Blum, Léon, 1872–1950. A non-Marxian socialist, Blum's work is included here for its perspective on the Comintern's shift towards a 'popular front' policy in 1934. A member of the French Socialist Party, he helped found the journals *L'Humanité* and later *Le Populaire,* which he edited. In 1919 he was elected deputy to the National Assembly, a position he held until 1940. He was head of the popular front government in 1936, and had a further brief spell as premier in 1938. In 1940 he was arrested by the Vichy government and interned in concentration camps. After his release at the end of the war he served as head of the French delegation to Unesco.

Bordiga, Amadeo, 1889–1970. A leading member of the left 'abstentionist' faction of the PSI, he opposed the Party's participation in the elections of 1919, and demanded the expulsion of the reformists. He led the PCI from its foundation at the Livorno Congress in January 1921, and was responsible for the formulation of the Party's policy in the Rome theses (1922). Although a delegate to ECCI, and subsequently a member of its praesidium, he maintained a determined opposition to its 'united front' tactics from 1921 onwards. At the Lyons Congress of January 1926 he was removed from the leadership of the PCI in favour of

Gramsci and Togliatti. He was arrested and deported in Mussolini's repression later that same year, but was expelled from the PCI for 'factionalism' on his return in 1930. He was active as an independent Communist in Naples in the post-war period.

Dimitrov, Georgi, 1882–1949. A left Social Democrat, he was opposed to Bulgarian participation in the world war, and was briefly imprisoned in 1918. A member of the Bulgarian Communist Party's Central Committee from its foundation in 1919, he attended the third World Congress of the Comintern in 1921, and was a member of ECCI from 1923. In that year he was forced to flee Bulgaria after the failure of the Communist uprising in the country. He settled in Berlin in 1929 as director of the Comintern's western European bureau. He achieved fame in 1933 with his courageous defence against the charge of burning down the Reichstag, of which he was acquitted. From 1935 until its dissolution in 1943 he was general secretary of the Comintern. He was granted Soviet citizenship in 1937. After the war he became general secretary of the Bulgarian Communist Party and prime minister of Bulgaria, a post he held till his death.

Gramsci, Antonio, 1891–1937. Left member of the PSI and secretary of its Turin section, he was one of the founders of the weekly *L'Ordine Nuovo* in 1919, and active in the factory council movement and the factory occupations of 1920. He was elected to the Central Committee of the PCI at its founding Congress in 1921. Although one of the few to take the fascist threat seriously, he was absent in Moscow as PCI delegate to the Comintern during 1922, the year which led to the fascist coup. In 1924 he was elected a deputy to the Italian parliament where he led the Communist group. Among the party factions he was opposed both to Bordiga on the left and Tasca on the right. At the Lyons Congress in January 1926 his faction captured the Party leadership from Bordiga, but he was arrested and imprisoned later that year. His letters and notebooks written in prison placed him at the forefront of the development of Marxist theory, though his influence was only felt after his death, due to ill health brought on by his imprisonment.

Hilferding, Rudolf, 1877–1941. Joint founder and editor of the theoretical journal of Austro-Marxism, *Marx-Studien,* he moved from Vienna to Berlin in 1906, where he also served as foreign editor of the SPD journal *Vorwärts.* He opposed voting for war credits at the start of the war, and joined the USPD in 1918, serving as editor of its journal *Freiheit.* He took German citizenship in 1920, was elected an SPD member of the Reichstag after the reunification of the Party, and became Minister of Finance in 1923 and again in 1928–9. From 1924 he edited the Party's theoretical journal *Die Gesellschaft*. He was forced to emigrate in 1933, and was murdered by the Gestapo under the Vichy Government.

Kautsky, Karl, 1854–1938. Leading theoretician of the Second International, he was editor of the journal *Neue Zeit* from its foundation in 1883 until 1917. He was responsible for formulating the Erfurt Programme of the SPD in 1891, and became exponent within the Party of a 'centrist' orthodoxy between the revisionism of Bernstein and the radicalism of Luxemburg. He joined the USPD during the war, and acted as political adviser to Karl Ebert's government immediately after it. He was bitterly opposed to the Bolshevik revolution, believing in the self-emancipation of the working class within bourgeois democracy as the only viable road to socialism. He moved to Vienna in 1924, but he remained influential within the SPD through his prolific writings until the defeat of 1933.

Löwenthal, Richard, (pseud. *Paul Sering*), 1908–   On the left wing of the SPD, he went into exile after the Nazi seizure of power in 1933, and was associated with the 'New Beginning' group, which sought to reconstruct the Marxist revolutionary tradition of the Party. During the war he worked as a journalist in England, gradually abandoning his early Marxism for a 'democratic socialist' position, which he set out in an influential book *Jenseits des Kapitalismus* (Beyond Capitalism), published in 1946. He returned to Germany to become Professor at the Free University, Berlin. His academic writing has been mainly concerned with the tension between the theory and practice of both communism and socialism.

Manuilski, Dmitrii, 1883–1959. A member of the Bolshevik faction of the RSDLP from 1903, he took part in the revolutions of 1905 and October 1917. In 1921 he was appointed secretary of the Ukrainian Communist Party. From 1924 he was a member of ECCI and its praesidium, and from 1928 the chief Soviet delegate to the Comintern. In that capacity he acted as leading exponent of the 'third period' line on fascism, etc. After the war he held various official posts, including Ukrainian minister for foreign affairs and permanent representative to the UN General Assembly.

Nin, Andrés, 1892–1937. A prolific writer and publicist, he was a member of the Spanish Socialist Party from 1911. In 1920 he served as general secretary of the National Confederation of Labour, and was briefly imprisoned for his activities. He joined the PCE in 1923, and worked in Moscow for the next few years as delegate to the Profintern. In 1927 he broke with Stalin over the latter's struggle with Trotsky, and was expelled from the USSR. On his return to Spain he formed a Communist opposition group, but broke with Trotsky in turn over differences of analysis of Spanish conditions. In 1935 he helped found POUM, which played an active part in the Spanish civil war, attempting to push the Republican cause in a revolutionary direction against Communist opposition. He joined the Generalitat (autonomous government of Catalonia) as minister of justice in September 1936, but was expelled from government along with his Party in December. After the abortive uprising in Barcelona in May 1937 he was tortured and killed by Communist agents, presumably at Stalin's behest.

Radek, Karl (born *Karl Berngardovich*), 1885–1939. A journalist and activist in the Social Democratic parties of Russia, Poland and Germany from 1904 till the outbreak of the world war. He attended the anti-war conferences at Zimmerwald and Kienthal in 1915–16. After the Russian revolution he accompanied Lenin and Zinoviev across Germany, and subsequently took part in the Brest–Litovsk peace negotiations. After the German revolution of 1918 he was sent to Berlin to help organise the KPD, and was briefly imprisoned. He rose to a leading position in the Comintern, specialising in German affairs, but lost influence in 1923–4 because of his support for Trotsky, and was expelled from the Party in 1927. He was readmitted in 1930 after a recantation, but was subsequently tried for treason in 1937 and condemned to ten years in prison.

Sas, Gyula (pseud. *Aquila*), 1893–1943. After serving in the Austro-Hungarian army during the war, he joined the Hungarian Communist Party when the Hungarian Soviet Republic was proclaimed in 1919, but fled to Austria when it was crushed later the same year. In 1920 he emigrated to Italy, using the name Giulio Aquila. In 1922 he moved to Berlin to work for the Comintern's department of information and statistics, also serving on its special commission on fascism. He wrote a number of works on fascism during the 1920s and was secretary to the 1929 anti-fascist congress in Berlin. In 1934 he was forced to leave Germany and moved to Moscow to work with Karl Radek on *Izvestia*. In 1937 he was arrested with Radek, and died in prison.

Schifrin, Alexander (pseud. *Max Werner*), 1901–51. Member of the Mensheviks, he emigrated from the USSR in the early 1920s, and joined the SPD. He edited the Party's newspaper in Mannheim, and also contributed to the *Socialisticesky Vestnik*, journal of the Mensheviks in exile. Besides articles for the SPD theoretical journal *Die Gesellschaft*, edited by Hilferding, he also wrote books on military questions and problems of international policy. He was forced to leave Germany in 1933, and was a frequent contributor to the SPD journal in exile, *Zeitschrift für Sozialismus*.

Seydewitz, Max, 1892–   Joining the SPD in 1910, he was editor of Party journals in Halle and Zwickau during the 1920s. In 1931 he became editor of the new theoretical journal *Der Klassenkampf*, which was founded by dissidents on the left opposed to the party's policy of 'tolerating' the Brüning government. The same year he was expelled from the Party, and helped found the SAP on a platform of united workers' resistance to the Nazis. In exile from 1934–45, he returned to Saxony after the war and became chief minister in the state government, and subsequently director of the state art collections in Dresden.

Silone, Ignazio (born *Secondino Tranquilli*), 1900–78. Was active in the youth wing of the PSI and then in the party leadership after 1918. He was a founder member of the PCI at the Livorno Congress in 1921, and editor of the Communist weekly *L'Avanguardia*. He was arrested and imprisoned in Spain in 1924 for organising Communist youth groups in the country. After a brief return to Italy, he sought refuge from Mussolini's police in Switzerland. His views brought him increasingly into conflict with the Comintern during the 'third period', and he left the Party in 1930, the year when he published his first novel *Fontamara*. He returned to political activity during the war, helping organise resistance to Mussolini as a member of the PSI. He served as a left wing Socialist deputy in the Constituent Assembly immediately after the war, but subsequently retired from politics to devote himself to his increasingly extensive literary output.

Stalin, Joseph (born *Iosif Vissarionovich Dzhugashvili*), 1879–1953. A member of the RSDLP from 1898 and of the Bolshevik faction from 1903, he was repeatedly exiled to Siberia and as often escaped. After taking part in the October revolution he served as a member of the revolutionary military council and as People's Commissar for Nationalities. In 1922 he was appointed General Secretary of the Russian Communist Party, a position which he used after Lenin's death to consolidate his personal power, and to destroy the opposition successively of Trotsky, Zinoviev, Kamenev and Bukharin. With the latter's demise in 1929 he attained an unassailable position, not only within the USSR, but over the Communist parties outside the Soviet Union as well.

Tasca, Angelo (pseud. *Valle, Rienzi, Serra, Leroux, Rossi*), 1892–1960. A member of the PSI from 1908, and active in its youth movement, he helped found the weekly *L'Ordine Nuovo* with Gramsci and others in Turin in 1919. From the foundation of the PCI in 1921 he was a centre of right wing opposition to its leader Bordiga, and in favour of a united front with the PSI. As a member of the PCI executive committee from 1924, he also opposed the Gramscian tendency within the Party. In 1928 he was a delegate to the Sixth World Congress of the Comintern and a member of ECCI, but he broke with Stalin over the 'social-facism' line of the third period, and was expelled from the party in 1929. He settled in Paris and took French citizenship, writing for the French Socialist daily, *Populaire*. In 1938 he published a classic study of the rise of fascism under the pseudonym of A. Rossi.

Terracini, Umberto, 1895–   Joined the PSI in 1916 and helped found the weekly *L'Ordine Nuovo* with Gramsci and others in Turin in 1919. He was appointed to the Central Committee of the PCI at its foundation in 1921 and edited the Party newspaper *Unita*. Like Bordiga, he opposed the united front tactics advocated by the Comintern in this period, although a member of its praesidium. In 1926 he was arrested by the fascists and sentenced to twenty years in prison, from which he was freed in 1943. After the war he served in the PCI directorate, and as a member of the Italian Senate from 1948.

Thalheimer, August, 1884–1948. On the left of the SPD before the war, he joined the Spartacus League under Liebknecht and Luxemburg in 1916, helping edit its clandestine journal. He was elected to the Central Committee of the KPD on its foundation in 1919, and appointed chief editor of *Rote Fahne*. With Brandler he led the dominant right faction of the Party, until both were dismissed from the Central Committee following the abortive insurrection of 1923. He then moved to Moscow to work in the central administration of the Comintern. In 1928 he returned to Germany, but was expelled from the Party for his opposition to the Comintern's line on 'social-fascism' etc. With Brandler he founded the opposition party KPD(O) and its theoretical journal *Gegen den Strom*. In 1933 he emigrated to France, and in 1940 to Cuba, where he died.

Thälmann, Ernst, 1886–1944. Member of the SPD from 1903 and the USPD from 1917. He took part in the Congress in 1920 uniting the Party's left wing with the KPD, and was appointed to the KPD Central Committee. In October 1923 he took part in the abortive insurrection in Hamburg, and was elected to parliament the following year. With Stalin's approval he became leader of the Party in 1925, from which position he stood for the Presidency of the Republic in both 1925 and 1932. After 1928 he faithfully expounded the Comintern line on 'social-fascism' etc. In 1933 he was arrested by Hitler's secret police, and held in concentration camps, where he was executed in 1944.

Togliatti, Palmiro (pseud. *Palmi, Ercoli, Correnti*), 1893–1964. Joined the PSI in 1914, and was active in Turin, becoming editor of the newspaper *Avanti* in 1919. He was one of the group along with Gramsci which founded the weekly *L'Ordine Nuovo* in the same year. In 1922 he was elected to the Central Committee of the PCI, and in 1924 to the Praesidium of the Comintern. He worked with Gramsci to remove Bordiga from the leadership of the Party at the Lyons Congress in 1926, and in 1927 was appointed general secretary, a post he held with only brief interludes until his death. After 1928 he became an increasingly important figure within the Comintern, acting as head of the secretariat for Central Europe and as co-ordinator of the Comintern's operations in Spain during the civil war. He returned to Italy in 1944 after the fall of fascism, and held office in various post-war governments until the PCI went into opposition in 1947.

Trotsky, Leon (born *Leon Davidovich Bronstein*), 1879–1940. Writer and revolutionary, he played a leading part in the revolutions of 1905, as head of the St. Petersburg's Soviet, and of October 1917, as chief military organiser. Although he only joined the Bolshevik Party in July 1917, he was immediately elected to its Central Committee. As people's commissar for foreign affairs, and then commissar for war, he played a central part in the consolidation of the revolution. After Lenin's death in 1924 he was successively outmanoeuvred by Stalin in the latter's bid for power, being expelled from the Party in 1927 and exiled in 1928. In exile he became Stalin's most powerful critic, exposing both the distortions of the revolution in the USSR and their fateful consequences for the workers' struggle elsewhere. He was murdered in Mexico in 1940 by Stalin's agents.

Zetkin, Klara, 1857–1933. A member of the SPD from 1878, she was active in exile from 1880 in the international socialist movement, particularly the women's movement. After her return to Germany in 1890 she became editor of the socialist women's journal *Gleichheit* and head of the women's section of the Second International. From 1907–17 she was on the Executive Committee of the SPD. Imprisoned during the war for pacifist activity, she joined the Spartacus

League with Luxemburg and Liebknecht, and subsequently the KPD, to whose Central Committee she was elected in 1919. She also served on ECCI and the Comintern Praesidium. From 1920 she was a Communist deputy in the Reichstag, and presided as senior parliamentarian at its opening session in August 1932. She left Germany on Hitler's accession to power, and died in the USSR in 1933.

Zibordi, Giovanni, 1870–1943. On the reformist wing of the PSI, he worked with Prampolini as joint editor of the socialist journal *Giustizia* in Reggio Emilia from 1904. In 1915 he was elected parliamentary deputy for Reggio. An outspoken opponent of fascist violence from its early emergence in 1921, he was himself subjected to an armed attack in March of that year, and was forced to flee from Reggio to Milan. He continued to help edit *Giustizia* when it was transferred to Milan as a journal of the newly formed PSU. He was arrested a number of times by Mussolini's police, and devoted his later years to literary activity.

Notes and List of sources

Introduction

(1) Collections already exist in German and Italian, and also secondary works (including English ones) which treat some of the material collected here. Among the former should be mentioned: Abendroth, W., ed., *Faschismus und Kapitalismus* (Frankfurt, 1967); Casucci, C., ed., *Il fascismo. Antologia di scritti critici* (Bologna, 1961); de Felice, R., ed., *Antologia sul Fascismo* (Bari, 1976); de Felice, R., *Il fascismo e i partiti politici italiani* (Bologna, 1966); de Felice, R., *Il fascismo. Le interpretazioni dei contemporanei e degli storici.* (Bari, 1970); Kühnl, R., *Texte zur Faschismusdiskussion* (Hamburg, 1974); Nolte, E., *Theorien über den Faschismus* (Cologne, 1967); Pirker, T., ed., *Komintern und Faschismus 1920–1940* (Stuttgart, 1965). Besides the introductions to the above works, discussions of Marxist theories from this period are to be found in collections published in *International Journal of Politics*, vol. 2, no. 4 (Winter 1972–73) and in *Journal of Contemporary History*, vol. 11. (1976), no. 4. See also Cammett, J., 'Communist Theories of Fascism, 1920–1935', *Science and Society*, vol. 31 (1967), no. 2; de Felice, R., *Interpretations of Fascism*, (Harvard, 1977), Kitchen, M., *Fascism* (London, 1976).
(2) A distinction can be drawn between those recent Marxist works on fascism which take a largely negative view of the inter-war theories, and those which use them to provide a starting point for their own analysis. To the former belongs Poulantzas, N., *Fascism and Dictatorship* (London, 1974); to the latter Kadritzke, N., *Faschismus und Krise* (Frankfurt, 1976).
(3) de Felice, R., op. cit. and Kitchen, M., op. cit., offer useful surveys of a range of different theories.
(4) For Gramsci's writings on fascism see Hoare, Q., *Antonio Gramsci, Selections from Political Writings 1921–1926* (London, 1978) and Gramsci, A., *Sul fascismo* ed. Santarelli (Rome, 1974). Of the three stages in the development of Gramsci's analysis of fascism identified by Santarelli, the present collection includes work from the second (1921–2) and third (1923–6). The relation between the categories of the Prison Notebooks and Gramsci's earlier analyses of fascism is outside the scope of the present study, though it still remains to be fully explored.
(5) See below, no. 2. The fullest account of the relations between the PCI and PSI during the period of fascist ascendancy is given in Spriano, P., *Storia del partito comunista italiano* (Turin, 1967), vol. 1, pp. 122–242. For works in English on the rise of fascism, see Rossi, A., *The Rise of Italian Fascism* (London, 1938); Lyttelton, A., *The Seizure of Power* (London, 1973).
(6) See below, no. 13.
(7) See below, nos. 3, 5, 6. See also the biographical outline.
(8) Admiral Horthy was leader of the army which defeated the Hungarian revolution in August 1919, and head of the regime responsible for the 'white terror' that followed.

(9) Hoare, Q., op. cit., pp. 255–266.

(10) Sas develops this aspect the least, see below, no. 6.

(11) See below, no. 11, p. 146.

(12) See below, p. 110.·

(13) Gramsci, A., ed. Santarelli, op. cit., p. 264, Hoare, Q., op. cit. p. 274.

(14) See below, no. 9.

(15) See below, p. 111.

(16) See below, pp. 125, 131, 145.

(17) See below, no. 8, and Hoare, Q., op. cit., pp. 346ff. ·

(18) See below, p. 131 cp. Togliatti, P., 'Le basi sociali del fascismo', Opere, vol. 2. (Rome 1972), esp. pp. 35–38.

(19) The term 'Social Democracy' was usually used by Communist writers as a generic term which included the Italian Socialists, the British Labour Party, etc., as well as those parties specifically called 'Social Democratic'.

(20) See below, p. 112.

(21) For the vagaries of the Comintern's 'united front' tactics, see Degras, J., 'United front tactics in the Comintern 1921–28', St. Anthony's Papers, 1960.

(22) See below, no. 8. See also Hoare, Q., op. cit., pp. 441–462.

(23) See below, no. 7.

(24) It is in fact possible to find occasional references by both Gramsci and Togliatti during 1924 to the reformists as 'semi-fascist' or a 'wing of fascism' (see e.g. Spriano, P., op. cit. pp. 348–9). This was consistent with developments in the Comintern line during that year. However, it formed part of Togliatti's subsequent attempt to achieve a more precise definition of 'fascism' that he should reject this misrepresentation along with others. See below p. 135.

(25) See below, no. 2, and Zibordi, G., Critica socialista del fascismo (Bologna, 1922), passim. Zibordi quotes Turati with approval: 'The war gave birth to two prodigies, communist and socialist on one side, nationalist and fascist on the other . . . The further apart they seem, the more they resemble one another. Both believe in the miraculous effects of violence, the one to consume the stages of history, the other to arrest it or divert its course'. op. cit. p. 58.

(26) Zibordi, op. cit., pp. 13–14, 46–7, 51–7.

(27) The most convenient source in English for Comintern policy on fascism is Degras, J., The Communist International 1919–43 (London, 1956–65), 3 vols. Histories of the Comintern from different perspectives can be found in Braunthal, J., History of the International, vol. 2, 1914–43 (London, 1967); Carr, E. H., A History of Soviet Russia, esp. The Bolshevik Revolution, vol. 3 (London, 1953), Socialism in One Country, vol. 3, pt. 1 (London, 1964), Foundations of a Planned Economy, vol. 3, (London, 1976). For the KPD and fascism see Pirker, T., Komintern und Faschismus (Stuttgart, 1965), pt. 2; Weber, H., Der deutsche Kommunismus, Dokumente (Cologne, 1963); Weber, H., Die Wandlung des deutschen Kommunismus (Frankfurt, 1970).

(28) Carr, E. H., Foundations of a Planned Economy, vol. 3 pt. 2 (London, 1976), pp. 562–8.

(29) Weber, H., Der deutsche Kommunismus (Cologne, 1963), pp. 157–60.

(30) The idea that Germany was not Italy provided a source of infinite solace to Communists and Social Democrats alike. A thoroughgoing critique of the idea under the title 'Deutschland und Italien' appeared in the journal of the KPD Opposition Gegen den Strom, vol. 6 (1933), no. 4.

(31) See below, no. 17.
(32) For discussions of the 'social-fascism' doctrine see Bahne, S., 'Sozialfaschismus in Deutschland', *International Review of Social History*, vol. 10 (1965); Carr, E. H., *Foundations of a Planned Economy*, vol. 3, pt. 2 (London, 1976), pp. 638–643; Poulantzas, N., op. cit., pp. 147–162.
(33) See below, no. 14. Both Bahne and Carr see Stalin's article as relatively unimportant compared with the German sources of the concept.
(34) See below, nos. 12, 16, 17.
(35) See S. Bahne, *Die KPD und das Ende von Weimar*, (Frankfurt, 1976).
(36) Carr, E. H., *Foundations of a Planned Economy*, vol. 3, pt. 1 (London, 1976), chs. 70–72.
(37) Quoted in Braunthal, J., op. cit., p. 425. See below, no. 20.
(38) See below, no. 21.
(39) Togliatti, P., *Lezioni sul fascismo* (Rome, 1970), translated as *Lectures on Fascism* (London, 1976), ch. 1.
(40) See Spriano, R., 'L'esperienza di Tasca a Mosca e il "socialfascismo" ', *Studi Storici*, vol. 10 (1969), no. 1.
(41) See below, p. 214.
(42) See below, p. 224.
(43) See Claudin, F., op. cit., pp. 210–242. A full account of the revolutionary dimension of the Spanish civil war is given in Bolloten, B., *The Spanish Revolution* (Chapel Hill, 1979).
(44) Summaries of Nin's life and work are provided in Nin, A., *Los problemas de la revolución española*, ed. Andrade, J. (Madrid, 1971), pp. 1–42, and Nin, A., *Por la unificación marxista*, ed. Castellote, M. (Madrid, 1978), pp. 7–22, 601–616. See below, nos. 30, 31.
(45) This is evident in most discussions available in English, e.g. Adler, F., 'Thalheimer, Bonapartism and Fascism', *Telos*, no. 40, (1979), Poulantzas, N., op. cit., pp. 59 ff. Martin Kitchen discusses Thalheimer's subsequent writings, though in my view he does not sufficiently mark the change they represent, nor the similarity between Thalheimer's analysis and Trotsky's. See Kitchen, M., 'August Thalheimer's theory of fascism', *Journal of the History of Ideas*, vol. 34 (1974), no. 1, and Kitchen, M., *Fascism* (London, 1976), ch. 7. A representative selection of writings from the KPO between 1928 and 1933 is to be found in Gruppe Arbeiterpolitik, ed., *Der Faschismus in Deutschland* (Frankfurt, 1973), and discussions of their work in Kadritzke, N., op. cit., and Tjaden, K. N., *Struktur und funktion der KPD–Opposition* (Meisenheim, 1964).
(46) It was not published, however, until 1930. See Gruppe Arbeiterpolitik, op. cit., p. 28.
(47) See below, nos. 20–22.
(48) Bauer, O., 'Das Gleichgewicht der Klassenkräfte', *Der Kampf*, vol. 17 (1924). In fact Bauer subsequently modified this analysis, cp. below, no. 46. For a survey of different uses of the Bonapartist analogy in treating fascism see Dulffer, J., 'Bonapartism, Fascism and National-Socialism', *Journal of Contemporary History*, vol. 11 (1976), no. 4. See also Tjaden, K. H. and Griepenburg, R., 'Faschismus und Bonapartismus', *Das Argument*, vol. 41 (1966).
(49) Adler misconstrues Thalheimer's theory by translating the German 'offen' as 'direct'. See *Telos*, no. 40, (1979), pp. 107, 115.
(50) See below, p. 200.

(51) See below p. 201.
(52) Gruppe Arbeiterpolitik, op. cit., p. 117.
(53) For discussions of Trotsky's analyses of fascism, see Kitchen, M., 'Trotsky's Theory of Fascism', *Social Praxis* (1975), Mandel, E., 'Introduction' to Trotsky, L., *The Struggle against Fascism in Germany* (Harmondsworth, 1975), Wistrich, R. S., 'Leon Trotsky's Theory of fascism', *Journal of Contemporary History*, vol. 11 (1976), no. 4.
(54) Trotsky, L., op. cit., p. 268 cf. below, p. 219.
(55) See below, p. 219.
(56) See below, p. 221.
(57) See the article 'What is National Socialism?' in Trotsky, L., op. cit., pp. 406–415.
(58) See below, p. 192.
(59) Trotsky, L., op. cit., p. 283.
(60) See below, no. 32.
(61) For the SPD in the Weimar Republic, see Hunt, R. N., *German Social Democracy 1918–33* (New Haven, 1964).
(62) Hilferding, R., *Das Finanzkapital* (Vienna, 1910), part 5.
(63) Wenlock, P., *The Theory of State Monopoly Capitalism*, unpublished Phd. University of Leeds, 1981.
(64) See below, no. 34. For contemporary critiques of Hilferding's concept of 'organised capitalism', see Leontjew, L., 'Der "organisierte Kapitalismus" und die "Wirtschaftsdemokratie"', *Unter dem Banner des Marxismus*, vol. 3 (1929); Siemsen, A., 'Von Hilferding bis Tarnow', *Der Klassenkampf*, vol. 5 (1931). A perceptive analysis of the shift in Hilferding's position is given in Gottschalch, W., *Strukturveränderungen der Gesellschaft und politisches Handeln in der Lehre von Rudolf Hilferding* (Berlin, 1962), esp. ch. 6.
(65) See below, nos. 33 and 39. The whole of Kautsky's article 'Einige Ursachen und Wirkungen des deutschen Nazionalsozialisimus', *Der Kampf*, vol. 26 (1933), is instructive as an extreme example of Social Democratic passivity.
(66) See below, nos. 35–36.
(67) See below, nos. 37–38. For a history of the SAP see Bremer, J., *Die Sozialistische Arbeiterpartei Deutschlands* (Frankfurt, 1978).
(68) See below, nos. 40–43. Edinger, L. J., *German Exile Politics* (London, 1956) is still the standard history of the SPD in exile. A copy of the 'Prague Manifesto' is printed on its covers. See also 'Miles', *Socialism's New Start* (London, 1934).
(69) The relevant sections are translated in no. 44. For a useful introduction to Austro-Marxism see Bottomore, T. and Goode, P., *Austro-Marxism* (Oxford, 1978); for a fuller history, Leser, N., *Zwischen Reformismus und Bolschewismus* (Vienna, 1968). Histories of Austrian fascism are to be found in Carsten, F. L., *Fascist Movements in Austria* (London, 1977) and Kitchen, M., *The Coming of Austrian Fascism* (London, 1980).
(70) Bauer's own account is below, no. 45.
(71) See below, p. 292.
(72) See below, no. 48.
(73) See below, p. 307.
(74) Bauer, O., *Zwischen zwei Weltkriegen?* (Bratislava, 1936), p. 198. The shift in Bauer's position was already noticeable in May 1934. See 'Die Strategie des Klassenkampfes', *Der Kampf*, vol. 27 (1934).

370   Notes on Introduction

(75) For an analysis of the different phases in Bauer's analysis of fascism, in relation to his changing political position, see Botz, G., 'Genesis und Inhalt der Faschismus-theorien Otto Bauers', *International Review of Social History*, vol. 19 (1974); Botz, G., 'Austro-Marxist Interpretations of Fascism', *Journal of Contemporary History*, vol. 11 (1976), no. 4.

(76) See below, no. 47. Bauer's volume, *Zwischen zwei Weltkriegen?* from which this and other extracts are taken, is a remarkable work of Marxist theorising, and deserves wider currency. For a critical analysis of Bauer's position from the left, see Loew, R., 'The Politics of Austro-Marxism', *New Left Review*, no. 118 (1979).

(77) The list of works grows apace. The following is a selection: Kühnl, R., *Formen burgerlicher Herrschaft* (Hamburg, 1971); Kühnl, R., *Faschismustheorien*. Texte zur Faschismusdiskussion 2 (Hamburg, 1979); Kuhn, A., *Das faschistische Herrschaftssystem und die moderne Gesellschaft* (Hamburg, 1975); Laclau, E., *Politics and Ideology in Marxist Theory* (London, 1977); Mason, T. W., 'The Primacy of Politics', in Woolf, S. J. ed., *The Nature of Fascism* (London, 1969); Opitz, R., 'Fragen der Faschismusdiskussion', *Das Argument*, no. 58 (1970); Poulantzas, N., *Fascism and Dictatorship* (London, 1974); Tjaden, K. H., ed., *Faschismusdiskussion 2* (Berlin, 1979); Vajda, M., *Fascism as a Mass Movement* (London, 1976); Winkler, H. A., *Revolution, Staat, Faschismus* (Gottingen, 1978).

(78) Togliatti, P., *Opere*, vol. 2 (Rome, 1972), p. 120; Bauer, O., 'Der deutsche Faschismus und die Internationale', *Der Kampf*, vol. 26 (1933), p. 312.

(79) See below, nos. 48, 52.

(80) See below, p. 333.

(81) See below, p. 351.

(82) The classic example of this analysis was Guérin, D., *Fascisme et grand capital* (Paris, 1936), translated as *Fascism and Big Business* (New York, 1939).

(83) See below, p. 315.

(84) See below, p. 352.

(85) See below, p. 318.

(86) Disagreement with the copyright owners has prevented the inclusion of Max Horkheimer's previously untranslated article 'The Jews and Europe' as originally planned. Writings on fascism from the inter-war period by Horkheimer and Marcuse are already available in English in Horkheimer, M., *Critical Theory: Selected Essays* (New York, 1972) and Marcuse, H., *Negations* (London, 1968).

(87) Horkheimer, M., 'Die Juden und Europa', *Zeitschrift für Sozialforschung*, vol. 8 (1939), pp. 115–37.

(88) Both ideas are given characteristic formulation in Pollock, F., 'State capitalism: its possibilities and limitations', *Studies in Philosophy and Social Science*, vol. 9 (1941). Pollock diverges from Horkheimer in allowing for a democratic as well as a totalitarian form of state capitalism; with this move, the theory becomes virtually indistinguishable from orthodox political science. The concept of 'totalitarianism' as a concept embracing Stalinist Russia as well as Hitler's Germany was obviously given impetus by the Nazi–Soviet pact of 1939; yet it was clearly prefigured in those aspects of Social-Democratic theory which identified a parallel between fascist and Bolshevik violence (e.g. Zibordi and Kautsky above).

(89) See in particular Nairn, T., 'The Modern Janus' in *The Break-up of Britain* (London, 1977).

Texts

(1) Examples of terrorist incursions by fascist gangs in the summer of 1921.

(2) The Popular Party, founded in 1919, was a Catholic, largely rural-based party of the centre.

(3) Zibordi's pamphlet was in fact written during the summer of 1921.

(4) The 'maximalist' section of the Socialist Party opposed parliamentary reformism in favour of a proletarian dictatorship.

(5) Hugo Stinnes was a German industrial magnate who had a considerable influence on industrial and economic policy. Andrew Bonar Law was British Prime Minister from 1922–3.

(6) The Wittelsbachs were the Bavarian royal family deposed in the revolution of November 1918. Friedrich Ebert, SPD leader, was elected first President of the Weimar Republic in 1919, and held office till his death in 1925. Heinrich Brandler led the KPD from 1921 until 1924.

(7) Fransesco Nitti was prime minister of Italy in 1919–20. The revival of Italian as well as German industry in the post-war years was heavily dependent on U.S. capital. D'Annunzio, who seized the town of Fiume in September 1919, was opposed to the successive Italian governments' failure to press Italy's claims to the eastern Adriatic.

(8) Mussolini's speech of 3 January 1925, denying all complicity in the murder of Matteotti, but taking responsibility for what had happened, brought the Matteotti crisis to a close.

(9) Erich Zeigner was head of the left SPD government in Saxony during 1923. In October the Communists joined the government under arrangements with Moscow to prepare for a general uprising to overthrow the Republic. The dismissal of the government by the *Reichswehr*, authorised by the SPD President Ebert, and the institution of a temporary dictatorship was a violation of the Weimar constitution.

(10) These were all right-wing members of the SPD leadership. For Ebert see note. 6.

(11) The Labour administration of Ramsay MacDonald in Britain lasted from 1928 to 1931, and the grand coalition administration of SPD leader Hermann Müller from 1928 to 1930.

(12) Heinrich Brüning's Centre Party-led administration of March 1930 marked the end of effective parliamentary government in Germany, as it was unable to command a parliamentary majority, and made wide use of emergency decrees. General Groener, as defence minister from 1928–32, played a considerable part in the downfall of the Republic. Otto Braun was Social Democratic premier of Prussia from 1925 to 1932, and the trade union leader Karl Severing his deputy.

(13) The *Reichsbanner* was the para-military defence organisation of the SPD, founded in 1924. Conceived as an organisation for the defence of the Republic, it was intended to act as a supplement to the official forces of the state, not in opposition to them. It was strengthened in 1930 under the so-called 'iron front' in response to the Nazi threat.

(14) The SPD supported Hindenburg's candidature for President in 1932 as the 'lesser evil' to Hitler, and in the hope that he would act as defender of the

constitution.

(15) Alfred Hugenberg, industrialist turned newspaper proprietor, was leader of the Nationalist Party (DNVP) from 1928, and responsible for the Party's alliance with the Nazis.

(16) The Socialist Workers' Party (SAPD) was a group of Social Democrats who broke away from the main Party in 1931. Heinrich Brandler was a leader of the right wing opposition (KPO) which was expelled from the main Party in 1929.

(17) Doriot was Communist burgomaster of St. Denis, who campaigned against the Party hierarchy for an early commitment to the popular front, and was expelled from the Party as a consequence.

(18) The attempted fascist uprising of 6 February 1934 was the occasion which brought the grass roots demands for a united front to a head in France, and led to co-operation between the Socialists and Communists in a general strike on 12 February.

(19) Joint demonstrations continued through early July 1934 as the two parties manoeuvred towards an agreement.

(20) Maurice Thorez was leader of the PCF during the popular front period.

(21) For a complete English version see F. Adler, 'Thalheimer, Bonapartism and Fascism' in *Telos*, vol. 40 (1979). See also note 49 above.

(22) Heinz Neumann and Hermann Remmele were leading exponents of the 'left-turn' within the KPD after 1928.

(23) Arkadi Maslow and Ruth Fischer led the KPD in its 'left' phase in the years immediately after 1924.

(24) Albert Grzesinski was the Social Democratic police chief of Berlin, responsible for banning the Communist May Day demonstration in 1929, and dispersing it at the cost of 29 lives. For Severing, see note 12.

(25) Gustav Noske was the defence minister in Ebert's post-war government. He made extensive use of the right-wing *Freicorps* units to suppress the revolutionary movement in Berlin in January 1919, earning the title 'butcher' of his class.

(26) Ernst Becker was author of the article to which Thalheimer was replying.

(27) For Maslow see note 23. Ernst Thälmann was appointed leader of the KPD in 1925 with Stalin's approval, and stood as Communist candidate for the German presidency in 1925 and 1932.

(28) Dmitrii Manuilski was secretary of ECCI from 1928 to 1943, and a chief spokesman of the ultra-left line of the 'third period'.

(29) 'Ercoli' was the pseudonym Togliatti assumed in exile.

(30) Gaston Doumergue was premier of France from February to November 1934.

(31) Edouard Deladier, Edouard Herriot and Pierre Laval were premiers of France during the 1920s and 1930s, and all were involved in the Franco-Soviet pact which was signed by Laval in May 1935.

(32) For the *Reichsbanner*, see note 13.

(33) The Reichstag coalition between the *Volkspartei* (People's Party) and the Social Democrats broke up in March 1930 over the issue of whether the increasing cost of unemployment should fall on industry or on those receiving benefits.

(34) This phrase was used by Engels in his 1895 introduction to Marx's *Class Struggles in France* to emphasise the threat to bourgeois class power posed by the parliamentary advance of German Social Democracy. The danger from

fascism, however, lay precisely in its ability to combine legal with illegal methods.

(35) After sweeping Nazi gains in the elections of July 1932, Hitler pressed to be given the Chancellorship and nothing else, but Hindenburg at this point refused.

(36) The decision by the Social Democrats not to oppose Brüning in the Reichstag succeeded in keeping the Nazis out of office on this occasion, but enabled Brüning to continue to govern by means of emergency decree.

(37) In May 1932 Hindenburg dismissed Brüning's administration, whose proposals for breaking up the bankrupt estates in East Prussia had alarmed the landowners. In place he appointed Papen, the protégé of the army command, amongst whose first acts was to lift the ban on the Nazi S.A.

(38) The Prague Manifesto was the revolutionary programme published by the SPD in exile in January 1934.

(39) In March 1933 the Chancellor Dollfuss took advantage of a parliamentary incident in which the president and both vice-presidents resigned, to allow the indefinite suspension of parliament.

(40) On 12 February 1934 a police search for arms in the SDAP headquarters in Linz was resisted by the Republican Defence Corps. Its leader gave the signal for an uprising against the government, which spead to Vienna and other towns, but was easily broken. The government used a ruthless show of force, particularly against the council housing blocks in Vienna, which were the pride of the Social Democratic municipality.

(41) Hugo Breitner was one of the architects of municipal socialism in Vienna.

(42) For a complete English translation of this chapter, see T. Bottomore and P. Goode, *Austro-Marxism* (Oxford 1978), pp. 167–186.

(43) Richard Löwenthal wrote under the pseudonym of Paul Sering. His views on fascism came to be considerably modified after the war.

(44) See Rossi, A. (pseudonym) *The Rise of Italian Fascism* (London, 1938).

List of sources

(1) Gramsci, A., 'Italia e Spagna', 'Forze elementari', 'I due fascismi', *L'Ordine Nuovo*, 11 March, 26 April, 25 August, 1921. Translated in Gramsci, A., *Selections from Political Writings 1921–1926*, ed. Hoare, Q. (London, 1978), pp. 23–4, 38–40, 63–5.

(2) Zibordi, G., *Critica socialista del fascismo* (Bologna, 1922), pp. 15–28.

(3) Partito comunista italiano, *Congresso di Roma* (Rome, 1922), Tesi, sections 51–5.

(4) *Internationale Presse Korrespondenz*, vol. 2 (1922), p. 1641.

(5) *Protokoll der Konferenz der EKKI* (Hamburg, 1924), pp. 204–32.

(6) Aquila, G. (Sas, G.) *Der Faschismus in Italien* (Hamburg, 1923), chapter 1.

(7) Gramsci, A., 'Democrazia e fascismo', *L'Ordine Nuovo*, 1 November 1924. Translated in Hoare, Q., ed., op.cit., pp. 267–72.

(8) Gramsci, A., 'Un esame della situazione italiana': report to the meeting of the PCI central committee on 2–3 August, 1926. Translated in Hoare, Q., ed., op.cit., pp. 400–11.

374   List of sources

(9) Togliatti, P., 'Rapporto alla commissione per il fascismo dell' Internationale Comunista': report to the commission on fascism of the Comintern, 12 November 1926.

(10) Togliatti, P., 'Osservazioni sulla politica del nostro partito', *Lo Stato Operaio*, vol. 2 (1928), pp. 324–36.

(11) Togliatti, P., 'A propos de fascisme', *L'Internationale Comuniste*, vol. 9 (1928), no. 18, pp. 1124–40.

(12) *Internationale Presse Korrespondenz*, vol. 3 (1923), pp. 1076–7.

(13) *Internationale Presse Korrespondenz*, vol. 4 (1924), p. 1581.

(14) Stalin, J., 'Concerning the International Situation', *Bolshevik*, no. 11, September 1924. Reprinted in Stalin, J., *Works*, vol. 6 (Moscow, 1953).

(15) *Internationale Presse Korrespondenz*, vol. 9 (1929), pp. 973 ff.

(16) Manuilski, D. S., *Die Kommunistischen Parteien und die Krise des Kapitalismus* (Hamburg, 1931), pp. 41–5.

(17) Thälmann, E., *Der revolutionäre Ausweg und die KPD* (Berlin, 1932), pp. 23–6, 36–9, 59–61.

(18) Togliatti, P., 'Sulla situazione tedesca', *Lo Stato Operaio*, vol. 7 (1933), pp. 84–93.

(19) *Cahiers du Bolchevisme*, vol. 11 (1934), no. 14–15, pp. 918–20.

(20) Blum, L., 'Les problèmes de l'unité', 'Le défense internationale contre le fascisme', *Le Populaire*, 7, 13 July 1934.

(21) Dimitrov, G., *The Working Class against Fascism* (London, 1935), pp. 7–10, 13–15, 17–23.

(22) Thalheimer, A., 'Über den Faschismus', *Gegen den Strom*, vol. 3 (1930), nos. 2–4.

(23) Thalheimer, A., 'Der sogenannte Sozialfaschismus', *Gegen den Strom*, vol. 2 (1929), no. 16.

(24) Thalheimer, A., 'Die Entwicklung des Faschismus in Deutschland', *Gegen den Strom*, vol. 3 (1930), no. 19.

(25) Trotsky, L., 'The Turn in the Communist International and the Situation in Germany', *Bulletin of the Opposition*, no. 17–18 (1930), reprinted in Trotsky, L., *The Struggle against Fascism in Germany* (Harmondsworth, 1975), pp. 9–32.

(26) Trotsky, L., 'For a Workers' United Front against Fascism', *The Militant*, January 1932, reprinted in Trotsky, L., op.cit., pp. 98–109.

(27) Trotsky, L., 'What Next? Vital Questions for the German Proletariat', *The Militant*, March–June 1932, reprinted in Trotsky, L. op.cit., pp. 110–244.

(28) Trotsky, L., 'Bonapartism and Fascism', *The New International*, August 1934, reprinted in Trotsky, L., *Writings of Leon Trotsky, 1934–5* (New York, 1971), pp. 51–7.

(29) Trotsky, L., 'An Open Letter to the Workers of France', *The New International*, August 1935, reprinted in Trotsky, L., op.cit., pp.305–15.

(30) Nin, A., 'La carta abierta de la IC y el congreso del partido', *Comunismo*, no. 10 (March 1932).

(31) Nin, A., 'La situación política y las tareas del proletariado', political thesis prepared for the national Congress of the POUM in May 1937.

(32) Silone, I., *Der Fascismus. Seine Entstehung und seine Entwicklung* (Zurich, 1934), pp. 273–85.

(33) Kautsky, K., *Materialistische Geschichtsauffassung* (Berlin, 1927), vol. 2, pp. 469–78.

(34) Sozialdemokratische Partei Deutschlands, *Protokoll des sozialdemokratischen Parteitages Kiel 1927* (Berlin, 1927), pp. 166–9, 172–3.

(35) Hilferding, R., 'In der Gefahrenzone', *Die Gesellschaft*, vol. 2 (1930), pp. 289–97.

(36) Hilferding, R., 'Zwischen den Entscheidungen', *Die Gesellschaft*, vol. 5 (1933), pp. 1–9.

(37) Seydewitz, M., 'Abwarten? – Nein! Handeln!', 'Unser Kampfprogramm', 'Der falsche Weg', *Der Klassenkampf*, vol. 4 (1930), pp. 577–80, 609–16, 641–5.

(38) Seydewitz, M., 'Die Mission der SAP', *Der Klassenkampf*, vol. 6 (1932), pp. 161–3.

(39) Kautsky, K., 'Einige Ursachen und Wirkungen des deutschen Nationalsozialismus', *Der Kampf*, vol. 26 (1933), pp. 235–6.

(40) Kautsky, K., *Neue Programm* (Leipzig, 1933), pp. 30–5.

(41) Hilferding, R., 'Revolutionärer Sozialismus', *Zeitschrift für Sozialismus*, vol. 1 (1933–4), pp. 145–52.

(42) Schifrin, A., 'Revolutionäre Sozialdemokratie', 'Die Konsequenzen des revolutionären Programms', *Zeitschrift für Sozialismus*, vol. 1 (1933–4), pp. 81–91, 281–93.

(43) Seydewitz, M., 'Die Überwindung der faschistischen Diktatur', *Zeitschrift für Sozialismus*, vol. 1 (1933–4), pp. 198–207.

(44) Sozialdemokratische Partei Österreichs, *Protokoll des Sozialdemokratischen Parteitages Linz 1926* (Vienna, 1926). Programm, section 3, 'Der Kampf um die Staatmacht'.

(45) Bauer, O., *Austrian Democracy under Fire* (London, 1934), pp. 15–23, 41–7.

(46–7) Bauer, O., *Zwischen zwei Weltkriegen?* (Bratislava, 1936), pp. 126–30, 321–5.

(48) Sering, P. (R. Löwenthal), 'Der Fascismus. Voraussetzungen und Träger', *Zeitschrift für Sozialismus*, vol. 2 (1935), pp. 775–80.

(49) Tasca, A., 'Proletariato, fascismo ed economia italiana', *Lo Stato Operaio*, vol. 1 (1927), pp. 41–8.

(50) Togliatti, P., 'L'Italie fasciste, foyer de guerre', *L'Internationale Comuniste*, vol. 8 (1927), pp. 179–84.

(51) Silone, I., *Der Fascismus* (Zurich, 1934), pp. 206–11, 227–30.

(52) Sering, P. (R. Löwenthal), 'Die Wandlungen des Kapitalismus', 'Der Fascismus. System und Widersprüche', *Zeitschrift für Sozialismus*, vol. 2 (1935), pp. 715–25, 839–48.

(53) Bauer, O., *Zwischen zwei Weltkriegen?* (Bratislava, 1936), pp. 70–8.

(54) Bauer, O., 'Der Faschismus', *Der sozialistische Kampf* (1938), pp. 75–83.

Index

380   Index

About the Editor

David Beetham was professor of political science at the University of Leeds UK from 1980 until 2001. His recent publications include *The Legitimation of Power* (second ed.), *Parliament and Democracy in the Twenty-Frst Century*, and *Democracy: A Beginner's Guide*.

About Haymarket Books

Haymarket Books is a radical, independent, nonprofit book publisher based in Chicago.

Our mission is to publish books that contribute to struggles for social and economic justice. We strive to make our books a vibrant and organic part of social movements and the education and development of a critical, engaged, international left.

We take inspiration and courage from our namesakes, the Haymarket martyrs, who gave their lives fighting for a better world. Their 1886 struggle for the eight-hour day—which gave us May Day, the international workers' holiday—reminds workers around the world that ordinary people can organize and struggle for their own liberation. These struggles continue today across the globe—struggles against oppression, exploitation, poverty, and war.

Since our founding in 2001, Haymarket Books has published more than five hundred titles. Radically independent, we seek to drive a wedge into the risk-averse world of corporate book publishing. Our authors include Noam Chomsky, Arundhati Roy, Rebecca Solnit, Angela Y. Davis, Howard Zinn, Amy Goodman, Wallace Shawn, Mike Davis, Winona LaDuke, Ilan Pappé, Richard Wolff, Dave Zirin, Keeanga-Yamahtta Taylor, Nick Turse, Dahr Jamail, David Barsamian, Elizabeth Laird, Amira Hass, Mark Steel, Avi Lewis, Naomi Klein, and Neil Davidson. We are also the trade publishers of the acclaimed Historical Materialism Book Series and of Dispatch Books.

Also Available from Haymarket Books

Clara Zetkin: Selected Writings
Clara Zetkin, edited by Philip S. Foner
Foreword by Rosalyn Baxandall, Introduction by Angela Y. Davis

The Comintern
Duncan Hallas

Eyewitnesses to the Russian Revolution
Edited by Todd Chretien

Fighting Fascism: How to Struggle and How to Win
Clara Zetkin, edited by John Riddell and Mike Taber

The German Revolution, 1917-1923
Pierre Broué, Introduction by Eric D. Weitz

The Nazis, Capitalism and the Working Class
Donny Gluckstein

The New Authoritarians: Convergence on the Right
David Renton

Toward the United Front: Proceedings of the Fourth Congress of the Communist International, 1922
Edited by John Riddell

The Washington Connection and Third World Fascism
The Political Economy of Human Rights: Volume I
Noam Chomsky and Edward S. Herman

Witness to the German Revolution
Victor Serge